Reconsidering Early Modern Spanish Literature

Juan de la Cuesta Hispanic Monographs

Reconsidering Early Modern Spanish Literature through Mass and Popular Culture: Contemporizing the Classics for the Classroom

Edited by

BONNIE L. GASIOR
California State University, Long Beach

MINDY E. BADÍA
Indiana University Southeast

Juan de la Cuesta
Newark, Delaware

On the cover: Equipo Crónica, *La antesala*, 1968, Acrílico sobre lienzo, 140,5 x 140,5 cm
Colección Fundación Juan March, Museu Fundación Juan March, Palma

Crédito imagen: Cortesía Fundación Juan March, Madrid. *Foto:* © Joan-Ramon Bonet/David Bonet

Juan de la Cuesta Hispanic Monographs
An imprint of LinguaText, LLC.
Newark, Delaware 19711 USA
(302) 453-8695

www.JuandelaCuesta.com

MANUFACTURED IN THE UNITED STATES OF AMERICA

ISBN: 978-1-58871-378-0 (PB)
E-ISBN: 978-1-58871-379-7 (PDF)

Table of Contents

Foreword
  CHARLES GANELIN and CATHERINE LARSON 7

Acknowledgments 19

Introduction. Leveraging Pop and Mass Culture in the Classroom:
  Pedagogical Possibilities
  MINDY BADIA and BONNIE GASIOR 21

PART I: THEORETICAL PRACTICE

  Harry Potter and the Buried Self: *Pureza de sangre*, Cryptonomy, and
    the Ethics of Concealment in J.K. Rowling's Potterverse
  BRUCE BURNINGHAM 33

  Not Your Father's Classroom: Looking Back at the Golden Age through
    the Lens of the #MeToo Movement
  DAVID CASTILLO 48

  'A Most Timely Message for This Tired and Cynical World': *Man of La
    Mancha* (1965) as the Depoliticization of Counterculture Quixotism
  WILLIAM CHILDERS 65

  Engaging Students on the #MeToo Movement: Framing Contemporary
    Crime Shows with Tirso and Zayas
  BRADLEY NELSON 87

  #MeToo in Early Modern Spain: Visual Pleasures and Silence Breakers
  SONIA PÉREZ-VILLANUEVA 106

PART II: PRACTICAL THEORY

  Representing Black Speech in Spanish Golden Age Poetry and U.S. Hip-
    Hop Culture: The Case of Góngora
  MINDY BADÍA 131

'Tan largo me lo fiáis' in the Era of '#TimesUp': *El burlador de Sevilla*
as Foil to Feminism in the Age of Trumpism
ROBERT BAYLISS 146

'Pop Don Quixote': *The Big Bang Theory* as Quixotic Emulation
YOLANDA GAMBOA TUSQUETS 159

Popularity, Paternity, and Porn: A Classroom Exploration of the
Twenty-First Century Don Juan in Film
ANTHONY GRUBBS 176

Teaching the *Mujer Varonil* as the Wonder Woman of Early Modern
Spain
VALERIE HEGSTROM..193

The Fastest Lance in the West: Don Quijote, High Plains Drifter
MARGARET MAREK 209

PART III: CLASSROOM AS CASE STUDY/POPPING PEDAGOGY

From the *Epopeya* to the *Narcocorrido*: The Hero in Hispanic Literature
and Popular Culture
LORI BERNARD 229

The Loves and Follies of Teaching Non-canonical Texts that 'Pop':
Morales' *Comedia de los amores y locuras del conde loco*
SIDNEY DONNELL 249

Enrique Iglesias, Madonna and ¿San Juan de la Cruz?: Using Pop Music
to Teach Spanish Mystic Poetry
BONNIE GASIOR..263

Drugs, Magic, Coercion, and Consent: From María de Zayas to the
'World's Scariest Drug'
JOHN SLATER 274

Students as Co-Architects at Hispanic Serving Institutions: Latinx
Students Building Knowledge in *Siglo* Studies
DARCI STROTHER...290

Afterword: The Faces of Relevance
EDWARD FRIEDMAN...301

NOTES ON CONTRIBUTORS 315

INDEX...321

Foreword

ONE OF THE MANY contributions of this volume of essays is its insistence on bringing together disparate things: early modern and (late) modern; cinema and classic texts; old school and new school. The collection includes studies intended to enrich the classroom experience of undergraduates in general education and major/minor courses; and essays that graduate students and faculty might find in the leading journals of our field. Far from a quixotic enterprise, the making of connections between unlikely partners has taken us on a variety of surprising journeys. We found ourselves considering the correlations between *Don Quijote* and Westerns, the points of contact between the *mujer varonil* and Wonder Woman, and the ways in which Spanish Golden Age poetry intersects with U.S. hip-hop culture. We found the essays insightful in and of themselves, but even more—individually and as a group—they suggested techniques and strategies for bringing together cultural elements that have helped twenty-first-century students better understand the sixteenth- and seventeenth-century Spanish texts and contexts that we teach. In like manner, these sixteen essays illuminate key elements of our students' cultural expertise and experiences, which then can enable us to see things that we had neither seen nor appreciated before. Taken as a whole, the essays both capitalize on recent pedagogical debates and movements and respond intelligently to colleagues who may continue to resist the incorporation of popular culture in a classroom dedicated to the "classics." By demonstrating respect toward our students through a consideration of the arts that speak to them, the authors not only respect students' potential limitations, but they also activate/tap into their knowledge wheelhouses. More importantly, they ultimately seek to deepen academic experiences that will empower students to find meaning well beyond the literary realm. Creative experiments like those detailed here can unlock intellectual potential across the spectrum.

To bridge the gap between "old" and "new," between early modern Spain and contemporary United states, Mindy Badía, in "Representing Black

Speech in Spanish Golden Age Poetry and U.S. Hip-Hop Culture: The Case of Góngora" considers how African-American English and hip-hop music have entered mainstream US culture in similar ways that Góngora's "En la fiesta del santísimo sacramento" shows Black Spanish (*sayagués*) as part of the linguistic tapestry of seventeenth-century Spain. Badía focuses on white artists who appropriate African-American English in a film that parodies it (*Airplane!*) and a television series that critiques hip-hop (*Atlanta*). Góngora, who received compensation for his poem, treads ground similar to a path followed by one of *Atlanta*'s characters, who is told he needs to pay cash to have his friend's newly recorded song get airplay. Language unites these scenes: Barbara Billingsley (from the "all-American" 1950s TV show *Leave it to Beaver*) speaking jive; and Dave, a white man who works at a radio station, employing African-American linguistic markers. Badía highlights linguistic and cultural borrowings between the non-dominant and dominant languages to teach students about surprising language-based similarities between the two periods as well as how to find common issues that connect these utterly disparate texts from greatly different times.

Rob Bayliss' contribution, "'Tan largo me lo fiáis' in the Era of '#TimesUp': *El burlador de Sevilla* as Foil to Feminism in the Age of Trumpism," proposes that Tirso's *Burlador* and other texts from the Golden Age can help our students understand their own cultural moment. He employs a perspective that seeks to avoid common pitfalls, such as "facile equivalencies or . . . pseudo-comparative conclusions," e.g., the idea that Don Juan is their generation's Weinstein. Bayliss asserts that "'Tan largo me lo fiáis" placed in dialogue with "#TimesUp" provides an opportunity to understand the past and the present, to understand the history of feminism and the patriarchy that shapes, defines, and necessitates it." To achieve those goals, he advocates for the discussion of terms and concepts associated with popular culture and its production, the digital age and engagement with celebrity culture, Reception Theory, and Cultural Studies. Bayliss further lays out strategies to help students navigate the various "waves" of feminism, including the "#TimesUp" movement and its implications for socio-cultural-historical responses to gender inequality, discrimination, and abuse. His approach involves giving his students an overview of the four "waves" of feminism and the ways in which oppression persists today, even though some despite the achievement of numerous significant gains. In addition, he applies this historical overview to the similarly evolving nature of literary criticism and its manifestation in readings of early modern Spanish texts, in particular, those treating gender inequality in the representation of women and the patriarchy. Bayliss advocates for a pedagogical approach that empowers students to rethink their relationship with popular culture and illustrate their expertise in its production and consumption, and he offers a variety of methods to elicit reflection on the degree to which things may or may not have changed in the intervening centuries. His essay illuminates the benefits of moving from an approach that uses the text as "an artifact to learn about early modern Spain to using it as a foil to critique contemporary society" and prepare students for the challenges they face in the twenty-first century.

Lori Bernard argues in "From the *Epopeya* to the *Narcocorrido*: The Hero in Hispanic Literature and Popular Culture" that with a focus on the "hero," medieval and early modern literature courses can bridge the cultural gap between these texts and today's students. Bernard proposes a reading of *The Poem of the Cid* and sixteenth-century *romance* versions, which compares the early texts to contemporary *narcocorridos* (popular songs that grew out of the pervasive drug trade). The first lines of the *Cid* yield a view of an emotional hero perhaps out of step with notions of "heroism," while the sixteenth-century *romances* permit students to note the differences in development and ending in order to show how both theme and hero become transformed over time and place. Discussion of the concept of "hero" and whether the Cid conforms yields an object lesson in cultural relativism and the challenge of reading the distinct codes belonging to periods distant from contemporary points of view. The greater contrast occurs between the widespread Mexican *narcocorridos* and popular poetry (both the epic *Cid* and its *romance* versions), which share characteristics such as the matter of transgressing both borders and social norms. Although students might find the Cid to be of questionable heroic stature—the poem's first known verse reveals the Cid in tears as he is forced into exile—, the protagonists of the *narcocorridos* present similar characteristics as they confront the State. Discussions of moral ambiguity and the sometimes-unheroic behavior of heroes round out the essay.

Sidney Donnell speaks to his experimentation with sixteenth-century Spanish plays in undergraduate second-language-learning classes in "The Loves and Follies of Teaching Non-canonical Texts that 'Pop': Morales's *Comedia de los amores y locuras del conde loco*." With a reliance on both canonical and non-canonical texts, Donnell compares the fleeting fame of sixteenth-century writers and their works to the pop artists on the Top 40 charts in order to help students understand the shifting ground of what constitutes mass or pop culture. When teaching *El conde loco* by Alonso de Morales, Donnell ambitiously incorporates sixteenth-century popular culture (songs and dances) and seventeenth-century court theater (*comedia cantada* [sung theater], a precursor to opera). To bring this segment to fruition, he has his students read/perform scenes from Morales's play; this, in turn, leads to a discussion about the play in a broader context. One aspect he highlights is the practice of male cross-dressing, given that relatively few women appeared on the sixteenth-century Spanish stage; the nature of characters who must "pass" for another gender leads to the questioning of gender fluidity. Performance of both gender and of the plays themselves is central to this approach: rehearsal and performance of selections follow the class's in-depth study.

Bonnie Gasior, with her essay "Enrique Iglesias, Madonna and ¿San Juan de la Cruz?: Using Pop Music to Teach Spanish Mystic Poetry," juxtaposes an unusual but insightful pairing of contemporary popular music and Spanish mystic poetry. As music is an integral aspect of students' lives, it affects their perceptions as well as responses not just to a particular piece but to other observations enriching in unsuspecting ways the texts they read. Gasior employs two seemingly distinct selections as a way into San Juan's "Noche oscura." Enrique Iglesias's "Experiencia religiosa" and Madonna's "Like a Prayer" present the sensuality/sanctity paradox, but while Iglesias sings an erotic love song easily interpreted both spiritually and physically with words that reflect those of San Juan's poem, Madonna takes the transgressive potential a step further in her at-the-time-controversial music video by employing the aura of mystery, solitude, prayer, and journey to address the social injustice of an African-American man wrongly accused of assault. The refuge Madonna seeks in a church in order to decide whether to call the authorities and the culminating "dream" of a sexual union with the black statue-turned-real enables students to tackle issues of self-expression and censorship, for instance, as expressed in responses to the Black Lives Matter movement. It is crucial, Gasior argues, to meet students where they are in the same way that San Juan did: using the human erotic to discuss the divine and the larger life questions.

Tony Grubbs uses the iconic figure of Don Juan as the focus of final projects in two undergraduate courses, a General Education class taught in English and a fourth-year Spanish literature class for majors and minors. His essay, "Popularity, Paternity, and Porn: A Classroom Exploration of the Twenty-First-Century Don Juan in Film," lays out the issues and techniques used in both courses, as well as the goals Grubbs has set for his students. In this culminating exercise, the instructor hopes that students will "identify and engage problems in their own situations, reinforce effective communication strategies, and, in the case of the Spanish course, practice the target language." After noting the reasons why Don Juan continues to attract university learners in a variety of media, including via popular culture, Grubbs explains that in both courses he follows Oscar Mandel's tripartite categorization of Don Juan: Classical, Romantic, and Molecular, with the final category offering a self-aware protagonist who struggles with his (self) definition. After early readings and discussions of adaptation theory, students are divided into three groups; each group will view, discuss, write about, and offer a multimedia presentation on a twenty-first-century film that centers on a Molecular Don Juan. Although filmed in English, the movies in both courses are easily adapted for students with differing linguistic and cultural backgrounds; in all other ways, the 400-level Spanish class engages with the final project in Spanish. The course analyzes the ways in which the three contemporary films (*John Tucker Must Die* [2006], *Don Jon* [2013], and *Broken Flowers* [2005]) reflect Classical, Romantic, and Molecular characterizations, cultures, and worldviews, while they simultaneously speak to modern university-level audiences. Grubbs's synthesizing project weaves together the various elements examined throughout the semester in an approach that has proven successful in uniting the classics with modern-day understanding of the figure of Don Juan and the complex socio-cultural issues he raises.

In an essay on the ways in which pop culture can serve students as they grapple with understanding early modern literature, Valerie Hegstrom elaborates on the similarities between past and present from the perspective of female protagonists and modern-day superheroes. In "Teaching the *Mujer Varonil* as the Wonder Woman of Early Modern Spain," Hegstrom underscores the power of Wonder Woman and the *mujer varonil* as potential platforms for motivating engagement with popular figures that, although separated by time and space, parallel one another as norm-questioning, groundbreaking wonder women. Hegstrom offers a blueprint for designing such a course in her list of guiding questions for students, which describe how well-known early modern texts written by both men and women can frame class discussions. Her representative examples include *Fuenteovejuna*, with Laurencia metaphorically joining the Justice League; the characterization of the strong and beautiful Gila in *La serrana de la Vera*; Tirso's *Antona García*, and struggles with relationship issues and "theme songs"; and Marcela from the *Quijote*, the "*mujer esquiva* who escapes enclosure." The approach elucidates contemporizing the classics for the classroom: using comic books and popular films, Hegstrom opens doors for students to consider seriously topics of contemporary and early modern concern and interest.

John Slater reminds us in "Drugs, Magic, Coercion, and Consent: From María de Zayas to the 'World's Scariest Drug'" that our students understand that their autonomy in decision-making "can be involuntarily stripped from them by someone else," a truth that is reinforced virtually every college week-end. They know about drug-related assault but had not realized that such knowledge could serve them as they seek to understand early modern litera-ture and culture. In his topics course on witchcraft and magic, Slater looks at the representation of medical and magical techniques described in *Siglo de Oro* literary texts and historical documents to show how magic, plants, pacts with the devil, and witches' incantations can be utilized to steal a person's free will, leaving him or her open to manipulation and sexual abuse. Rep-resentative literary examples include *La Celestina*, *El mágico prodigioso*, *La inocencia castigada*, and *El caballero de Olmedo*; readings from the Bible; Ber-nardo de Cienfuegos's *Historia de las plantas*; and historical documents on witchcraft and drugs. He concludes with a contemporary YouTube descrip-tion of a zombie-creating substance known popularly as the South American "devil's breath" or *burundanga* (aka the "World's Scariest Drug"), which can steal a person's free will, while the victim remains conscious. He details how the video grabbed the interest of his students and relates it to early modern fascination with the concept of free will, especially in Zayas's novella. Slater's use of popular culture demonstrates the connections between pedagogical practice and course goals: "better reading comprehension, more understand-ing, and notably higher engagement."

As an expert in the realities of post-secondary education for Latinx stu-dents, Darci L. Strother approaches from a different yet complimentary—if not overarching—perspective, the idea that professors can "harness the power of pop culture as we build a bridge alongside our students." "Students as Co-Architects at Hispanic Serving Institutions: Latinx Students Build-ing Knowledge in *Siglo* Studies" lays out the sobering statistics regarding the 416 Hispanic Serving Institutions, which indicate the disparity between the growing numbers of Latinx students and the age and cultural understanding of those who teach them, which can lead to greater problems for that set of learners. Strother urges us to consider new approaches, such as "the incorpo-ration of pop culture into our pedagogy," as a way to enhance the success of not merely twenty-first century but Latinx students. After giving examples of research and anecdotal evidence supporting the practice, Strother also warns the professoriate to be cautious that we do not doubly marginalize students who might have little or no experience with the faculty-chosen examples of contemporary pop culture. To make the project more inclusive of all stu-dents, Strother advocates encouraging them to be co-architects of the cur-riculum, beginning with the idea that it is important to remind our students that they know more than they think they do. She then follows with the example of her own early experience using popular songs in the classroom and her movement toward empowering her students to take over the selection of music and other approaches; she adds a table of student-selected examples of pop culture options created to enhance a variety of Siglo de Oro texts. Strother ends by advocating for a resource available on many campuses, M.A.-level Teaching Assistants, who are close in age to our undergraduate students and often crave the opportunity to work with them.

The good vs. evil scenarios of J. K. Rowling's *Harry Potter* novels and adapted films inform Bruce Burningham's "Harry Potter and the Buried Self: *Pureza de sangre*, Cryptonomy, and the Ethics of concealment in J. K. Rowling's Potterverse." The first essay in Part II, Burningham's contribution theorizes about issues of blood purity and racism among magicians and wizards. Although many see German anti-semitism in the Harry Potter series—acknowledged by Rowling as well—, Burningham views the attitude through the wider lens of Spanish history. He brings to bear the character Salazar Slytherin: the last name speaks for itself, but the first exhibits its Iberian roots and the name of the 20th-century Portuguese dictator. Rowling had lived in Portugal, a stay that may have influenced this particular character name. Throughout the series, wizards and witches born of Muggle families (those with no wizardry abilities) could be considered a crypto-Jewish community, and the questioning that many had to undergo in order to attend the Hogwarts School recalls that of the Spanish Inquisition into one's suspected lineage. At the end of the series, a scene in a metaphysical "King's Cross Station" (the port of entry to reach Hogwarts) of Harry Potter's mind, lies a crypt with an injured creature that can represent the evil that potentially lurks everywhere or the truth that cannot be faced. Regardless, this moment drives a narration, Burningham argues, that to be fully understood requires a reader schooled in the dark philosophy of Iberian blood purity.

David Castillo's "Not Your Father's Classroom: Looking Back at the Golden Age Through the Lens of the #MeToo Movement" brings to bear what he calls "reality literacy" as a primary goal of humanistic education for all students. One example of this would be transhistorical and transcultural discussions of, say, gender, in order to enable today's students to gain a wider understanding of early modern literature. Castillo proposes using Don Juan Manuel's exempla, honor plays by Lope de Vega, and *The Godfather* saga and TV series of a similar nature. By the same token, one could use Calderón de la Barca's *El médico de su honra* and María de Zayas's *Desengaños* with their calculated femicide and compare them to Stieg Larsson's The Millennium Trilogy: Salander suffers at the hands of the State and investigates crimes where femicide is not an aberration but part of a political stance. The next step could be to discuss women's voices as weapons, initiating the discussion with *La pícara Justina*, read in tandem with Angie Thomas's *The Hate U Give* as part of the Black Lives Matter movement. Another possibility would be the series *Alias Grace*. Justina is labeled with a "P" (for "*prostituta*") but fights back with her voice; for her part, Grace—after her release from an insane asylum where she served a sentence for allegedly abetting a murder—narrates while in an induced hypnotic trance the terrible events in her life, thus getting back at the man who had coerced and framed her. To round out class discussions, Sor Juana's *Respuesta* or any number of her sonnets serve as points of reference—sometimes surprisingly akin to today's questions—with regard to gender roles, misogyny, and representations of women.

In "'A Most Timely Message for This Tired and Cynical World': *Man of La Mancha* (1965) as the Depoliticization of Counterculture Quixotism," William Childers decries the "hollow sentimentalism" of Dale Wasserman's 1965 *Man of La Mancha* (based on his 1959 teleplay *I, Don Quixote*), yet he opts to teach the musical and its Cold War context, particularly focusing on the original lyrics—never incorporated by Wasserman—by W. H. Auden. Childers stresses the underlying ideological tensions of *Don Quijote* (and Don Quijote) in the era of the Cold War (for instance, bringing to bear George Balanchine's dance *Don Quixote*, a conservative, "romantic" view that was encouraged by a CIA arts-related front organization). He asks students to read Jack Kerouac's Cervantes-inspired *Dharma Bums* or to view Brue Baillie's *Quixote*, as well as having them study Auden's lyrics from *Man*. Wasserman sought to appeal across a political spectrum by removing controversy. *Man* "functioned like a form of group therapy for a nation in crisis . . . ." Even though other writers produced versions of the *Quijote* that focused on a Quijote-like character's struggles against prevailing norms, such as Kathy Acker's *Don Quixote* or Terry Gilliam's film *The Fisher King*. Wasserman's musical held a place in the culturally turbulent 1960s that allowed either the political left or right to draw conclusions from this adaptation. Until well near his death, the writer wished to ensure that *Man of La Mancha* continued in its depoliticized vein: he had a stranglehold on how productions could be mounted. Yet even with airtight authorial control, the underlying issues of the play's setting (a prison), the character's struggles against the official forces arrayed against him, and the universal nature of what we call quixotic come to the fore.

Don Quijote is ever a rich source for seeking ways to bring the early modern period to life through comparisons with contemporary popular culture, as Yolanda Gamboa shows in "Pop Don Quixote: *The Big Bang Theory* as Quixotic Emulation." She initiates her class by asking what it means to be "quixotic" and by assigning texts influenced by the *Quixote*; students are able to see how they encounter "Don Quixote" in their daily lives (statues, restaurant names, cartoon characters) which, in turn, enables them to forge a personal connection. Gamboa teaches in the Miami, FL, area, and its prevalent Hispanic culture presents her with a multi-cultural living laboratory for her approach. After reviewing selected critical writings on the *Quixote* and contemporary culture, Gamboa introduces the TV sitcom, *The Big Bang Theory*. Reading Cervantes and watching the show enable the students to perceive similar categories of humor and structure between the two works: the use of pairs, blurring boundaries between fantasy and reality, the experience of the journey, and reflections on contemporary issues. Gamboa concludes that similarities between Cervantes' time and our own—communication revolutions and the instability of "truth"—enhance twenty-first-century appreciation for the *Quijote* and the creations that ultimately derive from it. To see the truth is not a quixotic venture but a persistent question that engages everyone.

Margaret Marek likewise focuses on Cervantes' masterpiece by offering an examination of the points of contact between the Western and *Don Quijote* in "The Fastest Lance in the West: Don Quijote, High Plains Drifter." She suggests that the two have a great deal in common ("issues of national identity, violence, race, gender, and even religion"), thereby making the Western "an ideal form of pop culture for the teaching of the *Quijote* to today's undergraduate students." Marek traces the history, general characteristics, and popularity of the Western, inserting examples from the *Quijote* that appeared in Westerns from their earliest days: writers and filmmakers used the frontier much like Cervantes' fictional Don Quijote, who leaves his home to begin a quest and engage in a series of adventures where he can establish his new identity. She also discusses the Spanish Inquisition's procedures for approving publications and the burning of Don Quijote's library, which she compares to the censorship of the industry via the Motion Picture Production Code and the Catholic Church's Legion of Decency. Sub-section titles such as "The Good, the Bad and the Ugly: Showdown at the corral (*de comedias*)" illustrate the ways in which the conflicts between Cervantes and Lope reappear in divisions between advocates of the American and Spaghetti Westerns and between John Wayne and Clint Eastwood in creating the definition of the ideal Western.

Bradley J. Nelson compares and contrasts feminist questioning of early modern sexual violence and gender- and class-based injustice in Zayas's novella *El jardín encantado* and Tirso's *El Burlador de Sevilla*, and he further examines these issues from the perspectives of two twenty-first-century television programs, *Criminal Minds* and *Orange is the New Black*. The two late-modern television series portray sex crimes and the re-victimizing ways in which the criminal justice system treats female perpetrators and survivors of sexual violence. Nelson's goal is to teach students to consider how art can either affirm or interrogate power relations and to understand the ways in which public exposure and shaming often ironically exacerbate social biases and discrimination). Like several other essays in this volume, he also brings to the conversation relationships between art and the artist, as has recently been reflected in the situations of Woody Allen, Bill Cosby, and Harvey Weinstein and their relationship with the #MeToo movement.

In "#MeToo in Early Modern Spain: Visual Pleasures and Silence Breakers," Sonia Pérez-Villanueva discusses several of the same issues that Nelson tackles in his essay as she explores the cultural portrayal of violence against women. Pérez-Villanueva describes a course, "Representations of Violence against Women in Spain," which treats the topic via visual, literary, and cultural-history analyses. She examines the legal history of defining and dealing with rape as she sheds light on the true case of a seventeenth-century survivor of rape and breaker of silence who insisted on taking her complaint to court, and who ultimately lost her case due to the social and legal codes that protected Spanish men, especially those of the upper classes. Pérez-Villanueva then compares that early modern legal case with a contemporary one, noting current thinking on the ways in which women's words and bodies are devalued even today. The early modern vs. modern analogies include a discussion of the #MeToo movement and the concept of heroic rape, as exemplified by King Phillip II's commissions of works (principally nudes) by Titian.

Reconsidering Early Modern Spanish Literature through Mass and Pop Culture: Contemporizing the Classics for the Classroom offers a diverse exploration of the ways in which popular and mass culture can serve as valuable tools in the classroom. The summaries we have provided lay out the impressive array of possibilities we and our colleagues have at our disposal for making everything old new again or, in other words, for revealing that there is little new under the sun. This does not subvert the originality of either the early texts or today's popular ones. Rather, the ties that bind the medieval and early modern periods with our own late modernity reveal themselves as we and our students reach an increasing awareness of how fundamental aspects of the human condition remain constant and of how art attempts to respond to the challenges of daily life's joys, sorrows, inequities, and injustices. As the authors present their own pedagogical approaches and the theories that serve to guide them, we recognize ever more clearly the intertwined roles of context and relevance in the socio-cultural perspectives that help us understand texts that were written four or more centuries ago. The essays also remind us that when our students engage actively with these perspectives via contemporary media and culture, they learn strategies that not only aid them in understanding the Spanish classics, but also issues of great significance in their own lives. Ultimately, this collection advocates for an approach to teaching and learning that welcomes our students' contributions to the acquisition of knowledge in an ever-changing yet surprisingly consistent world.

CATHERINE LARSON
Professor Emerita
Indiana University

CHARLES VICTOR GANELIN
Professor Emeritus
Miami University of Ohio

Acknowledgments

WE SHOULD FIRST RECOGNIZE our fabulous colleagues who agreed to collaborate with us on a project when it was only in its infancy and whose commitment to teaching and research is unparalleled. We appreciate your friendship, your thoughtful contributions, your gracious acceptance of feedback, your attention to detail and deadlines, and your cooperation. We are also grateful for your patience when things did not go exactly as planned.

We would like to offer a special thanks to Charles Ganelin, Cathy Larson and Ed Friedman, our former professors. To say that we are lucky to have worked with you would be an understatement. We are indebted to you for not only bookending the manuscript—not to mention taking the initiative to provide feedback on the essays themselves—but also for your nearly three-decades-long mentorship. Our commitment to connecting students to the texts that we love and study stems from the experiences we had with you as our guides. We learned from the best, and we would not be where we are today without your encouragement, guidance and example.

Additional thanks go out to the following individuals for their suggestions, advice and interest in this project: Tim Rosenow, Marie Kelleher, Max Rosenkrantz, Christine Jocoy, Laura Vidler, Beth Manke, Jennifer Fleming, Jessica Pandya, Alessandro Russo, Anahit Manoukian, Alexis Pavenick, Lee Salkowitz, Carol Dzadony-Mancini, Eunha Choi, Pia Gupta, Yuwa Ho, Michelle Warren, Tracey Mayfield, Emily Tobey, Trace Camacho, Ali Iğmen, Markus Muller, Antonio Badía, Emma and Gabi Badía, the Damas Jóvenes, and last but not least, the best typing teacher Bonnie could have asked for in high school, Gigi DePascale.

Those responsible for bringing the book to fruition in more material ways are likewise worthy of mention. Bonnie would like to thank her Dean, David Wallace, for a converted assigned time award, which allowed her to hire two research assistants, Jaclyn Taylor, indexer extraordinaire, and Taylor Andrews, who gave valuable input as a third editor. Together, they accomplished what she, as an interim administrator with faculty carryover, would never have had time to complete otherwise. She would also like to thank the Chair of RGRLL, Aparna Nayak, for subvention support. Mindy was awarded an overseas travel grant from Indiana University Bloomington to participate in a conference that would ultimately become the basis for this book, as well as a Summer Faculty Fellowship from Indiana University Southeast to complete final revisions on the manuscript. And of course, we both applaud the all-star staff at Juan de la Cuesta.

Lastly, we'd—perhaps obviously—like to thank one another. Book editing is not easy, but it is much more fun when you do it alongside someone with an impeccable work ethic, a wicked sense of humor, and the ability to know when to take a break and just talk about retail therapy, pushups or Snoop Dogg.

Introduction

IN OCTOBER 2016, BOB DYLAN became the first singer/songwriter to receive a Nobel Prize in Literature for, as the award read, "having created new poetic expressions within the great American song tradition" (qtd. in Ellis-Petersen and Flood). Although some, such as Salman Rushdie and Joyce Carol Oates, praised the Swedish Academy's choice, others reacted to the news with far less enthusiasm (Ellis-Petersen and Flood). Tweets from American writer Gary Shteyngart ("I totally get the Nobel committee. Reading books is hard.") and, more colorfully, Irvine Welsh ("I'm a Dylan fan, but this is an ill-conceived nostalgia award wrenched from the rancid prostates of senile, gibbering hippies.")[1] illustrate that, in spite of the ways that cultural studies may have reshaped college curricula in the humanities, the intersection of "high" literary art and popular culture remains at a provocative crossroads. Assuredly, one could argue, and some have, that Dylan's work has more in common with literary masters like Keats and Shelley (for Anglophiles) or Rimbaud and Verlaine (for Francophiles). Nevertheless, the fact that several of his songs made it to Billboard's Top Ten List ("Like A Rolling Stone" and "Rainy Day Women" made it to number 2), as well as Dylan's own reluctance to identify himself as a poet, cements his place in the annals of popular culture.

If we examine the objections raised by Shteyngart and Welsh, a common tension emerges between the perceived rigor of the Nobel and the accessibility of Dylan's work. Indeed, Shteyngart's "reading books is hard" focuses on the relative ease of receiving Dylan's message (through song), while Welsh states that the rock star was chosen because his work connected with the selection committee on an emotional level (nostalgia) rather, we presume,

---

1   A Quevedesque comment, to be sure.

than an intellectual one. In both instances, their criticism of Dylan's selection as a winner rests on the perceived lack of intellectual challenge posed by his songs, a position that implies that in order to be great, a writer's work must also be difficult.

While we may not share these particular objections to Dylan's Nobel Prize, his receipt of the award, and especially the ensuing debates that his selection inspired, illustrates three key principles of this volume. First, and as the lively commentary from Shteyngart and Welsh shows, merging popular culture and so-called elite literature ignites a spark, which, as we argue, enhances student engagement with course material. Second, the accessibility of popular culture, an aspect that Shteyngart and Welsh both acknowledge and lament, eases the movement towards unfamiliar textual territory for novice readers of *Siglo de Oro* texts. This is similar to the way that Dylan's prize exposed some music fans to the history of the Nobel Prize and to the poets with whom Dylan has been compared, perhaps for the first time. And third, once students have practiced critical analysis of both Golden Age and popular texts, they are equipped to resist the facile assumptions that popular culture's accessibility masks in order to delve into its discourse analytically. That is, the academic study of the Spanish *Siglo de Oro*, examined in conjunction with examples from popular and contemporary media, prepares students to adopt a critical perspective on their own cultural milieux in ways akin to the examination of definitions of high literary art and popular song that Dylan's award stimulated.

Guided by these three teaching principles: student engagement, textual accessibility, and critical analysis, this volume explores the uses of popular culture— defined by Tim Delaney as "the vernacular or people's culture that predominates in a society at a point in time" (6) —and mass culture—broadly understood as the ideas and values that develop from a shared exposure to the media, news, music, and art—to inform pedagogical approaches to the cultural production of early modern Spain. Delaney furthermore points out that "Popular culture is also informed by the mass media" (6). Our book weaves together two principal theoretical strands. First, it is informed by pedagogical research that asserts the importance of meeting students where they are in their intellectual and academic journeys. (See, for example, the work of Ernest Morrell cited later in this introduction). Second, it reflects the work of scholars like Anna Creadick, who, when she asserts that "Michael Denning is correct that 'all culture is mass culture under capitalism'" (258), upholds a view of cultural transmission whereby the mass media perpetuate attitudes, values and behaviors that affirm the socio-political status quo and, in many instances, perpetuate inequalities. Creadick's perspective as an educator, combined with Denning's observation as a cultural historian, underscores the importance of developing the skills of cultural critique in the specific context of the classroom in order for students to become, borrowing Judith Fetterley's terminology, "resisting readers," those capable of recognizing the ways that popular culture engages power relationships.

Although many scholars of the Spanish Golden Age carry out their work at institutions that prioritize teaching, inquiries into the literature and culture of early modern Spain that focus on pedagogy are scarce. In fact, to our knowledge, and as of the writing of this introduction, only books exist: *Approaches to Teaching Spanish Golden Age Drama* (1989), *Approaches to Teaching Early Modern Spanish Drama* (2006), and most recently, *Spanish Golden Age Texts in the Twenty-First Century: Teaching the Old Through the New* (2019). While the gold standard for teaching literature from the *MLA Approaches to Teaching* series has inspired instructors to consider multiple angles of textual analysis, these first two limit their scope to theater. Our volume goes a step further. For one, we are exclusively concerned with the ways in which pop and mass culture can be used to inform the teaching of a greater corpus of early modern texts, rather than focus solely on one work or literary genre. Our collection, then, aligns with the pedagogical aims of *Approaches* as well as the accessibility goals of *Twenty-First Century* to advance the broader applicability of pop and mass culture to specific texts (and vice versa), while suggesting ways to reimagine others. Our contributors thoughtfully compare modern-day phenomena (such as #MeToo, popular music, and film) with concepts that shaped the discursive production of the sixteenth- and seventeenth-century Hispanic world (blood purity, the socio-cultural treatment of women, mysticism, and otherness to name a few) and ponder not only how pop culture influences our reading(s) of primary sources but also how those centuries-old sources can inform twenty-first century worldviews. In this way, students realize that their understanding of literature, while often linear, must also be two-directional. The use of popular culture, then, makes for an innovative pedagogical approach that generates a familiar context for unfamiliar material, respects the students' academic and intellectual development as a process, and establishes the habit of thinking critically. This last point takes students beyond achieving so-called mastery of the classics by equipping them to reflect on and engage more fully with their own cultural environment both inside and outside the classroom in the name of liberal arts education.[2]

---

2   Our use of the phrase "their own cultural environment" simply refers to the aspects of students' everyday lives that seem ubiquitous and, therefore, may never be

At our volume's core lie our students, whose perspective and authority are emphasized in the learning (and teaching) process. While some instructors may certainly consider themselves pop culture savvy, students are the true masters of this domain since pop culture is a market-driven, youth-oriented phenomenon. Our contributors suggest ways to empower students in the classroom by recognizing the knowledge they already have and allowing them to take a more active role in building on it. Our book thus suggests that we move beyond the debate of "*Does* pop culture have a place in the classroom?" to "*How* can pop culture have a place in the classroom?" This type of integrative approach also affords students the understanding that popular culture evolves over time and that trends in culture today might not be trending tomorrow or next year (and that every era, including the Spanish Golden Age, has its own sort of pop culture). By highlighting pop culture's ephemeral nature, we can broach more philosophical questions that are relevant to students' lives as well as to the texts we teach. Indeed, as it posits connections with contemporary culture, the volume also asserts the relevance of early modern Spanish literature for contemporary readers. From a pragmatic perspective, this leads to better enrollments in our literature courses, increases the likelihood of maintaining robust Spanish programs, and, in a wider context, sustains student interest in what many have described as the "imperiled" humanities.

Our approach combines theory and practice, encompassing essays that envision the *Siglo de Oro* and its relationship to popular culture in abstract ways (which can then inform teaching), as well as essays that outline specific lessons and exercises that exemplify the use of popular culture as a classroom resource. Whether specific or broad, the ever-shifting pop and mass culture parallels drawn in this volume are meant to be inclusive rather than exclusive in their approach to texts. Students come to our classes with varied interests and experiences, so we do not presume that all are familiar to an equal extent with the popular culture references offered (or that all are equally intimidated by Góngora, for that matter). While a song or a television show might not be immediately recognizable or relevant, its themes and examples can help students (and us) make connections to others that perhaps are, which again underscores the learning process as a negotiated ebb and flow. By suggesting metaphors that originate from outside academia, from an environment in which our students often feel more comfortable, we work our way inward together and on more equal footing. This is the case because, in order to accom-

---

examined critically. While these aspects are not the same for every student, they do exist for every student.

plish this task, most faculty will be required to do our own sort of homework and become more aware of our own zeitgeist and its classroom applicability and potential. Thus, the ideas offered in this volume mediate the array of cultural, historical and linguistic challenges that stem from the fact that our students are at least four centuries removed from the early modern period.

The effectiveness of popular culture as a pedagogical tool has been suggested by numerous scholars across disciplines. In some instances, their work addresses faculty resistance (both spoken and unspoken) to objects and instruments of inquiry that conventionally fall outside academia. Mark Lawrence Schrad lists common reasons why some educators reject popular culture as a teaching tool:

> [T]he assumption that any injection of "style" into a lecture necessarily comes at the expense of substance; arguments in favor of forcing students to adjust their styles of learning rather than requiring the instructor to adjust his or her style of teaching; instructors' desire not to 'pander' to the interests or purportedly shorter attention spans of students; or scoffing dismissals of student self-evaluations that claim that students do not properly understand what effective teaching is, and therefore anything that students actually enjoy—anything that holds their attention or keeps them engaged—is necessarily bad. (764)

Schrad uses results from surveys administered to students in his political science courses to make the case for the what he terms the "populist lecture," offering additional evidence of popular culture's ability to stimulate student interest, improve understanding and retention of course material, and encourage critical thinking (762-63). William Warner takes Schrad's observations a step further by impugning the deep-seated intellectual anxieties of faculty and their accompanying ironic underpinnings, which relates to Anna Creadick's notion of "the radical mutability of categories of cultural value" (17):

> When intellectuals show 'no respect' for the popular culture they consume, eschew, translate, and repress, they are feeling the allure of popular culture at the same time that [the] experience unsettles their vocation. The intellectual's resistance to popular culture becomes a way to sustain the moral claim to stand above the unmanageable flows of the popular. (732)

Our approach asks colleagues to resist this resistance to mass and popular culture in light of its usefulness as a teaching tool.

Researchers have identified popular culture's ability to enhance instruction in capacities that echo the three guiding principles of this volume mentioned previously: student engagement, reading comprehension, teacher/student relationships, and critical thinking. With respect to engagement, Ernest Morrell advocates for integrating popular culture in the classroom due to its unifying potential: "We, especially in the humanities, tend to set up this choice between pop culture and the "high" literature/art/culture we want to teach, but really pop culture is one of the main and most effective bridges between what our students know and what we want them to know" (Ace Alliance Blog). With respect to reading comprehension, Catherine G. Bellver writes of music as the "hook" that "taps into the readers' known information or experience" (889), and Ginger M. Eikmeier specifically addresses the ways that incorporating popular culture into our curricula enhances cognition, arguing that it forms part of students' prior knowledge and that "activating prior knowledge . . . is a major factor of reading comprehension. . . . It is what allows students to connect what they are reading to what they already know" (77). With respect to teacher/student relationships, Eikmeier also asserts that incorporating cultural references that form part of the students' realities outside the classroom shows them that faculty "do think about their needs and interests when we design instruction" (80) and, in a similar vein, Tiffany J. Hunt and Bud Hunt observe that "[Although] we have no requirement to be invested in our students' worlds, in the areas of culture that they find personally meaningful . . . [w]e suggest that teachers who are interested in building connections with students should spend time in their cultural worlds" (82). Finally, Maryan Mraz, Alison H. Heron and Karen Wood discuss the ways that using popular culture texts as pedagogical tools improves students' "critical media literacy," (the ability to think analytically about a variety of media), concluding that:

> Media literacy, particularly as it relates to popular culture, is a dimension of literacy that cannot be ignored by educators. By acknowledging and respecting the influence of media literacy on our adolescents' lives outside the classroom, teachers have a potential source for motivating student interest and eliciting their higher-order thinking abilities within the classroom. (55)[3]

---

3   Although the authors refer to the importance of media literacy for high school students, their observations are also relevant for university undergraduates.

Using these studies as a complement to our own experiences in the classroom, we show that in order to make connections between the cultural components of the material that we teach—those esoteric subjects such as mysticism, epic poetry, courtly love, and honor, for example—and those that constitute the worlds in which our students operate when they are not in class—rife with reality television, hashtags, vampires and Instagram— we must find common pedagogical ground in order to negotiate more fruitfully the learning process. Given this imperative, our volume explores ways in which we can make sixteenth- and seventeenth-century Spanish cultural production more accessible and less daunting for twenty-first century college students in the U.S. , helping them stay engaged, learn more effectively, and feel like experts—and thus, in control of and responsible for, if not motivated toward—their own learning.

Our approach to teaching the *Siglo de Oro* also dismantles the low/high culture binary, making the implicit argument that in significant ways, certain instances of early modern Spanish artistic expression existed as the popular culture of their time. The aesthetic disputes between Góngora and Quevedo (*cultistas* vs. *conceptistas*) and Lope and Cervantes (the latter of whom accused the former of being a sellout playwright), for example, bring to the fore issues such as the accessibility of the text, the role of the audience in shaping literary content, and culture as a commodity. In fact, with just these few examples, we see that the boundaries between high and low culture were already being negotiated, drawn, and redrawn in the early modern Hispanic world, and that our book, as well as the ideas that it rouses in our students, forms part of a longer history of the critical examination of the relationships between literature and society. By analyzing contemporary popular culture in light of its connections with the textual production of the early modern Spanish-speaking world, the latter becomes more familiar, while the former, de-familiarized, becomes a focus of critical engagement.

This book brings together the work of some of the most prominent scholars in the field of early modern Hispanic studies. These experts, working with a variety of genres and from multiple perspectives, illuminate the possibilities that discussions of popular and mass culture can bring to the literary experience. Most essays combine a defined theoretical approach with anecdote, the latter of which has been recognized as an effective means of synthesizing "particularity and universality as well as the theoretical and the practical" (Weber 1) in the context of pedagogical research. The volume's organization reflects the value we place on both theory and practice; although each essay contains both analysis and application, we have grouped the contributions into three units that move from the abstract to the concrete: Part I focuses primarily on theoretical readings, Part II combines theory and practice, and Part III offers specific examples of classroom exercises and approaches. Within this framework, the essays are arranged alphabetically. Additionally, we are honored to include contributions from our former professors, Charles Ganelin and Cathy Larson (who wrote the foreword), and Edward Friedman (who wrote the afterword). As professional role models, they instilled in us the profound respect for students and sprit of warm collegiality that helped shape this book.

The volume encompassses a wide range of early modern Spanish cultural production, incorporating all principal literary genres, art, and socio-cultural concepts (for example, "blood purity") that shaped aesthetic activity. We provide a wide array of examples from which our readers can choose as they determine which selections to emphasize in their own classrooms, thereby establishing the relevance of our book for the widest audience possible. References to popular and mass culture draw primarily from popular media in the United States because of its potential to engage our intended audience— scholars and teachers of early modern Spanish-language literature and culture working in U.S. universities—as well as their intended audience, the students. In sum, and mindful of recent trends in academia that emphasize the interconnectedness of scholarship and teaching, we envision the volume as a means of linking research and pedagogy without diminishing the seriousness of either endeavor.

There may be some who read our book and wonder how the theoretical approaches and classroom practices described in it, many of which emphasize establishing the contemporary popular culture context, help students understand the cultural production of early modern Spain. Because our book addresses an expert audience, it does not include ideas about how to provide students with an overview of the *Siglo de Oro*. Rather, we offer recontextualizations of the classics as a complement to instructors' own approaches in order to promote student engagement and enliven class discussions. We envision the volume being embraced by both junior and senior faculty in ways that inspire and invigorate both teacher and student. Ultimately, our goal is to motivate educators at all levels and in related disciplines to infuse their teaching with pop and mass culture as a way to level the academic playing field.

- *B.L.G.*
- *M.E.B.*

Works Cited

Bardsley, Alyson. "Girlfight the Power: Teaching Contemporary Feminism and Pop Culture." *Feminist Teacher*, vol. 16, no. 3, 2006, pp. 189-204.

Bass, Laura and Margaret Greer. *Approaches to Teaching Early Modern Spanish Drama*. The Modern Language Association of America, 2006.

Bellver, Catherine G. "Music as Hook in the Literature Classroom." *Hispania*, vol. 91, no. 4, December 2008, pp. 887-96.

Creadick, Anna. "Everybody's Doing It: Teaching Popular Culture," *Transformations: The Journal of Inclusive Scholarship and Pedagogy*, vol. 24, nos. 1-2, Spring 2013/Summer 2013 & Fall 2013/Winter 2014, pp. 15-24.

——Delaney, Tim. "Pop Culture: An Overview." *Philosophy Now*, vol 64, November/December 2007, pp. 6-7.

Eikmeier, Ginger M. "'D'oh!' Using *The Simpsons* to Improve Student Response to Literature." *The English Journal*, vol. 97, no. 4, March 2008, pp. 77-80.

Ellis-Petersen, Hannah, and Alison Flood. "Bob Dylan Wins the Nobel Prize in Literature." *The Guardian*. 13 October 2016, https://www.theguardian.com/books/2016/oct/13/bob-dylan-wins-2016-nobel-prize-in-literature. Accessed 11 November 2018.

Fetterley, Judith. *Resisting Readers: A Feminist Approach to American Literature*. Indiana UP, 1978.

Hesse, Everett Wesley, Ed. *Approaches to Teaching Spanish Golden Age Drama*. Spanish Literature Publications Company, 1989.

Hunt, Tiffany J., and Bud Hunt. "New Voices: Popular Culture: Building Connections With Our Students." *The English Journal*, vol. 93, no. 3, January 2004, pp. 80-83.

Mraz, Maryann, et al. "Research Into Practice Media Literacy, Popular Culture, and the Transfer of Higher-Order Thinking Abilities." *Middle School Journal*, vol. 34, no. 3, January 2003, pp. 51-56, www.jstor.org/stable/23043901?read-now=1&googleloggedin=true&seq=1#metadata_info_tab_contents. Accessed 10 October 2018.

——Puig, Idoya and Karl McLoughlin. *Spanish Golden Age Texts in the Twenty-First Century: Teaching the Old Through the New*. Peter Lang, 2019.

Schrad, Mark Lawrence. "In Defence of the Populist Lecture." *PS: Political Science and Politics*, vol. 43, no. 4, October 2010, pp. 759-65.

Shteyngart, Gary (@Shtyngart). "I totally get the Nobel committee. Reading books is hard." 13 October 2016, 5:10 a.m. Tweet.

Trier, James. "Teaching with Media and Popular Culture." *Journal of Adolescent & Adult Literacy*, vol. 49, no. 5, February 2006, pp. 434-38.

Warner, William. "The Resistance to Popular Culture in the Classroom." *American Literary History*, vol. 2, no. 4, Winter 1990, pp. 726-42.

Welsh, Irvine (@IrvineWelsh). "I'm a Dylan fan, but this is an ill-conceived nostalgia award wrenched from the rancid prostates of senile, gibbering hippies." 13 October 2016, 5:11 a.m. Tweet.

PART I
Theoretical Practice

Harry Potter and the Buried Self: *Pureza de sangre*, Cryptonomy, and the Ethics of Concealment in J.K. Rowling's Potterverse

BRUCE R. BURNINGHAM
Illinois State University

THIS ESSAY HAS ITS origins in a panel discussion that occurred in May 2014 at the "49th International Congress on Medieval Studies" held at Western Michigan University in Kalamazoo. The program of that year's congress included a session, apparently one of an annual series of ongoing Kalamazoo panels, titled "The Medievalism of J. K. Rowling's Harry Potter Volumes." Having spent several years reading the Harry Potter novels and seeing the subsequent film adaptations with my adolescent children, I was particularly drawn to this 2014 panel. None of the four papers presented as part of the session was directly related to general notions of "blood purity" (much less to the specific context of early modern Iberian *pureza de sangre* statutes). However, during the session's question-and-answer period, something interesting occurred that not only sparked my curiosity, but also led me to think that an essay on this specific topic would be an indispensable pedagogical tool for the current generation of *Harry Potter* fans who still comprise the vast majority of our undergraduate student population.

The Harry Potter series consists of seven novels and eight subsequent film adaptations (the seventh novel was split into two films). The first of these novels, *Harry Potter and the Sorcerer's Stone* (initially published in England under the title *Harry Potter and the Philosopher's Stone*), came out in 1997; the seventh novel, *Harry Potter and the Deathly Hallows*, was published in 2007. The various films, whose titles match each of the seven US novel titles, were released by Warner Bros. between 2001 and 2011. The films principally star Daniel Radcliffe as Harry Potter, Emma Watson as Hermione Granger, and Rupert Grint as Ron Weasley but also feature large recurring cast that includes such actors as Richard Harris, Maggie Smith, Robbie Coltrane, Alan Rickman, Michael Gambon, and Ralph Fiennes (among many others). As a global phenomenon, the Harry Potter novels have been translated into some 80 languages; the film versions have not only grossed nearly 8 billion dollars worldwide, but have also inspired a theme park area at Universal Studios in Orlando, Florida; and the entire Harry Potter enterprise has made Rowling a multimillionaire many times over.

Rowling's overarching narrative tells the story of a young, orphaned boy named Harry Potter who, after spending his first eleven years living with his suburban uncle and aunt (who treat him like a pariah, famously making him sleep in a cupboard under the stairs), discovers that he is, in fact, a wizard whose parents were murdered by an evil wizard named Lord Voldemort when he was just an infant. More to the point, Voldemort also attempted to obliterate Harry during the attack that killed his parents, and what makes Harry, therefore, special (and so famous among wizards) is that he is "the boy who lived" (*Sorcerer's Stone* 17). This initial violent encounter between Harry and Voldemort has left Harry with a permanent scar on his forehead in the shape of a lightning bolt, but has also left Voldemort far worse for wear: at the beginning of the first novel, Voldemort has been reduced physically to just barely more than a non-entity and socially to little more than a hushed rumor exchanged by people who can only bring themselves to call him "You-Know-Who" or "He-Who-Must-Not-Be-Named" (*Sorcerer's Stone* 11, 85). Over the course of the seven novels, each of which centers around a new academic year at Hogwarts School of Witchcraft and Wizardry, a larger struggle between the forces of good and evil plays out as Voldemort seeks little by little to reconstitute himself so that he can become the absolute dictatorial Lord over the entire wizarding world.

One of the key elements of Rowling's overarching narrative is a preoccupation with "blood purity," with the "Potterverse" (as scholars have come to refer to the fictional world of the Harry Potter series and its several spinoffs) being roughly divided into four "ethnic" groups. At one extreme there are "pureblood" wizards whose wizarding pedigree (going back countless generations) is unquestioned and unquestionable. At the other extreme, there are "Muggles," who are basically regular humans with no magical powers whatsoever. In between these two extremes, there are "Squibs," who come from well-pedigreed pureblood wizarding families but who exhibit no magical capacities, as well as people derisively referred to as "Mudbloods," who come either from pure Muggle families or from "mixed" families, but who do indeed display magical powers (Hermione Granger is just such a character). Over the course of the seven novels, various factions debate—and often fight over—the "proper" role of Muggle-borns in the wizarding world, with those factions allied with Voldemort believing that only pureblood wizards ought to hold positions of authority and those more "liberal" factions allied with Harry Potter believing in a much more "integrated" wizarding community.

And this brings us back to the aforementioned Kalamazoo question-and-answer period. During this panel discussion, the topic of conversation eventually turned to Rowling's representation of ethnicity and its relationship to twentieth-century German anti-Semitism. At this point, I raised my hand and mentioned that, for Hispanists, Rowling's discourse on "blood purity" in her novels necessarily carries echoes of earlier European anti-Semitic traditions, particularly the *pureza de sangre* statutes that were enacted in early modern Spain. My comments were basically met with vacant stares. Not only did my observation not engender any significant discussion, but after a moment or two of uncomfortable silence, coupled with a polite but somewhat dismissive nod from the panel moderator, everyone went back to talking about German anti-Semitism. At this point, I realized that most contemporary readers of the Harry Potter series, including students in undergraduate Spanish courses, usually don't even know what they don't know about the importance of the Spanish tradition and its continuing impact on the modern world, which is why an essay such as this one can help expand the "cultural literacy" of twenty-first-century media text readers beyond the narrow information they may have gleaned from watching films like *Schindler's List*, *Saving Private Ryan*, and *Inglourious Basterds*.

Still, the work of non-Hispanists on the issue of race and ethnicity in the Harry Potter novels is well worth examining. Most contemporary scholars see in this trope of "blood purity" an obvious connection to our own contemporary concerns regarding race and ethnicity, with many of these scholars exploring the issue from the general perspective of the Self and Other. Hillary Jones, for instance, examines what she calls the "Muggle/Wizard Binary" and notes that the discourse of the novels leads readers to "understand that Muggles constitute the derogated half" of the binary, and that the "wizard" half of the pair is to be viewed as "ordinary and normal" (97). Laura Loiacono and Grace Loiacono, for their part, highlight the ubiquity of such binary discursive tendencies even among those characters sympathetic to the cause of magical integration: "Wizards such as Dumbledore and his followers use polite terms when labeling people, but even they acknowledge the existence of social hierarchy based on blood" (184). Indeed, as Jennifer

Sterling-Folker and Brian Folker point out, "When magicals use the term *muggle* it is not meant as a compliment. Even among magicals who profess a fondness for muggles, there is an effort to disassociate from them" (119).

Other scholars explore the importance of Rowling's representation of the Potterverse's ethnicities from the more particular perspective of "whiteness studies." Raymond Schuck, for instances, notes that "The Harry Potter series occurs within a society that has been stratified by birthright, as the stories take place within the backdrop of the feud between 'pure' wizards and, basically, everyone else, though particularly those wizards not identified as 'pure'" (16). For Schuck, Rowling's "stratification of society into 'pure' and 'impure'" categories "connects to notions of purity associated with and utilized by white supremacist groups who condemn racial integration and miscegenation" (16). Moreover, notes Schuck, this stratification carries over even into the assignment (via the "Sorting Hat") of first-year Hogwarts students to the various "houses" (i.e., Griffindor, Slytherin, Hufflepuff, and Ravenclaw) around which their Hogwarts experience will revolve: "Muggle-born wizards do not get full choice; they are instantly ineligible for Slytherin" (19). Kristen Cole also notes the way in which "pure" wizard blood functions as a stand-in for "whiteness," particularly with regard to the Sorting Hat, and "white privilege" (154-56). Going further still, Elaine Ostry argues that the Harry Potter series "enacts a great 'race war,' in which the heroes fight against those wizards who possess a vision of racial purity" (89). Ostry notes, for instance, that within the Potterverse, magically coded racial epithets might even be considered a form of hate speech: "Ron explains that Mudblood is a 'really foul' term for a Muggle-born (as opposed to 'pure-blood') wizard. It is, in short, the N-word for the wizarding world. Perhaps Rowling is aware that one of the worst insults leveled against African Americans is 'mud people'" (92). (Ostry also mentions, not without irony, that Rowling's own apparent "color blindness" with regard to the "real world" of contemporary Britain is not unproblematic: "Minorities are mentioned, but they are not heroes; all the major players are Anglo-Saxon" [93-94].)

A third group of scholars specifically examine Rowling's representation of race and ethnicity from within the perspective of postcolonial theory. Hannah Lamb, for instance, argues that "The British wizards' relations with the Other present in their country, the Muggles, demonstrate further the nostalgia for a British imperial identity" (62). Along these same lines, Tess Stockslager examines the only three identifiable Potterverse characters—Tom Riddle (as he was known before he become Voldemort), Severus Snape, and Seamus Finnegan—who are, strictly speaking, magically biracial (that is, stem from one wizard parent and one Muggle parent) and argues that Seamus Finnegan's Irish ancestry is important:

> If Muggles and Muggle-borns are the Other, then half-bloods are somewhere in between the Other and the people who set the terms. Historically, the Irish occupy a similar position in the British consciousness. In British colonial writing, natives of Africa, Asia, and the Pacific islands are clearly the Other, but the status of the Irish is not so clear. (126)

For Stocklsager, magically "biracial" and "bilingual" characters such as Finnegan, Snape, and Riddle are not only forced to engage in a kind of magical "code switching" with their Muggle halves (128), but also carry with them a kind of postcolonial stigma that motivates their deepest desire for social acceptance. Moreover, Giselle Liza Anatol also notes the ways in which various giants, centaurs, and other magical folk function as stereotypical stand-ins for "First Nations peoples" and "indigenous peoples" who inhabit Rowling's postcolonial Potterverse ("Replication" 117-18):

> The travels of various British subjects outward in the name of Empire required a certain flexibility and porousness of England's borders. Not only could explorers, merchants, missionaries, and settlers travel *out*, but, in later years, multiracial, multicultural, and multinational subjects could travel back *in*. The borders between the nonmagical and magical worlds in the Harry Potter series are equally porous, making Hogwarts a pluralistic society, not only in terms of its pureblood and Muggle-born students, but also, ostensibly, in terms of other types of diversity. ("Replication" 112)

As Anatol argues in a different essay, however, such "porousness" lies behind many of the series' conflicts: "The fear of immigrant entry, reproduction, and take-over seems evident. Wizards and witches constantly worry about the threat of Muggles discovering and invading the magical realm" ("Fallen Empire" 170).

Beyond these more wide-ranging studies of the representation of race and ethnicity within the Harry Potter series, a few scholars—and working from the same knowledge-base that informed the aforementioned Kalamazoo panel—take a careful look at the specific connections between the Potterverse, European anti-Semitism, and the Nazi Third Reich. Such connections are by no means casual: "As J. K. Rowling herself notes, 'the Nazis used precisely the same warped logic as the Death Eaters' with regard to blood distinctions, and there are parallels between Voldemort's obsession with blood purity and Hitler's obsession with a pure Aryan race" (Sterling-Folker and Folker 118). As Sarah Wente further argues:

> Aryanism makes an appearance in the Harry Potter series through Draco and the Malfoy family. The Malfoys not only represent the antithesis of Harry's beliefs and values, but they also exemplify Hitler's idea of Aryan perfection. The physical appearance of the Malfoy family—blonde and presumably pale-eyed—makes them the embodiment of Hitler's Aryan profile. (94)

Of course, the most extended analyses of the connection between Harry Potter and National Socialism come from Nancy Reagin and Bethany Barratt. In an essay pointedly titled "Was Voldemort a Nazi?" (127), Reagin glosses a number of similarities between Voldemort's and Hitler's racist ideologies, but is supremely interested in the figure of Gellert Grindelwald: "Both Hitler and Grindelwald were from German-speaking Europe and were defeated in the watershed year of 1945 by British opponents" (132). Reagin later highlights the fact that "After Dumbledore defeated Grindelwald in 1945 and took the Elder Wand from him, Grindelwald was imprisoned in the topmost cell of Nurmengard Prison," adding that "the name *Nurmengard* resembles that of Nuremberg, the town where a series of famous trials of former Nazis and other war criminals was held after World War II" (148). Barratt, for her part, focuses specific attention on the Ministry of Magic's creation of its "Muggle-Born Registration Commission" as a prelude to the kinds of "ethnic cleansing" characteristic of the German Third Reich (68, 74). Indeed, as Reagin herself notes, the Commission's policy of confiscating the wands of Muggle-born wizards "paves the way for their economic destruction in the same way that Nazi policies of 'Aryanization' had done for German Jews, and the lack of a wand seems to stigmatize them almost as effectively as wearing a Star of David had for Jews" (143).

All this notwithstanding, Hispanists are likely to see in Rowling's overarching discourse of "blood purity" a reference not just to twentieth-century European anti-Semitism, but, more pointedly, to the Iberian Peninsula's own early modern preoccupations with *pureza de sangre*. For instance, Ruth Abrams, in the only published essay I have found that focuses specific attention on the Potterverse's Spanish connections, explores the ways in which the historical experience of Iberia's Jewish communities can inform our reading of the Potterverse. Taking as her point of departure the notion that "From the beginning of the Harry Potter series' popularity, Jewish readers have seen in its magical world a parallel to their own historical experience as a tiny cultural minority" (219), Abrams turns her attention to unpacking this connection, particularly through the socio-cultural similarities between Rowling's "pureblood" wizards and the *cristianos viejos* of the Iberian Peninsula:

> When we look at the position of Muggle-born wizards sent to Hogwarts while Lord Voldemort controlled the school and the Ministry of Magic, we can't help thinking of the people whose Jewish parents or grandparents were pressured into conversion to Catholicism, leaving them permanently suspect, neither Jewish nor Catholic. (221)

Over the course of some twenty-two pages, Abrams's essay serves as an essential primer on the Sephardic diaspora for a readership generally much more familiar with the Central and Eastern European Ashkenazi experience. Abrams gives an overview of Christian-Jewish relations on the Iberian Peninsula during the late Middle Ages; she notes the practice of forced conversion (especially after 1390 CE); she discusses the official enactment of the *pureza de sangre* statutes beginning in Toledo in 1449; and she traces the rise of the Spanish Inquisition, the autos-da-fé as well as the Catholic Monarchs' final expulsion of all non-converted Jews in 1492.

For Abrams, the most important connection between Rowling's representation of race and ethnicity in the Harry Potter series occurs through the way in which the Spanish Inquisition serves as a model for the Ministry's "Muggle-Born Registration Commission," which is overseen by what Wente calls its "High Inquisitor," Dolores Umbridge (109). Writes Abrams:

> Umbridge questions wizards and witches who have Muggle backgrounds with the assumption that they are guilty, just as the Inquisition chose its victims on the basis of ancestry, in the cases of the conversos and the moriscos. Like the Inquisition, Umbridge's tribunal keeps a bureaucratic record of everything that is said during the hearings. The Inquisitorial Instruction required that a scrupulous record of interrogations should be kept in all cases, with the macabre results that included fully documented screams of anguish and begging from the prisoners. (235)

Abrams then goes on to note—as does Henry Kamen, who insists that the central issue is really one of power far more than race or religion (20)—

that the Spanish Inquisition was "not an instrument of the Church of Rome so much as an instrument of the Spanish church and even more of the Spanish civil authorities" (Abrams 238): "Like the Inquisitors, Voldemort is most concerned with cementing his ideological position *within* wizarding institutions. Most of the *limpieza de sangre* statutes were enforced on people within church institutions, such as university faculty or students and members of religious orders" (238). In this way, Abrams argues, Voldemort uses the Ministry's inquisitorial Commission as a means of creating "a permanent class of persecuted people whose perceived threat would continue to justify his seizure of power" (238). I would only add to this that, by the time we get to *The Deathly Hallows*, blood purity becomes an even more obvious Iberian trope: "And it's also another way of weeding out Muggle-borns, because students must be given Blood Status—meaning that they have proven to the Ministry that they are of Wizard descent—before they are allowed to attend [Hogwarts]" (*Deathly Hallows* 210).

Scholars interested in linking Voldemort's anti-Muggle-born campaign to the murderous ideology of the Nazi Third Reich make much of Grindelwald's German ancestry and of the fact that this early supporter of magical blood purity was defeated by Dumbledore in the same year that the Allies defeated the Axis powers in World War II. Such a focus is not unimportant. As Reneé Ward rightly notes, "Many characters within *Harry Potter* have names that imply something about their natures, whether physical features or personality traits" (157). We need only think of Remus Lupin, Rowling's prominent werewolf character, or the kindly Xenophilius Lovegood, or even the aforementioned Dolores Umbridge, whose two names together suggest both her delight in inflicting "pain" on Muggle-borns as well as her preternatural "resentment" of all things non-pureblood. It is somewhat odd, then, that no one seems to have remarked on the crucial semantic value of the name of the character for whom Hogwart's most infamous house is honored: Salazar Slytherin. (As readers will recall, Slytherin is one of the four founders of Hogwarts—along with Godric Gryffindor, Helga Hufflepuff, and Rowena Ravenclaw—who established the school around the year 990 CE.)

Rowling's invented surname 'Slytherin,' of course, is foundational to the snake motif associated with Slytherin House and its members. And given that Rowling lived in Portugal during the early 1990s (Porto's Livraria Lello is said to be the inspiration for Hogwarts and its magical staircases), her decision to name at least one character after Portugal's dictatorial António de Oliveira Salazar—fellow-traveler of Spain's Francisco Franco as well as Adolf Hitler—is not unexpected. That said, unlike Gellert Grindelwald, Salazar

Slytherin is decidedly far removed from the Potterverse's more recent, twentieth-century history. As Stockslager notes,

> Salazar Slytherin is legendary as the Hogwarts founder who, after his demand that the school accept only pure-blood students was denied, built the Chambers of Secrets and placed within it the basilisk with the purpose of destroying Muggle-born students. Tom Riddle [young Voldemort], as the Heir of Slytherin, will open this chamber during his time at Hogwarts and later cause it to be opened again. (129)

Thus, as Sterling-Folker and Folker argue, "The Death Eater's obsession with blood purity is as old as Salazar Slytherin's participation in the creation of Hogwarts, and it seems to have been the central division among wizards and witches *since that time*" (109; my emphasis).

If we accept Reagin's aforementioned proposal for an onomastic connection between Nuremberg and Nurmengard, or Barratt's suggestion that Hogwarts' competitor school "Durmstrang" (which specifically excludes non-purebloods) is semantically connected to the German "Sturm und Drang" tradition "of which the anti-Semitic Richard Wagner was an adherent" (Barratt 75), a case can be made, I think, for connecting *Salazar* Slytherin not just to António de Oliveira *Salazar*, but also to the early modern Archbishop of Toledo: Juan Martínez Guijarro, who, as Robert Aleksander Maryks notes, "used the Latinized form of his name, *Silíceo*" (29; my emphasis), and whose preferred surname thus faintly echoes 'Salazar' in the same way 'Nurmengard' echoes 'Nuremberg,' and 'Durmstrang' echoes 'Sturm und Drang.' As Kamen pointedly reminds us, an "important step in *limpieza*" was taken when Silíceo "succeeded in imposing a statute on his cathedral" (21). Still, like Salazar Slytherin before him, Silíceo's preference for blood purity did not go unopposed (in ways that are uncannily similar to Rowling's description of Slytherin's unsuccessful attempts to impose *pureza de sangre* on Hogwarts). Says Robert Maryks:

> In none of the anti-converso laws did the 1449 *Sentencia-Estatuto* of Toledo leave its unlawful mark more than in the *Pureza-de-sangre* Statues (1547) of Juan Martínez Guijarro (1477-1557), Inquisitor General of Spain and Archbishop of Toledo. Even though Pope Paul IV and Guijarro's former pupil, King Philip II, ratified Guijarro's statutes in 1555 and 1556 Jesuit leaders would adamantly oppose the archbishop's attempt

to impose anti-converso laws on the Society of Jesus, which had been founded just a few years earlier. (29)

Likewise, as Kamen points out:

The growth of opinion against the statutes affected the Inquisition itself. In 1580 the Inquisitor General, cardinal Gaspar de Quiroga, who over thirty years previously had helped to vote for the statute in Toledo cathedral, began a move in favor of modifying the *limpieza* rules. His policy, followed by three subsequent Inquisitors General, developed into a movement to abolish the statutes completely. (22)

Yet, even if we discount any potentially echoing onomastic links between Salazar Slytherin and Juan Martínez Silíceo as perhaps too tenuous, it is nonetheless true that, at least discursively, the origins of the Potterverse's earliest obsession with blood purity lie not in nineteenth- and twentieth-century Germany, but in medieval and early modern Iberia. And this connection to an earlier tradition of Iberian blood purity—along with the social anxieties that arose because it of—is important because it has an impact on the larger issues at stake in Rowling's texts. As Abrams notes in her own essay: "Because wizards and witches keep their magical culture a secret from the wider Muggle culture, they seem like the crypto-Jews of late medieval Spain: people who were outwardly Christian but who secretly retained Jewish practices" (220). In fact, so crucial is the latent influence of Iberian crypto-Judaism on the Potterverse, that the entire Harry Potter narrative is haunted from start to finish by the specter of hidden identities, such that concealment of the "buried self" represents the dominant ethos of Rowling's master narrative, inspired, as it is, by what Jamie Warner calls a Foucauldian "Panopticon" at play in Rowling's text: "Someone must be watching" (Warner 148-51, 153).

The Potterverse's saturation with crypto-identities and buried selves takes place at all levels of the text. For instance, there are numerous individual characters who could be considered "passing as" something or someone else. The most basic of these individuals is the titular protagonist Harry Potter, who in the opening chapters of the first installment has spent his entire life so far living as a Muggle with the Dursleys. Indeed, this particular crypto-identity—deliberately engineered by Dumbledore to protect Harry during his childhood—is buried so deep that even Harry himself is unaware of his true identity until Hagrid ultimately divulges the secret: "Harry—yer a wizard"

(*Sorcerer's Stone* 50). Other characters who routinely hide their true identities in one way or another also include: the flamboyant and comically inept Gilderoy Lockhart, who spends much of his year at Hogwarts hiding the fact that he has not accomplished any of the great feats he credits to himself in his many autobiographical books (*The Chamber of Secrets*); the kindly Hogwarts professor Remus Lupin, who initially must conceal the fact that he is really a werewolf in order to maintain his social standing and employability (*The Prisoner of Azkaban, The Order of the Phoenix*, and *The Deathly Hallows*); the wicked Quirinus Quirrell, who hides the fact that his body serves as a physical host for what little remains of the weakened Voldemort (*The Sorcerer's Stone*); and the villainous Peter Pettigrew, who originally betrayed Harry's parents to Voldemort, and then spends several years hiding in plain sight as Ron Weasley's pet rat Scabbers (*The Prisoner of Azkaban, The Goblet of Fire, The Order of the Phoenix, The Half-Blood Prince*, and *The Deathly Hallows*). Also among this group of characters who "pass" for someone else are Riddle and Snape, both of whom are Muggle-born, and both of whom seem to be the characters most staunchly allied to Salazar Slytherin's original ideology of *pureza de sangre*. In the case of Riddle, his self-invented identity as Voldemort makes it easier for him to pass himself off as a pureblood (Barratt 73). In the case of Snape, his crypto-identity is actually a "double" buried self, since he not only hides his half-blood origins, but also (as we eventually learn in *The Deathly Hallows*) hides the fact that he has been a double-agent for Dumbledore all along.

At the level of society (both broadly and narrowly defined), crypto-identities also play an important role in the Potterverse. As mentioned above, the whole of the wizarding community—by hiding not just its magical identity, but even its entire population centers, institutions, and cultural traditions from the Muggle world—functions as a kind of early modern crypto-Jewish community hiding from its non-Jewish neighbors. Such a connection is far from coincidental, of course, as the 1689 decision by Rowling's Ministry of Magic to officially hide the entire wizarding community from Muggle eyes was the result of the kind of religious persecutions typical not just of the Spanish Inquisition in the late fifteenth century, but also the seventeenth-century Salem witch trials (de la Torre 52; Gupta 88). But beyond this macro-societal level of crypto-identities, Rowling also presents such micro-societal examples as the Dursley family, who know the truth about Harry's true identity (via his Aunt Petunia's sororal relationship to Harry's mother, Lily), but who also attempt to keep Harry's magical identity a secret from the rest of their Muggle friends and relatives in order to avoid what can only be called the stigma of suburban non-conformity. And then there are the Malfoys and the Lestranges, who spend much of the first several novels hiding their deep family loyalties to Voldemort until such time as it is safe to reveal their true identities as Death Eaters.

But even this societal level of buried selves pales in comparison to a more crucial metaphysical level of crypto-identity around which the entire Harry Potter narrative ultimately revolves. What allows Voldemort to essentially come back from the dead, following his encounter with an infant Harry Potter, is the existence of a series of "Horcruxes"—Tom Riddle's diary, Marvolo Gaunt's ring, Salazar Slytherin's locket, Hegla Hufflepuff's cup, Rowena Ravenclaw's diadem, Voldemort's snake Nagini, and, ironically, Harry Potter himself—into each of which he had previously concealed fragments of his soul. These Horcruxes not only lie at the heart of Rowling's seven-volume "quest narrative," in which Harry and his Hogwarts companions meticulously track down and destroy each of the dispersed shards of Voldemort's fragmented buried self (ironically, becoming Grand Inquisitors in their own right, rooting out all vestiges of what might be called the heresy of "Voldemortism"), but also constitute the core of what Nicolas Abraham and Maria Torok might call Rowling's metaphysical "cryptonomy": "The crypt works in the heart of the Ego as a special kind of Unconscious. Each fragment is conscious of itself and unconscious of the realm 'outside the crypt'" (80). Indeed, Voldemort's fragmented soul is hidden so profoundly within its scattered Potterversian Ego that even it is unaware that Harry Potter himself is one of its most important constituents. But there is still more. If, as Stockslager argues, Voldemort's passing as a pureblood "violently literalizes the concept of race as performance" (130), Harry Potter's status as an unwitting Horcrux can be read as a performance of Abraham and Torok's concept of the crypt: the place in the Unconscious where trauma is buried so deeply that only the barest hints of its existence manage to bubble up to the surface.

At the climax of the epic final encounter between Voldemort and Harry Potter in *The Deathly Hallows*, Harry actually allows Voldemort to kill him the second time around: "He saw the mouth move and a flash of green light, and everything was gone" (704). Or, so Harry thinks. At the beginning of the next chapter Harry wakes up in a kind of limbo, a metaphysical space that looks very much like King's Cross railway station, and where a pathetic and enigmatic creature figures prominently: "It had the form of a small, naked child, curled on the ground, its skin raw and rough, flayed-looking, and it lay shuddering under a seat where it had been left, unwanted, stuffed out of sight, struggling for breath" (706-07). Dumbledore also appears suddenly, and Harry and Dumbledore carry on a lengthy conversation (ever conscious of the presence of the "raw looking thing" [722]) in which all of the Potterverse's deepest secrets are finally divulged: that Harry was an unintended Horcrux; that he is somehow still alive because Voldemort used a drop of Harry's own blood to reconstitute his physical being; and that what has really died in this most recent deadly encounter was not so much Harry as the fragment of Voldemort's soul that had been encrypted within him.

More importantly, we also learn crucial information about Dumbledore's own trauma and about the resultant buried self that he too has kept secret since the beginning of the series. We learn that, prior to defeating Grindelwald in 1945, Dumbledore was actually an ally who shared Grindelwald's "pureblood" belief that Muggles should be "forced into subservience" (716). In this regard, Dumbledore's famous defeat of Grindelwald, it turns out, is less about the triumph of good over evil than it is about a power struggle between two like-minded wizards—a struggle that accidentally ends with the death of Dumbledore's sister Ariana. And this, then, is the core trauma that lies at the heart of all the Potterverse's buried secrets and crypto-identities: that Dumbledore himself is as responsible as Grindelwald for Voldemort's rise to power. And whether we read the presence of the "small, maimed creature" in King's Cross station as a figure of the dead Ariana (708), or as a symbol of the evil that can tempt even the noblest souls, or simply as a metaphor for the dreadful "truth" that cannot be faced (718), Rowling's metaphysical version of King's Cross—a place that explicitly exists inside Harry's head, but which Dumbledore insists is no less "real" (723)—turns out to be the Potterverse's most important "chamber of secrets." It is, in fact, Rowling's deepest crypt and one that is only fully accessible to readers who know something about early modern Iberian *pureza de sangre* and its aftermath.

But this brings me back to my point of departure. If a truly profound and nuanced appreciation of the multiple and interconnected buried selves that inhabit Rowling's Potterverse requires more than just an awareness of Nazi ideology and its horrors, then it behooves us as Hispanists to teach works like the Harry Potter series (both in its traditional print format and on film) alongside early modern Spanish texts, if for no other reason than to increase the chances—however slightly—that the next time someone references the Iberian *pureza de sangre* statues in a discussion of contemporary anti-Semitism there might be someone else in the room who can help move the discussion forward and thus broaden the horizons of those who still don't know what they don't know.

Works Cited

Abraham, Nicolas, and Maria Torok. *The Wolf Man's Magic Word: A Cryptonomy*. Translated by Nicholas Rand, U of Minnesota P, 1986.

Abrams, Ruth. "Of Marranos and Mudbloods: Harry Potter and the Spanish Inquisition." *Harry Potter and History*, edited by Nancy R. Reagin, Wiley, 2011, pp. 219-41.

Anatol, Giselle Liza. "The Fallen Empire: Exploring Ethnic Otherness in the World of Harry Potter." *Reading Harry Potter: Critical Essays*, edited by Giselle Liza Anatol, Praeger, 2003, pp. 163-78.

———. "The Replication of Victorian Racial Ideology in Harry Potter." *Reading Harry Potter Again: New Critical Essays*, edited by Giselle Liza Anatol, ABC-CLIO, 2009, pp. 109-26.

Barratt, Bethany. *The Politics of Harry Potter*. Palgrave, 2012.

Cole, Kristen L. "Transcending Hogwarts: Pedagogical Practices Engendering Discourses of Aggression and Bullying." *Wizards vs. Muggles: Essays on Identity and the Harry Potter Universe*, edited by Christopher E. Bell, McFarland, 2016, pp. 149-67.

De la Torre, Elizabeth. "The Muggle Hunt." *Hermione Granger Saves the World: Essays on the Feminist Heroine of Hogwarts*, edited by Christopher E. Bell, McFarland, 2012, pp. 52-64.

Gupta, Suman. *Re-Reading Harry Potter*. 2nd ed., Palgrave, 2009.

Jones, Hillary A. "'I'm a Wizard Too!': Identification and Habitus." *Wizards vs. Muggles: Essays on Identity and the Harry Potter Universe*, edited by Christopher E. Bell, McFarland, 2016, pp. 89-109.

Kamen, Henry. "Limpieza and the Ghost of Américo Castro: Racism as a Tool of Literary Analysis." *Hispanic Review* vol. 64, no.1, Winter 1996, pp. 19-29.

Lamb, Hannah. "The Wizard, the Muggle, and the Other: Postcolonialism in Harry Potter." *A Wizard of Their Age: Critical Essays from the Harry Potter Generation*, edited by Cecilia Konchar Farr, State U of New York P, 2015, pp. 57-72.

Loiacono, Laura, and Grace Loiacono. "Were the Malfoys Aristocrats?: The Decline and Fall of the Pure-Blooded." *Harry Potter and History*, edited by Nancy R. Reagin, Wiley, 2011, pp. 173-92.

Maryks, Robert A. *The Jesuit Order as a Synagogue of Jews: Jesuits of Jewish Ancestry and Purity-of-Blood Laws in the Early Society of Jesus*. Brill, 2010.

Ostry, Elaine. "Accepting Mudbloods: The Ambivalent Social Vision of J. K. Rowling's Fairy Tales." *Reading Harry Potter: Critical Essays*, edited by Giselle Liza Anatol, Praeger, 2003, pp. 89-101.

Reagin, Nancy R. "Was Voldemort a Nazi?: Death Eater Ideology and National Socialism." *Harry Potter and History*, edited by Nancy R. Reagin, Wiley, 2011, pp. 127-52.

Rowling, J. K. *Harry Potter and the Chamber of Secrets*. Scholastic, 1998.

———. *Harry Potter and the Deathly Hallows*. Scholastic, 2007.

————. *Harry Potter and the Goblet of Fire.* Scholastic, 2000.

————. *Harry Potter and the Half-Blood Prince.* Scholastic, 2005.

————. *Harry Potter and the Order of the Phoenix.* Scholastic, 2003.

————. *Harry Potter and the Prisoner of Azkaban.* Scholastic, 1999.

————. *Harry Potter and the Sorcerer's Stone.* Scholastic, 1997.

Schuck, Raymond I. "'The Anti-Racist-White-Hero Premise': Whiteness and the *Harry Potter* Series." *Wizards vs. Muggles: Essays on Identity and the Harry Potter Universe*, edited by Christopher E. Bell, McFarland, 2016, pp. 9-26.

Sterling-Folker, Jennifer, and Brian Folker. "Conflict and the Nation-State: Magical Mirrors of Muggles and Refracted Images." *Harry Potter and International Relations*, edited by Daniel H. Nexon and Iver B. Neumann, Rowman & Littlefield, 2006, pp. 103-26.

Stockslager, Tess. "What it Means to Be a Half-Blood: Integrity versus Fragmentation in Biracial Identity." *J.K. Rowling: Harry Potter*, edited byCynthia J. Hallett and Peggy J. Huey, Palgrave, 2012, pp. 122-34.

Ward, Reneé. "Getting Medieval in the Classroom." *Teaching with Harry Potter: Essays on Classroom Wizardry from Elementary School to College*, edited byValerie Estelle Frankel, McFarland, 2013, pp. 152-67.

Warner, Jamie. "Muggles, Magic, and Misfits: Michel Foucault at Harry Potter's Hogwarts." *Homer Simpson Ponders Politics: Popular Culture as Political Theory*, edited by Joseph J. Foy and Timothy M. Dale, UP of Kentucky, 2013, pp. 147-62.

Wente, Sarah. "The Making of a New World: Nazi Ideology and Its Influence on Harry Potter." *A Wizard of Their Age: Critical Essays from the Harry Potter Generation*, edited by Cecilia Konchar Farr, SUNY P, 2015, pp. 89-112.

Not Your Father's Classroom: Looking Back at the Golden Age through the Lens of the #MeToo Movement

DAVID R. CASTILLO

State University of New York at Buffalo

E ARLY IN MY CAREER, I used popular culture as a resource or *mesa de trucos* to get students interested in the authors, works, and histori-cal contexts of the Spanish Golden Age. Thus, I would pair the 1991 film about domestic violence, *Sleeping with the Enemy,* with María de Zayas's *Desengaños amorosos.* The *Godfather* saga would inform our reading of such honor plays as *El alcalde de Zalamea, La Estrella de Sevilla, Del rey abajo, ninguno* and *El burlador de Sevilla,* among others. We might look in the di-rection of Disney's *Pocahontas* in search for ways of explaining the histori-cal mystifications at work in Lope de Vega's *El Nuevo Mundo descubierto por Cristóbal Colón* and *Fuenteovejuna.* I would call upon *Easy Rider, Thelma and Louise, Diarios de la motocicleta* and other road movies to dramatize the significance of the open road in *Don Quixote.* Lately, however, I envi-sion these trans-historical and transcultural encounters as opportunities to encourage in-class conversations about our own time and place, our *medial-ogy* (see Castillo and Egginton, *Medialogies*), as much as about the cultural and historical contexts of the anonymous author of *Lazarillo de Tormes,* Cervantes, Velázquez, Lope, Zayas, Calderón or Gracián. In this essay, I re-trace this pedagogical trajectory while focusing on gender roles in an effort to foreground the potential of certain Golden Age works to promote reality literacy in the age of Trump and the #MeToo movement.

Words, images and stories are the building blocks of reality. They liter-ally make sense of our world. They help us figure out who we are and what we want to be. They frame our nightmares as much as our dreams. They define the relations of kinship within which we learn to recognize ourselves in accordance with certain norms and expectations. If our aim is to understand our reality—what we call *reality literacy* (see Castillo and Egginton, *Medialogies*)—, we must be willing to critically examine those key words, images and stories that frame what we know or think we know about ourselves and others, and about the world we all inhabit. My own teaching practice is guided by the conviction that *reality literacy* ought to be a primary goal of Humanistic education, regardless of our students' disciplinary fields of study and their specific areas of specialization.

In patriarchal societies, understanding reality requires looking into the ways in which gender roles are constructed and transmitted through recurrent words, images, and stories. Coming to terms with the culturally constructed nature of gender and gender roles might lead to the questioning of familiar behavioral patterns and the patriarchal norms that sanction them. In the context of the literature and culture classroom, and more specifically in the Spanish Golden Age classroom, we could encourage students to examine representations of gender roles in different works and genres, and to compare and contrast those representations with familiar images in our own cultural environment. We could also travel back to pre-modern times, in search for areas of continuity as well as potential changes in the ways gender roles are represented.

I have often used "Episode XXXV" of Don Juan Manuel's *Libro de los ejemplos del conde Lucanor y de Patronio* (1335) as a place to start this kind of trans-historical and transcultural discussion of gender roles. As it is well known, this short medieval "example" served as the basis for Shakespeare's full-length play *The Taming of the Shrew* (1590-1592). Don Juan Manuel's story describes how an ambitious and cunning young groom poses as a murderous madman in order to terrify his wealthy and notoriously rebellious bride into abject compliance. The young man's violent performance (he kills and dismembers his dog, his cat and his horse and threatens his wife's life on their wedding night) is celebrated in the text as an example of judicious behavior that sets the gender roles straight, a necessary precondition of a good marriage: "Al enterarse de cómo habían pasado la noche, estimaron en mucho al mancebo, que sí había sabido, desde el principio, gobernar su casa. Desde aquel día en adelante fue la muchacha muy obediente y vivieron juntos con mucha paz" (*Aproximaciones* 41). But when the bride's own father follows the example of his son-in-law, sacrificing a rooster in an attempt to frighten his wife into submission, we witness a very different outcome: "La verdad, don Fulano, que te has acordado tarde, pues ya de nada te valdrá matar cien caballos; antes tendríais que haber empezado, que ahora te conozco" (*Aproximaciones* 41). This final scene turns out to be central to the practical lesson provided at the conclusion of the story: "Si al principio no te muestras cómo eres, no podrás hacerlo cuando tú quisieres" (41). This is an interesting way to distil the story's meaning and its teachings; for one thing, the violent actions of the young groom and his father-in-law stand in stark contrast to their own temperate personalities. Theirs is a self-reflective performance of (violent) masculinity aimed at establishing the "proper" gender hierarchy in the context of marriage.

Today, we might resort to the lyrics of Luis Miguel's ballads to help us unpack the story's central lesson about the performative nature of gender relations. Their romantic content notwithstanding, such verses as "amarte como yo lo haría, como un hombre a una mujer" reveal a certain (unavoidable) gap between the speaking "I" that would love "you" and the gender type "man" that would love the gender type "woman." Such is the nature of the relation of similitude introduced by the grammatical marker *como*: To love you *as* I would, *as* a man [loves] a woman. There's a certain impersonation involved here, a form of role play, where "man" is invoked as a behavioral model that frames/conditions how "I would love you." We can now return to the seemingly paradoxical lesson of Don Juan Manuel's didactic example about the need to show your wife *who you are from the beginning* (of marriage). We can see that in the context of Patronio's exemplum, showing how or even who you are ("qui eres" in the original) refers to the culturally determined expectation/obligation to inhabit the symbolic placeholder *man/husband*: in this case, head of the household whose authority and dominion ought to be unquestioned.

Fast-forward roughly three centuries to the visual and mass-oriented culture of the Baroque. The "historical dramas" and "honor plays" authored by Lope de Vega, Calderón de la Barca and others for the stage of the new theater or *comedia nueva* treat their heterogeneous audiences to action-packed spectacles built on similar models of violent masculinity. Within the symbolic horizon of the honor play, a woman's *honra* is typically linked to her sexual virtue and her willingness to bend unquestioningly to the will of her father, husband or brother; for a man, however, the honor call takes the form of a mandate to protect and control his dependents (especially his wife and daughters) and to perform violent acts of retribution in defense of his family name. We can say that the honor code works as a gendered form of ideological interpellation (in the Althusserian sense) and a constant reminder of our differential social obligations; *a religion of obedience*, as José Antonio Maravall aptly called it in *Teatro y literatura en la sociedad barroca*. In this context, the masculine act of self-affirmation that is encapsulated in the honor mandate, *yo soy quien soy*, is literally a call to arms in defense of the family's reputation, as in the popular gangster movies and TV shows of our own age, from the award-winning *Godfather* saga of the late twentieth-century to the recent BBC series *Peaky Blinders*. Indeed, it is not difficult to find displays of violent masculinity in these and other gangster flicks which closely parallel climactic scenes in such classic plays as *Peribañez y el comendador de Ocaña* and *El alcalde de Zalamea*, to mention but two of the most canonical works of the Spanish Golden Age. As a matter of fact, the archetypal characters that populate these and many other baroque plays would also seem familiar to fans of the action-hero genre, going back to the classic Westerns of the 1950s and 1960s and forward to the typical Steven Seagal movies of the 2000s and the recent screen adaptations of the Jack Reacher novels authored by Lee Child. With relatively minor variations, these popular forms of entertainment reproduce, reify and capitalize on spectacular images of "protective" masculinity that glorify violence.

In the context of baroque theater, Calderón's *El médico de su honra* offers an extreme version of the sacrificial dimension of honor, as Don Gutierre arranges for the killing of his wife Doña Mencía at the hands of a medical surgeon who is himself threatened into compliance. The innocent woman is methodically bled in a sacrificial ritual meant to repair Don Gutierre's honor (which he wrongly believes has been damaged). Not only is the perpetrator not punished for his honor killing, he is actually rewarded with a new bride (his former lover Doña Leonor) by none other than the King himself, who expresses admiration for the judicious way in which his noble subject has set about mending his honor privately and discreetly. The play concludes with Don Gutierre's chilling reflection that honor's stains must be cleansed with blood ("que el honor / con sangre, señor, se lava," 3.2938-39) and his ominous warning to Doña Leonor: "Mira que médico he sido / de mi honra. No está olvidada / la ciencia" (3.2946-48).

While honor is the essential value by which the archetypal characters of the *comedia nueva* measure themselves and their actions, its symbolic weight is by no means uncontested in baroque culture. One of the most interesting responses came from María de Zayas, whose second collection of exemplary novellas known as *Desengaños amorosos* (1647) is explicitly framed as a feminine exposé of masculine violence and a denunciation of marriage and the honor code as death traps for women. Her third *Desengaño* "El verdugo de su esposa" reproduces much of the familiar plot of Calderón's *El médico de su honra* while foregrounding the victim's innocence and the calculating cruelty of her husband who uses the honor code as a cover for his crime. Here the focus in not on the tragic dilemma of the honor-bound husband, as in the Calderonian model, but on the monstrous nature of the aristocratic system that feeds on the blood of innocent women. Each of Zayas's *Desengaños* is designed to serve as an example of masculine hypocrisy, cruelty, and deceit and as a warning for women to avoid the prison-house of marriage. There is probably no better and more graphic illustration of the oppressive and confining *architecture of patriarchy* (Gilbert and Gubar) than the image of an innocent wife imprisoned inside a house wall in Zayas's fifth *Desengaño*, "La inocencia castigada." Having learned of his wife's rape, and despite her legal exoneration, Don Alonso conspires with her brother and sister-in-law to punish her for her involuntary desecration of the family honor. They bury her inside a wall where she is kept alive for six years. The narrator's graphic description of her decaying flesh is the literal embodiment of the putrid honor system, as Zayas sees it:

> En primer lugar, aunque tenía los ojos claros, estaba ciega . . . Sus hermosos cabellos, que cuando entró allí eran como hebras de oro, blancos como la misma nieve, enredados y llenos de animalejos, que de no peinarlos se crían en tanta cantidad, que por encima hervoreaban; el color, de la color de la muerte, tan flaca y consumida, que se le señalaban los huesos, como si el pellejo que estaba encima fuera un delgado cendal . . . los vestidos hechos ceniza que se le veían las más partes de su cuerpo; descalza de pie y pierna, que de los excrementos de su cuerpo, como no tenía dónde echarlos, no sólo se habían consumido, más la propia carne, comida hasta los muslos de llagas y gusanos, de que estaba lleno el hediondo lugar. (287)

Indeed, in the dark domestic world of *Desengaños amorosos*, the house itself works as "an instrument of torture employed against women" (Williamsen 144), even as a murder weapon. Thus, in the next *Desengaño*, "Amar sólo por vencer," we witness Don Bernardo's cold-blooded killing of his unmarried daughter, whose honor had been "stained" by a deceitful lover. A wall of the house is once again the patriarch's weapon of choice. The narrator's description of the young woman's death provides a powerful illustration of the asphyxiating architecture of patriarchy: "la pared le había abierto la cabeza, y con la tierra se acabó de ahogar" (330). As I argued elsewhere, the monsters come with the house in Zayas's baroque tales of domestic terror:

At the end of the last *Desengaño,* "Estragos que causa el vicio" (*Ravages Caused by Vice*), we are left with nothing but dead bodies and ruins everywhere. This is an implosion of the aristocratic house, not unlike Poe's vision of decay and destruction in 'The Fall of the House of Usher' . . . If indeed the code of honor may be seen as a fortification in service of the aristocratic dream of self-containment, then *Desengaños'* nightmarish parade of tortured and suffocating bodies and mangled corpses is a shocking reminder of the code's monstrous face. (*Baroque Horrors,* 118)

Zayas's *femicidal house* is a powerful representation of the oppressive and violent "architecture of patriarchy," which could indeed be linked to familiar tales of gothic terror, from the works of Anne Radcliffe and Edgar Allan Poe to Stieg Larsson's *Millennium Series,* including *The Girl with the Dragon Tattoo, The Girl Who Played with Fire,* and *The Girl Who Kicked the Hornet's Nest.* As Diana Russell notes, while *femicide* refers to "the killing of females by males because they are females . . . femicide is on the extreme end of a continuum of antifemale terror." Notably, Lisa Vollendorf has resorted to the work of Russell and other feminist scholars on *femicide* to support her interpretation of *Desengaños amorosos* as a work of early modern feminism (*Reclaiming the Body*). More recently, Bradley Nelson has built on Vollendorf's insights and the scholarship of Russell and her collaborators in a provocative essay that uses Larsson's *Millennium* series as the frame story for a close analysis of Zayas's "El traidor contra su sangre." Nelson argues that in the male dominated societies described by both Zayas and Larsson, violence against women is not an aberration but "a logical and necessary component of a patriarchal social, economic, political, and, yes, aesthetic order [that] depends on the cultivation and (violent) maintenance of a (gender) *politics of inequality*" (Nelson 66).

Lisbeth Salander's personal history of abuse and torture at the hands of representatives of State institutions reveals the structural feedback loops that provide cover to perpetrators who pose as protectors and benefactors. As the narrator explains in the first novel of the *Millennium* series, "this was the natural order of things. As a girl, she was legal pray, especially if she dressed in a worn black leather jacket and had pierced eyebrows, tattoos, and zero social status" (*The Girl with the Dragon Tattoo* 182). It is worth noting that the literal translation of the original Swedish title of the novel is not *The Girl with the Dragon Tattoo,* but *Men Who Hate Women.* As Nelson observes, Salander's personal history:

unveils the absolute inequality and violence of gender roles in Swedish law enforcement, correctional, judicial, and even medical institutions. As a consequence, men who violently and perversely exercise their power on female victims are not reformed . . . because the cause of their perverse and often psychotic behavior is their absolute hatred of women, a hatred Larsson finds firmly rooted in all of the previously mentioned modern institutions. (67)

Analogously, the tales of domestic terror included in Zayas's collection of *Desengaños* are explicitly framed as personal histories of female victimization meant to unmask the wolves in shepherds' clothing and to expose the misogynist social and cultural institutions that enable the perpetrators and offer them cover.

While Salander will eventually figure out how to use her marginal status and her brilliant hacking and camouflaging skills to exert a kind of vigilante justice over her abusers (outside of and often against the legal system), the female victims that populate the pages of *Desengaños* cannot escape the terrors that come with the house. They are the sacrificial victims of the "protective" architecture of patriarchy. Their tragic destiny is prefigured right from the beginning of each *desengaño* as martyrs in the waiting: *mártir, corderilla, inocente palomilla, inocente victima.*

In this sense, Salander's history of defiant survivalism in the face of unimaginable abuse and victimization would seem closer to the life-story of the rogue protagonist of *Lazarillo de Tormes* and the first female *pícara* in *La pícara Justina* (1605), the latter attributed to Francisco López de Ubeda. While the first-person voice of Lazarillo paints a dark picture of the Spanish society of the mid-1500s and denounces the lack of charitable souls and the rampant corruption of "protective" masters and institutions such as the Church and the State, Justina's own marginal gaze focuses on gender relations. Her in-your-face first-person account comes through in Ubeda's text against the background of a misogynist author; Friedman calls him "antifeminist" in his landmark study *The Anti-heroine's Voice.* Justina's relentless undressing of (male) authority figures and her unapologetic claim to matrilineal picaresque royalty sets up an intriguing gender-inflected conflict between the burlesque voice of the pícara-narrator and the moralistic, admonishing, and accusatory authorial presence that struggles to contain her within the familiar frame of didactic literature. As Friedman writes:

The author superimposes himself on the structure of the narrative, poetically at the beginning of each section and morally at the end . . . In the *aprovechamientos*, he appends instructive but commonplace adages to a blatantly antisocial text to remove *La pícara Justina* from the threat of inquisitorial stricture. The benefits are reciprocal in that the author enjoys moral superiority over his creation and the narrator enjoys a certain freedom of speech. (92)

Justina, like Lazarillo before her, is an unlikely narrator, a literary trope meant to represent the unspoken and unspeakable truth of a social body that is rotten to the core. But while Lazarillo's first-person narrative flows freely, unconstrained and unchallenged, even as it denounces the hypocrisy and corruption of his masters, the interventionist author of *La pícara Justina* brackets her voice within a moralistic watchtower perspective, similar to that of the "atalaya de la vida humana" in Mateo Alemán's *Guzmán de Alfarache*. The watchtower author is meant to diagnose, isolate and treat the cancer that is spreading through the social body; and the *pícara*'s life/gaze/voice is treated as both poison and antidote. This dual status of the pícara as venom and vaccine (*pharmakon*) explains why the author himself assumes the role of the (moral) doctor who must provide the proper medicinal dosage and usage instructions for his patients or readers:

Y advierto al lector que siempre que encontrare algún dicho en que parece que hay un mal ejemplo, repare que se pone para quemar en estatua aquello mismo, y en tal caso se recurra al aprovechamiento que he puesto en el fin de cada número y a las advertencias que hice en el prólogo al lector, que si ansí se hace, sacarse ha utilidad de ver esta estatua de libertad que aquí he pintado, y en ella los vicios que hoy día corren por el mundo. (466)

Referring in another section to the pícara's insightful (yet ill-intentioned) description of the religious festivities of León, the author makes the following comments: "personas mal intencionadas son como arañas, que de la flor sacan veneno, y así, Justina, de las fiestas santas no se aprovecha sino para decir malicias impertinentes" (247). The medical language is most explicit in those sections of the text that are reserved for authorial interventions. In fact, the presence of this kind of language has contributed to the book's attribution to Francisco López de Ubeda, a physician from Toledo who was known to have accompanied Phillip III to León in 1605. Here is an example from the introduction: "Si ello, el libro está bueno, bien provecho les haga, y si malo, perdonen, que mal se puede purgar bien los enfermos si yo me pongo ahora muy de espacio a purgar a la pícara" (79). As we can see here, the author pitches his picaresque book as medicine for the sick, which would lose its efficacy if he were to water down the active ingredient. In other words, the author must allow enough of the pícara's voice and worldview to come through for the *pharmakon* to work; that is, for us to be properly inoculated against the plague of free women.

The first words of the pícara-narrator are understandably tentative. Justina feels vulnerable, out of her element, intimidated by the very writing instruments she must use to tell her story. She expects to be scorned and stigmatized by masculine authorities. Yet, by the end of her introduction, she is fully ready to go. If she entered the realm of writing as a fearful writer ("melindrosa escribana"), she now feels empowered by the pen, as the heading of Chapter One indicates: "De la escribana fisgada." As noted by Nina Cox Davis and others, the word "fisga" and its derivatives function as phallic markers of power in the burlesque context in which the standard male critic—mockingly named "fisgón medroso"—is disqualified as vain, intrusive, nosy, and overly scrupulous, even as he pompously claims professional expertise in every imaginable subject: "yo, el licenciado Perlícaro, ortógrapho, músico, perspectivo, mathemático, arismético, geómetra, astrónomo, gramático, poeta, retórico, dialéctico, phísico, médico, flebótomo, notomista, metaphísico, y theólogo, que declaro ser este primer capítulo y todo el libro el segundo pecado nefando" (87). In her response, Justina notes that as a critic (and not a creator), her male accuser is a mere renter or borrower of words: "alquilador de verbos" (90). Her aggressive stance vis-à-vis masculine authority is best signified by the rallying cry that marks the start of her life story: "¡Agua va! Desvíense que lo tengo todo a punto, y va de historia" (69). As I note elsewhere, the implications of this cryptic warning to watch out for "dirty waters" are fully fleshed out in Chapter Five when Justina instructs a college graduate ("bachiller") to retrieve from under her bed a basket of honeycomb, which turned out to contain a pile of feces (*Awry Views* 69).

Justina's contempt for representatives of moral and cultural authority can be contextualized within her general view of men. She identifies a series of masculine types in Book Four, which deals with her search for a suitable groom, including the *presumptuous*, the *hypocritical*, the *self-centered*, and the *ostentatious*. Justina seems to suggest that men are only good for money, sex, and possibly to provide cover under a good family name. She playfully uses the list of Latin cases to mockingly paint a picture of her ideal man: he must be "dative" (obsequious) and "genitive" (sexually satisfying), as well as "nominative" (he must carry a reputable name). Despite her initial hesitations in the presence of ink, pen, and paper, Justina comes to think of her writing as a weapon that she can skillfully wield to expose masculine hypocrisy, short-sightedness, egotism and misogyny, even as her voice is ultimately contained within the profoundly anti-feminist frame provided by the author.

In making the connection to current popular culture, we could cite numerous examples of a similar understanding of a woman's voice as her weapon. Angie Thomas's best-selling novel *The Hate U Give*, which has been hailed as the literary anthem of the Black Lives Matter movement, offers a good illustration of this notion:

> "Who said talking isn't doing something?" she says. "It's more productive than silence. Remember what I told you about your voice?"
>
> "You said it's my biggest weapon."
>
> "And I mean that . . . You want to fight the system tonight? . . . Use your weapon." (410-11).

But in terms of a feminine voice effectively competing for narrative space, I can think of no better and more current example than the Netflix TV series *Alias Grace*, based on Margaret Atwood's award-winning fictionalization of the life of Grace Marks, a poor Irish immigrant working as a domestic servant in Upper Canada who was convicted of the infamous 1843 double murder of her employer and his housekeeper. Grace's tragic life story is framed by a series of personal interviews conducted by Dr. Simon Jordan. As was the case in *La pícara Justina*, the female protagonist is able to overcome her initial hesitations to take control of the narrative in an act of defiance that will force Dr. Jordan to confront his own hidden fears, prejudices and desires, pushing him to question his protective/authoritative role as expert inquirer, potential benefactor, and ultimate judge. The doctor's identity crisis is a direct consequence of the shattering of his own narrative frame, precipitated by a hypnotic session during which Grace channels a darkly aggressive persona, capable of the most scandalous insights, and not unlike the spider-like gaze of the "poisonous" Justina. The tables are turned in this powerful scene in which the subject of the scientific experiment undresses the good doctor, his companions, and, I would argue, the entire community. Dr. Jordan asks the hypnotized Grace whether she ever had "relations" with her alleged co-conspirator and partner in crime. Her shocking response comes with a series of confessions uttered in a notoriously unchained voice that identifies herself as the ghost of Mary Whitney, Grace's dead friend and confidante:

> Relations? What do you mean? Really, doctor? You are such a hypocrite! You want to know if I kissed him, if I slept with him . . . Is that it? Whether I did what you'd like to do with that little slut that's got hold of your hand. You'd like to know that, so I'll tell you. Yes. I would meet him outside in the yard. I'd press up against him and let him kiss me and touch me all over, doctor, the same places you'd like to touch me, because I can always tell. I know what you are thinking when you sit in that stuffy sewing room with me. That was all doctor. That was all I let him do. I had him on a string . . . After that, he'd say he'd do anything. Why? Oh, doctor? You are always asking why? Poking your nose in. And not only your nose. Such curious man, doctor. Curiosity killed the cat, you know? You should watch out for that little mouse beside you and her little furry mouse hole too! . . . I am not Grace . . . I told James to do it. I was there all along. Here, where I am now with Grace. . . . But Grace doesn't know, she's never known. They almost hanged her. That would have been wrong . . . I wouldn't want to hurt her. You mustn't tell her. . . . You want to see her back in the asylum? . . . You see, you are all the same, you don't listen. . . . You don't hear. (*Alias Grace*, part 6)

Whether a symptom of an acute case of multiple personality disorder (as the roguish hypnotist claims), a supernatural act of possession (as some members of the audience would want to believe), or a cunning deception (as Dr. Jordan suspects), Grace's hypnotic performance has the effect of reducing the doctor to silence and shame. The reputed physician was supposed to be able to penetrate the depths of Grace's psyche, access her lost memories, and ultimately author an objective judgement on Grace's mental state and her involvement in the murders. But instead of the expected authoritative report that would have established Grace's innocence (or guilt), the eager addressees of Dr. Jordan's letter (including the external audience) are left with nothing but the doctor's confession of utter impotence, wrapped in myriad conflicting feelings. If Dr. Jordan's document speaks truth, this is not the truth of Grace's soul, but that of the doctor's own shattered ego threatened by the mere existence of Grace, the whole of Grace:

> Was she really in a trance or was she play acting, laughing up her sleeve. . . . The truth eludes me; the whole Grace eludes me . . . I wonder if

[hypnotism and mesmerism] provide an opportunity for women to say what they think and to express their true thoughts and feelings more boldly and in more vulgar terms that they could otherwise feel permission too. I wonder about Grace's violent childhood and her experience as a young woman, abused constantly, harassed on every side. I wonder how much repressed rage she must have carried with her as a result. The question is, was this rage directed toward Nancy Montgomery and Thomas Kinnear, resulting in their murder, or at me, therefore making her confession during her hypnotism a fraud designed to hurt me. One thing is certain: I cannot write a report for your committee. I must forget Grace Marks. (*Alias Grace*, part 7)

These powerful scenes from *Alias Grace* might help illuminate certain passages of *La pícara Justina* in unexpected ways. Justina feels stripped in the presence of the pen and forced to stand naked in shame *(in puribus)* as the author piles on the blame. She is branded with the letter P that signifies deviancy, poverty, shamelessness, stained genealogy and venereal disease (pícara, pobre, poca vergüenza, pelona y pelada). Rather than retreating, however, the pícara manages to go on the offensive and return the blame. Thus, Justina suggests that the reason why the pen can brand her with this long list of stigmatizing marks and threaten her with yet one more P, the most definitive of all (prostitution no doubt), is that the letter P lives inside its own name: "qué he de esperar, sino que como la pluma tiene la P dentro de su casa y el alquiler pagado, me ponga algún otro nombre de P que me eche a puertas?" (62). Moreover, she comes to think of her own stigmas as battle wounds or even hunting trophies to be exhibited rather than hidden: "las manchas de la vida picaresca . . . son como las del pellejo de pía, onza, tigre, pórfido, taracea, y jaspe" (55). As with the scandalous confession that emerged from the depths of Grace's split voice, Justina's own "naked" confession works to expose the hypocrisy of her accusers and those moral and cultural authorities who hold power over her: "¿Seré yo la primera camuesa colorada por defuera y podrida por de dentro? ¿Seré yo el primer sepulchro vivo?" (57).

Could it be that by releasing Justina's voice, the moral doctor/author of *La pícara Justina* risks the same fate as Dr. Simon Jordan in *Alias Grace*? I would argue that as the voice of the pícara becomes stronger and more defiant, the commonplace accusations, warnings and disclaimers of the male author can no longer be trusted to contain her. Thus, the readers of *La pícara Justina* (as those of *Lazarillo* before her), as well as the spectators of *Alias*

Grace and the readers of Atwood's original novel, might welcome the chance to see the world through the eyes of the accused, even if momentarily.

Despite their vastly different content, Justina's fictionalized account of a female writer fighting off male critics and moral watchtowers may bring to mind the work of such women authors as Teresa de Jesús and Sor Juana Inés de la Cruz, both of whom were looked at with suspicion by their male superiors for their intrusion into the masculine realm of writing. In her *Respuesta a Sor Filotea*, Sor Juana defended the right of women to engage in intellectual pursuits and to teach other women. In fact, she went on to suggest that male teachers should be kept away from young women to ensure their safety and to protect the moral health of the community. She countered the Bishop of Puebla's admonishment that she should devote herself to prayer and activities appropriate to her gender by paraphrasing Teresa de Jesús's assertion that one can very well philosophize in the kitchen while cooking dinner. Known as the "tenth muse" and the "American Phoenix," Sor Juana was a self-taught scholarly wonder who was equally comfortable discussing philosophy and science, composing music and writing poetry. Her denunciation of male hypocrisy and misogyny led to her official condemnation. In 1694, a year before her death, Sor Juana ceased to write under pressure from the Bishop of Puebla and other high-ranking officials whose censure forced her to repent her waywardness, undergo penance for her sins, and dispose of her books, scientific tools and musical instruments.

As a poet, Sor Juana mastered the baroque style that had been popularized by Luis de Góngora and his followers while adding her own gender-inflected perspective. In her masterful sonnet known as "A su retrato," for example, Sor Juana makes use of such baroque tropes as the passing of time and the illusory nature of youth and beauty to criticize the blind conventionality of her portrait (possibly Juan de Miranda's work) and make a point about art's airbrushing of women:

> Este que ves, engaño colorido,
> que, del arte ostentando los primores,
> con falsos silogismos de colores
> es cauteloso engaño del sentido;
> éste, en quien la lisonja ha pretendido
> excusar de los años los horrores,
> y venciendo del tiempo los rigores
> triunfar de la vejez y del olvido,

> es un vano artificio del cuidado,
> es una flor al viento delicada,
> es un resguardo inútil para el hado:
> es una necia diligencia errada,
> es un afán caduco y, bien mirado,
> es cadáver, es polvo, es sombra, es nada. (*Aproximaciones* 162)

The final verse of Sor Juana's sonnet echoes Góngora's anamorphic un-veiling of the tragic end of youth and beauty "en tierra, en humo, en polvo, en sombra, en nada" (Góngora, "Mientras por competir con tu cabello"). Yet, by focusing on her *lying portrait* ("engaño colorido"), Sor Juana redirects the anamorphic gaze to the representational medium, turning (her) poetry into a weapon against art(tifice). Thus, the truth that is revealed from the right angle ("bien mirado" or rightly seen) in Sor Juana's poem is not (at least not only or primarily) the tragic end of aging flesh hidden behind youthful ap-pearances, but the blind spots of (conventional) art. She seems to be imply-ing that the lying conceits that erase the signs of aging from her face (*falsos silogismos de colores*) hide her existential truth (her life as well as her impending death). This is the failure of man's art(tifice) wrapped in thoughtless flattery: *lisonja, vano artificio, necia diligencia errada*.

As with the previously quoted texts, Sor Juana's work could certainly inform and animate class discussions of gender roles, misogyny and conven-tional representations of women in the age of Trump and in the context of the #MeToo and #Time'sUp movements. With regards to representations of women, for example, the vast majority of the images produced today by the retail, fashion and culture industries use Photoshop tools to remove wrin-kles, skin blemishes, and other signs of aging from women's faces and to alter the appearance of their bodies to fit unattainable ideals of shape, size and proportion. This, despite the fact that the American Medical Association officially identified airbrushing as a health issue back in 2011 and discour-aged "the altering of photographs in a manner that could promote unrealis-tic expectations of appropriate body image" (American Medical Association, Body Image and Advertising to Youth H-60.928).

As with misogynistic practices and discourses, unequal treatment of women, sexual harassment and other forms of abuse, some cultural commen-tators are wondering if the ongoing scandal of the Trump presidency might not also offer an opportunity to address the damage caused by airbrushed images of women. In a January 15, 2018 article published in the Fashion and Style section of the *New York Times*, for example, Vanesa Friedman noted that the recent galvanization of women, whether as political activists or as voices speaking up as part of the #MeToo movement, is resulting in a significant increase in anti-airbrushing pronouncements and possibly the first signs of real action (Friedman "Airbrushing Meets the #MeToo Movement. Guess Who Wins").

By way of conclusion, I would suggest that in allowing the work of such authors as María de Zayas and Sor Juana Inés de la Cruz and such texts as *El médico de su honra* and *La pícara Justina* to speak to our medialogy, the Golden Age classroom can help us contextualize and historicize our moment and encourage us to ask, "What next?" Understanding how we got here in the first place is half the battle, and the trans-historical and transcultural classroom can make us better prepared for the difficult conversations ahead. After all, as Margaret Atwood has recently reminded us in her urgent reflection "Am I a bad Feminist?"—a title that resonates with uncanny accents when placed side by side with Sor Juana's confession "Yo, la peor de todas"—, the question of *what next* must be borne of honest self-examination, with the long view in sight; and fiction can help. If the ultimate aim of ideology is to eliminate all ambiguity, as Atwood notes, and thus confine everything and everyone into ready-made models (of gender and otherwise), "fiction writers are particularly suspect because they write about human beings, and people are morally ambiguous" ("Am I a Bad Feminist?").

Works Cited

Alemán, Mateo. *Guzmán de Alfarache*. Edited by Benito Brancaforte, Cátedra, 1981.

Alias Grace. Directed by Mary Harron, CBC Television, 2017. Netflix, *www.netflix. com/watch/80119801?trackId=200257859*.

Anonymous. *Lazarillo de Tormes*. Edited by Joseph Ricapito, Cátedra, 1981.

Atwood, Margaret. "Am I a Bad Feminist?" *Globe and Mail*, 13 Jan. 2018, www.the-globeandmail.com/opinion/am-i-a-bad-feminist/article37591823/. Accessed 7 Oct. 2019.

"Body Image and Advertising to Youth H-60.928." American Medical Association, 2011, www.theglobeandmail.com/opinion/am-i-a-bad-feminist/article37591823/. Accessed 7 Oct. 2019.

Calderón de la Barca, Pedro. *El alcalde de Zalamea*. Edited by Valbuena Briones, Cátedra, 1990.

———. *El médico de su honra*. Edited by Valbuena Briones, Espasa-Calpe, 1965.

Castillo, David. *(A)wry Views: Anamorphosis, Cervantes, and the Early Picaresque*. Purdue U.P., 2001.

———. *Baroque Horrors: Roots of the Fantastic in the Age of Curiosities*. U. of Michigan P, 2010.

Castillo, David and William Egginton. *Medialogies: Reading Reality in the Age of Inflationary Media*. Bloomsbury, 2016.

Claramonte, Andrés. *La Estrella de Sevilla*. Edited by Alfredo Rodríguez López-Vázquez, Cátedra, 2010.

Davis, Nina Cox. "Breaking the Barriers: The Birth of López de Ubeda's *Pícara* Justina." *The Picaresque: Tradition and Dis-placement*. Edited by Giancarlo Maiorino, U. of Minnesota P., 1995, pp. 137-58.

De la Cruz, Sor Juana Inés. "A su retrato." *Aproximaciones al estudio de la literatura hispánica*. Edited by Edward Friedman, Teresa Valdivieso and Carmelo Virgillo, McGraw-Hill, 1999, p. 41.

———. "Respuesta a Sor Filotea de la Cruz." *Freeditorial*, freeditorial.com/es/books/respuesta-a-sor-filotea-de-la-cruz/related-books. Accessed 7 Oct. 2019.

Diarios de motocicleta. Directed by Walter Salles, Focus Features, 2004.

Don Juan Manuel. "Lo que sucedió a un mozo que casó con una muchacha de muy mal carácter." *Aproximaciones al estudio de la literatura hispánica*. Edited by Edward Friedman, Teresa Valdivieso and Carmelo Virgillo, McGraw-Hill, 1999, pp. 39-41.

Easy Rider. Directed by Dennis Hopper, Columbia Pictures, 1969.

Friedman, Edward. *The Antiheroine's Voice: Narrative Discourse and Transformations of the Picaresque*. U. of Missouri P, 1987.

Friedman, Vanessa. "Airbrushing Meets the #MeToo Movement. Guess Who Wins." *New York Times*, 15 January 2018, www.nytimes.com/2018/01/15/fashion/cvs-bans-airbrushing.html. Accessed 7 Oct. 2019.

Gilbert, Sandra and Susan Gubar. *The Madwoman in the Attic. The Woman Writer in the Nineteenth-Century Literary Imagination*. Yale U.P., 1979.

The Godfather. Directed by Francis Ford Coppola, Paramount Pictures, 1972.

The Godfather 2. Directed by Francis Ford Coppola, Paramount Pictures, 1974.

The Godfather 3. Directed by Francis Ford Coppola, Paramount Pictures, 1990.

Góngora. Luis de. "Mientras por competir con tu cabello." *Aproximaciones al estudio de la literatura hispánica*. Edited by Edward Friedman, Teresa Valdivieso and Carmelo Virgillo, McGraw-Hill, 1999, pp. 156-7.

Knight, Steven, creator. *Peaky Blinders*, BBC Studios, 2013.

Larsson, Stieg. *The Girl with the Dragon Tattoo*. Vintage, 2011.

———. *The Girl Who Played with Fire*. Vintage, 2011.

———. *The Girl Who Kicked the Hornet's Nest*. Vintage, 2012.

López de Úbeda, Francisco. *La pícara Justina*. Edited by Bruno Mario Damiani, Studia Humanitatis, 1982.

Maravall, José Antonio. *Teatro y literatura en la sociedad barroca*. Crítica, 1990.

Nelson, Bradley. "The Aesthetics of Rape and the Rape of Aesthetics." *Hispanic Issues on Line* (HIOL), vol. 8, 2011, pp. 62-80, cla.umn.edu/sites/cla.umn.edu/files/hiol_08_04_nelson_the_aesthetics_of_rape.pdf. Accessed 7 Oct. 2019.

Pocahontas. Directed by Eric Goldberg and Mike Gabriel, Buena Vista Pictures, 1995.

Rojas Zorrilla, Francisco de. *Del rey abajo, ninguno.* Edited by. Briggite Wittman, Cátedra, 2007.

Russell, Diana. "The Origin and Importance of the Term Femicide." www.dianarussell.com/index.html. Accessed 7 Oct. 2019.

Sleeping with the Enemy. Directed by Joseph Ruben, 20th Century Fox, 1991.

Thelma and Louise. Directed by Ridley Scott, Metro-Goldwyn-Mayer , 1991.

Thomas, Angie. *The Hate U Give.* HarperCollins, 2017.

Tirso de Molina. *El burlador de Sevilla.* Edited by Alfredo Rodríguez López-Vázquez, Cátedra, 2016.

Vega y Carpio, Félix Lope de. *El Nuevo Mundo descubierto por Cristóbal Colón.* Edited by Robert Shannon, Ibérica, 2001.

———. *Fuenteovejuna.* Edited by Juan María Marín, Cátedra, 1968.

———. *Peribáñez y el Comendador de Ocaña.* Edited by Juan María Marín, Cátedra, 1995.

Vollendorf, Lisa. *Reclaiming the Body: María de Zayas's Early Modern Feminism.* U. of North   Carolina P., 2001.

Zayas, María de. *Desengaños amorosos.* Edited by Alicia Yllera, Cátedra, 1983.

"A Most Timely Message for This Tired and Cynical World": *Man of La Mancha* (1965) as the Depoliticization of Counterculture Quixotism

WILLIAM P. CHILDERS

Brooklyn College and the *CUNY Graduate Center*

FROM 9:30 TO 11:00 PM on Monday, November 9, 1959, CBS's DuPont Show of the Month aired Dale Wasserman's *I, Don Quixote*, directed by Karl Genus and starring Lee J. Cobb as Cervantes/Don Quixote. This was a significant event in television history, as demonstrated by the self-congratulatory tone of reviews by TV critics who reveled in the fact that the small screen had proven itself capable of presenting a monumental novel in a single evening.[1] Against the grain of this mainly celebratory reception, Arthur Miller wrote the television editor of the *New York Times*, chiding those who give audiences a false sense of having *seen* works they had not *read*:

We are breaking the continuity of culture by passing on its masterpieces through mutilated distortions. This is not "better than nothing." The wholeness of viewpoint . . . is being fragmented so that the marvel of a complete experience . . . is denied millions of people who, worse yet, go forth under the illusion that they have actually had it. (*Theater Essays* 216)

Wasserman retorted that *I, Don Quixote* was not an adaptation, but an original play based on the imaginative recreation of Cervantes' life and some scenes from his works. Thus it could not be held to a standard of faithfulness.

---

1 Wasserman collected glowing reviews from *Variety, The Hollywood Reporter, Time,* and other newspapers and magazines (*Dale Wasserman Papers*, Box 13). A common thread running through many is the idea that *I, Don Quixote* set a new bar for television adaptations of classic literature, though the *New York Times* critic sounded a sour note: "the task of translating the dreams of Quixote into believable theatre was beyond the capabilities of TV" ("Tilting with Don Quixote").

Moreover, the show had renewed interest in a book that viewers had heard of but few had actually read. "The day after the broadcast hundreds of shops reported themselves sold out." Whether they were reading it or "merely buying it," who could tell? But at least it was sending them back to the original, contrary to Miller's claims ("Reply to Arthur Miller").

The Miller-Wasserman debate presents divergent views of the role of the writer, marking one possible distinction between "high" and "popular" culture. As Miller puts it in the preface to his own adaptation of Ibsen's *An Enemy of the People*, the "serious writer," whether creating original material or adapting work from the past, must find "a path through the wall of 'entertainment,'" so as to pose for the audience the essential contradictions of the present (*Theater Essays* 16). Wasserman claimed that *I, Don Quixote* was in fact "an attempt to push at the boundaries of the medium, in this case to present ideas which made demands of the audience and didn't assume it simple-minded" (letter to Henry B. Maloney, 6 Dec 1959, *Dale Wasserman Papers*, Box 13). Ultimately, though, he plays the ideologically conservative Lope de Vega to Arthur Miller's nonconforming Cervantes. His goal in *I, Don Quixote*, as elsewhere, is to give spectators what they want, rather than try to teach them what they *should* want.[2]

---

2   Behind this debate also lurks the shadow of the House Un-American Activities Committee (HUAC), whose anti-communist hearings of the 40s and 50s were frequently characterized as an "Inquisition." Although Lee J. Cobb caved in and "named names" to HUAC in 1953, in *I, Don Quixote* he portrays Cervantes standing up to the Spanish Inquisition in defense of freedom. Miller's first triumph in the theater had been *Death of a Salesman*, starring Cobb as Willy Loman and directed by Elia Kazan. Kazan had also named names in his testimony before HUAC, in 1952. Though Miller and Kazan had been very close friends, they had not spoken since. Called before HUAC in 1956, Miller refused to provide names and was found in contempt of Congress, though his conviction was overturned on appeal in August 1958. Just over a year after his HUAC troubles were finally cleared up, to see the informer Lee J. Cobb portray Don Quixote fighting for justice no matter the cost was too much to take. Implicitly at stake in the Miller-Wasserman debate, then, is whether the Inquisition can cease to be a stand-in for McCarthyism and instead be used to denounce the Soviets as enemies of the "open society." *I, Don Quixote* proclaims, via the new-ish medium of television and at the threshold of a new decade, that the time has come to forget McCarthyism. Miller has misgivings, and ultimately sees the adaptation as an over-simplification, not just of Cervantes, but of the current political moment. (For Miller's history with HUAC, summarized here, see Bigsby 528-80, Gottfried 191-97 and 288-98, and Miller, *Timebends* 328-35, 389-94, and 449-56.)

Although Wasserman sees himself as making demands on his audience, reflecting on the contradictions of the present is not among them. Comparison with Cervantes' own approach is suggestive. In the original novel, Don Quixote's confusion of fiction and reality draws attention to the gap between the elevated chivalric vision and the world as it is. This ironic gap, the basis of the parody that makes the original "a funny book," also creates an opening for satire, since readers become aware, by comparison, that human society does not live up to its professed ideals.[3] As we will see, the counterculture approach to *Don Quixote* exploits this opening to reactivate Cervantine satire, bringing it to bear on such contemporary issues as consumerism and militarism. In Wasserman's teleplay, however, as well as the musical that would later be based on it, Don Quixote's identity as a reader of chivalric romances, and with it the parody of what he has read, are essentially eliminated.[4] The double-edged irony of a reader who goes insane (a distorted mirror to the actual reader) is replaced in *I, Don Quixote* by the author's "inspirational" yearning after a higher, abstract truth unattainable in this world. Wasserman's Cervantes invites us to believe along with Don Quixote, and through our belief we enter an ennobling "bubble" of intimate identification with the hero (even if his heroism is only imaginary), which lifts us above the fray of this-worldly struggles. Of course, this amounts to neither more nor less than a staging of the Romantic approach to *Don Quixote* described by Close. Such simplification of the ideological tensions within Cervantes' *Don Quixote* will

---

3   Of course, the phrase "funny book" refers to Russell's polemical article, but his entire argument begs the larger question of whether the parody of chivalric romance is a pretext for a broader satire, and if so, against what target(s). The satiric reading pioneered by Efron was articulated with theoretical sophistication by Parr and has been defended against the British "funny book" school by Iffland, most recently in a 2015 essay for the online annual *El español en el mundo*.

4   That he was driven mad by too much reading is mentioned once in passing by the fictional Cervantes of *I, Don Quixote* as he introduces the character he is about to bring to life, though even then it is not specified that he read tales of chivalry: "[H]e has much time for books. He studies them from morn to night—and through the night as well. And all he reads oppresses him . . . fills him with indignation at man's murderous ways toward man. He broods . . . " (141, ellipsis in original). There is no further mention of his books in either the television version or the musical. In the version of the teleplay Wasserman later published (in *The Impossible Musical* as well as in the journal *Cervantes*), there is a scene in which Don Quixote's books are blamed for his mental illness and slated to be burned, as in *Don Quixote* I.6. However, this was cut from the teleplay as aired in November 1959, and then left out of *Man of La Mancha* altogether.

have very definite consequences for *Man of La Mancha*, where the immediacy and lyricism of live musical theater produce an effect nothing short of mesmerizing.

This ideological insularity was already present, however, for television viewers in 1959. On November 16th, a writer named Dorothy Thomas sent Wasserman a letter, which read, in part:

> Dear Dale Wasserman: I who never write fan letters am impelled to sit down – if belatedly! – and thank you – the actors, director, producer and the Du Pont Company – for your inspiring "I, Don Quixote." To me it seemed a most timely message for this tired and cynical world. There was so much in your play that I want to remember. What sticks in my mind is Don Quixote's reiteration of the importance of helping others, of dreaming, struggling, fighting, never giving up no matter how many times one falls. I am horrified at the Beatnicks [sic] who in youth turn their backs upon all that – upon life itself. Truly you have gleaned from Cervantes words that poor suffering ridiculous humanity needs to hear.[5]

Thomas' rejection of Beat nihilism ("youth [who] turn their backs . . . upon life") in favor of an abstract, optimistic quixotism contrasts, though she could not have been aware of this, with the reception of Cervantes by writers like Ferlinghetti, Ginsberg, and, above all, Jack Kerouac, who wrote

---

5   *Dale Wasserman Papers*, Box 13. The letter is from a freelance writer named Dorothy Thomas, of Ridgewood, New Jersey, who also appeared in 1954 on Edward R. Murrow's radio program "This I Believe," and spoke of the obligation to be happy, in a quintessential statement of 1950s conformity worthy of *Invasion of the Body Snatchers* (1956): "I feel embarrassed, ashamed, apologetic when I wallow too long in the slough of despond. I have a deep if an inexplicable conviction that somehow it is wicked to be long unhappy." It is this rejection of inconformity as immoral that lies behind her horror of the Beats. What is this, though, but a fear of recognizing her own deep dissatisfaction? As it turns out, by the way, this is *not* the same Dorothy Thomas who achieved a modicum of literary fame in the 1930s as the author of short stories about life on the Nebraska plains, collected in such volumes as *Ma Jeeter's Girls* (1933) and *The Home Place* (1936), who was living in Vernon, New Jersey in 1959. I was able to finally establish that they are not the same person by comparing the signature on the letter to Dale Wasserman with the one on a letter by the Nebraska writer. I am grateful to Erin Willis, Curator of the Jane Pope Geske Heritage Room of Nebraska Authors in Lincoln, for sending me a digital image of a letter by that Dorothy Thomas to compare with this one. Though the letters were written within a month of each other, the signatures are nothing alike.

his 1958 novel *The Dharma Bums* while reading *Don Quixote* and included in it several explicit references to Cervantes.[6] Far from seeing rejection of mainstream U.S. values as an abandonment of life, Kerouac celebrates, albeit somewhat tongue in cheek, the West Coast Beats' quixotic embracing of Zen as a neo-Transcendentalism capable of renewing America's commitment to its deepest professed value, human freedom. Japhy Ryder, his fictionalized Gary Snyder, exclaims ecstatically:

> [T]he whole thing is a world full of rucksack wanderers, Dharma Bums refusing to subscribe to the general demand that they consume production and therefore have to work for the privilege of consuming, all that crap they didn't really want anyway such as refrigerators, TV sets, cars, at least new fancy cars, certain hair oils and deodorants and general junk you finally always see a week later in the garbage anyway, all of them imprisoned in a system of work, produce, consume, work, produce, consume, I see a vision of a great rucksack revolution thousands or even millions of young Americans wandering around with rucksacks, going up to mountains to pray, making children laugh and old men glad, making young girls happy and old girls happier, all of 'em Zen Lunatics who go about writing poems that happen to appear in their heads for no reason and also by being kind and also by strange unexpected acts keep giving visions of eternal freedom to everybody and to all living creatures . . . . (73-74)

In contrast to *I, Don Quixote*, Cervantine satire is here brought to bear on the present, specifically the intensification of consumerism in the postwar period. Though caricatured, Japhy is half-seriously presented as a latter-day knight errant, whose hope for "rucksack revolution" sounds, from today's vantage point, like a prophetic announcement of the "turn on, tune in, drop out" movement of the mid-60s.

Over the next few years the youth movement expanded from its Beat infancy to include a growing number of the Baby Boom generation. It gained enough momentum to supply *Man of La Mancha*, the musical version of *I, Don Quixote*, with unexpected relevance to contemporary culture. While denying any interest on his own part in the Bohemian scene of Greenwich

---

6   Kerouac wrote to Allen Ginsberg on 30 Nov 1957 that he was writing *The Dharma Bums* and "reading *Don Quixote* which is probably the most sublime work of any man ever lived, thank God for Spain! All living creatures are Don Quixote of course, since living is illusion" (*Letters* 374).

Village in the mid-60s, Wasserman acknowledges, in his memoir, *The Impossible Musical*, that by 1965 the resonance between the Counterculture and the figure of Don Quixote was obvious and contributed significantly to the success of the musical:

> In November of 1965, *Man of La Mancha* slipped into this whirlpool of social change . . . the Knight of the Woeful Countenance is a world-class symbol of nonconformity, an idealist, posited against an overly rational, cynical age. He believes in love's power to prevail over all challenges, even death. And he imagines the world not as it is but as it might be . . . In this respect, *Man of La Mancha* was a child of the fifties and the sixties, an example of lucky timing that brought resonance to the already timeless import of the play. (121-22)

"Lucky timing" is more of an understatement than he knew. In fact, the currents of the counterculture were swirling around *Don Quixote* in 1965 with peculiar intensity. Several left-leaning, overtly satirical adaptations were completed or were underway. This was the year experimental filmmaker Bruce Baillie edited the first version of his feature-length *Quixote*, a critical vision of U.S. racism and imperialism, which he initially projected onto two side-by-side screens from two projectors.[7] Screenwriter Waldo Salt, formerly blacklisted for having been a member of the Communist Party, began work on his adaptation of *Don Quixote* in June 1965.[8] In 1964, John Kennedy Toole finished the first draft of *A Confederacy of Dunces*, which uses a Quixotic character, Ignatius J. Reilly, to comically assert a politically noncommittal, but decidedly satirical indictment of mainstream values in the Cold War U.S. Throughout 1965, Toole revised his novel under the tutelage of editor Robert Gottlieb at Simon and Schuster.[9] In November 1965, the very same month as the *Man of La Mancha* debut in Greenwich Village, in Madison, Wisconsin

---

7   In 1967, it would be released in its current form as a single edited film for one projector, with the simultaneous juxtapositions converted into linear sequences. The filmmaker himself uploaded this version to YouTube in 2015.

8   Though it made it to pre-production twice, it has yet to be filmed. On Salt's screenplay and its history, see my essay, "Surviving the Hollywood Blacklist."

9   When Gottlieb definitively rejected it early in 1966, Toole gave up writing; eventually he committed suicide. *Dunces* languished until 1980, when it finally appeared due to the persistence of Toole's mother and the support of Walker Percy. It won the Pulitzer Prize a generation after it was originally written. I make the case for the quixotism of the hero of Toole's *Confederacy of Dunces* in "Quixote Gumbo."

activist/editor Morris Edelson launched his little magazine of avant-garde writing, *Quixote*, with a light-hearted "anti-manifesto" beginning with the question, "well, quixote, what windmill?"

All of these projects have in common the use of Don Quixote as a figure to challenge existing values, satirically juxtaposing the anachronistic image of the knight with such ills as consumerism, militarism, racial inequality, and *laissez faire* capitalism. Yet in the same year, 1965, a mere six months before *Man of La Mancha*, an ideologically conservative adaptation appeared on the New York stage. On May 27th, George Balanchine himself played the title role in his original ballet with music composed by Nicolas Nabokov, in a gala performance at the recently completed New York State Theater at Lincoln Center. The Balanchine/Nabokov *Don Quixote* is, like *Man of La Mancha*, a Romantic celebration of the "timeless" (i.e. depoliticized), "indomitable" spirit of Cervantes' hero. Though Balanchine had his own private reasons for wanting to play the role (he was in love with Suzanne Farrell, to whom he assigned the role of Dulcinea), it can hardly be a coincidence that the composer, Nicolas Nabokov, was at the time Secretary General of the Congress for Cultural Freedom, the notorious CIA front that funneled millions of dollars annually into the promotion of a positive image of the United States around the world through covert funding of literary, intellectual, and artistic projects that hid their propagandistic purpose behind a defense of individual liberty and free speech. In fact, it was Nabokov's CIA handler who encouraged him to finish *Don Quixote* rather than undertake a planned trip to Moscow, which he considered inopportune. The classical ballet repertoire includes a well-known "Russian" adaptation of *Don Quixote* by Ludwig Minkus and Marius Petipa, which, although premiered in 1869 in St. Petersburg, was not performed in its entirety outside of Russia until the Soviet Union began promoting it in the 1950s. Undoubtedly this revival of the Minkus/Petipa ballet explains the CIA's interest in having Balanchine and Nabokov finish theirs: even Cervantes was dragged into the cultural Cold War.[10]

These battle lines lurk in *Man of La Mancha*'s "political unconscious," aligning the satiric re-contextualization in the present with the progressive New Left, and the overtly depoliticized, Romantic approach with anti-Soviet

---

10   Suzanne Farrell discusses Balanchine's fascination with her and *Don Quixote* in her memoir, *Holding on to the Air*. Frances Saunders has thoroughly researched the story of the Congress for Cultural Freedom, including Nabokov's role in it. For Nabokov's work on *Don Quixote*, see Giroud, 358-66, who explains it was Nabokov's CIA handler, Michael Josselson, who encouraged him to finish the ballet.

propaganda of a conservative cast.[11] Wasserman's aim of a successful Broadway show meant appealing to both sides through a careful tightrope walk that successfully tapped into the countercultural swirl into which the figure of Don Quixote had been caught up, without losing the abstract, timeless "idealism" that had so appealed to Dorothy Thomas. To bring these underlying ideological tensions to the forefront for our students, some of the extant materials referred to above can be brought into the classroom, such as (excerpts from) *The Dharma Bums* or Bruce Baillie's *Quixote* (which the director himself has made available on YouTube). We can teach them about the failed projects of Orson Welles, Waldo Salt, and Harold L. 'Doc' Humes, contextualizing them in relation to their creators' political engagement.[12] The bland sentimentality of *Man of La Mancha* stands out by contrast with the oppositional tone of other adaptations and appropriations of Cervantes from the same period. The key set of materials, however, that drives this point home most dramatically, are W. H. Auden's lyrics for *Man of La Mancha*, which were rejected because of their blatantly satirical content. Teaching the Broadway musical along with these texts provides a clear window into the ideological tensions that undergird *Man of La Mancha*, despite their being excluded from the spectator's conscious experience.

In pursuit of his goal of a Broadway hit, Wasserman had always intended to adapt his teleplay for the stage; only when director Albert Marre and composer Mitch Leigh became involved was a decision reached that the project would be a musical. But before lyricist Joe Darion was hired to write the lyrics, the first librettist was W. H. Auden, who wrote some 16 songs totaling 426 lines for the musical, none of which were ever used on stage.[13] While this

11   The term "political unconscious" is of course Fredric Jameson's, which he uses, in his seminal book of that title, to refer to the ideological tensions existing at the time a work is created, and which penetrate it, but in a repressed form that must be teased out by interpretation. In the case of *Man of La Mancha*, the production's own history is part of that process of repression, as the exclusion of Auden's lyrics attests.

12   On Salt, see my "Surviving the Hollywood Blacklist." I discuss Welles, Humes, and Salt in my forthcoming article "QuixoNation."

13   Auden published two of these during his lifetime, with all references to *Don Quixote* removed, as "Song of the Ogre" and "Song of the Devil" in *City Without Walls* (39-42). In his posthumous *Thank You, Fog,* "The Golden Age" and "Recitative by Death" were included as "Two Quixote Lyrics" (41-46). Wasserman published an ample selection with detailed narrative in *The Impossible Musical* (82-94), following up on earlier articles in which he told his version of events and included various smatterings of the lyrics: "Tilting at *Man of La Mancha,*" "Auden in Autumn" and

is not the place for a full-scale study of Auden's approach to *Don Quixote* in his critical writings and the lyrics for *Man of La Mancha*, some consideration must be given to the reasons for the failure of this collaboration, especially as it pertains to the subsequent success of the musical. References to *Don Quixote* began appearing regularly in Auden's writing in 1940, while he was in the midst of the crisis that led to his turning away from Leftist politics and returning to the Anglican Communion, the religion of his boyhood.[14] He began reading theological works, including Kierkegaard, from whom he may have first derived the understanding of Don Quixote as a "knight of the faith," in the modern, secular world.[15] In subsequent writings on *Don Quixote*, Auden insists on the importance of the ending, where the disillusioned Alonso Quijano renounces chivalry and dies.[16] The significance of this moment for Auden is the contrast between the lunatic knight's absurd faith and the debased reality in which the rest of us actually live. The value of *Don Quixote* for Auden was that it forces upon us this awareness between an idealized hero and the ironic truth of the modern secular world. Don Quixote's renunciation of chivalry is Cervantes' final acknowledgement of this unbreachable gap and is thus fundamentally tied to the pedagogical value of the work in the present. Auden emphatically chose to avoid giving spectators the comforting feeling of being ennobled by identification with the 'idealis-

---

"Pink-slipping a Poet Laureate." A fairly complete version of the lyrics Auden wrote for *Man of La Mancha* appeared in *Antaeus* in 1981, but the most complete edition is in the *Libretti* volume of the Princeton *Complete Works* of Auden, under the editorship of Edward Mendelson (507-22).

14   For a nuanced account of Auden's "conversion," see Carpenter, 209-10, 282-300.

15   Ziolkowski assumes Auden's view of Don Quixote reflects Kierkegaard's "direct influence" (209). Around the same time as he first read Charles Williams, however, Auden was a member of a group created by Ford Maddox Ford in New York, "Les Amis de William Carlos Williams," which met five times in 1939. Among the 18 members listed by Witemeyer in *Pound/Williams* (326), were Waldo Frank and Edward Dahlberg, both of whom published writings in the first half of the 20th century interpreting *Don Quixote* in "spiritual" terms. Dahlberg, in particular, discusses Don Quixote as a religious figure in "The Cross and the Windmills," a chapter from his 1941 volume *Do These Bones Live?* (92-101). Might Dahlberg have also been an influence on Auden's view of *Don Quixote*?

16   Auden's key texts on *Don Quixote* are "The Ironic Hero," part of the essay "Balaam and the Ass," and "Ishmael—Don Quixote" (a chapter in *The Enchafèd Flood*). However, references to quixotism as a particularly modern form of heroism are sprinkled here and there in Auden's work of the 40s and 50s.

tic' hero, even if that was what they wanted. Rather, he sought, like Arthur Miller, to confront them with what they *should* want, the truth about their current situation. Presumably neither Marre, nor Leigh, nor Wasserman had read any of Auden's seminal texts on *Don Quixote* before he was brought in as librettist. If anyone connected with the project had been familiar with the contents of Auden's interpretation of Cervantes' masterpiece, they would have foreseen that a positive outcome of his involvement with the project was impossible.[17]

The short-lived partnership between Auden and Wasserman was arguably the most significant confrontation between high culture and popular culture approaches to *Don Quixote* in the 20th century. As Wasserman tells it in *The Impossible Musical*, he recognized the quality of the material Auden was producing, but also saw that it was entirely wrong for *Man of La Mancha*. He emphasizes in particular a song-sequence in which Sin, Folly, and Death break the fourth wall to confront the audience, which was created by Auden for the scene of the traveling players (a scene based on the *carro de la muerte* episode in *Don Quijote* II.11, which was eventually dropped from the musical play). Auden's text calls for the house lights to be turned on so his medieval personifications can accuse spectators of hypocrisy and corruption, mentioning in the process such cultural practices and social mores of the mid-twentieth century as partying on Benzedrine, driving fast automobiles, playing loud pop music on radios and juke boxes, and watching television crime shows. At one point Sin bluntly exclaims, "Enjoy your dream. / I'm so bored with the whole fucking crowd / of you / I could scream" (*Libretti* 520). Concerning this *mise-en-scène*, Wasserman comments, "Wonderful! This piece of work I thought truly brilliant. Also, I thought, if allowed through the gates it would absolutely destroy *Man of La Mancha*." (*Impossible Musical* 93). Nonetheless, the specific reason he gives for their final parting of the ways is disagreement over the ending – he quotes Auden saying to him, after showing him a lyric he had written about Don Quixote's final disillusionment, "So you see, old boy, he does recant," to which Wasserman responded, "Only in your play" (94) – and their association was at an end. That the insurmountable sticking point was the ending does not mean, however, that Auden was merely insisting on remaining true to Cervantes' original out of traditionalism for its own sake.[18] Faithfulness, here, is not a general principle, but concerns the specific

17   Auden apparently did know, as he told the *Evening Standard,* that the script he had seen "will have to be rewritten" (quoted in Carpenter).

18   Lo Ré assumes (without having delved into Auden's writings on the subject) that the motive is a traditionalist's defense of faithfulness to the original:

point on which Auden's entire interpretation turns, the deathbed renunciation of chivalry. For Auden, the same thing is at stake in both the deathbed
scene and the Brechtian confrontation in which Folly, Sin, and Death mock
the audience in deliberately up-to-date terms, namely, the contrast between
Quixote's chivalric dream and the contemporary society in which the late
20th-century audience lives.[19] This is the contrast that *Man of La Mancha's*
lyrical escapism aims to make us forget. Wasserman rightly saw that Auden's
approach would fundamentally undermine *Man of La Mancha*, derail its
message, and make what he hoped would be a mainstream smash into a highbrow theater experience reserved for a minority. In the classroom, however,
truth, not entertainment, is the primary concern; placing Auden's *Man of
La Mancha* lyrics alongside the better-known final product creates a laboratory for exploring fundamental truths about the relations among literary
canons, popular adaptations, and the market values inherent in the mass culture industry. Once students have a sense of the context of reception of *Don
Quixote* into which Wasserman et. al. sought to insert their version, they can
examine the discarded materials and pose the counterfactual question: how
would the experience have been different if Auden's material had been used,
instead of replacing it with Joe Darion's?[20]

Students will grasp that Wasserman's rejection of Auden's work on the
musical amounted to a self-conscious choice for depoliticizing *Don Quix-*

"Auden, a scholar, insisted on fidelity to the novel" (106). Similarly, Fuller: "it was
Auden's traditional view of Quixote as a victim of comic delusions who has to repent
of his folly that caused his work to be dropped" (555). Auden's understanding of the
ending, however, is not as conventional as these critics seem to think.

19   I have not chosen the adjective "Brechtian" lightly, as the style of this section closely resembles that of Brecht's *Rise and Fall of the City of Mahagonny* and
Seven Deadly Sins, both of which Auden and Kallman translated, in 1957 and 1959-
60, respectively. Although Auden distanced himself from Brecht's ideological commitment to Communism, he clearly shared with Brecht (and, I would argue, with
Cervantes) the idea that the playwright's role is to disrupt the audience's comfortable, escapist identification with the theatrical spectacle. Willet's *Brecht in Context*
remains a privileged source on Auden's on-going, changing relationship to Brecht's
work (59-72).

20   Wasserman's published accounts of the "case," culminating in the chapter
devoted to it in *The Impossible Musical,* contain ample selections from the Auden lyrics as well as invaluable (albeit biased) testimony concerning the breakdown of the
collaboration. I recommend, however, initially presenting to students the versions of
the lyrics published in the *Libretti* volume of the Princeton edition of Auden's *Complete Works,* in order to avoid framing them entirely from Wasserman's perspective.

ote, even while he was tapping into the unconscious ideological implications Cervantes' hero had at the time. The satire against a society addicted to immediate thrills and throwaway convenience is crucial to both the counterculture approach to *Don Quixote* and to Auden's understanding of the juxtaposition of the idealized world of chivalric romance with the debased society of 20th-century America.[21] Moreover, not only did Auden intend the two to be brought together in a patently contradictory manner, he also sought to impede the audience's identification with Don Quixote. The bubble the spectators entered with Cervantes and his hero would be burst when the house lights went up and Folly, Sin, and Death underlined our unbridgeable separation from the hero; thus, when we saw him recant before dying, we would be prepared to recognize the truth, that the "real" Alonso Quijano was no more a hero than we are. The result would not be uplifting, but disillusioning. Wasserman did at this point what he had to do: he fired Auden from the project, swerving away from any politicized, countercultural appropriation of Cervantes, and went on to have a worldwide hit that has gone through multiple revivals on Broadway, and to this day is seemingly always being produced somewhere.[22] What conclusions will students choose to draw from this object lesson about the cultural mechanisms of the 'society of the spectacle' as Debord dubbed our era? What does the tension between the two versions of *Man of La Mancha*, the one actually produced and the one that was repressed, reveal about the ideology embedded in what Castillo and Egginton have recently termed our 'medialogy'? Classroom discussion of such issues expands the immediate problematic surrounding the adaptation of a single

---

21   In this context, it is helpful to recall that connections between Auden and the Beats were stronger than is sometimes assumed, based, I would argue, on a misreading of Auden's so-called "traditionalism." "Auden's influence was formative and widespread for a startlingly diverse range of poets . . . for many of [whom] . . . , as with Ginsberg, the distinctions critics are used to making about competing traditions in American poetry—with often an implied or explicit claim of the superiority of one over another—don't always add up quite so neatly" (Wasley 48).

22   At least, this is Wasserman's claim in *The Impossible Musical* (9) where he tries to show that it is the most successful musical of all time. He is particularly proud of its international diffusion: "Musicals successful on Broadway . . . may go on to play in German, Swedish, Hebrew, or Japanese. Not many also play in Urdu, Icelandic, Gujarati, Uzbekistani, Siamese, Magyar, Slovenian, Swahili, Polish, Finnish, Ukranian, or nine distinctly different dialects of Spanish. *Man of La Mancha* has played or is playing in all of these" (12).

literary classic to a larger debate concerning the contradiction inherent in the notion of a 'culture industry'.[23]

To present students with a balanced view, we cannot deny that *Man of La Mancha,* as produced, is a cleverly conceived adaptation of *Don Quixote.* The play within a play through which Cervantes justifies himself to his fellow prisoners during a mock trial functions well as a trope on which to hang a handful of incidents from the episodic plot of the original. But I would argue that we want them to recognize that the real secret to its tremendous impact was that it offered a spectacle that appealed to both sides in the widening generational divide in the mid-1960s United States. Both sides could perceive Don Quixote figuratively through the lens of their own politics; indeed, as we have seen, many already did, going back at least to the late-1950s. For counterculturalists, his attack on the windmills, though doomed to failure, was a bold assault on the powers that be. His willingness to fail could in itself be seen as a rejection of *laissez faire* capitalism's ethos of worldly success, which inculcates a division of the entire population into "winners" and "losers." For those who found the politics of the New Left threatening, however, Don Quixote also represented to them their "higher ideals," albeit emptied of any concrete contents. *Man of La Mancha* safely avoids getting into specifics where contemporary issues are concerned. The enemies of quixotic heroism are limited to the Spanish Inquisition and the vulgar muleteers who abuse Aldonza. Absence of controversy allows it to be all things to all spectators.[24]

---

23   Depending on the teacher-scholar's own bent and the context within the course, a large body of theory is available raising such issues. An apt approach could be to sample Cold War theory by beginning with critiques of mass culture by, say, Benjamin and, especially, Horkheimer and Adorno, then considering Marcuse's *Eros and Civilization,* that is, another Frankfurt intellectual's more 'idealistic' call for a liberating form of cultural production. Alternatively, Castillo and Egginton's *Medialogies* provides a roadmap for posing the same problems in the early 21st century.

24   This account clarifies, I hope, the diametric opposition between the two critics who have analyzed *Man of La Mancha* from an ideological standpoint. For John Bush Jones, "the play brings together the counterculture's visionary desire for escape . . . and the increasingly militant New Left's visionary agenda for change" (238-39). For Alberto Sandoval-Sánchez, however, *Man of La Mancha* is a profoundly conservative reaction against the counterculture, an anachronistic return to the 1950s, "an antidote to the social and political unrest of the era" (201). That it could mean both of these things to different audience members, and repress awareness of its own contradictory position vis-à-vis contemporary sociopolitical conflict, is the source, precisely, of its appeal.

In the classroom, the goal should not be to revile the musical, of course, but to examine how, in the context of mid-60s turmoil, Wasserman, with help from Leigh and Darion, was able to create a piece that could appeal across the political spectrum. *Man of La Mancha* harnessed the cultural energy that had become invested in Cervantes' mad knight, but that had not as yet found an outlet capable of explicitly articulating quixotism as self-ironic activist satire. Thus the musical siphoned away that cultural energy from any more overtly progressive understanding of *Don Quixote*. By appropriating the countercultural reading, emptied of any specific political content, Wasserman created an uncontroversial space of agreement, one could even say of national reconciliation, during a time of violent confrontation. (It debuted two years to the day after the assassination of John F. Kennedy, and around a year and a half before the two-month period linking those of Martin Luther King, Jr. and Robert F. Kennedy.) Audiences cried, rather than laughed, and the relief it brought them was then interpreted by each member in accordance with his or her own needs. *Man of La Mancha* functioned like a form of group therapy for a nation in crisis, helping theater-goers to put the all-too-obvious contradictions of the present out of their minds, rather than forcing them to reflect on those contradictions.[25] Students may reasonably disagree about whether such a role for culture should be disparaged. Situating the musical at the crossroads between two very different ways of understanding the function of cultural products vis-à-vis the controversies dividing society can be a way of getting them to test their own unexamined assumptions about the relations between politics and the arts.

Sapped of its cultural momentum by the popularity of the musical, the countercultural quixotism Wasserman had appropriated withered after 1965 but did not die altogether. Among the impressive late manifestations of this spirit, one could try exposing students to "punk" novelist Kathy Acker's *Don Quixote* (1986), a surreal satire drawing on the anarchism of the Spanish Republic in constructing an alternative to neo-liberalism.[26] Much of Terry Gilliam's output as a director falls within countercultural quixotism, above

---

25   Testimonials of tears abound in Wasserman's fan mail. Anecdotally, I have been told by several people who saw *Man of La Mancha* as adolescents in the 60s and 70s that it was personally liberating and inspirational in ways that went beyond insipid abstract "idealism," and indeed involved, in some instances, a memorable flood of tears. The impact of the musical on individual audience members could be lasting and profound, and certainly, in its way, went beyond mere "entertainment."

26   I discuss Acker's *Don Quixote* as apocalyptic satire with utopian overtones in "Not These Bones."

all *The Fisher King* (1991), in which a Hunter College English professor, specializing in the Grail legend, is driven mad by a traumatic experience and transforms himself into a questor knight, fighting indifference to human suffering during the heyday of Reaganomics. Having succeeded, finally, in making *The Man Who Killed Don Quixote*, which had its world premiere at the 2018 Cannes Film Festival, Gilliam has remained faithful to the understanding of Cervantes' masterpiece as a challenge, not just to the debasement of a contentless "idealism" by "materialism," but to the occlusion of imagination by the "organized system" (as counterculture guru Paul Goodman termed it in *Growing Up Absurd*) with its perverse overvaluation of fame and money, quixotically denounced by Kerouac decades ago.[27]

Meanwhile, Wasserman did all that was in his power to ensure that *Man of La Mancha*, even after its initial success, remained a force depoliticizing *Don Quixote*. The contractual agreement licensing *Man of La Mancha* strictly regulated the staging of the musical, prohibiting reinterpretation or recontextualization of any kind. Wasserman took it upon himself to serve as the enforcer of this contract. One instance in particular stands out, the Denver Center Theatre Company's 1988 production, which changed the setting to an unnamed Central American country whose brutal right-wing dictator is supported by the United States. The stage is littered with rubble and prominent money bags with dollar signs on them; the windmill Don Quixote attacks is Uncle Sam; a Spanish-language radio broadcast supporting the Sandinistas plays at the beginning. The merits of this particular production, or even of the idea of recasting Cervantes' hero as an opponent of Yankee imperialism, are beside the point here. What is interesting in this context is that Wasserman, having gotten wind of what was happening in Denver, boarded a plane and attended the play incognito, to see for himself. He then brought legal action against the theater company to force them to remove the offending aspects of the staging. In his affidavit, he argued they were damaging *Man of La Mancha*'s reputation by giving audiences a political message they did not expect, and falsely creating the impression that Wasserman, Leigh, and Darion shared it:

---

27   As I write, *The Man Who Killed Don Quixote* is still tied up in legal battles delaying its U.S. release. In any case, Gilliam's best counterculture appropriation of *Don Quixote* remains *The Fisher King*, which is widely available and readily lends itself to a continuation of the classroom debate over the role of the arts in expressing opposition to mainstream values.

The production of 'Man of La Mancha' that I witnessed went beyond al-
teration and bordered on mutilation by employing unlicensed deletions
and additions to the play which . . . inserted political messages never
present in the play, as licensed. . . . I believe that the play implies that
the authors, including myself, ascribe to anti-American and other political beliefs never written into and never intended to be suggested by
the original script and score of 'Man of La Mancha.' (Dale Wasserman
Papers, Box 17 folder 12)

The director, Michael Penny, defended himself in a letter in which he
insisted that, "unless you meant *Man of La Mancha* merely as a frothy entertainment, which I doubt, you must admit that the 'concept' did not interfere
with your original intentions which were to show that people's spirits can
soar above their circumstances." Wasserman, in his response, bristled at the
implication:

I'm surprised at your reference to *Man of La Mancha* as "a frothy entertainment." Of all things it has been, it never was that. Indeed, the huge
difficulties in getting the original production produced and financed
arose from producers' opinions that it was intellectual, abstract and far
out of the genre of "entertainment." (Dale Wasserman Papers, Box 17
folder 12)

What Penny means by "entertainment" is close to what Arthur Miller
meant by the same term thirty years earlier, a theatrical spectacle the audience is invited to enjoy without being challenged to establish a link to their
own lives outside the theater. Wasserman seems to have sincerely believed he
deserved recognition as a 'serious' writer because of the abstract, 'philosophical' themes dealt with in his plays, even though they were detached from any
connection to the present. He never accepted the notion that a writer's role
involves a critique of contemporary society that the audience cannot avoid
recognizing. In any case, Wasserman succeeded in getting an out-of-court
agreement that saved the Denver production while eliminating as much of
the offending, "anti-American" material as possible. The Denver Center also
agreed to print copies of the following disclaimer and distribute them with
every program:

The material in this production which precedes the opening scene in
prison is not a part of 'Man of La Mancha' as written by the authors. The

authors of 'Man of La Mancha' have not approved this material, nor have they approved they Denver Theatre Center's change of the locale of the play from 16th-century Spain during the Inquisition to contemporary Central America. (Dale Wasserman Papers, Box 17 folder 12)

As this example shows, any attempt to read back into *Man of La Mancha,* the political satire excluded in 1965, would have to wait until old age led the vigilant Wasserman, concerned to protect his artistic and financial legacy, to finally drop his guard. The legal battle over the Denver production is a further opportunity for students to debate the competing claims of those who would reintroduce immediate relevance to the present, arguably more in the spirit of Cervantes' original, as opposed to the copyright holder's desire to keep his adaptation free of controversy in order to ensure its broad appeal.[28]

In March 2008, a group called Room5001 Theater created a bold reimagining of *Man of La Mancha* under the direction of Joshua William Gelb, with an all-male cast of eight actors. As Gelb himself explains on his website, "the atrocities of Guantanamo and Abu Ghraib had come to light, both terrifying narratives of corrupt political-prison systems that recalled in my mind the brutalities of the Spanish Inquisition." He was "determined to relate the renowned story of madness waging war against the cruel, real world as simply and brutally as possible" in order to bring out its "inherently provocative politics." By "asking to what extent live-performance is capable of engaging with/affecting the horrors of life well beyond the insular world of musical-theater," Gelb was effectively inverting Wasserman's original intention of isolating Cervantes and the audience in a bubble of good feeling about their shared humanity, however corrupt the world outside the theater might be. Like the Uncle Sam windmill and money bags of the Denver Center's 1988 production, the orange jumpsuits of the prisoners in Gelb's 2008 production aimed to harness Quixote's passion for justice as part of a critique of U.S. foreign policy. This time, however, Wasserman, then 93 years old, did not respond. In fact, he died later that year, while Mitch Leigh, the last of the original collaborators, died in 2014. Since, a new era in the history of the

---

28   Material relating to the Denver Center production occupies folders 12-14 of Box 17 of the Dale Wasserman Papers. In addition to the legal documents and personal correspondence quoted above, the files include both favorable and negative reviews of the production, and some, such as Alan Stern in the *Denver Post,* who explicitly defended the director's artistic right to re-interpret the musical play. In the end, however, Wasserman insisted upon his *legal* right to curtail the director's artistic expression, as per the contract.

musical has begun, in which it is possible to tinker freely with its ideological underpinnings. A few of the most recent examples will suffice. In 2016, an all-female production, set in a women's prison and starring Louise Pitre was directed by Gordon Greenberg in Toronto. In an interview with Playbill.com, Greenberg justified the directorial choice in the following terms:

> The prison setting of *Man of La Mancha* is central to its richness and resonance. . . . It underscores the idea that this story is being constructed in the moment. Freedom, for them, comes through narrative and music—and a belief in the possibility of a better world. Setting the show in an all-female prison keeps this framing idea alive as the women assume various roles (male and female) in the story. It's a way to heighten theatricality and keep the prison present throughout the show. And, in a male-dominated world, it throws the female roles into relief. As we talk more and more about the nature of gender in all realms of public and private life, it's an engaging way to view this robust and transcendent story.

In 2017, a new Brazilian version of *O Homem de la Mancha* premiered in Sao Paulo, which in June 2018 opened in Rio de Janeiro under Miguel Falabella's direction. The setting, instead of a prison of the Spanish Inquisition at the turn of the 17th century, is a Brazilian mental hospital in the 1950s; thus the denunciation is directed at local politics within living memory. Late in 2017 the Arizona Theatre Company launched a version set in Spain during the Franco dictatorship, directed by David Bennett. In summer 2018, as I write, audiences in the Los Angeles area can see A Noise Within's production in Pasadena, California, directed by Julia Rodriguez-Elliott, set in a modern prison. Presumably, it will now become difficult to find any new production that does *not* adapt the setting and themes to make the story politically relevant in the present. At long last, the real-world connections, originally so central to Cervantes' story, but excluded by Wasserman and his collaborators, are finding their way back in. Yet the question remains: is the damage *Man of La Mancha* did to U.S. audiences' perception of *Don Quixote* reversible? To take a recent case, in the HBO series *The Newsroom*, which I have studied elsewhere, the playful mixing of references to *Man of La Mancha* and to Cervantes' original novel across multiple episodes heightens the Romantic idealization of the anchorman's heroic role of delivering the truth to his audience even at personal cost, with none of the self-ironic undercutting we find in Cervantes (Childers, "Quixo-Journalism"). A good way to end the exploration of *Man of La Mancha* and its political unconscious is to ask students to imagine the kind of *mise-en-scène* that would contribute to un-doing its legacy of a depoliticized *Don Quixote*. In particular, one might fo-cus attention, as several of the recent productions mentioned above do, on the prison setting and its resonances, both literal and metaphorical, in the present historical moment. What is our equivalent today of the Inquisition? What, if anything, can Quixotism still offer us in our quest to free ourselves of its coercive presence in our lives?

Works Cited

Acker, Kathy. *Don Quixote, Which Was a Dream.* Grove Press, 1986.

Auden, W. H. "Balaam and the Ass: The Master-Servant Relationship in Literature." *Thought: Fordham University Quarterly*, vol. 29, no. 2, Summer 1954, pp. 237-70.

———. *City Without Walls and Other Poems.* Random House, 1966.

———. *The Enchafèd Flood; or, The Romantic Iconography of the Sea.* Random House, 1950.

———. "The Ironic Hero. Reflections on *Don Quixote*." *Horizoni*, vol. 20, August 1949, pp. 86-93.

———. "Lyrics for *Man of La Mancha*." *Antaeus*, vols. 40/41, Winter-Spring 1981.

———. *Thank You, Fog. Last Poems.* Random House, 1974.

Auden, W. H., and Chester Kallman. *Libretti*. Edited by Eward Mendelson. Princeton UP, 1993.

Baillie, Bruce, director. *Quixote.* Canyon Cinema, 1965-1967. www.youtube.com/watch?v=D5p6Igg-O10. Accessed 4 October 2019.

Benjamin, Walter. "The Work of Art in the Age of Mechanical Reproduction." *Illuminations*. Translated by Harry Zohn. Schocken, 1969, pp. 217-52.

Bennet, David, director. *Man of La Mancha.* Arizona Theater Company, 2017.

Bigsby, Christopher. *Arthur Miller. 1915-1962.* Harvard UP, 2009.

Brecht, Bertold. *The Rise and Fall of the City of Mahagonny* and *The Seven Deadly Sins of the Petty Bourgeoisie.* Translated by W. H. Auden and Chester Kallman. Eyre Methuen, 1979.

Carpenter, Humphrey. *W. H. Auden. A Biography.* Houghton Mifflin, 1981.

Castillo, David R. and William Egginton. *Medialogies: Reading Reality in the Age of Inflationary Media.* Bloomsbury, 2017.

Childers, William P. "Not These Bones: Apocalyptic Satire in Baroque Spain and the Cold War United States." *Writing in the End Times. Apocalyptic Imagination in the Hispanic World,* edited by Bradley Nelson and David R. Castillo. *Hispanic Issues On Line*, vol. 23, 2019, pp. 125-64. cla.umn.edu/sites/cla.umn.edu/files/hiol_23_06_childers.pdf. Accessed 4 October 2019.

———. "Quixo-Journalism." *A Polemical Companion to Medialogies: Reading Reality in the Age of Inflationary Media.* Edited by Bradley J. Nelson and Julio Baena.

Hispanic Issues On Line Debates, vol. 8, 2017, pp. 91–110. cla.stg.umn.edu/sites/cla.umn.edu/files/hiold_08_07_childers_0.pdf. Accessed 4 October 2019.

———. "QuixoNation" *Cervantes and the New Millenium*. Edited by Bruce Burningham. U of Nebraska P, forthcoming.

———. "Quixote Gumbo." *Cervantes*, vol. 5, 2015, pp. 17-47.

———. "Surviving the Hollywood Blacklist: Waldo Salt's Adaptation of Don Quixote." *Don Quixote. The Re-accentuation of the World's Greatest Literary Hero*. Edited by Slav N. Gratchev and Howard Mancing. Bucknell UP, 2017, pp. 153-80.

Close, Anthony. *The Romantic Approach to* Don Quixote. *A Critical History of the Romantic Tradition in Quixote Criticism*. Cambridge UP, 1978.

Dahlberg, Edward. *Do These Bones Live?* Harcourt, Brace and Company, 1941.

Debord, Guy. *The Society of the Spectacle* [1967]. Zone Books, 1994.

Edelson, Morris. "anti-manifesto." *Quixote*, vol. 1, no. 1, Nov. 1965, p. 3.

Efron, Arthur. *Don Quixote and the Dulcineated World*. U of Texas P, 1971.

Falabella, Miguel, director. *O Homem de la Mancha*. Atelier de Cultura, 2017.

Farrell, Suzanne. *Holding on to the Air: An Autobiography*. UP of Florida, 2002.

Fuller, John. *W. H. Auden: A Commentary*. Princeton UP, 1998.

Gelb, Joshua William, director. "Man of La Mancha." www.joshuawilliamgelb.com/lamancha/. Accessed 4 October 2019.

Genus, Karl, director. *I, Don Quixote*. DuPont Show of the Month, 1959.

Gilliam, Terry, director. *The Fisher King*. Columbia-TriStar, 1991.

———. *The Man Who Killed Don Quixote*. Alacran Pictures, 2018.

Giroud, Vincent. *Nicolas Nabokov. A Life in Freedom and Music*. Oxford UP, 2015.

Goodman, Paul. *Growing Up Absurd. Problems of Youth in the Organized System*. Random House, 1960.

Gottfried, Martin. *Arthur Miller. His Life and Work*. Da Capo, 2003.

Greenberg, Gordon. Interview with Playbill.com. 17 Nov 2016. www.playbill.com/article/all-female-la-mancha-set-in-womens-prison-gets-staged-presentation-today. Accessed 4 October 2019.

Iffland, James. "¡Que siga la fiesta! Reflexiones sobre el humor de la segunda parte del *Quijote*." *El español en el mundo*. Anuario 2015. cvc.cervantes.es/lengua/anuario/anuario_15/iffland/p01.htm. Accessed 4 October 2019.

Horkheimer, Max and Theordor Adorno. "The Culture Industry: Enlightenment as Mass Deception." *Dialectic of Enlightenment* [1944]. Translated by Edmund Jephcott. Stanford UP, 2002, pp. 94-136.

Jameson, Fredric. *The Political Unconscious. Narrative as a Socially Symbolic Act*. Cornell UP, 1981.

Jones, John Bush. *Our Musicals, Ourselves. A Social History of the American Musical Theatre*. Brandeis UP, 2003.

Kerouac, Jack. *The Dharma Bums*. Viking, 1958.

Kerouac, Jack, and Allen Ginsberg. *Jack Kerouac and Allen Ginsberg: The Letters*, edited by Bill Morgan. Penguin, 2010.

Lo Ré, A. G. "Dale Wasserman's *Man of La Mancha* and Miguel de Cervantes' *Don Quixote*." *Essays on the Periphery of the Quixote.* Juan de la Cuesta, 1991, pp. 103-18.

Marcuse, Herbert. *Eros and Civilization: A Philosophical Inquiry Freud.* Beacon, 1956.

Miller, Arthur. *The Theater Essays of Arthur Miller,* edited by Robert A. Martin, Viking, 1978.

———. *Timebends. A Life.* Grove Press, 1987.

Parr, James A. *Don Quixote: An Anatomy of Subversive Discourse.* Juan de la Cuesta, 1988.

Rodríguez-Elliott, Julia, director. *Man of La Mancha.* A Noise Within (Pasadena), 2018.

Russell, P. E. "*Don Quixote* as a Funny Book." *Modern Language Review,* vol. 64, no. 2, 1969, pp. 312 -26.

Sandoval-Sánchez, Alberto. "Cervantes Takes Some Detours to End up on Broadway: Re-imagining Don Quixote in *Man of La Mancha.*" *Cervantes and/on/in the New World*, edited by Julio Vélez-Sainz and Nieves Romero-Díaz, Juan de la Cuesta, 2007, pp. 179-212.

Saunders, Frances Stonor. *The Cultural Cold War. The CIA and the World of Arts and Letters.* New Press, 2000.

Thomas, Dorothy. Letter to Dale Wasserman, 16 Nov 1959. Dale Wasserman Papers, New York Public Library, Box 13.

———. "This I Believe." Essay for Edward R. Murrow's *This I Believe* radio broadcast. Tufts Digital Library. dl.tufts.edu/catalog/tufts:MS025.006.009.00010.00001. Accessed 4 October 2019.

"Tilting with Don Quixote." *New York Times* 11 Nov 1959.

Toole, John Kennedy. *A Confederacy of Dunces.* Forward by Walker Percy. Louisiana State UP, 1980.

Wasley, Aidan. *The Age of Auden: Postwar Poetry and the American Scene.* Princeton UP, 2010.

Wasserman, Dale. "Auden in Autumn." *American Theatre*, vol. 26, no. 10, Dec 2009, pp. 46, pp. 48-52.

———. *The Dale Wasserman Papers.* New York Public Library, Lincoln Center, Billy Rose Collection.

———. *I, Don Quixote* (1959). *Cervantes*, vol. 21, no. 2, 2001, pp. 125-213.

———. *The Impossible Musical: The Man of La Mancha Story.* Applause Theatre and Cinema Books, 2003.

———. *Man of La Mancha. A Musical Play,* lyrics by Joe Darion, music by Mitch Leigh, Random House, 1966.

———. "Reply to Arthur Miller." *New York Times,* 6 Dec 1959, p. 15.

———. "Tilting at 'Man of La Mancha.'" *Los Angeles Times*, 5 Mar 1978, p. 60.

———. "W.H. Auden and *Man of La Mancha.* On Pink-Slipping a Poet Laureate." *The Dramatist*, May/June 1999, pp. 16-23.

Willet, John. *Brecht in Context: Comparative Approaches.* Methuen, 1983.

Witemeyer, Hugh, editor. *Pound/Williams: Selected Letters of Ezra Pound and William Carlos Williams.* New Directions, 1996.

Ziolkowski, Eric J. *The Sanctification of Don Quixote. From Hidalgo to Priest.* Pennsylvania State UP, 1991.

Engaging Students Critically on the #MeToo Movement: Framing Contemporary Crime Shows with Tirso and Zayas

BRADLEY J. NELSON

Concordia University

I AM SURE THAT I am not the only person to be struck by the historical, rhetorical, and aesthetic homologies between María de Zayas's collections of *novelas* and the #MeToo movement. Zayas's novelistic spectacles, comprised of tales told by aristocratic women about the violent abuse of women at the hands of men, offer tantalizing and useful parallels with the #MeToo movement as well as the virulent backlash against it. This essay seeks to explore ways to engage students with the complex issues surrounding the question of moral responsibility in societies in which economic, juridical, political, and medical institutions place men and women in asymmetrical power relations. The intent here is to analyze how different aesthetic modes reveal or conceal these institutional biases through their treatment of the ritual structure of scapegoating in both early modernity and today. One of my hypotheses is that due to her indirect and often subtle exposure and critique of sexual violence and injustice in a repressive social and religious environment, learning how to read Zayas teaches our students to analyze the current situation more reflectively and productively. But this is not a one-way street, since approaching Zayas through contemporary aesthetic renderings of sexual violence also allows us to begin to recognize the devastating irony that runs through her novels. The overall goal of my courses is to create entanglements between nonlocal or historically remote, i.e., anachronistic, cultural artifacts and contemporary social issues, leading to critical dialogues and equipping students to engage with issues inside and outside of the classroom.

I will model this approach by setting up a conversation between Zayas's *El jardín encantado* and Tirso de Molina's *El burlador de Sevilla*, on the early modern side, and *Criminal Minds* and *Orange Is the New Black*, on the late modern side. The specific learning outcomes include teaching students to analyze how aesthetic frameworks act to substantiate and/or question gendered power relations as well as the ways in which public exposure and shaming, rather than weakening these inequitable and violent social and legal structures, often serve to occlude and even fortify said inequities through a dialectic of guilt and punishment. Catherine Bell follows René Girard in describing scapegoating as an act that "lies . . . at the beginning of a sociocultural process that continually repeats and renews both the violence and the repression that renders the violence deceptively invisible" (16). Seen from this angle, the public exposure and shaming of the sexual criminality of famous individuals (Harvey Weinstein, Bill Cosby, Eric Schneiderman) can serve to normalize the institutional structures and practices that facilitate and conceal these actions in the first place. As I state in an earlier essay on Zayas, "framing sexual violence as socially unnatural or deviant contributes to the maintenance and legitimization of a symbolic order in which it is a banal part of daily existence" ("The Aesthetics" 66). I am not suggesting that sex crimes and criminals not be pursued through the criminal justice system; nor am I suggesting that Weinstein, Cosby, etc., are innocent of the crimes they are accused of committing; rather, I propose that a focused study of texts that stage sex crimes and their prosecution can help us and our students reflect on the relationship between public castigation (scapegoating) and social and institutional transformation. Critically informed discussions of these texts can help us understand that sex crime laws and the institutional practices and procedures ostensibly designed to apply them are constitutive elements of sexist power relations, whether early or late modern, and are thus at the heart of the problems being investigated and mapped by #MeToo.

Tirso de Molina's foundational text clearly exposes the relationship between power, sexual violence, and feminine victimization, as well as the role of scapegoating in reifying and legitimizing all of the above. *El burlador* situates itself within Counter Reformation discourses and values concerning personal responsibility (free will, sin, punishment), and in this context many critics have focused on the ways in which Don Juan's victims—Isabela, Tisbea, Aminta[1], and Ana—all seem to bear responsibility for their own dis-

---

1   Rodríguez López-Vásquez's edition of the play refers to Aminta as 'Arminta' throughout.

honor.[2] Ruth Lundelius counters this trend by showing how "Tirso . . . is able to exhibit and castigate a number of traditional exemplars of errant women: the inordinately proud and disdainful, the irresponsible rebel against paternal authority, the incontinent flouter of the precepts of church and state, and the foolish social climber" (13). For Lundelius, Tirso domesticates aesthetic tropes and narrative frameworks that had long served to question and challenge patriarchal dominance and, in so doing, renders the systemic sexual violence of the plot "invisible," to echo Bell (16).[3]

One interesting detail that has received little attention is that Juan's false promises of marriage may be considered legal as well as moral crimes. Renato Barahona's archival work on the legal prosecution of sex crimes in early modern Spain suggests that Don Juan's promises of marriage have legal standing.[4] As Barahona explains, it was not uncommon for the victims of such crimes to seek redress in what today would be considered a civil lawsuit (122). Accordingly, since Doña Isabela and Doña Ana have promised themselves to Don Octavio and the Marqués de Mota, respectively, their dishonor by Don Juan and the king's reluctance to punish him would seem to shed light on how women and men are held to different standards where promises of marriage are concerned. At the very least, it shows that aristocratic behavior is out of step with legal practices and institutions. In the case of the peasant women, Tisbea and Aminta, the first "falls victim" to her own *excessive* pride in rejecting the fishermen around her as potential suitors[5]—Don Juan's false promises notwithstanding—while Aminta's rape involves the consent of her father and fiancé. Juan is probably correct in calling Aminta his great-

---

2   See, for example, the debate between José María Ruano de la Haza and Vicente Cabrera concerning whether or not Doña Ana was actually seduced by Don Juan, a debate not unlike the one revolving around whether or not Laurencia was raped by the Comendador in Lope de Vega's *Fuenteovejuna* (see Parker Aronson). In my view, these debates miss the point that the violence is not limited to the physical act, but produces terror in the ways through which patriarchal institutions reify as well as conceal how violence is produced and legitimized.

3   Encarnación Juárez Almendros argues that this devaluation of female role models and social power begins in the Middle Ages with the replacement of mythologies of motherhood with the Holy Trinity and continues into modernity with the marginalization of female healers, midwives, etc., as seen in early modern medical treatises, especially on the subject of childbirth (84-86).

4   For a more complete presentation of Barahona's work, see my essay "Poet or Pimp."

5   Constance Rose states that "[Tirso's] Tisbea is a serious study in self-deception" (48).

est seduction, as the peasant woman is *burlada* in two ways: sexually and in a social sense through the mocking and moralistic jokes of the courtiers who receive her when she travels to the court to make Juan follow through on his promise of marriage. In addition, the rape of Aminta is orchestrated by rural and urban patriarchal institutions together, as Juan convinces her father and fiancé that Aminta, herself, helped initiate her elopement with her seducer, instead of wringing hard fought promises of marriage from the inveterate liar when he threateningly approaches her bedside in the middle of the night.[6] From a pedagogical perspective, the social, legalistic, and, yes, *scholarly* victimization of these women makes for a productive comparison with current juridical practices involved in the investigation and prosecution—and sensationalization—of sex crimes as well as the importance of social media in disseminating attenuated, exaggerated, or false versions of the crimes. It is also significant that Tirso is recognized as one of the most theologically knowledgeable playwrights of the Spanish Golden Age; indeed, a better question from a modern perspective might be how theology participates in, perpetuates, and justifies sexual violence, something that would take Tirso studies in a different direction, one much closer to contemporary discussions of the Weinsteins and Cosbys of the entertainment industry.[7]

In act 2, Juan kills Don Gonzalo, the father of Doña Ana, when Gonzalo interrupts his attempt to rape Ana. Ana has arranged a secret tryst with Mota—the man Juan is pretending to be—in order to frustrate her father's negotiations with a man she does not want to marry. According to Elena del Río Parra, Ana's seemingly wilful actions are supported by the Council of Trent's edicts concerning marriage and free will (160).[8] As such, one could see Gonzalo's death as a kind of divine punishment for interfering with Ana's free will. The king's and Gonzalo's reactions, however, demonstrate that the

---

6   Perhaps it is just me, but I am struck by the structural similarities between Juan's night visit to Aminta's bedside and the angel Gabriel's visit with the Virgin Mary: both are betrothed when they are accosted by unearthly creatures. See my essay "Religion and Sex Crimes in Baroque Spain."

7   See my essays "Zayas Unchained," and "Religion and Sex Crimes in Baroque Spain" for examples of how Zayas and Calderón bring theological and religious doctrine and practices into their very different representations of sexual violence in early modern Spain.

8   Río Parra cites the Council of Trent: "Manda el Concilio a todos . . . que de ningún modo violenten directa ni indirectamente a sus súbditos, ni a otros ningunos, en términos de que dejen de contraer con toda libertad sus matrimonios" (160). The edict is especially directed against the rich nobles who subject their children to arranged marriages for material interests.

aristocracy is out of step with Tridentine doctrine as well as legal customs concerning marriage. Indeed, neither the murder of Ana's father nor Juan's serial rapes are enough to trigger anything other than a whitewashing of the latter's crimes—and they are crimes according to the legal codes of the time—along with the subsequent reification of the systemic power differential between men and women. As Catherine Connor Swietlicki argues in her Freudian reading of the play, "societies attempt to order and control the perverse, thereby sublimating perverted energies into civilization-building" (101). The king's answer to Juan's many crimes is to marry him to the victim of another of his rapes and lift him up even higher in the aristocracy[9]: "Conde será desde hoy Don Juan Tenorio / de Lebrija, él la mande y la posea; / que si Isabela a un Duque corresponde, / ya que ha perdido un Duque, / gane un Conde" (vv. 2646-49). The other rapes are also dealt with through arranged marriages, which seems to show that a major goal of the play is the (trans)substantiation of a class- and dynasty-based system of arranged marriages rather than to celebrate the concept of free will. For Tirso, however, these earthly arrangements are not a solution in and of themselves, and Juan is punished not by the king's justice but by something that looks more like divine retribution. As Resina puts it: "[Tirso] voices the internal contradictions of a society organized by the honor principle while lifting this principle not only above feudatory contingencies but also above the intervention of the king, who in the *comedia* is always the arbiter and guarantor of social order" (547).

And this is probably the most effective aesthetic and rhetorical strategy of the play where the perpetuation of legalized rape is concerned. The king is unable to make satisfactory matches, attempting to insert, first, Octavio and, then, Juan into the place of the Marqués de Mota at Doña Ana's side, until Juan is removed from the picture. One might argue that this outcome is progressive, if not for the fact that when the punishment finally occurs, the world returns to "normal"; in fact, it's better than ever, since all of the potential mates are now paired with the people they were "destined" to be with, at least according to the plot and social caste ideals held by the nobility. Resina again: "The partners are sorted out in socially restrictive combinations under the pretense of a natural (i.e., uncompelled) affinity" (571). In this sense,

---

9   See also a recent editorial by Nicholas Kristoff: "One Down, but 49 States Still Allow Child Brides." Kristoff writes how pedophiles are often married to their child victims with the parents' permission in order to keep from prosecuting the men as child rapists and simultaneously provide the children conceived during the rapes a "stable" home.

Juan's sex crimes come to be seen as abnormal, an aberration, in a world that would be perfect if it were not for the perverse desire of men *and* women to act outside of established patterns of thought and social institutions. They are definitely *not* seen as a natural and mundane outcome of gendered power relations in the aristocracy. Institutions, including marriage, are cleansed of any potential responsibility for the perverse actions of the *burlador*, which is precisely the role of the scapegoat. Thus, the criminal prosecution—or otherworldly punishment—of a rapist does not mean that structural injustices and violence have been recognized and redressed, however satisfactory, i.e., cathartic, it may feel.

This ritualistic relationship between juridical and law enforcement institutions and sex crimes is something I bring to the attention of students when I ask them for analogies with popular television crime shows. If the institutions charged with investigating and prosecuting sex crimes consistently remain out of frame when the crimes are taking place, then their aesthetic representation is not unlike what we have seen in *El burlador*, where the king arrives at the scene of the crime after the rapist has left. *Criminal Minds*, for example, pits a team of FBI criminal profilers against ever more perverse criminals whose minds are placed under a microscope, so to speak, by the FBI's Behavioral Analysis Unit. In this exemplarily masculine representation of law enforcement, we see female characters literally relegated to the sidelines, as occurs in the first episode of season 11 titled "The Job." In this episode, JJ, a female agent who has been on parental leave for several months, is brought in, one can only surmise, to bring a sense of familial normalcy to the FBI unit, in marked contrast with one of the criminals brought to justice: a woman who unknowingly sets up her husband to be the victim of a contract killer. In one scene, JJ complains about the fatigue of motherhood on a Skype call while expressing her desire to return to the job. After the male agents assure her that she is missed, we shift to the other (criminal) wife, who accidentally brings her husband to the attention of a hitman. Her "blond" moment is followed by an equivocal encounter between Derek Morgan, uber-masculine FBI agent, and his sidekick/groupie/techie, the actually blond Penelope Garcia. At a key moment in the plot, Garcia throws up her arms in frustration while combing through digital bank records for a transaction trail leading to the hitman. Morgan steps in with a number of directives that eventually zero in on the killer's bank account while Garcia watches with her mouth literally agape. The unintentional irony runs thick when Derek congratulates "baby girl" on a job well done, while she dreamily replies, "this never gets old." The lessons here would seem to be that women are: a. not necessary; b. not conscious of their criminal acts; and c. incompetent crime fighters, in any case.

One thing that sets this show apart from other crime shows is its use of literary culture to buttress the moral and intellectual superiority of the BAU and legitimize its treatment of the criminal minds it analyzes and brings to justice. The episode "Inner Beauty" features a quote by James Baldwin: "I imagine one of the reasons people cling to their hates so stubbornly is because they sense, once hate is gone, they will be forced to deal with pain." The problem with this episode, however, is that the object of hate, at least structurally, is women. It begins with a woman fumbling with her keys in a dark hallway while a large man walks towards her. She gets into her flat and slams the door, just as the man (a repairman, it turns out) walks by and sets up his ladder to fix the broken light bulb. Later, the repairman discovers two dead female bodies in a water tank in the building, as the first woman's shower turns into a blood bath thanks to the dead bodies. Her "irrational" fear of the man is seemingly punished by the disgusting water. The plot of the episode revolves around a man who kidnaps women who look like his deceased girlfriend, except for the fact that his former girlfriend had disfiguring tumors on her face, leading her to commit suicide. The killer imprisons the women and attempts to mimic his girlfriend's looks by performing plastic surgery on them. His perverse love for these newly disfigured women apparently sublimates his hatred of the former girlfriend for abandoning him. This is the context into which a quote by the inexorably misogynistic St. Augustine is introduced: "Since love grows within you, so beauty grows. For love is the beauty of the soul." The lesson would appear to be that the killer's love for his dead girlfriend is pure for overlooking her ravaged exterior. Conversely, his hatred of his victims is triggered by her abandonment of him and his victims' resistance to playing the role he assigns them; he prefers their death to his abandonment. Continuing the theme of abandonment, agent Rossi runs into his former first wife while babysitting his/their grandson. Rossi's daughter is a journalist whose job often requires her to be away from home, which explains the presence of the grandparents. Rossi has been harboring a resentment against his first wife because she did not tell him she was pregnant when they divorced. The show emphasizes that her decision was not mean-spirited, nevertheless, what does become clear is that male resentment and hatred of women is related to their feelings of abandonment, both in the main plot and the frame tale. This makes the eventual capture of the murderer problematic, since the difference between him and Rossi is not one of kind but of degree. If we pull on the thread of the abandonment theme, the punishment of the murderer touches all of the women in the story: the murderer's dead girlfriend, Rossi's ex-wife, and his daughter. They are stained by blood just like the unlucky woman from the hallway whose flight from the repairman foreshadows the flights of the other women connected to the plot and subplot. Thus, what is ritualistically cleansed here is the male conscience and the institutions set up to guard it, voiced through the hatred at the heart of Baldwin's quote.[10] I should point out that this is not a straight reading of the episode, but a structural one that finds tragic irony where the writers probably did not intentionally put it. Of course, one could posit that the writers are intentionally excavating and inspecting the internal antagonisms and contradictions of the criminal justice system, but I think I would need to see more obvious signs of authorial control to be swayed in that direction.

Moreover, *Criminal Minds'* transhistorical literary framework, moving from Baldwin to Augustine—are there two more different takes on hate?—parallels Tirso's use of Counter Reformation theology to legitimize his theater as well as the plots and characters contained therein. In both cases, although the human victims and criminals are immersed in the immorality and chaos of the mundane, the criminal justice system is lifted out of this confusion along with its actors and institutions. Like *El burlador*, *CM* reifies the criminal justice system through the ritualistic purging of society of the violent perverts that interrupt what would otherwise be its rational functioning. At the same time, female characters are made to bear much of the responsibility for the hatred and violence against them, when they are not simply marginalized or relegated to the status of accidental criminal.

No such purification, or trivialization, is allowed to take place in the Netflix sensation *Orange is the New Black*. *OITNB* revolves around the story of Piper Chapman, a white middle-class woman in her thirties who is arrested and put in a women's prison for having worked as a drug mule for a previous female lover's drug cartel. The narrative structure of the popular series can be described as an inverted picaresque in the sense that a member of the dominant social class and racial identity is submerged into a marginal world where all of her and the audience's assumptions about law and order, race, ethnicity, sexuality, etc., are challenged and questioned. Indeed, the contingent and arguably unnecessary existence of Litchfield Prison is underlined by the fact that Piper is already rehabilitated, engaged to be married to

---

10   This buttressing of the patriarchy reaches absurd heights when the figure of the "good-hearted" pimp is introduced to provide background on the killer's latest victim. It appears that all of the victims are former drug addicts, which adds a sense of inevitability to their capture and death.

her boyfriend, when she is arrested. Her incarceration converts an accidental criminal into a "criminal mind," a transformation that is repeatedly staged through flashbacks of other inmates' previous lives. It is a good analog for both the #MeToo movement and Zayas's collections of tales because the vast majority of the stories are centered around and told by women.

The story I would like to focus on concerns Nathalie Figueroa, the executive assistant to the warden. Figueroa is an instructive character due to her apparently superior position in the administrative hierarchy of the prison. One might assume that her senior standing would allow her to make positive changes in the daily lives of the inmates, however, she is principally concerned with maintaining her own public profile, a compromise that reinforces the sexist power structure of the prison. Figueroa manages a crisis involving Mendez, an abusive guard who sells methamphetamines and heroin in the prison and coerces inmates into trading sex for drugs. When he is placed on involuntary leave because of his possible involvement in an inmate's death, he instructs a fellow guard to intercept the drugs on their way into the prison and implicate an inmate in the drug trafficking. When the unwitting accomplice, the guard John Bennett, discovers the drugs in a grocery shipment, he informs his superior, Officer Healy, and dutifully accuses Red, a Russian inmate who runs the kitchen. Healy informs Joe Caputo, the Director of Human Activities—one of the strangest job titles ever imagined—who proceeds to inform Figueroa. One gets the impression that Red is going to take the fall, until Figueroa intervenes in the investigation. She has shown throughout seasons 1 and 2 more interest in saving money than providing the inmates with the medical, educational, and therapeutic services to which they are entitled. It becomes apparent, in fact, that she is embezzling these funds and thus cannot afford the negative attention she would receive for her administrative negligence or financial malfeasance, were the drug bust to go public. Together, Mendez and Figueroa bring a darkly ironic meaning to the concept of "the criminal justice system."

When Figueroa interviews Bennet about his discovery, she puts him ill at ease by sitting on a desktop in front of him and flashing her long slender legs. When Bennet tells her that he found the drugs before the delivery truck had entered the grounds, the executive assistant purses her lips and explains that, in fact, *he* is the one responsible for bringing the drugs into the institution. She also tells him that he should probably not submit an official report on the incident even as she gives him a substantial pay raise. It is a masterful performance that mimics the intimidating actions of the guards with the inmates, including the sexual undertones and not-so-subtle threat of a criminal prosecution. When Figueroa drives away in her brand-new Mercedes, no doubt purchased with embezzled public money, the viewers instinctively intuit that they are watching a "bad" person who is manipulating the system for her own profit.

There are two things I'd like to take away from *OINTB*. In the first place, the distance between the criminals and the authorities is collapsed to the point where all are shown to be simultaneously victims and complicit in a corrupt and unjust system that envelops them all. In subsequent episodes, Figueroa will be shown to be a victim of her husband's demand that she embezzle funds from the prison to fund his political campaign. This does not, of course, excuse her actions, which help perpetuate a lethal drug trade in the prison she is supposed to be running; however, removing her from the prison system will not change how it functions. This is not a case of an apparatus of power looming over and manipulating its victims. Everyone—inmates, guards, administrators and, outside of the prison, family members, friends, employers, even fiancés—participates and questions, resists and embodies the discourses and bureaucratic positionings provided by a habitus (Bourdieu) that is obsessed by crime (and sex).

And this includes Figueroa, who becomes more interesting and instructive once we stop dwelling on whether she is a good or bad person. If we criticize her for acting immorally, or unethically, then we set up a Don Juan kind of a situation in which we imagine that the system would not be broken if people like her would simply do their jobs correctly. But since we have learned that many of the women are in prison for "crimes" that seem literally meaningless, or based on fabricated evidence by excessively enthusiastic police officers, or excessively punitive laws, Figueroa's actions point to something different: not broken people, but a broken institution that invests the desire of individuals to succeed or simply survive in its networks, converting those investments into affordances for a very small minority. Moreover, what Figueroa's actions show us is that sexual harassment and criminality are embedded in institutions and that an individual's "crimes" should not be separated from the institutional contexts in which they are produced. *OITNB* teaches us that there is no separating what goes on in prison from what goes on in the social relations and legal practices that create prisons and inform how they operate. Extending this to the #MeToo movement, the show demonstrates that imprisonment is not a solution to institutionalized sexism but a leading actor and location of systemic misogyny in the first place.

Both *OINTB* and the #MeToo movement also foreground the importance of the extradiegetic space in which the narratives are placed. María de

Zayas's aristocratic *sarao* is a largely theatrical social space, where ladies and gentlemen have come together to listen to oral performances that include poetic and musical interludes, sumptuous meals, and seemingly amicable debates over the moral messages of the stories. I have written a number of essays on Zayas's fiction dealing with issues such as femicide, monstrosity, and the relation between Counter Reformation theology and sex crimes.[11] When I am teaching, however, I usually begin with a discussion of *taste*, since taste bridges the aesthetic and moral worlds of religion, politics, and patriarchy. Taste establishes in an intuitive and corporeal manner the limits of what is permitted—good taste—and what is prohibited—bad taste. This is even more interesting in Zayas because she shows that what may be seemingly prohibited or in bad taste, say, rape or wife murder, can become tasteful depending on the aesthetic fabric into which it is sutured.

Like all of the artifacts we have considered up to now, *The Enchanted Garden* assembles an overwhelmingly patriarchal world with limited and limiting roles and channels of conduct for both men and women; moreover, the way that Zayas stages sexual relations in this world reveals that its primary limitation on self-determination is family rank and money. The story begins with a description of the two main rivals, Doña Costanza and Doña Teodosia: "eran llamadas, por renombre de riqueza y hermosura, las dos niñas de los ojos de su patria" (515). It is significant that the narrator, Doña Laura, mentions the daughters' wealth *before* their beauty, while doing the inverse with the male hero, Don Jorge: "mozo galán y rico, único heredero en la casa de sus padres, que aunque había *otro* hermano, cuyo nombre era Federico, como Don Jorge era el mayorazgo le podemos llamar así" (515). The women's wealth takes precedence over their beauty, and vice-versa with Don Jorge, inverting the normal gender values right at the beginning of the story. Zayas also doubly emphasizes Jorge's primogeniture in a sentence that provides one of a number of grammatical curiosities in the tale. Jorge has just the one brother, so why say that Federico is *another* brother? It inserts an interesting rhetorical hiccup in a story where the *naturally* matched pairs never work out. Jorge pursues Costanza, and Federico courts Teodosia, but this is where the plot starts to loop around itself. Costanza treats Jorge coolly, deferring decisions on her conjugal destiny to her parents, as obedient daughters do. Teodosia, in the meanwhile, pines for Jorge, leaving Federico out of the equation. It is understandable, of course, since there is only one first-born son, as Zayas repeatedly points out in the introduction. Unlike *El burlador*,

---

11   See "The Aesthetics of Rape."

where Don Juan must be removed for the world to return to its "normal" functioning, the math should work here. But Jorge murders Federico after being falsely told by Teodosia that Costanza and Federico are in love and secretly planning to marry. After his crime of passion, the heir flees to Naples.

Jorge returns, of course, after four years, at which point people have forgotten about the circumstances of Federico's death. He is still madly infatuated with Costanza, who has married a con man, "Don" Carlos, who feigned a deathly illness in order to name Costanza the sole heir of his fictional 100,000 ducats, prompting her mother to command Costanza to promise to marry Carlos if he recovers, which of course he does. He eventually tells Costanza about the marriage ruse, she forgives him, and they proceed to have kids and enjoy a very happy marriage. None of this deters Jorge, who presses his case so forcefully that Costanza fears for her and her husband's reputations, and so she pulls Jorge aside to tell him that the only way they will ever be friends is if Jorge agrees to marry Teodosia, who, like Carlos, falls "deathly" ill when she sees that Costanza's marriage has made no difference in Jorge's affections. When Jorge hears Costanza's proposal, he reacts violently, swearing that he will never love her sister and that he will love Costanza until he dies. Hearing this, Costanza stands up "y en modo de burla" (527) tells Jorge mockingly that if he can build her a magnificent garden by the following morning, one that competes with the hanging gardens of Babylonia, she will do anything he wants. If he cannot, then he must marry Teodosia: "Este es el precio de mi honra" (527). What happens next takes our story into the realm of the fantastic, as Jorge's despair lures the devil, who promises to make the fabulous garden appear in exchange for Jorge's soul. Jorge gladly agrees, setting up the even stranger denouement of the *novela*.

When Costanza's conman husband Carlos wakes up the following morning, he sees the fabulous garden and immediately shows his wife. Upon seeing the garden, where an arrogant Jorge is ambling along its groomed paths, Costanza faints. When she wakes up, she tells Carlos to kill her if he wants to preserve his honor because she made the mistake of "putting a price" on their honor. Carlos refuses and proceeds to laud Jorge's ingenuity and desire, in other words, his merit as Costanza's "true" husband. He then takes out his sword and attempts to plunge it into his own heart, at which point Jorge steps in to stop him. Overcome, Jorge releases Costanza from her pledge, prompting the devil to release Jorge from his. Jorge proceeds to marry Teodosia, and they live together for many years and have many children; only upon Jorge's death does Teodosia tell the truth about Federico's murder. Laura ends this last story of the soirée with a question about which of the three

is the most understanding (*entendido*) character—Carlos (Costanza's decep-
tive husband), Jorge (the fratricidal and soulless stalker), or the devil—due
to their redemptive gestures in the denouement. More in a moment about
Zayas's devastating irony in having Laura's listeners discuss "at length" the
various merits of these three intrepid heroes; but first a word about the complex machinery of Zayas's plot and how it relates to the rest of our discussion.

My severe reduction of several pages of Zayas's courtly and suspense-
building prose is designed to zero in on the basic elements of the plot, some
of which are amplified and aesthetically inflated through the author's controlled baroque rhetoric of light and shadows. As the principal motor of the
action, much light is shone on Jorge's passion for Costanza and her coolness
and eventual disdain for it. And, of course, much light is shone on the enchanted garden and the exaggerated effects that it has on Costanza, Carlos,
and Jorge. In the shadows we have Jorge's first-born status, Carlos's deceitful
seduction of Costanza, Teodosia's role in the murder of Federico, and, in the
darkest place of all, Federico's murder, about which very little is said until the
end, where it briefly appears as a trivial, if disturbing, afterthought. Emphasis
is placed on Jorge's firstborn status and Teodosia's jealousy early in the story,
but as the plot develops these initial clues are overridden by Jorge's increasingly violent emotions, especially when the story surges towards its bizarre
and incredible conclusion. Federico's murder, on the other hand, is described
in a single sentence, and Teodosia's dangerous lies to Jorge are all but forgotten when she "falls ill" at the beginning of the climax of the narrative. It is
left to the reader to recall that she is willing to do absolutely anything to win
Jorge's heart. . . .and inheritance. It is also up to the reader to flesh out the
whys and wherefores of Federico's murder, and I will now focus on his role in
Zayas's plot since it connects directly with the central thesis of this pedagogical paper concerning how an author's or director's use of the ritual of violent
scapegoating can be used as a barometer for gauging the sexual climate, or
economy, of the world rendered by the artist.

The younger brother's death, based on a lie and committed out of jealousy, fails to open the path for Teodosia to marry the man she wanted; in
fact, Costanza, the true target of the lie—an exemplary instance of slut-
shaming—remains undiminished in Jorge's mind. Thus, there is no relation
between the brother's death and Teodosia's marriage to Jorge. It is Costanza's
and then Carlos's attempted suicides that lead Jorge to marry the younger
sister. But the murder does necessitate Jorge's flight from the city, opening
the way for Carlos to proceed unimpeded toward his deceitful marriage with
Costanza. The basic lesson here is that the able liars and connivers, Teodosia

and Carlos, end up achieving their ends. By comparison, what do Costanza and Federico receive for their obedience? A liar for a husband and a violent death, respectively.

Returning to Costanza's challenge to Jorge, Zayas's narrator communicates to her reader that she considers it a joke, a rhetorical ploy designed to force Jorge to see how ridiculous his obsession has become. But he takes the jest as a serious, albeit impossible, challenge, proving just how poor he is at reading signs, implicitly drawing an equivalence between Jorge's failure to recognize the other's desire and evil, since his desperation and blind love invite the devil into the affair. Nevertheless, it is Costanza who is explicitly made to take responsibility for Jorge's contract with Satan when she confesses that she failed Carlos by putting a price on their honor. Even the devil is allowed his moment of redemption, a dodgy theological sleight-of-hand by Zayas as well as a warning to the reader that we should be very careful when considering what is revealed and concealed in the story.

Again, Laura ends her story by inviting her listeners to debate who is the most understanding character in the narrative—Carlos, Jorge, or the devil—since all three have redeemed Costanza's "sin" in their own way. What remains unstated is that Costanza has arrived in this place because she has obeyed her parents, first by turning away Jorge when he does not ask Costanza's father for her hand in marriage and, then, by obeying her mother's desire that she marry Carlos. Finally, when she is married to Carlos and fending off a very aggressive Jorge, she makes a jest that leads indirectly to Jorge's damnation, thanks to his inability to take a joke. All of which leads me to believe that Laura's challenge to her listeners is an enormously witty and potentially subversive joke. Costanza's subtle wink—in fact, the only glimpse of what we can take to be her 'real feelings'—reveals the falseness and deception in the actions of the nobility; just as Jorge's violent wilfulness exposes a society in which the accident of primogeniture leaves anyone who is not firstborn out of the inheritance, and subtly identifies this custom as source and catalyst for the violence and asymmetrical economies of sexual desire that surge through the plot. The fact that Federico is the only victim of violence in a story that pretends to serve as a morally exemplary *novela* is disturbing on any number of levels. He is guilty only in the sense that his mere existence as a secondborn son is extraneous to the functioning of Spanish aristocratic society and genealogy. I would argue that Zayas uses his death to underline the injustice and unreason of the legal and genealogical institution of primogeniture. In combination with Costanza's stubborn insistence on deferring to her parents' prerogative where her choice of mate is concerned, it serves to expose the rot at the center of early modern Spanish social and legal institutions.

All of which brings me back to the #MeToo movement, the ways that media sensationalize individual cases of male sexual predation, the complex nature of the struggle for gender equality and sexual justice, and the relevance of Spanish Golden Age texts to these issues. If we take the cases of Harvey Weinstein and Bill Cosby, both accused of rape, we can start to see the nature and size of the problem.[12] In both cases, it took many allegations of sexual criminality and harassment to force the criminal justice system to act. Still, I would argue that one of the weaknesses of the #MeToo movement is the tendency of its social media campaigns to leave the impression that once a Bill Cosby is judged guilty in a court of law, substantial change has occurred. If we look to Tirso de Molina, one can argue that the opposite actually happens in the Counter Reformation criminal justice system, whose most effective strategy for "dealing" with rape is the double-victimization of the victims of sexual assault through interrogations, legal wrangling, and, eventually, arranged marriage.[13] Such a punitive process for the survivor of rape, molestation, pedophilia, etc., is extremely effective in turning victims and survivors away from criminal justice procedures, thus skewing the statistics concerning sexual criminality in both early and late modern society. And we see it in the eagerness of Tirso's female characters to get married and perpetuate the very system that put them at risk in the first place.[14] The punishment of Don Juan, like the prosecution of Bill Cosby, leaves the impression that the criminal justice system can work just fine if the proper people (dead or alive) are in charge and if the victims of rape are "real" victims who were not provoking or enticing the rapist.

What Zayas and *OITNB* show us, on the other hand, is that these institutions—marriage and the criminal justice system—are the root of the problem, and they do this in a number of ways. In *The Enchanted Garden*, wealth and primogeniture are identified early on as fundamental traits, or condi-

---

12   See Ronan Farrow's "Harvey Weinstein's Secret Settlements," Jeannie Suk Gerson's "Bill Cosby's Crimes," Doreen St. Félix's "The Rush of Seeing Harvey Weinstein's Perp Walk," Jia Tolentino's "What Bill Cosby's Accusers Have to Endure," as well as the extensive coverage in *The New Yorker* and *The New York Times*.

13   See Evans's analysis of the way the king silences Isabela when she attempts to tell the king what has happened with Don Juan (239).

14   It is instructive to compare the scholarship on the moral weaknesses of Tirso's female characters with exposés on rape survivors published in print and online news media.

tions, of the protagonists. Costanza and Federico obey established traditions and customs and end up suffering death or a near-death experience. Teodosia and Jorge commit horrible acts—and perhaps they do deserve each other—but their murder conspiracy goes completely unpunished. In fact, the audience is left to debate the *merits*, not the *sins*, of Jorge, Carlos, and the devil. The fact that this is even debatable with the devil in attendance constitutes a delightfully vicious swipe at aristocratic society. *OITNB*, in the meanwhile, collapses the distance between the actions of female criminals and the penal code and institutions to which they have been subjected. Both productions provide instructive paths of inquiry into the #MeToo movement.

What is to be done, for example, with the relationship between art and the artist? Woody Allen's well-regarded films and his very questionable behavior towards women, including his adopted daughter; Cosby's advancement of black culture in mainstream America and his alleged use of date rape drugs; Harvey Weinstein's alleged predatory behavior and his production of edgy independent films such as *Sex, Lies, and Videotape*, *The Crying Game*, and *Pulp Fiction*, to name a few. If anything, this aesthetic-behavioral knot underlines yet again the structural nature of gender inequality and the embeddedness of sexual abuse and criminality in our economic, juridical, political, and artistic institutions and industries. This is not meant to excuse criminal behavior but rather bring into focus the entanglements between these institutional *habiti* while presenting the claim that it is not enough to subject criminals to the rigors of prosecution; rather, we must challenge legal definitions and prosecutorial practices where sex crimes are concerned. In the case of Zayas, the murderer embodies aristocratic primogeniture, the conman and the importance of money, and the devil stands in for the religious discourse of sin and salvation. Zayas's devastatingly ironic critique of all three provides a roadmap for contemporary feminisms.

The same can be said for Tirso de Molina and the aforementioned dilemma concerning the relationship between the criminal and his art. I am not suggesting that Tirso the author belongs in this company, but I will say that literary and cultural studies have been navigating this divide between the artist and the work, the work and changing traditions and customs, for a long time. There is no getting around the fact that *El burlador* seems to advocate for a culture in which rapists marry their victims, where peasants cannot marry aristocrats, and where the criminal justice system is a mere tool and alibi in the hands of the king and the nobility. The question for my students, as Pendzik puts it, is "how shall I read his plays as a feminist?" (165). Although the outing and public shaming of figures like Weinstein and Cosby are signs that sexual harassment and criminality are being recognized in ways that potentially challenge the status quo, focusing on their individual crimes can actually work against the broad goals of feminist activism, as Tirso and *Criminal Minds* have illustrated. What Zayas and *OITNB* show us is that focusing too hard on individuals, and their punishment, conceals or deflects our attention from the institutional structures that allow, disguise, and often redeem sexual violence through the very attempt to bring it to light. Rather than accept the criminal justice system's handling of sex crimes as a truism, the practices and procedures that victimize and often silence survivors of sexual violence in the attempt to provide due process to the accused, along with the aesthetic modes in which their violence is disguised, ought to become the object of our critical reflection, as cultural critics and anthropologists.

Works Cited

Barahona, Renato. *Sex Crimes, Honour, and the Law in Early Modern Spain: Vizcaya, 1528-1735*, U of Toronto P, 2003.

Bell, Catherine. *Ritual Perspectives and Dimensions*, Oxford UP, 1997.

Cabrera, Vicente. "Doña Ana's Seduction in *El burlador de Sevilla.*" *Bulletin of the comediantes*, vol. 26, no. 3, 1974, pp. 49-51.

Connor Swietlicki, Catherine. "Don Juan: Cultural Trickster in the *Burlador* Text." *New Historicism and the* Comedia: *Poetics, Politics and Praxis*, edited by José Antonio Madrigal, Society of Spanish and Spanish-American Studies, 1997, pp. 83-109.

Farrow, Ronan. "Harvey Weinstein's Secret Settlements." *The New Yorker*, November 21, 2017, https://www.newyorker.com/news/news-desk/harvey-weinsteins-secret-settlements.

———, and Jane Mayer. "Four Women Accuse New York's Attorney General of Physical Abuse." *The New Yorker*, May 7, 2018, https://www.newyorker.com/news/news-desk/four-women-accuse-new-yorks-attorney-general-of-physical-abuse.

Gerson, Jeannie Suk. "Bill Crosby's Crimes and the Impact of #MeToo on the American Legal System." *The New Yorker*, April 27, 2018, https://www.newyorker.com/news/news-desk/bill-cosbys-crimes-and-the-impact-of-metoo-on-the-american-legal-system.

Gómez-Moriana, Antonio. "Pragmática del discurso y reciprocidad de perspectivas: sobre las promesas de don Juan y el desenlace del *Burlador.*" *Gestos*, vol. 7, 1989, pp. 33-46.

"Inner Beauty." *Criminal Minds: The Complete Eleventh Season*, written by Jeff Davies and Haben Merker, directed by Alec Smight, CBS, 2016.

"The Job." *Criminal Minds: The Complete Eleventh Season*, written by Jeff Davies and Erica Messer, directed by Glen Kershaw, CBS, 2015.

Juárez-Almendros, Encarnación. *Disabled Bodies in Early Modern Spanish Literature: Prostitutes, Aging Women and Saints*, Liverpool UP, 2017.

Lundelius, Ruth. "Tirso's View of Women in *El burlador de Sevilla.*" *Bulletin of the comediantes*, vol. 27, no. 1, 1975, pp. 4-13.

Molina, Tirso de (atribuida a). *El burlador de Sevilla*. Edited by Alfredo Rodríguez López-Vásquez, Cátedra, 1989.

Nelson, Bradley J. "The Aesthetics of Rape, and the Rape of Aesthetics." *Hispanic Literatures and the Question of a Liberal Education*, edited by Luis Martín-Estudillo and Nicholas Spadaccini, Hispanic Issues Online, vol. 8, 2011, pp. 62–80.

———. "Zayas Unchained: A Perverse God or Theological Kitsch?" *Writing Monsters: Essays on Iberian and Latin American Cultures*, edited by Adriana Gordillo and Nicholas Spadaccini, Hispanic Issues Online, vol. 15, 2014, pp. 42-59.

———. "Poet or Pimp? Theatricality and Sex Crimes in Lope de Vega and Cervantes." *¿Promete el autor segunda parte? Cuatrocientos años de una promesa cervantina*, edited by Antonio Cortijo Ocaña and Francisco Layna Ranz, *eHumanista Cervantes*, vol. 4, 2015, pp. 178-95.

———. "Religion and Sex Crimes in Baroque Spain: The *Avemaria* as Alibi in *His Wife's Executioner*, by María de Zayas." *Théologiques*, Special Number on Praising and Cursing God Through Music, edited by Éric Bellavance and Vivek Venkatesh, vol. 26, no. 1, 2018, pp. 61-82.

Parker Aronson, Stacy. "They Said, She Said: Making the Case for Rape in *Fuenteovejuna.*" *Bulletin of the comediantes*, vol. 67, no. 2, 2015, pp. 33-47.

Pendzik, Susana. "Female Presence in Tirso's *El burlador de Sevilla.*" *Bulletin of the comediantes* vol. 47, no. 2, 1995, pp. 165-81.

Resina, Joan Ramón. "What Sort of Wedding? The Orders of Discourse in *El Burlador de Sevilla.*" *Modern Language Quarterly: A Journal of Literary History*, vol. 57, no. 4, 1996, pp. 545-78.

Río Parra, Elena del. "Sobre el alma: matrimonio, confesión y casuística en torno a *El burlador de Sevilla.*" *Revista de literatura*, vol. 68, no. 135, 2006, pp. 151-71.

Rose, Constance. "Reconstructing Tisbea." *The Golden Age Comedia: Text, Theory, and Performance*, edited and introduction by Charles Ganelin and Howard Mancing, Purdue UP, 1994, pp. 48-57.

Ruano de la Haza, José María. "Doña Ana's Seduction in *El Burlador de Sevilla*: Further Evidence Against." *Bulletin of the comediantes*, vol. 32, no. 2, 1980, pp. 131-33.

St. Félix, Doreen. "The Rush of Seeing Harvey Weinstein's Perp Walk." *The New Yorker*, May 25, 2019, https://www.newyorker.com/culture/annals-of-appearances/the-rush-of-feeling-seeing-harvey-weinsteins-perp-walk-arrest?mbid=nl_Daiy%20052618&CNDID=41190558&spMailingID=13586914&spUserID=MTMzMTgoODczNTIzSo&spJobID=1402348413&spReportId=MTQwMjMoODQxMwS2.

"Take a Break from Your Values." *Orange is the New Black*, written by Constantine Makris, directed by Nick Jones, Netflix, 2014.

Tolentino, Jia. "What Bill Cosby's Accusers Have to Endure on the Stand." *The New Yorker*, June 8, 2017, https://www.newyorker.com/culture/jia-tolentino/what-bill-cosbys-accusers-have-to-endure-on-the-stand.

Wickenden, Dorothy. "The End of the Weinstein Era." *The New Yorker*, October 12, 2017, https://www.newyorker.com/podcast/political-scene/the-end-of-the-weinstein-era.

Zayas y Sotomayor, María de. *Novelas amorosas y ejemplares*. Edited by Julián Olivares, Cátedra, 2000.

#MeToo in Early Modern Spain: Visual Pleasures and Silence Breakers

SONIA PÉREZ-VILLANUEVA
Lesley University

> Y en la soledad de este silencio y encierro, me le hallé delante, cuya vista me turbó de manera que me quitó la de mis ojos y me enmudeció la lengua; y así no fui poderosa de dar voces, ni aun él creo que me las dejara dar, porque luego se llegó a mí.
>
> — *Don Quijote de la Mancha* (I, XXVIII, 21)

THE RECENT PUBLIC SURGE of stories about violence against women, and women standing up to such violence, has revealed just how much gender-based aggression is part of our popular culture.[1] The visibility of gender-based violence in today's media also makes apparent how many voices have been previously silenced by the unwillingness of those in power to protect women from this epidemic of violence. Fortunately, survivors are now finding social support to speak up against their perpetrators as shown by the Silence Breakers (time.com) and the #MeToo movement. Although such movements might suggest that a certain progress has been made with respect to our responses to gender-based violence, Tarana Burke, founder of the #MeToo movement, said in a *Time* interview, "now the work really begins" (Chan). Burke's call to action provides educators with an opportunity to integrate issues of harassment of and violence against women

---

1   The elaboration of this essay has been possible thanks to a research fellowship from Faculty Life and Development at Lesley University. I am grateful to Margaret E. Boyle and. Elena Cueto Asín for their thoughtful comments after I delivered a version of this chapter at Bowdoin College. Special thanks are due to Bonnie Gasior and Mindy Stivers Badia for their thorough reading of the final draft and their generous edits.

into the curricula so that students can explore the interplay between cultural representations of violence against women and historical accounts.

While #MeToo and other movements have raised social awareness and influenced governments to pass new laws, there is still work to be done as to how violence against women is portrayed culturally.[2] Many cultural representations of violence are gender biased; women who are portrayed as subjects of violence are mystified, eroticized, and depicted as heroic, thereby camouflaging and trivializing the act of sexual violence as a norm in society. Women must endure suffering with beauty and grace, which minimizes the shock of violence.

My course "Representations of Violence against Women in Spain" uses pop culture to analyze society's acceptance of gender-based violence. The visual, literary, and legal histories of early modern Spain offer a particularly rich textual tapestry for an examination of the cultural roots of gender violence. The course introduces students to early modern authors and artists such as Miguel de Cervantes, Calderón de la Barca, Lope de Vega, Titian and Francisco Rizi, among others, who portrayed their female subject matters as victims of intimate violence, rape, and murder in an aesthetically beautiful way. These portrayals show a society too accustomed to seeing "beautiful" pain and too comfortable with an understanding of female suffering as an essential and even pleasurable element of culture. Nowadays, the #MeToo movement reveals, in Salma Hayek's words, that "women are talking today because, in this new era, we finally can" (newyorktimes.com). However, this course shows a powerful history of women such as Ana Ramírez who dared to speak out in early modern times. There is precedent for women to decry violence; the important question is: will they be heard this time?

This essay is based upon material from the first part of the "Representations" course, *Sexual violence in Early Modern Spain: From Silence Breakers to Visual Pleasures*, which introduces, among others, the important testimony of Ana Ramírez, a seventeenth-century survivor of rape. Just like the #IBelieveYou and the #MeToo movements, Ana Ramírez's case illustrates the difficulties of women winning rape cases in court because of the contradictions between legal theory and legal practice. The law condemned rape in early modern Spain as it does in current times. However, the oppressive cul-

---

2   For example, in 2017, Honduras and El Salvador banned child marriage. India also reviewed its laws on child marriage, amended its anti-rape laws and as of September 2018 stopped considering adultery a crime. France, in turn, has started an initiative for awareness and prevention of sexual harassment as well as a revision of its rape laws.

ture of the Counter-Reformation, influenced by the moralists of the time, considered rape plaintiffs to be unreliable because of women's "natural state" of lust and propensity to give in to temptation. Moreover, some important artistic representations of women in early modern times supported the definition of "beautiful" women as seducers and therefore portray them as visual objects of sexual pleasure. To illustrate this point, the final section of this essay introduces the greatest patron of the Spanish arts and owner of one of the largest collections that eroticized female suffering: Philip II.

Contemporary social movements against gender-based violence provide an opportunity to educate young people about the deep historical roots of how we perceive women and how those perceptions are influenced by art, law, and religion. The #MeToo movement has many important historical precedents, as do current cases of gender-based violence. My course offers a platform for students to recognize the cultural patterns in representations of violence against women that allow for its continuation and acceptance. Like Ana Ramírez in early modern Spain and the women who have accused Harvey Weinstein of rape, such as Lysette Anthony, Annabella Sciorra and Paz de la Huerta, among others, students can be silence breakers themselves and can also bring a voice to the silenced.

ANA RAMÍREZ: A 17ᵗʰ CENTURY SILENCE BREAKER
Sexual violence was a reality in early modern Spain, as the hundreds of legal complaints found so far in the Spanish archives attest.[3] However, as Juan

---

3   See, among others, Alonso García y Agustina García, su hija, y Catalina Caparrós, viuda de Alonso de Mula, todos ellos vecinos de Ceheguín, contra Manuel de Chinchilla y consortes, por violación de Agustina García y asesinato, 1575. Alonso López, vecino de Iniesta, contra Vicente Pajarón, vecino de dicha villa, y consortes, por la violación de su hija, Mari Sánchez. 1565. Catalina Martín, vecina de Siruela (Badajoz), contra Alonso Sánchez Seciliano, por intento de violación. 1572. Cristóbal Prieto, en nombre de su hija Juliana, vecinos de la villa de Vara del Rey, pide al Consejo se haga justicia en contra de Diego de Locoya y Andrés Escribano, vecinos del mismo lugar, por haber intentado violar a su hija. 1575. Juan de Salinas y consortes, parientes de Juan del Castillo, difunto, contra Francisco de Arellano, que se dice clérigo, hermano del provisor, todos vecinos de Salamanca, por haber corrompido a una hija de Juan del Castillo, y otros delitos, 1524-1525. Juan de Ybar, vecino de Villarejo (Medinaceli), con Alonso López, sastre, por llevarle a su hija Ana de casa y violación, y a sus consortes, justicia y abadesa del monasterio de Buenafuente, que le apoyaron después de haber sido condenado. 1567. Carta de poder otorgada por el Convento de Santa María de Gracia de Baeza (Jaén), de la Orden de Santo Domingo, a favor de Pedro Serrano, para que en su nombre se querellase contra Melchor de

José Iglesias Rodríguez argues, there are not as many judicial reports as rapes committed because many victims feared being accused of defamation (81). The case of Ana Ramírez (1654) is a remarkable story of one young woman willing to report her rape by Juan Gallego, a man of nobility, and call upon the protection of the laws of her time. Ana stands as an important precedent for the #MeToo movement as she tried to overcome her position of weakness in Spanish society, both in terms of how the law was applied, but also with respect to the influence of deep-rooted cultural biases. As already argued by Iglesias Rodríguez, Ana's testimony illustrates the vulnerability and exposure of lower-class victims of rape:

> Con ánimo de delinquir y afrentarme abrá un año poco más o menos
> . . . estando yo en las casas de mi morada, sola y sin compañía ninguna,
> siendo como soy mossa honrada, onesta y recogida, me solisitó de amo-
> res, persuadiéndome una y muchas besses a que se quería cassar conmigo
> y que de ello me da[ba] palabra, con que me dejase gossar del susodicho,
> y aunque muchas beses me resist, disiendole que yo era muger pobre y él
> hombre rico y no se abía de cassar conmigo, que escussase sus pretençio-
> nes, todavía me ynstó y dio palabra de caseamiento diséndome que no
> abría de ser otra su muger si no era yo y que en ello podia estar muy sierta,
> y debaxo desta palabra y en fee de que abía de ser mi marido me rendí y
> entregué al susocicho, el cual me gozó, estrupó y ronpió mi birginidad en
> uno de los días de las Carnestolendas passadas de sinquenta y tres en la
> noche, y dende en adelante el dicho Juan Gallego prosiguió en gozarme
> cada bes que quería, entrando y saliendo en mi cassa de día y a deshoras

---

Quesada y otros compañeros de éste por irrumpir en dicho convento, forzar a una monja y cometer otros sacrilegios. 1566. Pleito de Beatriu Joan Veçes y de Morales y de Hieronima Morales y de Miranda contra Jaume Danón, vecino de Oliva (Valencia), por realizar un robo y la violación de Caterina Magdalena Callado. 1592. Proceso, autos y sentencia dados en Marchena (Sevilla) contra Juan de Escobar, hijo de regidor de dicha villa, por haber escalado el muro y fortaleza del castillo de Paradas (Sevilla), haber sacado de él a su prima hermana Catalina Escobar, hija de Bartolomé Escobar, alcaide, y habérsela llevado para usar de ella a su voluntad. 1523. Autos del Real Oficio formado contra Juan Escudero, Escribano Real, y un sastre llamado Robledo, sobre haber forzado a Lucia Gómez. 1656. Ejecutoria del pleito litigado entre Juan de Castroverde y Elvira Castroverde, su menor, vecinos de Pozuelo de la Orden (Valladolid), con Pedro Sobrino y sus hermanas María y Ana Sobrino, vecinos de dicha villa, sobre la agresión e intento de violación que sufrió la menor. 1624. (pares. mcu.es/ParesBusquedas/servlets/Control servlet)

de la noche por los corrales de las cassas de la morada del dicho su padre.
(qtd. in Iglesias Rodríguez, 83)[4]

Juan Gallego refused to marry Ana. At the time of the court case, he was
preparing to marry another woman who shared his social status. As Barahona observes in his study of sex crimes in Early Modern Vizcaya:

> Damage to a woman's good name was due more to aborted marriage
> plans and abandonment than to loss of chastity and charges of promis-
> cuity. Having been taken advantage of—deceived, seduced, sometimes
> impregnated, and then repudiated—a woman opened herself to public
> scorn, shame, ridicule, and insults. (33)

Ana became pregnant as a result of her rape, and her pregnancy could
very well have encouraged her to bring the case to court to seek legal protection for herself and her child. The law provided for reparations in the case of
rape, which included a pardon of the victim's family and marriage between
the victim and perpetrator, the latter of whom would pay the parents an
agreed upon amount. While there are some historical cases of such "reparations," authors amplified the concept as a literary device where kidnapping,
courtship, seduction, rape and abandonment would result in in a "happily-
ever-after" marriage.[5]

Ana's testimony in the first-person singular reveals important information about the legal system of the time. Her words carefully describe the
crime, which the accuser committed "with intention" (Iglesias Rodríguez,
83). The place where the rape occurred is important because the rapist broke
into the victim's house, committing the crime in a domestic environment.
There were no witnesses, as she was alone, thus making this a he-said/she-
said case. Juan Gallego was part of an upper social class and therefore his testimony would have had more weight in court. That is why it is important for
the victim to portray herself as an "honorable, honest and reserved" virgin, so
that she can be protected by the law.

---

4   The transcriptions of Ana Ramirez's case are taken from Iglesias Rodriguez's thorough work on sexual violence in early modern Spain (see works cited).
Iglesias Rodriguez documents in detail Ana Ramirez's case, which he found in the
archives of Niebla (Archivo Municipal de Niebla), box 697, exp. 32.

5   One of the most striking narratives of rape is Cervantes' *The Force of Blood*.
The story exemplifies the resolution of rape when Leocadia (victim) marries Rodolfo
(rapist) at the end of the novella.

There is another key detail in her testimony: "he enjoyed me, deflowered me and broke my virginity one day of the Carnestolendas." Carnestolendas is the carnival season, and numerous writers of the time, including Miguel de Cervantes, Lope de Vega and Calderón de la Barca, use the Carnestolendas as backdrops for their plots, accentuating the masquerades, hidden identities, and carnal pleasures associated with the season. The Carnestolendas were rituals with pagan roots, emphasizing freedom of sexuality in opposition to the severe liturgy of Lent. It was a spring festival, involving abundant food and drink, joy and merriment. Ana's testimony is important because it shows how women, and particularly women of a lower social status, were vulnerable and fragile sexual targets of predators in these times of excess. Centuries later, sexual assaults and gender-based violence are still reported during Carnival festivities in Spain and around the world.[6]

María de Zayas also situates her work *Disenchantments of Love* (1647) during the Carnestolendas, but with a different emphasis. Contrary to her contemporaries, Zayas portrays the reality of violence against women with gory details, avoiding any idealization of their abuse.[7] In her legal testimony,

---

6   For example, during the Carnival celebrations of 2020 in La Paz (Bolivia), the Special Force to Fight Violence (FELCV) attended to more than 50 cases involving intimate-partner violence and rapes, reported the FELCV's Chief of Security, Lieutenant Diego Aruquipa (https://www.atb.com.bo). Like the #MeToo movement, women in the Spanish-speaking world and the Caribbean have started their own campaigns to bring awareness to sexual violence during the Carnival. "In Carnival, not everything is allowed" is the slogan of the campaign that went viral in Jujuy, Argentina, so that women could enjoy the festivities in the Andean province without fear of abuse. The idea was promoted by the feminist collective of the towns of Tilcara and Maimará, where reported cases of gender-based violence increases by more than 50% during the celebration (elciudadanoweb.com). Similarly, Amnesty International has launched a campaign to stop sexual violence against girls in Haiti during Carnival, citing that a large number of rapes take place each year during the carnival festivities. Many are perpetrated at gunpoint and carried out by gangs of young men. Scores of survivors have stepped forward and bravely denounced their experience. Many, however, are hesitant to report their attackers to the police because they fear retaliation, or the shame and stigma that survivors of sexual violence often face. (amnesty.org). In Brazil, there has been an increase of feminist voices since 2015 with campaigns such as #carnavalsemassedio (carnival without harassment) and the blog "Agora é que são elas", which stress the need to prevent sexual assault during the public festivities.

7   Zayas narrates more than thirty cases of physical and sexual violence against women and "incorporates the spectacle of violence seen in public life, literature, and theatre, and the aestheticization of violence seen in hagiography" (Vollendorf 39).

Ana Ramírez portrays herself as if she were a character of Maria de Zayas's *Disenchantments of Love*. She narrates in the first person singular her physical and sexual abuse in order to, as critics have observed about Zayas, "open the eyes of all the dangerous illusions of love and the faithlessness and cruelty of men" (Greer, 38). Despite her brave testimony, it must have been a great disenchantment for Ana that Juan Gallego went free, having to pay only a fine of 2,000 ducats to "atone for" his crime (Iglesias Rodríguez, 82).

The creation and application of the law were heavily influenced by cultural norms and codes of honor at the time. While rape was a crime defined by Spanish law, it was not often punished. Rape was denounced because it was viewed as a sin and an indignity against the code of honor; however, many rape cases were not tried because of an accepted notion that women pretended to be virtuous and men were deceived by them. Juan Gallego went free with a minor fine. There are also many contemporary examples of misplaced cultural assumptions undermining the application of law in the case of rape.

In a recent legal case in Spain, a group of judges found no evidence of violence in a situation where five men, known as the Wolf Pack, abused and raped a young woman. During the attack, the victim appeared to be passive, quiet, and in her own words "removed." This form of escape is a natural response to sexual violence in an attempt to avoid emotional turmoil.[8] The legal conclusion of the judges was that because she was passive and did not

---

Zayas transgresses the parameters of the *imitatio* and creates, in Elizabeth Grosz's words, "a biography, a history of the body, for each individual and social body" (142). She creates a space where "only women will narrate the disenchantments, to defend the reputation of women so maligned that virtually no one speaks well of them" (Greer 38).

8   This case is a particular example where the law does not match human behavior, where the law does not contemplate a natural response—a survival response—to violence, where the law ignores the violence of rape and disguises it with the invisibility of sexual abuse. Psychologist scholar Stephen Porges proposed the polyvagal theory to understand how the nervous system responds to safe, dangerous and life-threatening situations. When the situations are fearful and life-threating, the nervous system brings defensive strategies—freeze behaviors. The Polyvagal Theory explains why in extreme situations when there is intimidation and fear of being attacked, our nervous system adapts and provokes immobilization and passivity. Porges's theory explains why a nineteen-year old woman did not actively resist in a life-threatening situation of danger; her nervous system opted for survival, a response of silence and immobilization. This passivity was not consent. Rather, it was a natural neurobiological response to avoid her own death.

fight back, there was no evidence of violence and consequently no rape, just a lesser verdict of sexual abuse. The accused men were originally fined 6,000 Euros, the modern equivalent of the paltry sum of 2,000 ducats charged to Juan Gallego. The accused were freed following the case, pending a sentencing decision for the lesser crime of sexual abuse. Outraged by the decision, Spaniards took to the streets in protest and created #IBelieveYou in support of the victim. Since then, the Spanish government has reviewed its laws regarding rape in response to such demonstrations and social outrage. The case was taken to the Supreme Court in July 2019, three years after the attack, where it was concluded that the five members of La Manada acted "with full knowledge," and that the victim did not consent. The court stated in the sentence that the victim was attacked in a hidden place, which was done on purpose. Moreover, the behavior of the perpetrators implied a clear denigration of the victim as a woman. The five rapists were condemned to 15 years in jail. This is a case that brings hope and progress in the battle to stop and prevent gender-based violence in Spain and around the world. However, there is a long history of cases in Spain where cultural interpretations of behavior carry more weight than the letter of the law.

RAPE AND THE LAW IN EARLY MODERN SPAIN
According to moralist decrees, such as José de Jesús María's *De las excelencias de la virtud de la castidad*, women incited carnal sin or lust. Theological reasoning could be a stronger arm of law since criminal law in Spain was closely influenced by theology. Additionally, as Rodríguez Ortiz has remarked:

> Indudablemente, la mentalidad de la época influía en los tribunales de justicia, que, con frecuencia, argumentaban que los hechos no habían quedado suficientemente probados o que una mujer no podía ser violada por un solo hombre. Y es que socialmente la mujer seguía siendo considerada [...] un ser desequilibrado e inclinado hacia la lujuria y la perversión, de modo que se mantuvo la sospecha de que la resistencia ofrecida por la mujer en el acto sexual era más fingida que real. Por este motivo, la prueba de la resistencia ofrecida por la víctima ocupaba un papel esencial en el castigo del delito. (116-17)

Women who issued a public complaint of being raped could be seen as "*desviada* en el sentido de que propiciaba la violación, independientemente de que el violador también fuera señalado por el desbordamiento infrene de sus apetitos" (Mantecón Movellán, 161). Pseudoscientific treatises supported this idea of women as aberrant characters. For example, Francisco Nuñez de Coria's *Treatise on the Use of Women* (1572) considered women "insatiable" (fol. 290v) and "more lustful than men" (291r).[9] The book defines women as the temptation from which not even the strongest man can escape.

In early modern times, accusations of sexual assault were kept private within the family so that the victim's honor would not be jeopardized in the public sphere since it was difficult to prove the act of rape. Covarrubias' dictionary (1611) defines "violar" (rape) as "corromper la donzella por la fuerça" (to corrupt a maiden by force), considering the act of "violar" only against virgin women or maidens. The word "force" is important in this definition since it is the use of force that will define "rape" in legal terms in order to consider it a crime. Thus, victims had to prove that there was use of force in the act, as sometimes the perpetrator used false flattery and persuasion to rape his victim. In that case, it was not considered a crime, "y contra quien llevar mujer por fuerza pero no por la desflorar por halagos y suasiones y engaños; salvo cuando por fuerza pública la deflorase" (Barahona, 202, n.22). Accordingly, Covarrubias defines "forçar" as "Necesitar a alguno que haga por fuerza lo que no hiciera de grado. Forçar, a veces significa conocer muger contra su voluntad." As proved by the verdict in the case of the Wolf Pack, these early modern definitions of rape continue to influence the current Spanish legal code.

An earlier code of civil law, The *Siete Partidas* (1265), created by Alfonso X, condemned rape as a sexual crime characterized by a man lying with a woman without her consent and by the use of force. Law 1 of title 20 of the *Siete Partidas* reads:

> Forzar o robar mujer virgen, casada o religiosa o viuda que viva honestamente en su casa, es yerro y maldad muy grande; y esto es por dos razones: la primera es porque la fuerza es hecha contra personas que viven honestamente a servicio de Dios y por bienestar del mundo; la otra es

---

9   *Tractado del vso delas mugeres, y como sea dañoso, y como provechoso, y que cosas se ayan de hazer para la tentacion dela carne, y del sueño y vaños.* Coira understands the difficulties of men and recommends "andar los pies descalços, dormir sobre cosas frias y humedas," although he also adds that this remedy is "muy pernicioso y peligroso para la salud corporal y muy perjudicial para la vida." (303r) In other words, there is no remedy to avoid temptation because the only remedy would be harmful to men's health. Although the advice in this treatise is not to have sex outside the marriage, the temptation is too big and men have to "expelle lo superflo de la postrera digestion, ordenado para la conseruacion del indiuiduo y especie" (303r).

que hacen muy gran deshonra a los parientes de la mujer forzada, y además hacen muy gran atrevimiento contra el señorío, forzándola en menosprecio del señor de la tierra donde es hecho. (667)

Title 20 covers two specifics crimes, kidnapping and rape, and defines them both in relationship to God and the concept of honor. In other words, a man who commits this crime is not only attacking the victim but also the Church and the honor of the Paterfamilias: the father (a virgin woman), the husband (a married woman), the son (a widow) and God (a religious woman). Being considered a serious crime, rape was punished with death if it was proven that there was force in the act, which is why it was crucial for the victim to bring evidence of her resistance. To complicate matters further, according to law 2 of title 20, only relatives of the victims—and not the victim herself—could accuse the perpetrator. And if the family members did not want to accuse him, then neighbors could. As mentioned above, the legal complaint was a family matter, and the victim needed the support and protection of her father, who would start the legal process in behalf of his daughter. Although women were allowed to give testimony of the attack, their fathers, husbands, or male relatives would testify for them and narrate the event in the third person singular: "La esturpó de su virginidad," (Barahona, 45) "Ha solicitado y persuadido . . . a mi hija para que tubiera acesso y copula carnal," (Barahona, 49) etc. Furthermore, social class was also important to consider because the law sometimes only protected upper classes, "personas que viven honestamente," since the crime threatened the aristocratic values of the code of honor, a "gran atrevimiento al señorío." People from poor, rural and humble backgrounds also gave less importance to marriage, honor and chastity, which made it more difficult for them to prove that a crime had been committed (Poska 116).

Proving rape became more difficult with the Laws of Toro, disseminated in 1505 in the city of Toro, following Germanic and Roman law. The Laws of Toro were meant to complement the *Siete Partidas* and the Royal Jurisdiction by bringing some unity to the legal system in Spain, which was at the time a "labyrinth of justice" based on municipal sets of laws (Carrión 27-31). The Laws of Toro contained several aspects of civil law, from inheritance disputes to matrimonial legislation, and also included criminal and procedural law. Surprisingly, the Laws of Toro did not include the crime of rape—to force or steal a woman—even though it affected inheritance and family legislation. Thus, the crime of "rape" depended on complicated sets of laws that punished the offense differently and according to local regulations. These rules, in turn, were supplemented during the Counter-Reformation (1545–1648) by the New Compilation of the Laws of the Kingdoms and "by the publication of numerous *edictos* and *pragmáticas* (royal decrees) designed to cleanse and order urban spaces. These new laws and decrees mainly targeted ethnic and religious minorities, the poor, and women" (Boyle 5). These new laws and the complication of the system benefited the offender, particularly if he was from a higher social class than the victim, since he would obtain a lesser penalty or one of the pardons allowed by law (Rodríguez Ortiz 102). In the case of nobles, punishment was even often avoided by paying the Royal Chamber directly (Rodríguez Ortiz 104).

With the new royal decrees of King Charles I (1552) and King Philip II (1566), the crime of rape was considered a lesser crime and the punishment changed from the death penalty to time in prison. It was also becoming more difficult for the victim and her family to win a lawsuit, particularly if the woman was of a lesser social status. The weight of society was against women who were victims of sexual violence, and the role of powerful King Phillip II provided greater context for Ana's world. Rape victims of early modern Spain were alone: they either had to keep quiet about the rape or live a life of public shame.

Testimonies of record in early modern Spain show the bravery of women who did accuse their rapists because they broke the silence in a society that systematically condemned the victim and pardoned the offender. Likewise, Rose McGowan and Ashley Judd showed their bravery for being the first women to come forward with their allegations against Weinstein in October 2017. Their public accusations started what has come to be known in popular culture as the "Weinstein Effect," a new cultural norm in which the words of sexual assault victims are taken more seriously than they previously were. In the context of the Weinstein Effect, another 150 cases of rape, harassment, and abuse against powerful men have been brought to court. Leaders in their respective fields including Bill O'Reilly (journalist), Matt Lauer (journalist), Kevin Spacey (actor), Stephen Wynn (casino magnate), Patrick Meehan (congressman), Al Franken (senator), and many others have experienced public recrimination and left their jobs due to the testimonies of their victims.

But will the #MeToo movement succeed where the brave women of early modern Spain did not? The #MeToo movement has shown the power of speaking out, destigmatizing the issue of sexual violence and giving attention to the prevalence of the crime. However, as in early modern times, the #MeToo movement has also shown how irregular the legal process is when accusing powerful men. Perhaps the most paradoxical case of all concerns the election of the President of the United States, Donald Trump. Mr. Trump proudly talked about grabbing women by their genitals, and he has been accused of sexual harassment and abuse. As Jia Tolentino argues, "Individual takedowns and #MeToo stories will likely affect the workings of circles that pay lip service to the cause of gender equality, but they do not yet threaten the structural impunity of powerful men as a group" (*New Yorker*). Despite the power of the #MeToo movement, application of the law appears to still be subject to cultural norms that remain, on balance, tilted against the protection of women. The symbiotic relationship between culture and male power appears to persist and the application of the law remains in too many cases subverted.

HEROIC RAPE: POWER AND PARADOX

In Spain, King Phillip II (1527-1598), "the Prudent," son of Emperor Charles V and Empress Isabel of Portugal, became the most powerful figure in shaping not only the civil and religious laws of early modern Spain, but also its culture through his voracious collection of art. Philip II was a devout Catholic and the greatest advocate of the Counter-Reformation. He was also a fervent reader and art collector and became the most important patron of Titian, the influential Italian painter. He first commissioned Titian to paint the series that would come to be known as the *Poesie,* a series of six mythological inventions that portray beautiful women, feature nudes, and narrate aesthetically pleasing rapes such as the ones found in *Danae* (1553) and the *Rape of Europa* (1562). The paintings were kept in private rooms where only men were allowed to view them, presenting rape as a private pleasure for powerful men to enjoy. As such, the great art of Titian becomes a source of misogynistic pleasure.

Considering the rigid religious, cultural and social context of the Counter-Reformation and the Inquisition, this commission transgressed the norms of the time regarding nudes in art. The *Poesie* portray women as sensuous and erotic characters in a celebratory way. However, this paradox was acceptable because the monarch kept the collection in a reserved private room, thus maintaining the artistic depiction of rape within a domestic environment. Literature of early modern Spain, highly influenced by Classical mythical works, used rape as a motif and portrayed sexual violence as "heroic rape." The heroic rape tradition, a term coined by Susan Brownmiller in 1975 in her book *Against our Will*, conceives the violent act committed by kings, soldiers or gods as aesthetically pleasing, almost erotic, hiding the reality of pain and suffering that the victim undergoes. As Marcia Welles argues in *Persephone's Girdle*, the female figures depicted in this manner become mere objects of exchange. Outside Spain, Renaissance and Baroque French, Dutch, Flemish and Italian art celebrated the "beauty" of female victims and the "courage" of the perpetrators; in Diane Wolfthal's words, "these works glorify, sanitize, and aestheticize sexual violence" (7).[10]

In most of these representations of rape, women are portrayed as beautiful passive objects who cannot—or do not want to—escape. Their faces reflect an absent calmness, and in most cases, they are looking up, showing their left arm raised in a delicate gesture, as if they were about to dance.[11] Some of the victims are completely naked or their clothes are torn, showing their bare arms and feet, and in some instances one of their breasts is exposed, which creates a perverse erotic scene. As Leo Currant has observed in

---

10   There are more than one hundred examples of canonical masterpieces that use heroic rape as a central theme in their productions; examples are *Rape of the Sabine Women* (c 1500) by Sodoma (1477-1549), *Rape of the Sabine Women* (1583) by Giambologna (1529-1608), *The Rape of the Sabine Women* (1633-34) by Nicolas Poussin (1594-1665), *The Rape of Ganymede* (1611-1612) by Rubens (1577-1640), *Rape of Ganymede* (1635) by Rembrandt (1606-1669), *Rape of Ganymede* (mid-16th century) by Francesco Salviati, *Rape of Europa* (c 1660) by Jacob Jordaens (1593-1678), *Rape of Europa* (1548-1588) by Paolo Veronese (1528-1588), *Rape of Lucretia by Tarquin* (ca. 1520) and *Rape of Europa* (1562) by Titian (1488-1576), *Rape of Lucretia* (mid-16th century) by Andrea Schiavone (1500-1563), *Rape of Lucretia* (1537-1594) by Jacopo Tintoretto (1519-1594), *Rape of Helen* (mid-16th century) by Francesco Primaticcio, and so on.

11   It is worth noting the paintings of 17th century female artist Artemisia Gentileschi, and in particular the work *Susannah and the Elders*, which provides a contrast to how rape was depicted at the time. In Gentileschi's work, women are portrayed realistically, revealing pain and suffering in their gestures. (Wolfthal 25). Gentileschi was a survivor of rape herself, and records of her trial in 1612 show similarities with the case of Ana Ramirez. As Mary Garrard observes: "She described her honourable conduct and avoidance of improper advances, and narrated the rape incident in graphic detail. Artemisia's account checked all the boxes that the court required in rape cases. She dramatized her active resistance, which included wounding Tassi [the perpetrator] with a knife in self-defence, and descried her pain on penetration and the bleeding that followed, and Tassi's subsequent promise to marry her" (83). Tassi, the rapist, was absolved, and Gentileschi was subjected to public shame. Later on, in the 1620s, and in spite of being illiterate, Gentileschi was able to narrate symbolically her story through art where female subjects are strong and take revenge into their own hands.

his study of Ovid's *Metamorphoses*, "sexual desirability is enhanced by disarray of clothing or hair, by discomfort and embarrassment, or by fear. For the rapist these are all aphrodisiacs" (qtd. in Wolfthal 21). With over one hundred visual representations, rape became more than a motif in renaissance and baroque art; it portrayed an allegory of supreme power in the imagination of male viewers, particularly those with political or religious power such as kings or princes (Wolfthal 23).

The collection of *Poesies* arrived in Madrid between 1553 and 1662.[12] Titian created his *Poesies* as dramatic pieces of art with a clear goal of satisfying the senses of the viewer, who in turn receives aesthetic pleasure. All the *Poesie* pieces are large-scale canvas that exhibit female nudes and in some of them, forced sexuality. The sense of movement, palpability of textures, and the richness of color and sensuality contained in his work made Titian one of the greatest masters of the Renaissance. The pieces of the *Poesies* are magnificent and have become one of the most influential collections in the history of Western art. It is not at all surprising, then, that the women in his pieces become beautiful objects of desire, as the following passage in a letter the artist sent to Philip II suggests:

> Because the figure of *Danae* which I have already sent to Your Majesty is seen entirely from the front, I wanted in this other *poesia* to vary the pose and show the opposite side, so that the room in which they are to hang will appear more agreeable. Shortly, I hope to send you the *poesia* of Perseus and Andromeda, which will have an appearance different from these two; and likewise Medea and Jason.[13] (Translated in Mulcahy 8-9)

---

12   The collection consisted of six pieces: *Danae* (129.8 x 181.2 cm), *Venus and Adonis* (106.7 x 133.4 cm), *Perseus and Andromeda* (175 x 189.5 cm), *Diana and Acteon* (184.5 x 202.2 cm), *Diana and Calisto* (187 x 204.5) and the *Rape of Europa* (178 x 205 cm). At the time of the commission, Titian started working on a seventh painting to add to the collection, the *Death of Acteon*. However, he never sent it to Phillip II and remained unfinished until the artist's death in 1576.

13   "E perché la Danae, che io mandai già a vostra Maestà, si vedeva tutta dalla parte dianzi, ho voluto in quest'altra poesia variare, e farle mostrare la contraria parte, acciocché riesca il camerino, dove hanno da stare, più grazioso alla vista", Giovanni Gaetano Bottari, *Raccolta di lettere sulla pittura, scultura ed architettura* (Milano: Giovanni Silvestri, 1822, voll. I-VIII), vol. II, pp. 27-2

With the first two paintings of the collection, *Danae* and *Venus and Adonis*, Titian presents his patron with a complete nude; when seen together, the two women in the paintings form a single woman's body, viewable from front and back.

In Lucia Binotti's words, "Titian's recommendation that his paintings be placed in a *camerino* where they would be more 'pleasing to the sight,' supports the view that the author composed this series with the Prince's *diletto* in mind, where *diletto* included sensual and erotic pleasure" (32).[14] Indeed, both pieces are highly sensual and communicate a desire that goes beyond the beauty of the nude. Titian had already painted other versions of Danae before his commission of the *Poesies* and continued creating copies due to its growing popularity among clients. Titian's composition portrays a princess, Danae, lying nude on her bed while she is being violated by Jupiter, disguised as golden rain. The scene is peaceful and beautiful; Danae is at the forefront of the canvas, reclining on her pillows comfortably while she waits for Jupiter to finish his act of possession. The nude is frontal while the position of the elevated right thigh hides the genitalia of the princess.

The second piece of the collection, *Venus and Adonis,* portrays a narrative not included in Ovid's *Metamorphoses,* where Adonis leaves Venus in order to hunt while she holds to him in protest of the abandonment. Venus is at the forefront with her body facing into the painting, such that a viewer gazes upon her nude body from the back as she looks up at Adonis. Titian requested the paintings of *Danae* and *Venus and Adonis* be kept together in the same room. The physical appearances of the women used in each painting are similar, and could have been based on the same model, likely a Venetian prostitute. Kept in the same room, the position of the nudes could create a "mirror" effect, which in turn might have created the feeling of submersion in a setting of naked female flesh. The mythical characters, Danae and Venus are secondary; the purpose of the painting is to delight the viewer, in this case Philip II, who enjoys both the aesthetic beauty of the paintings and the repeated nude presentation of the model. Eroticism in the *Danae* painting is heightened as the male viewer is invited to see himself as the warrior or god in the scene who, like Jupiter, takes possession of the female naked

---

14   There is no written or visual evidence of where the collection was kept during the 16th century. As Fernando Checa has observed, "su primera adscripción a un lugar concreto es tardía: se trata de las salas del cuarto bajo de verano del Alcázar, donde fueron vistas por Cassiano dal Pozzo en 1626, sitio en el que, con las variaciones que señalaremos, se localizan a lo largo del siglo XVII." (99).

body.[15] The private consumption of the woman in the painting might reflect the public treatment of women as consumable possessions, a trend that has continued over time. Nowadays, as Rhonda Garelick has observed, in the entertainment industry of Hollywood, "the gaze the moguls train on women in private is also the gaze with which they frame them for our public consumption" (thecut.com).

In the context of the strict codes of the Counter-Reformation, Philip II started a tradition of commissioning heightened visual depictions of rape for consumption by men in private spaces. The trend was picked up by members of the aristocracy. Titian's sixth painting of the *Poesie* series, *The Rape of Europa*, attracted substantial attention from collectors of the time. Many commissioned copies of the piece, as reflected in the registries of Juan Sánchez, Regent Montoya, the Marquis of Heliche, or the Marquis of Carpio among others (Portús Pérez 84). Titian continued creating replicas for other clients (Falomir 17). Rubens created his own copy of the painting during his visit to the Alcázar in 1628-1629, and Velázquez created a copy in the form of a tapestry for the background of his painting *The Spinners* (1657).

---

15   Philip II was married to Mary Tudor in 1554—his second wife after the death of Maria Manuela of Portugal—a year after he received the first painting of the series and coinciding with the arrival of *Venus and Adonis*. To this respect, Anne Cruz has argued that "the Danae relies on its erotic attraction to perform the role expected of the Venus of Urbino: that of finding fulfillment in marriage. It is a painting that depicts the woman's legs open and foreshortened, actively encouraging female fecundity" (11). Nonetheless, Mary Tudor did not have children, and the monarchs lived separate lives. The result was an unhappy marriage, hinted at in *Venus and Adonis* where, as Rosemary Mulcahy has astutely observed "the subject showing Adonis resisting the charms of Venus and leaving for the hunt, while Cupid sleeps, seems prophetic of Philip's unsuccessful marriage" (8) It is unclear how much attention Philip II paid to the *Poesies* collection as he collected more than 1,500 paintings and thousands of items, including "armour, scientific and musical instruments, maps, books and prints, jewellery, coins and medals, furniture, tapestries, fabrics and household items, as well as a collection of relics and natural and man-made wonders." (Mulcahy, 4). The *Poesies* could have been just another collectable item in the King's large collection. His tastes in art also evolved. It is important to note that Philip II continued a close relationship with Titian who kept producing art for his patron until he died in 1575. However, the subjects and themes in Titian's art for the King become less erotic. This evolution coincided with Philip's ambitious project to build the monastery and palace of *El Escorial* (1563-1582). The paintings he commissions from Titian begin to focus on religious themes, "reflecting the changing concerns of Philip as he grew older" (Mulcahy, 9).

Titian (Italian, 1488-1576), *Rape of Europa*, 1562.
© Isabella Stewart Gardner Museum, Boston.

In his study about the collection of nude paintings in the Spanish Court, Portús Pérez maintains that:

> En circunstancias normales las copias constituyen un índice expresivo de la fama de ciertas obras, de las que son al mismo tiempo testigos y transmisores. Pero en el caso concreto que nos ocupa, a ello hay que sumar lo mucho que revelan sobre la dialéctica entre lo público y lo privado, entre lo prohibido y lo permitido, en torno a la cual bascula el tema de las salas reservadas de los Austrias. Estas obras realizadas como objetos de carácter personal por un pintor (Rubens); o como piezas destinadas a grandes (marqués del Carpio) y pequeños coleccionistas, constituyen testigos importantes sobre las condiciones de accesibilidad a los gabinetes secretos y sobre la fortuna que—a despecho de las condenas de los moralistas—tuvo la pintura del desnudo. (84)

Indeed, the Council of Trent (1545-1563) prescribed new rules regarding images and prohibited nude or semi-nude paintings or drawings. The Spanish Inquisition, in turn, included in its *Index* of prohibited books an important decree (rule XI) about the visual arts:

> Para obviar en parte al grave escándalo y daño no menor que ocasionan las pinturas lascivas, mandamos que ninguna persona sea osada á meter en estos reinos imágenes de pintura, láminas, estatuas, ú otras de escultura, lascivas, ni usar de ellas en lugares públicos de plazas, calles ó aposentos comunes de las casas. Y asimismo se prohíbe á los pintores el pintarlas, y á los demás artífices que no las tallen ni hagan, pena de excomunión mayor. (Carbonero y Sol 43)

Artists in Spain were threatened with excommunication and punishment if they produced nude art. They were only permitted to portray classic mythology that would not stimulate any desire of "lust or incontinence of spirit"; that is to say, images that were not lascivious in nature and would not incite viewers to perverse passions (Pérez-Villanueva 154-55).

It is difficult to believe that Titian's *Poesies* and all its subsequent copies did not present a threat to this mandate. In 1554, Francisco de Vargas, serving as an Ambassador in Venice, wrote a letter to Philip II about Titian's *Venus and Adonis* describing the painting as lascivious, "es cosa de grande estima en que Tiziano se ha esmerado mucho, sino que es demasiado lascivo" (Checa 100). Moreover, nude paintings (including the *Rape of Europa*) were not considered appropriate for women and were reserved for the private enjoyment of male viewers. Philip IV (1605-1665), for example, asked to have the paintings covered when the queen visited him in his private rooms in the Alcázar, as Casiano del Pozzo narrates in one of his letters describing the rooms, "cada vez que la reina se dirige a las salas se hacen cubrir antes de que llegue todos los cuadros en los que hay desnudeces" (Portús Pérez 91). Nude paintings, as well as rape scenes portrayed in them, belonged to the privacy of the reserved room and, as such, were not banned by the Inquisition, which was more concerned about the scandal and damages that lascivious images might cause in open spaces, "common rooms" or "public squares." Kings, aristocrats, and noble men could enjoy *The Rape of Europa* in the privacy of their reserved chambers.

But how lascivious is *The Rape of Europa*? The painting is a visual representation of Ovid's *Metamorphoses* book II, 838-875, which tells the story of the rape of the daughter of Agenor, King of Tyre, who was abducted by

Jupiter after he had taken the form of a bull. It is not surprising that artists and collectors felt attracted to this particular piece. As Ovid's poem shows, Europa is deceived by Jupiter, who emerges in the disguise of a wild animal—a bull—but, at the same time appears to be beautiful and calm.[16] Titian's composition reflects Ovid's description of the bull. The animal becomes the protagonist of the canvas and shows his magnificence, strength and beauty. His presence and power are overwhelming, creating a symbolic meaning of masculinity with which male viewers could have identified. However, the painting also reflects the paradoxes of the poem. The flowers on his horns and his tender look juxtapose with the violent act of the kidnapping, communicating an unusual aesthetic empathy. The sense of movement created by placing the bull almost outside the canvas, as if he were going to jump out, anticipates the next scene of the poem: the rape. The ferocious performance is in turn contradicted by the flying cupids who have their bows and arrows ready for the "act of love." Europa's dynamic portraiture is highly dramatic: she holds tightly to one of the decorated horns in an attempt not to fall while she raises her other arm that carries a red cloth flying with the wind. There is a strong sense of movement in the scene. Viewers cannot see her face, since she is looking back at shore and her arm hides part of it. Nevertheless, we can discern her eyes, which look up almost in a state of ecstasy (Fitzroy 46). Europa is not completely naked, but the erotically charged scene shows the wet texture of her torn clothes attached to her body, exposing one of her breasts. The bull is about to become a beast and possess the beauty. However, the whole composition of the scene is dramatically and aesthetically beautiful, representing the anticipation of rape as a grand act of love. It seems as if this last piece of the *Poesie* series would bring viewers back circularly to the first one, *Danae*, where the princess rests peacefully on her bed, in a domestic environment, waiting to be taken by Jupiter in the shape of golden rain. The victim becomes, to use Mulvey's terminology, the "to-be-looked-at-ness":

---

16   Majesty is incompatible truly with love; they cohabit / Nowhere together. The father and chief of the gods, whose right hand is / Armed with the triple-forked lightning, who shakes the whole world with a nod, laid / Dignity down with his scepter, adopting the guise of a bull that / Mixed with the cattle and lowed as he ambled around the fresh fields, a / Beautiful animal, colored like snow that no footprint has trodden / And which no watery south wind has melted. His muscular neck bulged, / Dewlaps hung down from his chin; / his curved horns you might think had been hand carved, / Perfect, more purely translucent than pearl. His unthreatening brow and / Far from formidable eyes made his face appear tranquil. (Ovid, 846-875).

In a world ordered by sexual imbalance, pleasure in looking has been split between active/male and passive/female. The determining male gaze projects its phantasy onto the female figure, which is styled accordingly. In their traditional exhibitionist role women are simultaneously looked at and displayed, with their appearance coded for strong visual and erotic impact so that can be said to connote to-be-looked-at-ness. (589)

Titian, like a stage manager, creates a composition of rape that is aesthetically pleasing and titillates (male) viewers in the privacy of their dressing rooms.

While over time, some audiences have moved from high art to pop culture, and have exchanged the private rooms of Philip II for movie theaters, TV rooms, or phone screens, the issue of gender-based violence persists. The prevalence of how women continue to be depicted today as objects of desire, sources of titillation, and flesh to be consumed has consequences, and it is our duty to speak out and challenge these images. In Garelick's words, "we are accustomed to a pop culture universe—to film and TV plots, advertisements and fashion shoots—in which men "do" and women mostly "are"—are pretty, are looked at, are victimized, are desired, are dressed and undressed" (thecut.com). But our cultural norms also have private consequences. Like Philip II so many years before, our modern heads of industry continue to apply male power in private spaces. Harvey Weinstein, the king of Hollywood for many years, relished depicting male sexual fantasy in film. What is more troubling is the sexual violence so many women have testified that he perpetrated in his private spaces. Violence against women continues to be misrepresented in contemporary popular media, and too many powerful men continue to perpetuate a cycle of sexual violence in private. This is why it is important to bring these pressing issues into the classroom.

CONCLUSION

In her seminal book, *Persephone's Girdle: Narratives of Rape in Seventeenth Century Spain*, Welles states:

> That the motif of rape joins these three realms—myth, history and politics—is not fortuitous. It corresponds to the same mythic plot, wherein the woman's body becomes the object of exchange – between kings, with national and international consequences, or simply between men, with merely domestic repercussions. (7)

The repercussions of rape were—and are—all too real, traumatic and torturous. We do not know the number of sexual assaults that happened in early modern Spain because women were not encouraged to make a legal complaint against their rapists. Although the legal provisions known as the *Siete Partidas* and the *Fuero Real* included sets of laws to condemn sexual violence, women found it difficult to file legal complaints against their perpetrators. Rape, after all, was a private issue that was kept within the family. Ana Ramírez's trial proves to be a case of a silence breaker, a brave predecessor of the #MeToo movement. Gender violence keeps happening and has become a global epidemic that affects 35.6% of women in the world (WHO); therefore, movements that highlight and attempt to eliminate it are still necessary, even now. As a result of public demonstrations denouncing gender-based violence, many countries have changed, modified, or created new laws to protect victims of it. However, as the #MeToo movement has shown, many women have feared for decades that powerful men would damage their careers and, thus, have kept quiet in case of the repercussions. Political and artistic leaders continue a cycle of abuse. Powerful men like Harvey Weinstein and Donald Trump are current manifestations of the relationship between power and the acceptance of sexual violence that results when women are represented as beautiful objects to be consumed. In the words of actress Salma Hayek, speaking of Weinstein, "in his eyes, I was not an artist. I wasn't even a person. I was a thing: not a nobody, but a body" (nytimes.com). The cautionary tale of early modern times is that brave women have spoken up before, and the #MeToo movement has its precedents and does not stand alone in history. We can only hope that the movement will change the relationships between power, culture and the law.

Works Cited

Barahona, Renato. *Sex Crimes, Honour, and the Law in Early Modern Spain: Vizcaya, 1528-1735*. U of Toronto P, 2003.

Binotti, Lucia. "Visual Eroticism. Poetic Voyeurism." *Signs of Power in Habsburg Spain and the New World*, edited by Jason McCloskey and Ignacio López Alemany, Bucknell U P, 2013, pp.27-58.

Boyle, Margaret. *Unruly Women: Performance, Penitence, and Punishment in Early Modern Spain*. U of Toronto P, 2014.

Brownmiller, Susan. *Against our Will: Men, Women and Rape*. Simon and Schuster, 1975.

Carbonero y Sol, León. Índice de los libros prohibidos por el Santo Oficio de la Inquisición española. Madrid, Imprenta de D. Antonio Pérez Dubruij, 1873.

Carrión, María M. *Subject Stages. Marriage, Theatre, and the Law in Early Modern Spain*. U of Toronto P, 2010.

Cervantes Saavedra, Miguel de. *La fuerza de la sangre*. Alfar, 2010.

———. *Don Quijote de la Mancha*. Edited by Francisco Rico. Alfaguara, 2013.

Chan, Melissa. "'Now the Work Really Begins.' Alyssa Milano and Tarana Burke on What's Next for the #MeToo Movement." *Time*, 6 Dec. 2017, time.com/5051822/time-person-year-alyssa-milano-tarana-burke/. Accessed 5 June 2018.

Checa, Fernando. *Tiziano y la monarquía hispánica. Usos y funciones de la pintura veneciana en España (siglos XVI y XVII)*. Madrid, Nerea, 1994.

Covarrubias Orozco, Sebastián. *Tesoro de la lengua castellana*. fondosdigitales.us.es/fondos/libros/765/16/tesoro-de-la-lengua-castellana-o-espanola/. Accessed 3 March 2018.

Crowther, Paul. *How Pictures Complete Us. The Beautiful, the Sublime, and the Divine*. Stanford U P, 2016.

Cruz, Anne. "Titian, Philip II and Pagan Iconography." *Signs of Power in Habsburg Spain and the New World,* edited by Jason McCloskey and Ignacio López Alemany, Bucknell UP, 2013, pp.3-26.

Falomir, Miguel and Paul Joannides. "Dánae y Venus y Adonis: origen y evolución." *Dánae y Venus y Adonis, las primeras 'poesías' de Tiziano para Felipe II*, edited by Miguel Falomir, Madrid, Museo del Prado, 2014.

Fitzroy, Charles. *The Rape of Europa. The Intriguing History of Titian's Masterpiece*. Bloomsbury, 2015.

Gaetano Bottari, Giovanni. *Raccolta di lettere sulla pittura, scultura ed architettura*. Milano, Giovanni Silvestri, 1822, vol. I-VIII.

Garelick, Rhonda. "All Consuming Women. The Same Industries that Exploit us Turn around and Sell our Exploitation back to us." *The Cut*, thecut.com/2017/10/harvey-weinstein-hollywood-beauty-standards-and-abuse.html. Accessed 12 July, 2018.

Garrard, Mary. *Artemisia Gentileschi and Feminism in Early Modern Europe*. Renaissance Lives, 2020.

Greer, Margaret. *María de Zayas Tells Baroque Tales of Love and the Cruelty of Men*. Penn State UP , 2000.

Grosz, Elizabeth. *Volatile Bodies: Toward a Corporeal Feminism*. Indiana UP, 1994.

Hayek, Salma. "Harvey Weinstein is my Monster Too." *The New York Times*, 12 Dec. 2017, nytimes.com/interactive/2017/12/13/opinion/contributors/salma-hayek-harvey-weinstein.html. Accessed 5 June 2018.

Hazen, Helen. *Endless Rapture: Rape, Romance and the Female Imagination*. Scribner, 1983.

Iglesias Rodríguez, Juan José. "Tensiones y rupturas: Conflictividad, violencia y criminalidad en la Edad Moderna." *La violencia en la historia. Análisis del pasado y perspectiva sobre el mundo actual*, edited by Juan José Iglesias Rodríguez, Universidad de Huelva, 2012.

Jesús María, José de. *Primera parte de las excelencias de la virtud de la castidad*. Alcalá, Viuda de Juan Gracián, 1601.

Las siete partidas del Rey don Alfonso el Sabio. Madrid, Imprenta real, 1807.

Mantecón Movellán, Tomás. "Mujeres forzadas y abusos deshonestos en la Castilla moderna." *Manuscrits,* vol. 20, 2002, pp. 157-85.

Mulcahy, Rosemary. *Philip II of Spain, Patron of the Arts.* Four Courts Press, 2004.

Mulvey, Laura. "Visual Pleasure and Narrative Cinema." *Literary Theory: An Anthology.* Edited by Julie Rivkin and Michael Ryan, Blackwell, 1998, pp. 585-95.

Núñez de Coria, Francisco. *Tractado del vso delas mugeres, y como sea dañoso, y como provechoso, y que cosas se ayan de hazer para la tentacion dela carne, y del sueño y vaños.* biblioteca-antologica.org/es/wp-content/uploads/2017/10/NU%C3%91EZ-DE-CORIA-Tratado-del-uso-de-las-mugeres.pdf. Accessed 8 March 2018.

Ovid. *Metamorphoses.* ovid.lib.virginia.edu/trans/Metamorph2.htm. Accessed 12 March 2018.

Pérez-Villanueva, Sonia. "Misericordia y justicia. La representación del cuerpo de la mujer en la Inquisición" *Mulieres Inquisitionis. La mujer frente a la Inquisición en España,* edited by María Jesús Zamora Calvo. Madrid, Editorial academia del Hispanismo, 2017.

Perry, Mary Elizabeth and Anne J. Cruz. *Culture and Control in Counter-Reformation Spain.* U of Minnesota P, 1992.

Porges, Stephen. *The Polyvagal Theory: Neurophysiological Foundations of Emotions, Attachment, Communication, Self-Regulation.* Norton, 2011.

Portús Pérez, Javier. *La Sala reservada y el desnudo en el Museo del Prado: [Exposición]: Museo Nacional del Prado, 28 de junio al 29 de septiembre de 2002.* Turner, Madrid, 2002.

Poska, Allyson. *Women and Authority in Early Modern Spain: The Peasants of Galicia,* Oxford UP, 2005.

Rodríguez Ortiz. Victoria, *Mujeres forzadas. El delito de violación en el Derecho castellano (siglos XVI-XVIII).* Universidad de Almería, 2003.

Titian. *Danaë.* 1553, oil on canvas, The Wellington Collection.

———. *Venus and Adonis,* 1554, oil on canvas, Museo del Prado.

———. *Perseus and Andromeda,* 1556, oil on canvas, The Wellington Collection.

———. *Diana and Acteon,* 1556-1559, oil on canvas, The National Gallery.

———. *Diana and Calisto,* 1556-1559, oil on canvas, The National Gallery.

———. *The Rape of Europa,* 1562, oil on canvas, Isabella Stewart Gardner Museum.

Tolentino, Jia. "Harvey Weinstein and the Impunity of Powerful Men." *New Yorker,* 30 Oct. 2017, newyorker.com/magazine/2017/10/30/harvey-weinstein-and-the-impunity-of-powerful-men. Accessed 7 June 2018.

Val Cubero, Alejandra. *La percepción social del desnudo femenino en el arte (siglos XVI y XIX). Pintura, mujer y sociedad.* Madrid, Minerva, 2003.

Vollendorf, Lisa. *Reclaiming the Body: María de Zayas's Early Modern Feminism.* U of North Carolina P, 2001.

Welles, Marcia. *Persephone's Girdle: Narratives of Rape in Seventeenth-Century Spain.* Vanderbilt UP, 2000.

Wolfthal, Diane. *Images of Rape: The "Heroic" Tradition and its Alternatives.* Cambridge UP, 1999.

Zayas, María de. *Parte segunda del sarao y entretenimiento honesto: (desengaños amorosos).* Edited by Alicia Yllera Fernández, Cátedra, 20

PART II
Practical Theory

Representing Black Speech in Spanish Golden Age Poetry and U.S. Hip-Hop Culture: The Case of Góngora

MINDY E. BADÍA
Indiana University Southeast

AS A SCHOLAR AND teacher of early modern Spanish literature, I am always in search of new ways to connect the textual production from the early modern period to issues that resonate with my students. In this respect, I echo comments expressed by Edward Friedman, who describes a common conflict that teachers of Renaissance and Baroque poetry face between making the material "interesting and even relevant" and, at the same time, "respecting the historical contexts and parameters . . . of the texts themselves" (59). Friedman sketches out a balanced approach that would link what he terms "the old and the new," combining tried and true methods of close reading with recent theoretical approximations to the literary text. Inspired by Friedman and informed by Gerald Graff's writing about the productive potential of "teaching the conflicts," this essay sketches out a metacritical encounter between the Spanish Golden Age lyrical tradition and the lyrics of popular music.

Graff's methodology asserts that, in response to what many have referred to as the "culture wars," professors should not take sides but, rather, should bring students into the fray by helping them understand dissenting points of view and by teaching them to engage critically with such perspectives (132). "Teaching the conflicts" eschews definitive readings, be they traditional or progressive, in favor of alerting students to the ways that accepted knowledge is created through contention and debate. Graff's notion of conflict, which he likens to "connection," allows me to explore the possibility that early modern Spanish culture and contemporary U.S. culture (my version of Friedman's "old" and "new") may not necessarily be as removed from one another as their chronological and cultural contexts would suggest, and to propose that the conflicting critical interpretations of the phenomenon of white artists imitating Black[1] speech exists as a provocative connection between these two historical periods.

Specifically, I suggest an approach to teaching Spanish Golden Age poetry that situates early modern Spanish representations of *habla de negros*[2]— Black or Africanized Spanish—within current conversations about the performance of blackness in contemporary music in the United States. Using Luís de Góngora's "En la fiesta del santísimo sacramento" as my Golden Age example, and integrating scholarship focused on the cultural implications of a white artist's mimicry of Black speech in both Golden Age Spain and the contemporary U.S., I connect what is almost certainly an unfamiliar seventeenth-century text (at least for the undergraduates at my institution) to theoretical discussions of race, identity, and language as they relate to hip-hop, a musical genre that has received considerable critical attention for its linguistic features in both popular media and among scholars.[3] By establishing these critical connections between Golden Age poetry and hip-hop, I situate my students' engagement with Góngora's poem within the more familiar context of current popular music. This contextualization facilitates students' comprehension of the Golden Age text, affirms Góngora's relevance to present realities, and positions students to adopt a critical stance in their consumption of popular culture.[4]

---

1   I have chosen to capitalize the word "Black" when I refer to people as an acknowledgement of the shared sense of identity and culture that the word denotes. In citations, I use the capitalization of the original quote.

2   Scholars have used a variety of terms to refer to literary representations of the Spanish spoken by Blacks in early modern Iberia; *bozal* and *sayagués* are two examples. I use the phrase *habla de negros* throughout this essay because it makes explicit the role of language in literary representations of Blacks.

3   My approach could also be expanded to include poetry by authors such as Nicolás Guillén and Candelario Obeso, writers whose poetic depictions of Black speech function explicitly to address socio-political realities. For a discussion of Guillén as an heir to Spanish Baroque poets in general and to Góngora in particular, see Roberto González-Echevarría, especially pages 304-05.

4   As I revise this essay in July 2020, I am struck by the poignancy of the subject matter. Conflicting accounts of the killing of George Floyd and Breonna Taylor (the latter of which occurred in my hometown), as well as differing media portrayals of the ensuing protests, illustrate the all-too-real consequences of representation within social systems that perpetuate racial inequality.

To establish a context for the ways that Black English has emerged as a distinct feature of U.S. popular culture I offer two definitions, one of African-American English (AAE)[5] and one of hip-hop, as well as three concrete examples that illustrate how instances, appropriations, and misappropriations of African-American speech have shaped, over time, the cultural landscape in the United States. I begin with the definitions. First, Walter Edwards defines African-American Vernacular English as "the variety (dialect, ethnolect and sociolect) of English natively spoken by most working- and middle-class African Americans and some Black Canadians, particularly in urban communities" (383). Within the context of Edwards's broad definition, it is helpful to remember Lisa Green's contention that "African Americans from different regions, age groups, education status and socioeconomic classes will know many of the words . . . but may not identify themselves or be identified as AAE speakers" (13). Green's point prompts a clarification of the examples that I use to make my own arguments, which I limit to the forms of AAE characteristic of hip-hop culture. Second, Tricia Rose offers the following definition of hip-hop as a cultural phenomenon: "hip hop culture emerged as a source of alternative identity formation and social status for youth that started in the South Bronx in the early 1970s. Its central forms are graffiti, breakdancing and rap music" (74). Rose also stresses the importance of hip-hop in the formation of community and, most significant for this essay, lists language as a key feature of this community building by which "[a]lternative local identities were formed in fashions and language, street names and most importantly, in . . . neighborhood crews or posses . . . local source[s] of identity, group affiliation and support system[s]" (78). As we shall see, Rose's emphasis on hip-hop and the formation of community occupies a central space in critical discussions of linguistic appropriation because it raises the question: To what extent does exhibiting certain features of a group, in this case its language, entitle a person to self-identify legitimately as one of its members?" [6]

Turning to the historical examples, I find that my students benefit from a discussion of how representations of Black speech in hip-hop form part of a much longer tradition within the United States and that this sort of

---

5   AAE is also referred to as African-American Vernacular English (AAVE).

6   Rachel Dolezal and Jessica A. Krug's cases illustrate how polemical this question of identity can become. Additionally, my daughter Gabriela has informed me of an even more recent trend: "blackfishing." Blackfishing is the phenomenon of white social media influencers who, through make-up, hairstyles and fashion associated with Black culture, present themselves as Black.

contextualization helps them view Góngora's poem as less removed from the environment–both its present and its past– in which they live and study.[7] The appearance of AAE in U.S. popular culture goes at least as far back as the minstrel shows of the 19th century.[8] Most scholars agree that minstrelsy, with respect to the role of language and speech in the forging of identities and affinities, far from creating community between African Americans and whites, constituted an instance of mimicry that denigrated Blacks. Minstrel shows featured white performers acting out comic skits, dancing, and playing musical instruments. These performers donned blackface and mocked African Americans for comic effect; in minstrel shows, Blacks were depicted as lazy, slow-witted and superstitious (among other things). While minstrelsy's popularity had faded by the early 20th century, some critics link this early portrayal of Blacks to contemporary racist structures within the U.S. (Eberhart and Freeman 304-05).

My second historical example is taken from the 1980 film *Airplane!*. It is important because it suggests a continuum of performing Black speech insofar as it bridges the chronological gap between early parodies of AAE in minstrel shows and more recent instances in popular entertainment. In the scene, two African-American passengers on an aircraft (first Jive Dude and Second Jive Dude in the excerpt below) attempt to communicate with a flight attendant (Randy). When the flight attendant cannot understand the two men due to their use of "Jive," the name given to the parodic representation of AAE, a third passenger, Jive Lady, acts as a translator.

> RANDY: Can I get you something?
> SECOND JIVE DUDE: 'S'mofo butter layin' me to da' BONE! Jackin' me up . . . tight me!
> RANDY: I'm sorry, I don't understand.
> FIRST JIVE DUDE: Cutty say 'e can't HANG!
> JIVE LADY: Oh, stewardess! I speak jive.
> RANDY: Oh, good.

---

7   Although my primary goal is to make early modern Spanish culture accessible to my students, I am not opposed to teaching them some U. S. history along the way.

8   Robert Hornback argues that early modern European representations of Black speech lay the foundation for minstrelsy in later centuries and states that literary texts that mock Black speech for comic effect first appeared in the Iberian Peninsula in the fifteenth century (143).

JIVE LADY: He said that he's in great pain and he wants to know if you can help him.

RANDY: All right. Would you tell him to just relax and I'll be back as soon as I can with some medicine?

JIVE LADY: [to the Second Jive Dude] Jus' hang loose, blood. She gonna catch ya up on da rebound on da med side.

SECOND JIVE DUDE: What it is, big mama? My mama ain't raise no dummies. I dug her rap!

JIVE LADY: Cut me some slack, Jack! Chump don' want no help, chump don't GET da help!

FIRST JIVE DUDE: Say 'e can't hang, say seven up!

JIVE LADY: Jive-ass dude don't got no brains anyhow! Shiiiiit!

(qtd. in Crow)[9]

Viewers familiar with the cultural reference in the film will recognize the "translator" as Barbara Billingsly, the actress who portrayed June Cleaver in the television series *Leave it to Beaver*. As June Cleaver, Ms. Billingsly became a model of mid-century middle-class white womanhood—the epitome of a 1950s *americana* (and thus, a key element of the racist stereotype portraying Black men as sexually aggressive)—as well as an iconic image of the cultural history of United States, a slice of americana. Ms. Billingsly's role in *Airplane!* illustrates how popular culture can exist as both an instrument and object of inquiry, engaging with important social shifts, many of which related to language and race, that occurred in the U.S. during the second half of the twentieth century. The inter-textual reference to the mid-century television program establishes a chronological connection with the Civil Rights movement of the 1950s and 1960s, while its inclusion in a film from 1980 coincides with the formal academic recognition of African-American English, a phenomenon that emerged as a source of much scholarly debate in the late 1970s.[10] Looking forward, the movie's release year also anticipates the emergence of hip-hop culture, and in particular its linguistic register, as

---

9   In Jonathan Crow's "The Making of the Famous Jive Talk Scenes from *Airplane!*," Norman Alexander Gibbs and Al White, the actors cast as First Jive Dude and Second Jive Dude, describe how they improvised the dialogue. During auditions, the scriptwriters were so impressed with the actors' improvisation that they removed the dialogue they had previously written and allowed Gibbs and White to improvise in the actual film.

10   William Stewart's experiments with dialect readers—written in African-American English and Standard English—for Black schoolchildren in the late 1960s

both an expression of African-American identity and an instance of its appropriation.

For efficiency's sake—the list of hip-hop performers I could cite is a long one—and because I am not sure how familiar this particular reading audience is with contemporary popular music, I have chosen to share an example of hip-hop culture that functions as both a primary and secondary source; that is, this scene from the television series *Atlanta* constitutes both an illustrative summary and implicit commentary on the phenomenon of white hip-hop artists appropriating traits of African-American culture and, in particular, language. *Atlanta*'s protagonist Earn (who is African American), has been expelled from Princeton and is looking for a job. He attempts to work as a promoter for his cousin Alfred, a rapper who goes by the stage name Paper Boi. In the exchange below, Earn tries to convince Dave (a white man), who works at a radio station, to ensure that Alfred's new song receives airplay. Although Dave presents himself as Earn's friend, he refuses to do Earn this favor and, instead, attempts to take advantage of Earn's desperate situation by suggesting that Earn pay him to have the song played. I argue that the scene broaches, among other things, three critical issues that relate to the use of *habla de negros* in Góngora's text: the idea of language and culture as constructs, the commodification of culture, and, in relation to this second point, the question of cultural ownership.

EARN: Yeah, whatever. Have you ever heard the song "Paper Boy"?
DAVE: "Paper Boy" by Paper Boy? Hell yeah I've heard that. Shit is fire. Streets is loving it.
EARN (relieved): You guys should play it on the radio then.
DAVE: Yeah, for real.
(Both nod in agreement for a moment while looking at each other.)
EARN: Nah, but seriously y'all need to play "Paper Boy."
DAVE: My n[. . .],[11] if it were up to me? Yeah. But you know KP picks all the music.
EARN: Well tell him to play it. It's important.
DAVE: Well I mean KP will usually spin some records for some scratch up top.
EARN How much?

---

and 1970s are but one example of the recognition of AAE as a distinct dialect in the second half of the twentieth century.

11   One of Dave's most marked linguistic characteristics is his use of the n-word, which suggests, among other things, an obliviousness to his own privilege.

DAVE: Half stack.

EARN: Five hundred dollars? Am I buying the station?

DAVE: Everybody's gotta eat, right? That's just how it goes.

EARN: I don't have five hundred dollars to give. I got fired today and I
still gotta pay rent. My parents locked me out of their house. Like
those meth commercials, only not funny.

DAVE: Sorry, my n[. . .]. You know how it is out here. He usually charge
a full C.

EARN: Fuck! I need this man.

DAVE: It's probably for the best, man. Music is gross. Alright, if you're
around come by the booth. I'm taking over for the Dirty Boyz tonight at six. Keep it locked!

(Dave walks back towards the entrance to the radio station. A group of
black employees head toward the door at the same time. DAVE engages them in small talk. EARN can slightly hear DAVE talk to the
employees. DAVE's voice is much more professional and a different
pitch. Almost a surfer tone.)

DAVE (CONT'D) (To employees): What's up, my dudes. Whaddup
bro!

(Glover 23-25)

In the *Washington Post* article "How Iggy Azalea Mastered Her 'Blaccent,'" Jeff Guo discusses the specific linguistic tropes that white hip-hop
artist Azalea uses in performance, many of which appear in Dave's dialogue
from *Atlanta* and in the speech of the Jive dudes in *Airplane!*.[12] Some of
the features that Guo notes are: ng=n (*goin'*); devocalization (*ma'*=man,
mistah=mister); copula absence (the omission of "is" or "are," for example:
"*she not here*"); the habitual "be"; the use of "*ain't*" to describe past events
that never happened (for example: "*he ain't even graduate*"); t=f (*mouf* vs.
mouth); and language that is generally non-rhotic (dropping the "r"). In the
selections from the film and the series, such language markers, as well as the
use of particular slang expressions (among them, the n-word in the case of
Dave's dialogue) are portrayed as features of a linguistic performance that
both unites and divides. With respect to the film, audiences are left to grapple with the matter of the scene's racism, while Dave's obvious cooptation
of Black speech in the television series makes clear Glover's implied contention that both language and culture are products that can be bought and

12   Some of these language markers are easier to appreciate when hearing the
dialogue.

sold. Dave's imitative use of AAE functions to manipulate Earn (who incidentally sees right through Dave's linguistic blackface) and runs counter to the so-called friendship between the two characters, as well as to the sense of community suggested by their linguistic and cultural affinities, affinities which, in this case, are only simulated. While Dave's use of AAE reinforces his white privilege, Earn's forays into so-called white culture (Princeton, his use of standard English) afford him little social or economic advantage. At the same time, Earn's "authentic" connection to African-American culture, exemplified by his cousin Alfred's budding fame as a hip-hop artist, constitutes a cultural currency that is controlled by whites, in this case, by Dave.

Assuredly, important differences exist among these three examples—the crude mimicry of minstrel shows, the uncomfortable parody of *Airplane!*, and the linguistic imitation of hip-hop artists as critiqued by the series *Atlanta*. Nevertheless, they do provide a collective context for our understanding the performance of Black speech as a relatively common cultural practice in the United States, and one that interacts with institutionalized racism in ways both affirming and subversive. As I suggest to my students, Góngora's representation of Black speech in this *letrilla* operates similarly within its own historical situation.

Composed for the Corpus Christi festivities in Córdoba in 1609, "En la fiesta del santísimo sacramento" uses a white poet's *idea* of the Spanish spoken by Blacks to create and profit, both monetarily and artistically, from a fabricated image of Black women. Like white hip-hop performers' imitation of Black speech, Góngora's use of *habla de negros* is performative, and the dialogic structure of the poem, as well as its oral recitation as part of the Corpus Christi celebrations, point to a fundamentally dramatic essence that seeps into everyday life in a fashion similar to the workings of the performative aspects of hip-hop culture. Additionally, given that the poet was commissioned to write for the Corpus Christi festivities (and thus, paid), and in light of the financial difficulties that Góngora faced due to mounting gambling debts, the poet's mimicry of Black speech for financial benefit operates in ways not unlike Dave's manipulative use of AAE in the scene from *Atlanta*.[13]

Below, I share a fragment from Góngora's text, followed by an overview of some of the salient features of Golden Age literary depictions of Black Spanish:

---

13   In his introduction to a bilingual edition of Góngora's poems, John Dent-Young writes that the poet was "notoriously fond of gambling" (XI).

Hablan dos negritas Juana y Clara

Juana: Mañana sá Corpus Christa
mana Crara;
alcoholemo la cara
e lavemonó la vista.

Clara: ¡Ay, Jesú, como sa mu trista!

Juana: ¡Qué tiene, pringa señora!

Clara: Samo negra pecandora,
e branca la Sacramenta.

Juana: La alma sá como la denta,
Crara mana.
Pongamo fustana,
e bailemo alegra;
que aunque samo negra,
sá hermosa tú.
Zambambú, morenica de Congo,
zambambú.
Zambambú, que galana me pongo,
zambambú.

Juana: Vamo a la sagraria, prima,
veremo la procesiona,
que aunque negra, sá presona
que la perrera me estima.
A esse mármolo te arrima. (1-23)

John Lipski's work provides us with an idea of how Africanized Spanish actually developed as well as how white poets represented *habla de negros* in literature.[14] Some of the features of Black speech that we see in early modern Spanish poetry, exemplified by the way Clara and Juana "speak," include lapses in noun/adjective and subject/verb agreement; paragogic additions (*rioso, dioso*); the substitution of letters (r=d, l=r); nasalization (with introduction of written "N" to show this: "*nengro*"); and nonstandard use of the copula (98-99).

Teaching Góngora's Corpus Christi poem to today's undergraduates poses at least two main challenges, one linguistic and practical, and the

14   I cite Lipski because his work focuses on descriptions of the linguistic and phonetic characteristics of *habla de negros*.

other cultural and theoretical.[15] Many students learning Spanish as a second language would find this non-standard rendering particularly difficult, and for this relatively solvable problem, a resource such as Johs Beusterien's "Talking Black: An Unfinished Black Spanish Glossary" serves as a useful guide. In order to ensure basic comprehension (and depending on the needs of the class), students can also work in groups to write sections of the poem in standard Spanish. Once linguistic hurdles are cleared, however, there remains the problem of how to contextualize effectively the poet's portrayal of Black speech. From a pedagogical perspective, one of the risks of a text like "Santísimo" is that it may not challenge student assumptions about otherness. Indeed, because the denigration of Black speech, and by extension, of Black people, seems apparent, what remains for us to wrestle with is the matter of how to respond. Readers might well react with understandable outrage, envisioning the Golden Age socio-historical context in monolithic opposition to their own, but this leaves little room for the sort of transformative experience that we seek for our students. By considering appropriations of Black speech in their own era and culture in which they live, as well as the scholarly and cultural conflicts that emerge from these more familiar instances of imitation, students move discussions of a troubling text beyond a simplistic binary of us (so-called post-racial, enlightened) vs. them (white, racist).

In the spirit of "teaching the conflicts," I offer examples of two divergent scholarly reactions to early modern poetic depictions of Black Spanish. Nelson González-Ortega writes, "In the Spanish Golden Age . . . the Black is represented as a comic figure who 'deforms' the Spanish language . . . writers such as Góngora . . . use blacks as poetic objects of caricature" (63). Here, González-Ortega argues that any instance *habla de negros* is inauthentic and essentially casts Blacks as the butt of a racist joke. Nicholas R. Jones, on the other hand, and in reference to this particular text by Góngora, asserts that the performance of Black Spanish constitutes a subtle subversion of white authority. Jones argues that Clara and Juana affirm their beauty through an explicit reference to the Song of Songs, positing it as more natural than that of white women who attempt to lighten their skin cosmetically: "Góngora defends black beauty by indirectly contrasting its naturalness with the facial cosmetics typically linked to white women" (34). Further, he contends that "Góngora develops his image of black women, in relation to cosmetic adornment and fine clothing, through elevating *habla de negros* speech as part of the *culterano* repertoire or *culto* style" (6). This aspect of Jones's argument

---

15   Of course, Góngora's poem is but one example of early modern Spanish *habla de negros*. Sor Juana's *villancicos* offer additional examples, as do various *comedias*.

rest, in part, on the relationships between poetic incorporations of African-ized Spanish and *culteranismo*, particularly with regard to the ways that both traditions result in a deliberate linguistic difficulty.[16]

Critics of contemporary U.S. popular culture evince a similar lack of consensus about the implications of depictions of Black English in hip-hop. My first example represents the point of view of those critics who see non-Blacks' use of AAE as a potential means of productive cultural exchange and of forging social and political affinities. As Sonia Fix asserts:

> [L]anguage and style continue to be available as resources for acts of identity, acts of belonging, and potent signifiers of one's personal ide-ologies about the boundaries of racial identification far past adolescence. AAE phonological features function as an available symbolic resource with which white participants may reflect ethnic allegiance and cultural alignment with the African-American community. (72)

The second illustration represents the perspective of academics who argue that whites' use of Black speech affirms racist stereotypes and under-mines racial equality. Maeve Eberhart and Kara Freeman contend that "even seemingly authentic language use involving appropriation of racially-linked forms is at its core not different from the linguistic minstrelsy and mock lan-guage that reflect whites' ongoing participation in and upholding of the sta-tus quo racist structure" (304-05).

Rather than resolving these critical conflicts for students, and in keeping with Graff's model, I encourage reflection by considering them in light of the following questions.

---

16   Jones' fascinating *Staging Habla de Negros* was published just as I was completing final edits to this essay. His revision of previous critical assessments of *habla de negros* that contend its unequivocal (and univocal) denigration of Blacks illustrates precisely the critical conflicts that I discuss here. Jones' book situates early modern Blacks in Iberia within African diasporic communities (93-105) and argues for their agentic position in early modern Spanish performances of *habla de negros* (113). This is in contrast to the only other book length study of representations of Blacks in early modern Spanish literature, Baltasar Fra Molinero's *La imagen de los negros en el teatro del Siglo de Oro*, in which the author observes that theatrical depic-tions of *habla de negros* served to portray Blacks as objects of laughter (21), leaving the possibility of Black agency in these texts unexamined.

- What role does the concept of authenticity play in discussions of contemporary cultural products that create/appropriate/incorporate/commodify Black speech?

- How does this concept (authenticity) relate to scholarly discussions about the use of *habla de negros* in early modern Spanish poetry as well as to notions of cultural, social and artistic legitimacy in early modern Spain?

- If we accept that a hip-hop persona is a performance, like the Blacks who speak in early modern Spanish poetry, how are such performances used selectively by both Black and white artists? What are the socio-political consequences of their performances?

At this point, I need to address a few caveats to my approach. First, I am not arguing that the lyrical production of Góngora is comparable to that of Vanilla Ice, at least not in this particular essay.[17]

The method that I propose is meta-critical, in that I look for links between the Golden Age and the contemporary age as they emerge in scholarship about white mimicries of Black speech. Second, and in this meta-critical vein, it is also important to acknowledge that, as far as I know, the racist implications of Black Spanish were not being discussed in the Golden Age (although it bears remembering that we have only begun to address the ways that performance traditions such as minstrel shows, a film as recent as *Airplane!*, and musical genres like hip-hop interact with societal racism in the U.S.). A third critical difference between the two instances of white appropriation of Black speech that structure my approach is that scholars of early modern Spanish poetry do not assert that a text like Góngora's expresses an affinity with Black people or with African culture in any sort of intentional way. This stands in contrast to arguments made by some contemporary hip-hop performers and cultural commentators who see non-Blacks' use of AAE as appreciation rather than appropriation. Finally, we must keep in mind the diversity of our classrooms and of our students' experiences and perspectives and handle difficult texts with due sensitivity. The unexpected proximity of a Spanish Golden Age poem, which many would assume to be linguistically, temporally, and culturally remote, can stimulate a particularly sharp sense

---

17   I realize that these images appear a bit unconventional in a scholarly essay. I include them because I have used them with great success to elicit discussion among students and because I like to think that my colleagues appreciate a good chuckle as much as I do.

self-awareness. For some students, this acute sense of recognition can reduce distance, increase accessibility and enhance their engagement with the text; for others, this sharpness cuts a bit too deeply. Nevertheless, and in spite of these differences and challenges, both groups of scholars do share an interest in how performances of Black speech engage racial hierarchies in their respective historical contexts and, in so doing, they provide a provocative point of convergence for my students' discussion of "Santísimo" and, by extension, of their own cultural milieux some 400 years later.

This connection between Góngora's early modern text and my students' present-day realities prompts a reflection on the notion of "realness" itself, one of hip-hop's core values and an issue that Jones's reading of "Santísimo" also addresses in its discussion of Black women's beauty.[18] I would submit that a notion akin to "realness" was, in fact, a defining socio-cultural concept in early modern Spain, and one with which we, as scholars and teachers of Golden Age culture, are all familiar. Perceived threats to the idea of what was essentially or authentically Spanish abounded, and literary depictions of Blacks, as well as those of religious minorities, existed to delineate and affirm, by means of contrast, what it meant to be a real Spaniard. Take, for example, this final illustration, a *décima* written by Quevedo that equates Góngora's verbal *suciedad* with having an impure (Jewish) bloodline:

> En lo sucio que has cantado
> y en lo largo de narices,
> demás de que tú lo dices,
> que no eres limpio has mostrado. (1-4)

This poetic snap, which I see as a Quevedesque take on the African-American pastime of playing The Dozens *avant la lettre*, illustrates how language usage, as well as the ways one's use of language was imagined and performed by others, formed part of what we might call an early modern Spanish pretension to "keep it real."[19]

---

18   Jonathan D. Williams observes "[h]ip-hop's fascination with authenticity is unique to the genre and is the function of its roots as the cultural expression of socially and economically marginalized African-Americans" (2).

19   According to Wikipedia, "'The Dozens' is a game of spoken words between two contestants, common in Black communities of the United States, where participants exchange insults until one gives up. It is customary for the Dozens to be played in front of an audience of bystanders, who encourage the participants to reply with

Works Cited

Beusterien, John. "Talking Black': An Unfinished Black Spanish Glossary." *Bulletin of the Comediantes*, vol. 51, nos. 1 and 2, 1999, pp. 83-104.

Bucholtz, Mary and López, Quiana. "Performing Blackness, Forming Whiteness: Linguistic Minstrelsy in Hollywood film." *Journal of Sociolinguistics*, vol. 15, no. 5, 2011, pp. 680-706.

Crow, Jonathan. "The Making of the Famous Jive Talk Scenes From *Airplane!*." *Open Culture*, 24 Dec. 2014, www.openculture.com/2014/12/the-making-of-the-famous-jive-talk-scenes-from-airplane. Accessed 5 Jul. 2018.

Dent-Young, John, ed. *Selected Poems of Luis de Góngora*, U of Chicago P, 2007.

Eberhardt, Maeve and Freeman, Kara. "'First Things First, I'm the Realest': Linguistic Appropriation, White Privilege, and the Hip-Hop Persona of Iggy Azalea." *Journal of Sociolinguistics*, vol. 19, no. 3, 2015, pp. 303-327.

Edwards, Walter "African American Vernacular English: Phonology." *A Handbook of Varieties of English: A Multimedia Reference Tool*, edited by Edgar Werner Schneider and Bernd Kortmann, Walter de Gruyter & Company, 2004, 366-82.

Fix, Sonya. "AAE as a Bounded Ethnolinguistic Resource for White Women with African-American Ties." *Language and Communication*, vol. 35, 2014, pp. 55-74.

Fra Molinero, Baltasar. *La imagen de los negros en el teatro del Siglo de Oro*, Siglo Veintiuno, 1995.

Friedman, Edward. "Teaching Golden Age Poetry: The Old and The New." *Calíope*, vol. 11, no. 2, 2005, pp. 59-68.

Glover, Donald. "Pilot." *Atlanta*, Sept. 2016, la-screenwriter.com/wp-content/uploads/2016/10/Atlanta_1x01_-_Pilot.pdf. Accessed 5 Jul. 2018.

Góngora, Luís de. *Letrillas*, edited by Robert Jammes, Castalia, 1980.

González-Echevarría, Roberto. "Guillén as Baroque: Meaning in *Motivos De Son*." *Callaloo*, no. 31, 1987, pp. 302–317. *JSTOR*, www.jstor.org/stable/2930748.

González-Ortega, Nelson. "Representing the Black Other." *In and Out of Africa: Exploring Afro-Hispanic, Luso-Brazilian and Latin-American Connections*, edited by Joanna Boampong, Cambridge Scholars Publishing, 2005, 58-85.

Graff, Gerald. "Organizing the Conflicts in the Classroom. *The Journal of the Midwest Modern Language Association*, vol. 25, no. 1, 1992, pp. 63-76.

Green, Lisa J. *African-American English: A Linguistic Introduction*, Cambridge UP, 2002.

Guo, Jeff. "How Iggy Azalea Mastered Her 'Blaccent.'" *The Washington Post*, 4 Jan. 2016, www.washingtonpost.com/news/wonk/wp/2016/01/04/how-a-white-australian-rapper-mastered-her-blaccent. Accessed 5 Jul. 2018.

Hornback, Robert. *Racism and Early Blackface Comic Traditions*, Palgrave, 2018.

more egregious insults to heighten the tension and, consequently, to be more interesting to watch."

Jones, Nicholas R. "Cosmetic Ontologies, Cosmetic Subversions: Articulating Black Beauty and Humanity in Luis de Góngora's 'En la fiesta del Santísimo Sacramento.'" *Journal for Early Modern Cultural Studies*, vol. 15, no. 1, pp. 26-54.

————— *Staging Habla de Negros: Radical Performances of the African Diaspora in Early Modern Spain*, Penn State UP, 2019.

Lipski, J.M. "The African Connection." *Latin American Spanish*, Longman, 1994, pp. 93-135.

Quevedo y Villegas, Francisco de. *Obras completas*, edited by Felicidad Buendía, Aguilar, 1966.

Rose, Tricia. *Black Noise: Rap Music and Black Culture in Contemporary America*, Wesleyan UP, 1994.

Wikipedia contributors. "The Dozens." *Wikipedia, The Free Encyclopedia*. Wikipedia, The Free Encyclopedia, 27 Jun. 2018. Web. 6 Jul. 2018.

Williams, Jonathan D. Williams, Jonathan D., "'Tha Realness:' In Search of Hip-Hop Authenticity." *College Undergraduate Research Electronic Journal*, U. of Pennsylvania, 14 Dec. 2007, repository.upenn.edu/curej/78. Accessed 6 Jul. 2018.

"Tan largo me lo fiáis" in the Era of "#TimesUp": *El burlador de Sevilla* as Foil to Feminism in the Age of Trumpism

Rob Bayliss
University of Kansas

THE TITLE OF THIS chapter cites two utterances taken from distinct discursive contexts, one from the early modern Spanish verse encoding the narrative of *El burlador de Sevilla* and the other from the contemporary American English codes of Twitter. If the first represents what we teach, discursive context and conventions included, the second better reflects the discursive milieu of our students. At first glance, the contrast in messaging could not be more striking: Don Juan Tenorio's continual utterance of "tan largo me lo fiáis" and its variants throughout *El burlador* capture the misogynist's delight in the deferral of justice as he wreaks havoc on early modern society, while #TimesUp constitutes a rallying call for twenty-first century women and an explicit admonition to their overwhelmingly male abusers. The #MeToo and #TimesUp movement appeared in an era in which, after the anticipated shattering of the U.S. political system's ultimate glass ceiling by Hillary Clinton was denied by the Electoral College victory of Donald Trump, the victims of sexual abuse and harassment insisted on the end of such deferrals. In fact, one could argue that the cultural relevance of *El burlador* would differ significantly had "Crooked Hillary" actually secured the presidency as expected—not because the movement's call for justice would have been automatically answered, nor because it necessarily would have been further deferred by the symbolic victory of her election, but because of the fact that Trump's election constituted a kind of *desengaño* for the majority of the popular vote. The anticipation of progress in the struggle for gender equality was replaced by the realization of how illusory many aspects of that progress really were, and by the revelation that the very perception of gender inequality was one of the many fault lines separating the two sides of an ideologically polarized nation. It is in this political context that college students come to our classrooms, often still developing their own political awareness, preferences and identities, and attempt to decode Spanish Golden Age literature.

The argument I propose here is not that we leverage current circumstances to make this literature more engaging to our students, but rather that *El burlador* and similar Golden Age narratives can facilitate the development of how they understand their own cultural moment. My argument will directly engage this specific play because of its particular thematic saliency, but it is my hope that the broader message regarding our role in contributing to our students' education is recognized as equally applicable to the many other canonical Golden Age texts in which the *código de honor* and related patriarchal structures impact the representation of women. "Tan largo me lo fiáis" placed in dialogue with #TimesUp provides an opportunity to understand the past and the present, to understand the history of feminism and the patriarchy that shapes, defines and necessitates it. In short, this dialogue affords an intercultural long-view of the struggles that will define the generation with which our students identify, and their shared practices of critical engagement with popular culture can inform and amplify their historical awareness in powerful ways.

To operationalize *El burlador* and related Golden Age narratives in this way, students must first learn about the context in which those narratives were generated; they must be equipped with the tools necessary for critically examining their own cultural context; and perhaps most importantly, they must be encouraged to synthesize these very different worlds while avoiding two common pitfalls of such comparative analysis. On the one hand, students often seek consolation by dismissing early modern Spanish narratives as simply too distant (historically, linguistically and culturally) to have any connection to their own experiences. On the other hand, from my experience students are often tempted to seek facile equivalencies, or to jump to pseudo-comparative conclusions, such as "Harvey Weinstein is just like Don Juan Tenorio" or "The *Comedia* is the early modern Spanish equivalent to the series I binge-watch on Netflix." Both tendencies are understandable, and the case can be made that many such assertions of difference and similitude are not entirely invalid. But more importantly, they can be channeled productively as steps in a process whose ultimate end is to learn more about the broader historical narrative in which both our students and Don Juan

Tenorio play a part. In this sense, they are not so much "pitfalls" as they are "teachable moments," or opportunities that educators can learn to identify and exploit to the benefit of their students' learning of a far more complicated but consequential mode of comparative analysis.

THE FIELD OF POPULAR CULTURAL PRODUCTION IN THE AGE OF SOCIAL MEDIA

To more clearly articulate what I mean by such learning, it will first be necessary to unpack some of the critical terminology that informs our discipline. To begin, we should note that "popular culture" is itself a notoriously amorphous and frustrating term, and one that does not really mean what it did even at the turn of the present century. Its resistance to a concrete and stable definition has frustrated scholars since at least 1980, when Tony Bennet labeled it "virtually useless, a melting pot of confused and contradictory meanings" (18). While considerable effort has been made in the last four decades to articulate more useful ways to theorize the term, the fact that popular culture is inherently dynamic and subject to continual change suggests that, in our efforts to study it, we do well to embrace its fluidity and to resist the urge to pin down the concept to a fixed and static characterization. A strong case in point is how within the last decade, social media have restructured the ways in which individuals inhabit what might be called, with a nod to the vocabulary of Pierre Bordieu, the field of popular-cultural production.

The Marxism-inflected discourse that characterizes earlier eras of Cultural Studies implies a certain degree of passivity in how readers, listeners and viewers engage with popular culture. In its earliest critical iterations, Cultural Studies worked to unmask the ways in which corporate industries and state institutions influenced the consumers being targeted through popular culture. As such it is a mode of critical analysis that was first oriented toward the exposure of the machinations by which culture shaped the lives of the citizenry, and to a lesser degree toward the study of the capacity of consumers to appropriate popular culture for purposes that work independently of (if not against) those machinations. While I do not mean to suggest that this mode of study is no longer useful or valid, or that the power of culture to shape the consumer has somehow subsided, I would argue that the popular-cultural landscape has been reshaped in the digital age in ways that call for rethinking many of the implicit assumptions of the original paradigm.

While Reception Theory and related critical frameworks were developed to address the degree to which readers and viewers "make meaning" in how they decode the objects that they consume, our understanding of "reception" itself has evolved considerably since the turn of the century to make room for the communities and relationships formed by social media users. What was appropriate in the study of post-industrial developed nations during the previous century, when the degree of agency ascribed to the mass consumption of cultural production was largely understood as being limited to the choice by individual consumers of which products to consume, is now unable to account for today's digital environment. Reception Theory can't account for phenomena like crowdsourcing (for example, when the lines between "original" artistic productions and derivative "fan fiction" become blurred, as with many of the Disney Corporation's projects after acquiring intellectual property rights of George Lucas's *Star Wars* franchise) and "crowdfunding" (consumer-driven campaigns to fund new productions tied to earlier brands or franchises whose corporate producers had deemed obsolete or unprofitable, such as the crowdfunded 2014 film *Veronica Mars* based on the 2004-2007 television series of the same name). This influence on the production of popular culture challenges the capacity of the critical paradigm of Cultural Studies, first developed in the waning years of the Cold War and well before online activity, always only a click away on their smartphones, had become a constitutive part of the developing identities and communities of most college-bound students.

In short, contemporary college students now engage with popular culture (including the celebrities it features) far more actively than ever before. Adjusting the discourse of cultural studies to this new, more dynamic environment requires our accounting for a new kind of consumer agency vis-à-vis the institutions (public and private) that produce and regulate it. This agency is no doubt facilitated by the fact that current technology offers an unparalleled degree of consumer choice in what to consume, thus leaving producers of content far more attuned to the feedback that technology has empowered consumers to express. A tradition of stable and finite corporate producers (television networks, record labels, film production companies) has been replaced by a vast number of new competitors, both small (independent artists relying on digital media to reach consumers directly) and large (Netflix, Hulu, Amazon, Spotify). A hashtag campaign on Twitter can now attract the kind of attention that had previously been reserved for the entertainment industry's elaborate corporate marketing efforts. In the age of social media, corporate industries enjoy less control over their consumers' choices, and they are held accountable for the ethical and political implications of their products in real-time. This change constitutes a new ecology in the field of popular-cultural production that is inherently more horizontal, and for which twentieth-century critical approaches to popular culture in many ways are not equipped.

This new ecology is further complicated by the fact that our oft-lamented "celebrity culture" now positions artists both as participants in popular cultural production and as individual voices participating in social media. Celebrities are among the most "followed" users of social media and thus can communicate with consumer-fans without the control that we have associated with corporate "producers" (often referred to by the nebulous term "the industry") in the past, and their voices have been empowered and amplified in the process. We should note that the benefits of this direct communication with fans can also entail increased accountability for what they express: the telling example of Roseanne Barr, whose top-rated ABC sitcom was abruptly cancelled after she posted racially charged tweets, is an object lesson of the consequences of offending fans directly in a politically polarized environment, and it is further evidence of the increased agency of consumers—including our students—in the digital age.

In sum, changes to the field of popular-cultural production tied to globalization, digital entertainment and social media have created a new environment in which consumers enjoy more choices than ever; they feel more empowered to take issue with what the industry chooses to represent and how they represent it; and they engage popular culture as co-participants rather than as passive consumers and admirers. It should come as no surprise that this generation of students would therefore engage the injustices represented in early modern Spanish texts like *El burlador* from a perspective that is less inclined to accept the institutionally sanctioned silencing of victims of abuse (as when Don Juan's first victim Isabel is locked away by the King of Naples), and that is more inclined to find fault with a society whose system of justice requires divine intervention to stop the abuser. In this sense, the deferral of "tan largo me lo fiáis" has been supplanted by the agency of #TimesUp in the brave new digital world inhabited by our students. Regardless of how we feel about these developments, we ignore their epistemological and ontological implications at the risk of misunderstanding how students now experience the texts, whether early modern or contemporary, that we bring to them.

Navigating the "Waves" of Feminism

As mentioned at the opening of this essay, the #TimesUp movement gathered steam during a confusing and contradictory moment in U.S. cultural and political history, indeed perhaps because of that confusion and those contradictions. The *engaño* of the anticipated election of a woman as president gave way to the *desengaño* of a president and an overwhelmingly white-male congress dedicated to reversing gains that were regarded by feminists as important progress (healthcare policy and Title IX protections for abuse victims in colleges and universities, for example). These developments stimulated a feminist awakening that began with the January 2017 Women's March, in which millions of women made manifest their resistance to the freshly inaugurated President Trump. While our students have seen a presidential candidate elected despite being caught on tape boasting of sexual assault with impunity (later dismissed as "locker room talk"), they also see a growing list of elected officials, private-sector power brokers, high-profile celebrities—and yes, even professors and administrators at institutions of higher learning—held accountable for sexual harassment and abuse, and forced to surrender the power that they had used to cover their tracks. Our students develop an understanding of what is meant by the term "feminism" in a climate in which even activists proudly identifying with the label have difficulty agreeing on precisely what the term means, and on who it includes. What is sometimes called feminism's "fourth wave" (a term contested by many) addresses longstanding issues within feminist politics and theory—questions of inclusion and the place of LGBTQ issues and identities, for example, and related subjects tied to the intersectionality of race and class—the complexities of which can challenge college students with little previous exposure to feminist theory.

Rather than insist on a thorough and complete account of the history of feminism, and of a nuanced understanding of its progression through various "waves" that also accounts for national and regional variations in that chronology (with significant differences in twentieth-century Spain, for example), I have found it most effective to present an efficient but admittedly simplistic overview of that history, with an emphasis on how each phase or wave contributes to the developing movement as it relates to our current circumstances. The emphasis in such a presentation is not on learning the names of historically important feminists, from Susan B. Anthony to Betty Friedan to bell hooks, but instead on presenting a coherent narrative to aid students as they work with the various forms of oppression apparent in *El burlador* and that persist today.

This narrative coheres around the straightforward premise that feminism is a movement dedicated to promoting the rights and opportunities of women as equal to those of men. With this point of departure, students can be primed with a basic understanding of how, after centuries of isolated instances of proto-feminists writing and acting to promote this cause of equality (often through a critique of the patriarchy's obstacles to it), the nineteenth century witnessed the first collective effort or movement that can be called "feminist", with the immediate goal of securing a woman's right to vote; armed with that right, mid-twentieth-century feminists targeted the institutional and cultural barriers that impeded equality through a range of remedies including reproductive rights (abortion, birth control) and the prohibition of gender-based discrimination, abuse and harassment. More recently (in what is often called feminism's "third wave"), late twentieth-century activists pushed for the realization in practice of the equality that previous generations had secured in principle—in other words, to reinforce legal protections from inequality for which the letter of the law was changed but for which the spirit in which such laws was implemented left much to be desired. Tangible gains since the turn of the present century include improved access to reproductive healthcare, tighter regulations to eliminate gender-based discrimination and income inequality, and new policies to prevent federally funded institutions from hiding or denying sexual harassment and abuse.

This broad-brush narrative effectively brings students up to date with the legacy of the feminist movement inherited by their generation. It will also put into clear relief how these tangible gains proved to be far more tenuous and fragile than most feminists had imagined. Since January 2017, a series of executive orders and legislative actions has placed the security of those gains in serious doubt, and this unanticipated rollback of policies and protections for women has in turned spurred a kind of reawakening among feminists. Whether or not we choose to embrace the term "fourth wave" to describe the present-day politics and concerns of feminists, there is little doubt as to the importance that new digital technologies and especially social media have come to assume in the current crisis—for better or for worse, a fact bearing many of the consequences outlined above regarding our students' evolving relationship with popular culture. Most notable of these consequences in the context of feminism is the increased sense of agency among users of platforms like Twitter, which cited #feminism as the most popular hashtag of 2017 and fostered a participatory culture of feminist activism often called "hashtag feminism."

Social media have reoriented the praxis of feminism and rendered the movement more self-reflective and horizontal than it had been in previous centuries, but college students unfamiliar with "pre-hashtag" feminism will therefore need the broad narrative of feminism's history described above to revisit earlier periods of cultural history and to appreciate the struggles of earlier generations of feminists. Armed with this basic historical knowledge, students are better prepared to engage a text like *El burlador* and understand its connection to the feminist movement of their own generation—in other words, they are prepared to place "tan largo me lo fiáis" within the same narrative thread that has led us to hashtag feminism.

This approach to historicizing feminism in the classroom can be enhanced by adding that the narrative applies to the context of literary criticism and early modern Spanish studies as well; like any discursive practice, academic treatments of *El burlador* and other Golden Age Spanish texts have evolved over the last century according to the broader cultural and political contexts in which they were produced. Critical assessments of this play in particular are influenced by the moment in the history of feminism in which they were written. This is why a sample of arguments made about the play from various historical periods can be mapped onto the broader narrative of feminist history, and put meat on the proverbial bones of the skeletal history of feminism being presented to students. In the context of a graduate course, entire articles from distinct periods can be assigned; for undergraduates, brief samples of these articles can be extracted for the sake of comparison. This allows students to understand that scholars like Otis H. Green and Joaquín Casalduero focused on the character of Don Juan himself in the context of the 1930s, with little interest in the women whose lives he ruined; that John Varey would treat Don Juan's treatment of women as indicative of broader institutional and societal corruption in the 1970s; and that Susana Pendzik and Mercedes Maroto-Camino would treat the play's exclusion of women as subjects and agents as a function of the same patriarchal ideology that informed the campaigns of conquest and colonization during the early modern Spanish Empire. All of these readings of the play are functions of the times in which they were published, and as such they provide useful and concrete examples of the evolving narrative of feminism that we want students to acquire. What arguments, we should ask our students, will you make in light of how you too are culturally and historically situated subjects?

While the present space does not allow for a full exploration of the topic, it should also be noted that a similar substantiation of feminism's evolution can be achieved, when appropriate and when time in the course calendar allows, through the study of the many adaptations of the Don Juan legend across the centuries and across the globe. Each adaptation, just like each critical study, is a product of its own discursive context. For the sake of brevity I will cite one obvious example: Zorilla's Romantic *Don Juan Tenorio* presumably elevates the status of women in comparison to *El burlador* through the vital role of Inés—the woman responsible for inspiring selfless love in Don Juan—and for reversing the original play's narrative by saving his soul. A critical reading of the 1844 play in dialogue with the history of the movement reveals that the ostensible feminism of this *refundición* proves illusory, and that Inés functions as a rarified and purified model of femininity whose ultimate purpose is to reinforce the patriarchal order. The fact that the play was written when Spain was still nearly a century away from granting the right to vote to women offers useful context for such a critique of Zorilla's passive (even if idealized) treatment of Inés and the play's other female characters. Sarah Wright's comprehensive study of the many iterations of the Don Juan legend in Spanish culture is recommended reading for teachers interested in further exploring this alternative strategy in the classroom.

LEARNING THROUGH COMPARING

As agents of higher learning, we see the potential of leveraging our students' engagement with popular culture (however we choose to define or understand it) to bridge the historical and cultural distance between them and the Spanish Golden Age, but we also recognize that such a premise entails flipping the balance of authority in the classroom, and allowing our students to teach us about the forms of popular cultural production on which they as consumers are the experts. From my experience, however, privileging that expertise in the classroom requires carefully structured affordances in order to move beyond the use of comparative analysis as a pretext for simply sharing what they enjoy in popular culture (an extension of their non-academic social media usage), and beyond the facile then-and-now cultural comparisons described above to which the so-called "selfie generation" seems especially vulnerable. Our empowered-as-expert students must be made responsible for rethinking their relationship—with a critical distance that it is our job to foster—with popular culture. If we are able to prompt a reflective comparison of how their generation and our collective society now respond to sexual injustice vis-à-vis the early modern Spanish society represented in *El burlador*, the lessons learned from that process can then inform their future choices of what to consume (and how to consume it), and more importantly, it can prompt critical reflection on contemporary cultural issues and their role in addressing them. From my experience, the prompting of such re-thinking is the most effective means of converting critical thinking and awareness from vaguely articulated learning objectives described in course syllabi to tangible student learning that can make a difference.

As a first step, students should examine how they have read *El burlador* and then be prompted to reflect on how their own experiences and sensibilities inform that reading. Identifying common elements shared between the experiences of women in the play and women today—the protagonist's and victims' behavior and psychology, as well as the social mechanisms that permit Don Juan and his modern analogues to continue unimpeded for so long—is a logical starting point. Do Don Juan's exploits seem comparable to any patterns of the sexual harassment and abuse we witness today? Is Don Juan's "tan largo me lo fiáis" an early modern equivalent to "yolo" ("you only live once")? Is his banter with the Marqués de Mota about Sevilla's brothels connected to the toxic masculinity of college fraternities and other "rape culture" environments? Are our contemporary methods of protecting the powerful from accountability for their actions (non-disclosure agreements, forced arbitration and other purchases of victim silence) simply more sophisticated versions of how Don Juan's sociopolitical *enchufe* as son of the Castilian King's confidant was used to shield him from any consequence for the lives and reputations he ruined? The answers to these questions, you might surmise, are both yes and no, or more accurately, "yes, but. . ." and "no, but. . ."—with each "but" representing an opportunity to learn.

Prompting students to identify the play's tangible evidence of patriarchal machinations to protect male aggression and suppress justice, for example, invites reflection on both how much and how little things have changed since the early modern period. From the play's opening scene, in which Isabela discovers *post-coitus* that Don Juan had impersonated the man she had hoped to marry, we see a series of actions that are in many ways parallel to the experiences of twenty-first century victims, and that are now frequent targets of hashtag feminism. The Neapolitan king's initial reaction to discovering this crime is neither to attend to the victim nor to pursue the perpetrator; instead, it is to foreground the crime's implications for himself and his crown, as evinced by his first *aparte* comment, "Esto en prudencia consiste" (ll. 24). As Pendzik's study examines in greater detail, Isabela is promptly silenced by the king and imprisoned, while his system of justice fails to apprehend her rapist—his escape, as we know, is facilitated by his uncle, just as his presence in Naples was arranged to shield him from the consequences of similar tricks committed in Spain. The patriarchal machinations continue throughout the play, with a crescendo in the third act when Aminta, Tisbea and Isabela converge at court to demand justice (a #TimesUp moment?). True to the character of his person and the monarchy/patriarchy he represents, the king expresses outrage at what he learns about Don Juan, but he also fails do more than had already been attempted unsuccessfully, by ordering his arrest. Don Juan's ultimate comeuppance remains in doubt until God Himself intervenes, leaving the king to clean up the mess by pairing his victims with husbands now that the *burlador*'s death can be said to have cleansed the stain of their dishonor.

This generational close reading will, of course, invite deconstruction from the disciplinary perspective that we as instructors bring to the discussion. The urge to create equivalencies will also invite blind spots, as will the perception of historical and cultural difference. For example, the theological implications of "tan largo me lo fiáis," effectively studied by Barbara Simerka and others, offer an important qualifier (a "yes, but. . ." teachable moment, so to speak) to the facile equivalence many students will make between Don Juan and Harvey Weinstein or Bill Cosby. Pendzik and Maroto Camino explain that the appearance of justice and resolution is in fact, from a feminist perspective, rather illusory. Acknowledging the female presence of Don Juan's victims, both those who are named and those who are not named explicitly in the play, requires acknowledging that the closure achieved before the final curtain falls is ultimately realized at the service of the patriarchy, which in early modern Spain was understood to mean the natural order of society. The social order restored by Don Juan's death at the hand of the divinely empowered stone guest, insofar as it allows this society to maintain its patriarchal structures and machinations unchanged, exposes for students the considerable gap between what Alexander Parker would call "poetic justice" in early modern Spain and the twenty-first century justice pursued by hashtag feminism.

Reading *El burlador* as a foil to our students' cultural circumstances thus invites them to understand that the experiences of victims empowered by the #MeToo movement are nothing new, but also that this empowerment and the social media through which it has been achieved are indeed very new and promise to address injustices that are as old as the patriarchy itself. Whereas the poetic justice that Parker and many other scholars have associated with the play's conclusion is dependent on an early modern Spanish spiritual and theological conception of divine providence, that authority is democratized and secularized today, with agency transferred from the divine Patriarch to the voices of the victims themselves and the virtual social spaces they inhabit, powered by hashtags and other discursive practices that allow for the kind of empowerment that eluded Don Juan's early modern victims.

As noted at the outset of this chapter, I would argue that many of the pedagogical strategies described above, not to mention the broader goal of teaching our students to better understand present struggles through discursive artifacts of the past, are applicable to innumerable texts written in the Hispanic Golden Age. The representation of male sexual aggression and its sociocultural implications for both male and female subjects is a thread connecting a preponderance of the period's canonical narrative texts, from Cervantes' *La fuerza de la sangre* and *Don Quijote* (Fernando and Dorotea's interpellated story among many others) to the popular *comedias de capa y espada* and most points in between. Indeed, the early modern patriarchy's articulation of honor itself offers an extreme iteration of the same gendered values and hierarchies that inform many of the retrograde beliefs and policies against which feminists continue to struggle. A broader case can be made that early modern Spanish culture's efforts to regulate, sublimate and channel male desire—featuring literary production as but one of many discursive practices, both secular and religious, working in this spirit—afford us a unique opportunity as educators to contribute to the intellectual formation of consumer-agents in the era of hashtag feminism.

Despite the common understanding of ours as an age in which we are closer to the ideal of gender equality than ever before, public awareness of sexual abuse has shown how far from that ideal we remain, despite the progress that has been achieved with the stimulus of feminist activism and thought. In our polarized cultural and political climate, this awareness invites "teachable moments" like those presented by *El burlador* explored here, from a presumed "safe" distance of four centuries that proves far from truly safe in light of current events and debates. Studying this play as a foil to both our current problems and to how we confront them—in social media, journalism and popular cultural production—prompts students to take stock of their own role in the problem and our collective efforts to fix it. In other words, by flipping how we approach this play pedagogically—from using the text as an artifact to learn about early modern Spain to using it as a foil to critique contemporary society—it is possible to convert the *Comedia* and other texts written in the Hispanic Golden Age into vital components of an education that prepares students for the challenges we face in contemporary society.

Works Cited

Aitken, Mel. "Feminism: A Fourth to be Reckoned With? Reviving Community Education Feminist Pedagogies in a Digital Age." *Concept*, vol. 8, no. 1, 2017, pp. 1-18.

Bennet, Tony. "Popular Culture: A Teaching Object." *Screen Education*, vol. 34, 1980, pp. 17-29.

Bordieu, Pierre. *The Field of Cultural Production: Essays on Art and Literature*. Columbia UP, 1993.

Casalduero, Joaquín. *Contribución al estudio del tema de Don Juan en el teatro español*. Smith College Studies in Modern Languages, 1938.

Friedan, Betty. *The Feminine Mystique*. W.W. Norton & Co., 1963.

Green, Otis H. "New Light on Don Juan: A Review Article." *Hispanic Review*, vol. 7, no. 2, 1939, pp. 117-124.

Hooks, Bell. *Feminism is for Everybody: Passionate Politics*. Pluto Press, 2000.

Mandrell, James. *Don Juan and the Point of Honor: Seduction, Patriarchal Society, and Literary Tradition*. Penn State UP, 1992.

Maroto Camino, Mercedes. "'Las naves de la conquista': Woman and the Fatherland in *El burlador de Sevilla*." *Bulletin of the Comediantes*, vol. 55, no. .1, 2003, pp. 69-86.

Parker, Alexander A. "The Approach to Spanish Golden Age Drama. *The Tulane Drama Review*, vol. 4, no. 1, 1959, pp. 42-59.

Pendzik, Susana. "Female Presence in Tirso's *El burlador de Sevilla*." *Bulletin of the Comediantes*, vol. 47, no. 2, 1995, pp. 65-181.

Simerka, Barbara. "Early Modern Skepticism and Unbelief and the Demystification of Providential Ideology in *El burlador de Sevilla*." *Gestos*, vol. 23, 1997, pp. 39-66.

Tirso de Molina. *El burlador de Sevilla*, Edited by Alfredo Rodríguez López-Vázquez, Cátedra , 1995.

Varey, John. "Social Criticism in *El burlador de Sevilla*." *Theatre Research International*, vol. 2, 1977, pp. 197–221.

Wright, Sarah. *Tales of Seduction: The Figure of Don Juan in Spanish Culture*. Tauris Academic Studies, 2007.

"Pop Don Quixote": *The Big Bang Theory* as Quixotic Emulation

YOLANDA GAMBOA TUSQUETS
Florida Atlantic University

E ARLY MODERN LITERATURE—particularly the character of Don Quixote, who is prevalent in contemporary culture at multiple levels—can still be relevant to a multi-tasking generation for whom technology has occupied most available reading time. Some years ago, I designed and taught a class that made those contemporary connections apparent: "Pop *Don Quixote* in Literature, Art and Film." It was in English and discussed *Don Quixote*'s influence on different genres, from ballet, to comics, to movies.[1] I began by asking the class what it meant to be "quixotic" and then assigning a task involving a comparison with another "quixotesque" work of their choice.[2] As I discovered, this was enough to keep my students (millennials and Generation Z—or even my own generation) engaged throughout a semester and beyond.[3] By encountering Don Quixote in their everyday life (from statues, to restaurant names, to chocolates, to movies), students become aware of the extent to which *Don Quixote* has permeated contempo-

---

1   I successfully taught this class for undergraduates at Florida Atlantic University in 2013.

2   I use "quixotesque" for the type of works that follow the particular pattern I propose in this essay and "quixotic" in a more general sense.

3   The comparison with another quixotesque work is a technique I learned from Howard Mancing while taking his class in the early nineties, and I have never stopped seeing quixotesque works since. Likewise, as soon as undergraduate students grasp the concept, they start seeing images of *Don Quixote* and the quixotesque in their everyday life. Note that millennials are the generation born in the early 80s and 90s. Generation Z, born in the mid-90s to early 2000s, constitutes the current generation of students (who are often mistakenly referred to as millennials).

rary culture. Moreover, they end up establishing a meaningful connection with the character, seeing Don Quixote's humanity and forging an emotional bond with the character that is precisely what students need in order to relate to the material, according to recent studies in cognitive science.[4]

In recent years, several Spanish Golden Age critics have addressed the correlations between *Don Quixote* and contemporary culture. They have searched for paradigmatic elements, the ones that constitute the essence of the quixotesque in their minds, and have gone on to highlight the effects of *Don Quixote* on contemporary comedy, cultural history, and postmodern culture. It makes sense to connect *Don Quixote* with contemporary culture because it is precisely what Cervantes' novel was doing in its time, incorporating all types of popular genres (not only literature but also storytelling, cultural stereotypes, and proverbs, among others), and also because we know Cervantes himself was concerned with mass media and its effects on the spectator (Castillo 32).

For example, looking specifically at comedy, Antonio Carreño Rodríguez described *Don Quixote*'s style of comedy as "the focus on physically and morally contrasting characters, pervasive verbal humor, parody, irony and intertextuality" (80). Carreño Rodríguez claimed that the most important comedic element in the novel was "the Cervantine duo" of contrasting characters, who evolve through their dialogue, and which he regards as "a paradigm that has the characters of Don Quixote and Sancho Panza at its center" (80). In his opinion, this model has repeatedly appeared on the American stage, from the genre of vaudeville, to movies and television and, more recently, to situation comedies such as *Seinfeld*. "Laurel and Hardy" come to my mind, while my students, who are Miami-adjacent, inevitably mention *El gordo y la flaca*, a television program on the Spanish network *Univisión* that features a portly man and a thin woman as hosts.

From the perspective of cultural history, David Castillo explored the pedagogical possibilities of placing "the literary classics side by side with the products of our media culture" (26) as "practical exercises of strategic re-historicization" (26). He evaluated other approaches and cautioned the reader by quoting Gonzalo Navajas's claim for a "transhistorical method of textual commentary that ought to be capable of integrating disparate media and sign systems while preserving their circumstantial specificity" (31). According to Castillo, this recognition of trans-historical bridges—a metaphor belonging to Walter Benjamin—helps students connect with the text and feel that the

---

4   See Carrera.

works "speak their language" (32). Castillo himself placed *Don Quixote* as a road narrative alongside road movies, claiming that "the Cervantine story is shaped, first and foremost, by the experience of the journey" (33), which is in itself transformative.[5] Reality cannot be lived vicariously, as doing so, according to Castillo, equates with conformity. Instead, it needs to be experienced, and this is where road movies and *Don Quixote* converge: "they are the direct result of an act of affirmation of experience over the vicarious consumption of illusions" (33).[6] Therefore, we can add the transformative journey to the list of components that constitute the quixotesque.

In addition to the previously mentioned elements that link *Don Quixote* and contemporary culture (comedy and cultural history), Cervantes' novel has also been connected to postmodernism, understood, according to Terry Eagleton, as "a cultural style characterized by a playful, derivative, and self-reflexive discourse blurring the boundaries between high and low culture (qtd. in Burningham 158). One such instance is Bruce Burningham's "Walt Disney's *Toy Story* as Postmodern *Don Quixote*," where the movie *Toy Story* appears to be a postmodern rendition of the work. Arguing that Don Quixote (the character) has become an archetype in Western tradition, with many new incarnations, Bruce Burningham offers a compelling postmodern reading of Cervantes' novel in Pixar's animated movies *Toy Story* and *Toy Story* II. Burningham claims that, in these films, instead of the knightly adventures and damsels in distress that Don Quixote believes he sees, the characters' delusions are movies, television shows, video games, and science fiction, and the characters themselves have morphed into toys (157-8). In particular, the quixotesque Buzz Lightyear refuses to accept his status as toy. He often misreads reality and tries to play his self-assigned role as "Space Ranger," savior of the galaxy. His friend and companion, a toy cowboy, Woody, who argues with Buzz and reminds him that he is a toy, is the down-to-earth character of the duo who eventually ends up playing along and joining him in his quest.[7] Burningham's article is particularly accessible for undergraduate students

---

5   Note that Castillo is not the only one who has taken this approach. See Hutchinson.

6   Castillo is actually highlighting the difference between active experience vs. passive spectatorship and claims that Don Quixote's problem is not the inability to distinguish between fiction and reality but the desire to participate and write the story according his expectations (33).

7   Burningham's analysis of contemporary culture via media, literature, and other contemporary films can be found in his book *Tilting Cervantes: Baroque Reflections on Postmodern Culture* (2008).

and provides a model for approaching the quixotesque from the angle of pop culture. We can now add the blurring of boundaries and self-reflexive discourse to the list of characteristics of the quixotesque.

Toy Story, however, is not the only postmodern rendition of *Don Quixote*.[8] One of the latest emulations of *Don Quixote* in contemporary culture, as I contend, is an extremely popular TV sitcom, *The Big Bang Theory*.[9] The show exhibits many of the constitutive elements of the quixotesque: humor, a Don Quixote-like character, several Cervantine duos, a blurring of boundaries, the experience of the journey, and a constant confrontation between reality and fantasy, the latter of which serves as a bridge between the Renaissance and contemporary times.[10] Despite the limitations of doing a comparative study, there is value in having contemporary viewers engage with *Don Quixote*, particularly through the quixotesque character of Sheldon Cooper. *The Big Bang Theory* takes a nostalgic leap when including the world of *Star Trek*, as well as action heroes from comics (the same way *Don Quixote* does by including Amadís and Orlando and, to a lesser extent, characters from other chivalric novels written long before Cervantes' time).[11] Contemporary

---

8   Shortly after its release in 1998, DreamWorks released *Shrek* and *Shrek 2* (2001; 2004), which are reminiscent of part I and part II of *Don Quixote*, respectively, as well as other animated movies which also present quixotesque elements such as *Bolt* (2008), an actor dog who believes he has retained the magic powers he had when acting in real life, and *Up* (2009), where an older man and a child go in search of a dream. I thank the students who took my classes on *Don Quixote*, and especially the group from spring 2013, for pointing out some of these movies and sitcoms.

9   I need to clarify that despite *The Big Bang Theory* currently airing its 11th season, I am limiting the scope of this article to seasons 1 through 7, and particularly to the Sheldon that is presented in those seasons.

10   Although there are two basic approaches in *Don Quixote* scholarship, reading it as funny (the hard approach) or tragic (the romantic approach), I will primarily follow the line of interpretation of *Don Quixote* "as a funny book," which according to P.E. Russell was the tone of its initial reception when it was first published. It also seems to be the tone of contemporary imitations, which tend to draw their comparisons from the first volume. However, it may not hold so well when looking at the second volume, which is more serious and sarcastic in nature. Indeed, in his review of P.E. Russell's book, John J. Allen concludes that Russell's cogent interpretation of *Don Quixote*, "seems inadequate to the last fifteen chapters" (220).

11   Comics first appeared in the *New York Sunday World* in 1898. They lost popularity due to the appearance of television (McLuhan, Pop Culture, 89-90). The first comic books appeared in 1935 (McLuhan, Pop Culture, 92). *Star Trek* was a science-fiction TV series, which aired in the US from the 1966 to 1969. Although

audiences, already drawn to *Star Wars* and comic heroes, can then be moved to examine the relationships between reality and fiction, or rather the nature of reality itself.[12]

According to P.E. Russell, in the context of the novel's purpose, "Cervantes simply wanted to give his readers something to laugh at" (313). This "funny" interpretation draws from the personality of Don Quixote himself as a ridiculous madman created in response to treatises on mental illness which claimed that "imprudent reading could lead to insanity" (Russell 315). Humor also emerges from the relationship between Don Quixote and Sancho, the two of whom were soon "established as traditional figures of fun in the popular mind" (Russell 318). The comedic pair appears to be one aspect of the quixotesque that has been consistently maintained in popular culture, and particularly in comedy, especially in the latter part of the 20th century and the first decades of the 21st, as Carreño-Rodríguez claims (82).

The Big Bang Theory, belonging to the genre of the "situational comedy," is also quite funny.[13] Created by Chuck Lorre and Bill Prady, who serve as executive producers along with Steven Molaro, the show premiered on CBS in 2007, and as of June 2018, it is currently in its 11th season. It features five main characters: roommates Leonard Hofstader (Johny Galecki) and Sheldon Cooper (Jim Parsons), physicists; Penny (Kaley Cuoco), their next-door neighbor and aspiring actress; and their two friends and equally socially awkward coworkers, aerospace engineer Howard Wolowitz (Simon Helberg) and astrophysicist Rajesh Koothrapalli (Kunal Nayyar). The show revolves around the daily lives of these characters and the issues the four male friends (in particular) have at work, with women and dating, and with their families, especially their mothers, who figure occasionally in the stories. Even though the IMDb website lists these five as the main characters, most of the action revolves around Sheldon, who resembles Don Quixote himself in myriad ways.[14] Both works employ similar techniques for the creation of humor,

---

ratings were low and the show was cancelled after only three seasons, it became tremendously popular in syndication during the 1970s and 1980s.

12   The *Star Wars* franchise is the main current form of science-fiction entertainment, while comic heroes are again popular through the Marvel and DC movies now that cinema has won in popularity over television.

13   If *Seinfeld* "brought the Cervantine comedy duo paradigm into the 1990s sitcom" (86), as Carreño-Rodríguez claimed, *The Big Bang Theory* brings it again in the 2010s.

14   At the risk of making a stretch, I believe that, besides his acting talent, the reason for Sheldon Cooper and actor Jim Parsons' rise in popularity (beyond

starting with the personality of Don Quixote himself and the Cervantine duos, but also including other elements such as language, setting, and the conflicts themselves. Such a comparison speaks to Castillo's trans-historical bridge, which allows us and our students to reflect on current times though our reading of the early modern novel.

A QUIXOTIC CHARACTER

Sheldon Cooper's appearance and personality are similar to those of Don Quixote who, according to Tobias Smollet, exhibits: a "ludicrous solemnity and self-importance" (qtd. in Russell 316). Russell further describes the character's "sad countenance" or "ill-favored face" [*triste figura*] (referring to his lank, ungainly, and ridiculous appearance) (317). In addition to these shared characteristics, Don Quixote and Sheldon are both prone to literal readings of reality and outbursts of anger. Regarded by strangers and even at times by his closest friends as socially awkward and somewhat off-balance, Sheldon's actions and words—never politically correct—represent the unspoken desires or truths of other characters or society. This makes one question whether he is a hero or a fool, a question some Cervantes' scholars have asked regarding Don Quixote.[15] Cervantes exploited Don Quixote's intervals of sanity for comedic purposes, making readers think "that madness speaks at times with a voice which is indistinguishable from the voice of sanity" (Russell 310). We can therefore regard Don Quixote as similar to a fool from Renaissance social and literary history, as we see in Shakespeare's comedies, the character who tells the truths nobody dares say while showing us a mirror of our own follies and prejudices. In a similar way, Sheldon is incapable of sarcasm since he cannot understand the nuances of language, nor social situations or human emotions. He is like Don Quixote, but even more so, akin to the *Star Trek* characters and comic heroes (such as Batman) that he idolizes, which itself is often a source of humor. Moreover, from the perspective of contemporary culture, Sheldon, who is quick to make judgements about others and label them, makes us realize that we sometimes act the same way. Sheldon's

---

that of Parson's coworkers) is due to the similarity of his character's role with that of Don Quixote with respect to their connection with audiences. Indeed, Sheldon, the series' main character, is the one who, like Don Quixote, has captured the imagination of viewers. In fact, CBS started airing a new sitcom called *Young Sheldon*, also created by Chuck Lorre and a prequel to *The Big Bang Theory*, on November 2, 2017. I will refer to Sheldon by his first name hereafter.

15   See John Jay Allen, *Don Quixote: Hero or Fool? A Study in Narrative Technique*.

lack of social filters, though comical and exaggerated, causes uneasiness, because he tells the truths everybody thinks but does not say, thus becoming a
mirror to our masked behaviors.

Sheldon exhibits similar behaviors to those of Don Quixote regarding
the imitation of heroes: an aversion to bodily functions, an uneasiness with
romance, and a lack of empathy (albeit for slightly different reasons). He is
as immersed in the *Star Trek* universe and in reading comic books as Don
Quixote is in the reading of chivalric novels, and both Sheldon and Don
Quixote appear to eschew reality as a result. For example, Don Quixote, who
idolizes chivalric heroes, assumes he is immune to feeling pain and does not
need sleep, to pay for lodging, or to defecate because none of those aspects
were applicable to knights of chivalry. Likewise, Sheldon attempts without
success to imitate his idols, the two-dimensional characters from *Star Trek* or
from comic books. Like his hero Mr. Spock, Sheldon relies on logic to navigate the world and appears unaware of affective aspects of social interaction.
When his friend and neighbor Penny teaches him about "gift giving," "the art
of conversation," or "apologizing," his attempt at producing those behaviors
appears feigned, thereby highlighting the performative quality of all social
conventions to the audience in ways similar to Don Quixote's obvious imitation of a chivalric script.

Don Quixote's repulsion of bodily functions provokes Sancho's laughter
and creates many of the comedic episodes in the first part of the novel, for
example, chapter 8. Sheldon, for his part, is preoccupied with having an orderly life, to the extent that he ensures that he and everybody else defecates
according to a schedule. He has no trouble speaking about the scientific and
natural act itself, which becomes a great source of humor, especially for a
North American audience for whom talking about bodily functions is still
taboo. In fact, by making a human, natural function so regulated it becomes
less "bodily," which is precisely what Don Quixote tries to do as well.

Of romance, Don Quixote only understands the courting stage and, like
Sheldon, does not appear to have any interest in sex, though the way these
two characters express themselves in that regard is slightly different. Whereas Don Quixote, influenced by his readings on courtly love, dreams about
his idealized Dulcinea, Sheldon, influenced by science fiction, justifies his
lack of interest in sex by claiming that a highly evolved creature like himself
does not succumb to carnal urges. Burningham has discussed this quixotic
characteristic in relation to quixotic Buzz Lightyear who, like Sheldon, follows *Star Trek* conventions, arguing that while "the tradition of courtly love
insists that each knight have a lady to whom he can command himself, the

code of science fiction does not provide such a proviso for space rangers" (160-161). Sheldon, who idolizes and imitates the characters in *Star Trek*, and especially Mr. Spock, believes that being a lover does not have a place in his understanding of reality. Sheldon again rejects the sexual/bodily in favor of the intellectual in the same way that Don Quixote, favoring the ideal, rejects the advances from women, such as that of Maritornes during the episode that takes place at the inn.

Like Don Quixote, Sheldon is unaware of his peers' perception of him, as he is incapable of empathy, and occasionally, he experiences fits of rage while lecturing his (often disinterested) friends. These moments are reminiscent of Don Quixote's long-winded speeches on "arms vs. letters" (Cervantes I; ch. 38), when the goatherds pay him little attention. Because Sheldon was as immersed in research as Don Quixote was in reading, his emotions, as well as his perception of the world, have remained stunted. In fact, even his closest friends, Leonard and Penny, treat Sheldon like a child at times, sometimes with compassion, other times with reprimands, just like Sancho treats Don Quixote. Sheldon and Don Quixote, however developed they are intellectually, are emotionally underdeveloped, and their transformational journey occurs through their dialogue with their peers. It is human interaction that allows both characters to slowly open their minds to the possible validity of another person's worldview and, therefore, to grow.

CERVANTINE COMEDIC DUOS

Five main characters form the sitcom: four male friends and a female. These characters interact as pairs during their daily lives, and their dialogues and journeys drive their personal transformations. The four male friends share meals at the university cafeteria, movie nights, and evenings at home, but their personalities and sources of humor are often structured in pairs, as is common in comedy. Sheldon Cooper and Leonard Hofstader exemplify what Carreño named "the Cervantine duo," a comedic paradigm from "the tradition of paired physiological and psychological opposites" (84), with its origins in the theater and which has constantly reentered the cultural space, albeit through different media (80-83). Despite their different personalities and occasional arguments, these roommates stick together and grow to be good friends, very much like Don Quixote and Sancho. Leonard is an experimental physicist and Sheldon a theoretical one, a distinction Sheldon often makes clear, stating that he is of a superior intelligence, which will one day earn him a Nobel Prize. He often undermines Leonard for what he regards as his "inferior" (applied) research, which signals his insecurities behind the

mask of the exemplary scientist he attempts to portray; just like Don Quixote knows he is no hero beneath his armor. Leonard, nevertheless, displays
immense patience with Sheldon, just as Sancho does with Don Quixote. This
binary is very similar in the novel as Don Quixote's pursuits are more intellectual whereas Sancho's are more material and experiential. Don Quixote
initially tends to treat Sancho condescendingly, at least in part I, though
their interaction changes over time, affecting their transformations so that
Sancho (like Leonard) will be wiser and more confident, and Don Quixote
(like Sheldon) humbler and more open to other people's ideas.

Howard Wolowitz, an engineer and the only one of the four male characters without a PhD—though he has a master's from the Massachusetts Institute of Technology, as he often boasts—emphasizes his need (and ours) to
create our identities by association. He and Rajesh Koothrappali, an astrophysicist, are another notable duo. Rajesh is portrayed as a hopeless romantic, shy, and unable to talk to women unless he is inebriated; he is an unmanly
and exoticized "other," as this marginalization often happens in American
comedy TV shows that portray Indian characters.[16] The sitcom's humor in-
tensifies with Howard and Rajesh, who are often depicted as a romantic pair
exhibiting homosocial undertones. They end up in compromising situations,
like kissing by mistake, or falling asleep together on the couch, and serve as a
reminder that the representation of homosexuality still tends to be portrayed
with comic undertones.[17]

Cast as stereotypically nerdy and childlike, together these four male
friends engage in adolescent pursuits, such as Dungeons and Dragons, and
they argue endlessly about events from comic books or *Star Trek*, with Sheldon leading the discussions and always having the last word. Their encounters are reminiscent of the encounters of Don Quixote and Sancho with the
priest and the barber, who join in the readings and discussions of charac-

---

16   According to *Representations in Sitcoms*, Indian men rarely appear in sitcoms and, if they do, their representation is narrow: "The characters are all one sided
and are never given the chance to branch out like their fellow Caucasian cast members. The stereotypes of the Indian men keep the men from being seen as equal or
normal. It confines them to remain foreigners and allows the groups to keep them as
outcasts." Referring specifically to Raj, it says that having overbearing parents leads
him to appear unmanly.

17   From *Will and Grace* (1998), with a reboot 2017-2020, eleven years after
the initial seasons, to *Modern Family* (2009), there appears to be a change in the societal view of homosexuality, and yet the topic is still treated with humor, probably
to appeal to a majority audience who may not be completely accepting of otherness.

ters from the chivalric novels or go along with Don Quixote's adventures but have less compassion for Don Quixote than Sancho does. Likewise, even though they partake in these games, Howard and Rajesh are more interested in experiencing the outside world than living vicariously through the world of comics, so they represent a different approach to living reality. They function as the priest and the barber, a point of contrast to the main characters.

One character deserves a special mention since she is connected to all the characters, especially to Sheldon and Leonard, with whom she forms separate comedic duos. Penny is their neighbor and friend; she works as an aspiring actress/by-day waitress at the *Cheesecake Factory* while she awaits her "big break." An attractive blond from Nebraska—as well as an embodiment of stereotypes of both blondes and rural women—she is streetwise, less intellectual than the male characters, yet she is savvy and evolves. She teaches them life lessons, especially Sheldon, as Sancho does with Don Quixote. All the men around her desire her, but she has no success with relationships until she pairs off with Leonard later in the series, again functioning as a Sancho in her duo with Leonard. Adding to her complexity is her Dulcinea/Dorotea role. Her external beauty in combination with her street smarts mirrors the duality of Dulcinea, be it as Don Quixote imagines her, a beautiful damsel from the chivalric novels, or as Sancho describes her: a rough, manly, peasant woman.[18]

Penny is Sheldon's friend, confidant, and social mentor, and she is also the one to use *his* language and manipulate him. Penny also takes on Dorotea's role as she works together with the priest, the barber, and Sancho (Howard, Rakesh and Leonard) to speak Sheldon's language and lead him wherever they want him to go, as Dorotea does (Cervantes, Part I; ch.37), when she performs as Princess Micomicona in order to convince Don Quixote to return home.[19] Some of the scenes that exhibit the most tenderness are those in which she maternally lulls Sheldon to sleep by singing "Soft Kitty," Sheldon's favorite song from his childhood. As a character, Penny is well aware of her different selves, very much the same way Dorotea is with Don Quixote. In fact, Penny is the most versatile and complex of all the characters, as she is capable of moving between the worlds of reality and fiction seam-

---

18   This duality appears embodied in Sophia Loren's Dulcinea from the movie *Man of La Mancha* (more present in contemporary North American culture than the actual novel of Cervantes), since she is both beautiful and an uneducated inn server, and could hypothetically be the inspiration for the character of Penny.

19   For a more detailed description of the Sierra Morena adventure as a case of performance see Larubia-Prado.

lessly. Not only is she secure in her identity, which puts her in touch with her selves,[20] but also in her knowledge of both social and dramatic conventions, an awareness that the other characters do not appear to have, and one that puts her in a leading position.

BLURRING BOUNDARIES

The language and theme of both the sitcom and *Don Quixote* are also comparable as they mix references to "high" culture for the highly educated and references to "low" culture, for the masses, thus appealing to both audiences. For example, the title of the sitcom, *The Big Bang Theory*, is misleading as it is not an educational science documentary. It refers to the world of science but weaves in popular culture: quixotesque Sheldon and his friends combine often incomprehensible (for most) discussion of scientific concepts with ideas from science-fiction, comic book heroes, and action movies. Likewise, *Don Quixote*'s title, "Don Quixote of la Mancha" is misleading, since it is not a chivalric novel, as it would seem, but a parody, and it contains everything from philosophical discussions, to literary works, to common sayings, alluding to the surrounding reality of the author. *Don Quixote* includes chivalric novels, since they were popular and consumed in Cervantes' time; in the same spirit, *The Big Bang Theory* includes comic books and *Star Trek* references, appealing to both the younger generation, now enthused by action movies based on comic heroes, but perhaps even more so to the older one, able to recall the *Star Trek* series.

Sheldon obsesses over details in stories, which he discusses with his friends, who figure in his life centrally, very much like the priest and the barber with whom Don Quixote discusses books. The fictions that form Sheldon's and his friends' universe range from the *Star Trek* series to the original comic books they avidly collect and which influence their language, whereas Don Quixote's thoughts and language are colored by his reading of chivalric novels from a century before his time but in vogue among his contemporary readers. We see Sheldon quoting from his heroic universe, for example, by saying "I'll be back" (from *Terminator*), or "I am Batman," (even imitating the voice inflection) and above all, from his adored *Star Trek,* including the Klingon language which he can even speak and write. Likewise, Don Quixote invokes *Amadis de Gaula* and *Orlando Furioso*, quoting from these novels or having daily conversations in their archaic language. All in all, both Sheldon's and Don Quixote's speech patterns are odd: in both cases, they appear

---

20   *Idem.*

disconnected from the contemporary reality of their respective audiences. Since both characters seem to live in the past, language serves to highlight their resistance to change and their wish to live strictly by their own values and codes which helps them connect with an older generation of viewers, the ones who watched *Star Trek* and are currently facing tremendous social and technological change.

THE TRANSFORMATIVE JOURNEY

At first glance, the world of *The Big Bang Theory* would seem more cosmopolitan than that of *Don Quixote* since the characters live "Somewhere in California, in a place . . ." called Pasadena and work as assistant professors at the rigorous California Institute of Technology. However, the truth is that their world is as limited as that of Don Quixote's La Mancha since they do not have a wider sphere than their research and their small group of friends around whom their lives revolve. Hence, in order to represent the limitation of the setting, the spaces in *The Big Bang Theory* are mostly enclosed, like the car in which Leonard drives Sheldon to work; the university cafeteria; either of their offices; the Cheesecake Factory, where they occasionally gather for dinner; the comic shop; or Sheldon's and Leonard's apartment. Likewise, if Don Quixote's escapades in La Mancha with Sancho make one think of two kids playing in a backyard, for the most part, the characters in *The Big Bang Theory* do the same and yet, in both instances, the limitation of the setting in no way hinders their personal transformation.[21]

Even the conflicts or misadventures in which Don Quixote and Sheldon find themselves are similar. Don Quixote ends up in trouble by his own actions, through his disregard of the law out of a desire to "undo all wrongs," and also by helping people who may not need to be helped, as is the case with the very well-known chapters of the goatherd (Cervantes I; ch. 2); the wine skins (Cervantes I; ch. 36); and, most interestingly, the convicts (Cervantes I; ch. 22). In this last episode, Don Quixote decides to take justice into his own hands and releases the chained convicts, who then wreak havoc as they wander around free in the towns of La Mancha.

Sheldon displays his own chivalric nature in an episode in which Penny dislocates her shoulder and he has to help her dress and get to the ER. He declares: "Let it not be said that Sheldon never saved a damsel in distress."[22] On two other occasions, following his own code to an extreme, as Don Quixote

---

21   This limitation of the setting appears to be a characteristic of sitcoms as it allows for better character development.

22   Season 3, episode 8.

does, Sheldon creates trouble for himself and ends up in jail. The first time, he proudly goes to court to defend himself for a traffic violation. He is found guilty and must pay a fine, causing him to address the judge disrespectfully; subsequently, he is declared in contempt of court, landing him in jail.[23] His disregard for the law and codes of conduct takes him to jail a second time when he approaches the home of revered author of Marvel comics, Stan Lee. When Sheldon knocks at the door to get Lee's autograph, the author refuses to open and asks a reluctant Sheldon to leave. Shortly after, he again tells Sheldon to leave, but he does it by asking him sarcastically: "What are you doing here, want to come in and watch basketball?" Sheldon, unable to understand sarcasm, walks right in, earning a restraining order for trespassing.[24] Even though Don Quixote and Sheldon see reality, they impose their own interpretation, based on their desires and worldview and which doesn't coincide with that of the people who surround them. In turn, people decide to play along up to a point, but often with consequences for everyone involved.

Even though *The Big Bang Theory* is not anchored by the experience of the journey, some episodes include journeys and one in particular, "The Bakersfield Expedition," akin to a road movie, bears an uncanny resemblance to *Don Quixote*.[25] In this episode, the four male friends take a road trip to Comic-Con International, a decades-old convention that brings together the world of comic books and video games for enthusiasts and which takes place annually in July in San Diego. In the sitcom, Comic-Con is held in Bakersfield, and on the way the characters pass through a barren desert landscape not unlike that of La Mancha. Halfway through the trip, Sheldon insists that they stop and choose a spot in the desert to dress up and take some pictures that would look just as if they were characters in *Star Trek: The Next Generation* (1987-1994). Their performance of the literary and cultural conventions of *Star Trek* is akin to Don Quixote's performance of Amadís and other chivalric heroes. They are not motivated by an inability to distinguish fiction from reality but by a desire to actively experience it, "to participate in the scene in order to rewrite the story" (Castillo 33). It was a moment they thoroughly enjoyed, as it represented "an act of affirmation of experience over the vicarious consumption of illusions" (Castillo 33); the more they posed for pictures the more they relived the scene, partaking in their imagined realities, and the happier they appeared. In a similar fashion, Don Quixote emulates

---

23 Season 3, episode 16.

24 Season 3, episode 16

25 Season 6, episode 13.

his heroes, affirming his experience during his performative knighting at the inn (Cervantes, part I; Ch.3).

While they were taking the desired pictures, someone stole Leonard's car, throwing a wrench in their Comic-Con plans. They were forced to walk through scorching dry heat of Southern California's Central Valley until they found a place from where they could call Penny to pick them up. The effect on the contemporary spectator watching them enter a roadside diner, sweating and distressed, dressed up in the outfits from *Star Trek* while the other customers were not wearing costumes, was probably very similar to the effect the scenes of Don Quixote arriving at the inn wearing his own garb as a self-made chivalric hero (Cervantes, part I; ch. 2-5) had for Cervantes' contemporary readers and listeners. Moreover, this scene epitomizes the contrast between "real" life and "the life of the imagination" or rather, the different realities that Don Quixote as well as Sheldon and his friends inhabit. In the end, the significance of the road trip does not lie in the never-reached destination but in the journey itself where the most important is the interaction among the main characters and experiencing their shared imagined reality, which contributes to building their personalities as well as their friendship.

REFLECTING ON OUR TIMES AND THE NATURE OF REALITY

Indeed, *The Big Bang Theory* bears many of the characteristics that we have come to identify as quixotesque. These include: the quixotesque character who often misreads reality, the comedic duo, the blurring of boundaries between fiction and reality, and multiple misadventures along the journey of discovery which ends up transforming the characters, all the while making the viewers question the nature of their own reality. Furthermore, since *The Big Bang Theory* stars college-aged characters, students in our classes might find it relatable, thus being a useful medium to teach the complexities of *Don Quixote*.

Through the character of Sheldon Cooper, the one who can speak without a filter, saying what other people think but don't dare say, viewers can see themselves in a mirror: the values they uphold, and the realities that they themselves inhabit. They are faced with an inordinate amount of stereotyping which, though funny, and at times decidedly uncomfortable, makes them question their propensity to emit quick judgements of people. Also, the emphasis on performance makes them realize the performative quality of their behaviors and especially of their social conventions, raising awareness of their own follies and encouraging change. In fact, whether one resorts to reading chivalric novels or comics, roaming through La Mancha or through California's desert, both Don Quixote and Sheldon remind us of—and at the same time make us question—the orderly, predictable fictions that we have *chosen* to inhabit in the face of the fast pace of information and transformation of reality. Between (fake or not) news and social media, our contemporary reality is no longer a visual world but rather a "simultaneous happening" (McLuhan and Fiore 167); it is a plural, chaotic, multisensory reality which is more difficult to apprehend every day, or perhaps another fiction.

Looking at both works trans-historically, as Castillo suggests, it turns out that *Don Quixote* continues to resonate among contemporary audiences, not only because of its similar sources of humor, but because of the similarity of the time periods with respect to the idea of a communication revolution.[26] Moreover, "the Cervantine dialogue with the cultural practices of his day [...] calls for a critical examination of prevalent literary, theatrical, and social conventions" (Castillo 31). If the printing press as well as the age of discovery marked the communication revolution of the Renaissance, creating instability in the time of Cervantes and making Don Quixote's desire to live in the chivalric past funny but justifiable, we are currently experiencing a point beyond the communication revolution that Marshall McLuhan predicted would occur with "the progressive disappearance of print, with the advancement of TV and the technological era" (Comics 90). Thus, Sheldon's resistance to change, though excessive, is at once funny and relevant today as we no longer seem to have the luxury of resisting the immense speed of change.

Both *The Big Bang Theory* and other quixotic contemporary emulations bring Cervantes' themes and motives to new cultural contexts and at the same time affirm it (Carreño-Rodríguez 86). In *The Big Bang Theory*, the emphasis on science and technology corresponds to the world of the 21st century, with the overload of information and misinformation from the media, web culture and social media, new forms of high speed communication in which we see that "the contrast between reality and fantasy breaks down" (Stainer Kwale qtd. in Johnson xix). Discerning what is "real," or rather, affirming which reality we care to inhabit, is no longer quixotic but rather an everyday human question. Hence, one can predict that quixotesque emulations such as the one I describe here are unlikely to disappear any time soon.[27]

---

26   Juan Luis Suárez Sánchez de León regards Don Quixote's time, the time of Humanism, as "the first globalization in the modern world" (11) also characterized by "a high level of change and the destabilization of fundamental notions such as the idea of Man, the experience of time and space, and the organization of the past" (16).

27   Terry Gilliam's *The Man who Killed Don Quixote*, some 29 years in the making, was released on May 2018.

Works Cited

Allen, John J. *Don Quixote: Hero or Fool? A Study in Narrative Technique.* U of Florida P, 1969.

———. Review of *Cervantes* by P. E. Russell. *The Modern Language Review,* vol. 83, no. 1, 1988, pp. 217-20.

Burningham, Bruce R. "Walt Disney's Toy Story as Postmodern Don Quixote." *Cervantes: Bulletin of the Cervantes Society of America,* vol. 20, no. 1, 2000, pp. 157-74.

———. *Tilting Cervantes. Baroque Reflections on Postmodern Culture.* Vanderbilt UP, 2008.

Carreño-Rodríguez, Antonio. "Costello + Panza = Constanza: Paradigmatic Pairs in Don Quixote and American Popular Culture." *Journal of Popular Film and Television,* vol. 37, no. 2, 2009, pp. 80-88.

Carrera, Elena. "Embodied Cognition and Empathy in Miguel de Cervantes's 'El celoso extremeño.'" *Hispania, v*ol. 97, no. 1, 2014, pp. 113-24.

Castillo, David R. "The Literary Classics in Today's Classroom: Don Quixote and Road Movies." *Hispanic Issues Online,* vol. 8, 2011, pp. 26-41.

Cervantes, Miguel de. *Don Quixote.* Translated by Edith Grossman, introduction by Harold Bloom, Harper Collins, 2003.

Hutchinson, Steven. *Cervantine Journeys.* 2nd ed., U of Wisconsin P, 1999.

Johnson, Carroll B. "Introduction," *Cervantes and his Postmodern Constituencies,* edited by Anne J. Cruz and Carroll B. Johnson, Garland, 1998, pp. ix-xxi.

Larubia-Prado, Francisco. "*Don Quixote* as Performance." *Revista Canadiense de Estudios Hispánicos,* vol. 33, no. 2, 2009, pp. 335-56.

Man of La Mancha. Directed by Arthur Hiller, musical play and screenplay by Dale Wasserman, performed by Peter O'Toole, Sophia Loren, et al., 1972. IMDb, www.imdb.com/ /title/tt0068909/?ref_=nv_sr_1. Accessed July 2018.

Mc. Luhan, Marshall. "The Comics." *The Pop Culture Tradition,* edited by Edward M. White, Norton, 1972, pp. 89-94.

———. and Quentin Fiore. "'Time' has Ceased and 'Space' has Vanished." *Global Literary Theory,* edited by Richard J. Lane, Routledge, 2013, pp. 166-77.

"Representations in Sitcoms: Indian Men." *Representation in American Sitcoms,* 5 June 2018, jcpasiec.wordpress.com. Accessed July 2018.

Russell, P.E. "Don Quixote as a Funny Book," *The Modern Language Review,* vol. 64, no. 2, 1969, pp. 312-26.

Star Trek. Created and Produced by Gene Roddenberry, performed by William Shattner, Leonard Nimoy, Deforest Kelley, et al., NBC, 1966-1969, 3 Seasons, *IMDb,* www.imdb.com/title/tt0060028/?ref_=fn_al_tt_1. Accessed July 2018.

Suárez Sánchez de León, Juan Luis. *Tecnologías del humanismo.* Universidad de Huelva, 2011.

The Big Bang Theory. Story by Chuck Lorre and Bill Prady, produced by Chuck Lorre, Bill Prady, and Steven Molaro, directed by Mark Cendrowski, performance by Johnny Galecki, Jim Parsons, Kaley Cuoco, Simon Helberg, Kunal Nayyar, et al., CBS, 2007- 11th season 2018, *IMDb*, www.imdb.com/title/tt0898266/?ref_=nv_sr_1. Accessed July 2018.

Popularity, Paternity, and Porn: A Classroom Exploration of the Twenty-First Century Don Juan in Film

Tony Grubbs

Michigan State University

Introduction

DON JUAN IS ONE of the most recognized figures in Western literature. He has graced the page, stage, and screen since the early seventeenth-century as a personification of societal preoccupations and
problems. Don Juan's ability to change with the times allows him to survive
and thrive in contemporary mainstream culture. Over the years, he has been
represented in a number of ways including a libertine, an idealist, a loser, a
woman, a Chicano hoodlum, and a pedophile, just to name a few.[1] Indeed,

---

1 Don Juan is characterized as a libertine in the early manifestations: Tirso de
Molina's *El burlador de Sevilla,* Moliere's *Dom Juan o le Festin de pierre,* for example.
He is an idealist in José Zorrilla's *Don Juan Tenorio* and a woman in *Doña Juana
Tenorio* by Rafael Liern. The Marqués de Bradomín, the protagonist of Ramón de
Valle-Inclán's *Sonatas,* is portrayed in various stages of his life; especially notable is
the decadant elderly iteration in *Sonata de invierno,* who knowingly seduces his own
daughter. Don Juan is a defeated veteran and vagabond in Valle-Inclán's *Las galas del
difunto.* Jacinto Grau also created two versions of Don Juan. The *Marqués de Carillana* is replete with symbolism as it introduces the title character as a decadent and
ridiculous nobleman who unwittingly attempts—and fails—to seduce his daughter.
The later work, *El burlador que no se burla,* is highlighted by Don Juan being tried
by the Devil and a jury of 3 demons. He does not repent for his actions and dies
happy. Two Chicanx adaptations exist. Carlos Morton adapts Zorrilla's work in a
modern version set in a cantina in San Antonio, Texas. Clear echoes of Tirso's *Burlador* are heard in Octavio Solís's *Man of Flesh.* In it, the Juan Tenorio is a gardener
who seduces women of all social classes. See Armand Singer for an extensive list of

Don Juan has become a universal myth after more than four centuries.[2] In his 1993 annotated bibliography *The Don Juan Theme*, Armand Singer identifies hundreds of works based on or inspired by the famous figure, and this number has continued to grow in many forms of media over the past twenty-plus years.

The universality of the Don Juan character is unquestionable. Since his beginning in the seventeenth century, the Sevillian nobleman has embodied the preoccupations and crises that plague humanity. The countless versions of Don Juan and his diverse characterizations validate his relevance. In *Historia universal de Don Juan*, Edgardo Dobry notes that Don Juan not only seduces women, but also authors, historians, and critics. He states that Don Juan is not a canonical figure, like Hamlet or Don Quixote, due to the character's different manifestations throughout the world and across time (10). This malleability contributes to the universal nature of Don Juan. He is also relatable. Dobry suggests the following:

> Miremos, entonces, a Don Juan como figura contemporánea de nosotros. Como plasmación, en cada ocasión momentánea y provisoria, del impulso por alcanzar alguna forma duradera y consolidada de identidad y de satisfacción; como silueta de la ansiedad, de la errancia y el recomienzo, alimentados por la imposibilidad de sostener el deseo una vez que se ha poseído un objeto. (15)

Indeed, Don Juan's pervasiveness in all forms of mass media confirms his prominence in modern culture. Sarah Wright's *Tales of Seduction: The Figure of Don Juan in Spanish Culture* considers his impact in numerous media, including in chat rooms (1-5). She concludes: "Don Juan as a sign has come to stand in the popular imagination for seduction with its attendant ambivalent connotations" (15-16). She correctly asserts that "The cult of Don Juan shows no sign of dissipating as we move into the twenty-first century" (16).

In my experience, university learners have an inkling of Don Juan as a literary figure, and they understand a "Don Juan" as womanizer. In fact, a brainstorming activity in the classroom typically yields a comprehensive description of Tirso's Don Juan Tenorio in *El burlador de Sevilla*. However, Don Juan's relevance in a contemporary context is sometimes lost on the students as we move through the semester. Of course, his influence is recognizable to

---

representations of the Don Juan character up to 1992. Pierre Brunel's *Dictionnaire de Don Juan* is also a useful resource.

2   See Carmen Becerra Suárez for a preliminary study of Don Juan as myth.

all of us who teach early modern literatures and cultures to a twenty-first century audience, but numerous hurdles, both material and thematic, commonly
hinder attempts to connect distant times and places. The students might be
wary of the genres—especially poetry—of the classical works, or they might
not be convinced that the themes from such "old" materials are germane to
modern life. These presuppositions are precisely what instructors must address as they guide the class to recognize the relationship between the past
and the present. One way is to approach foundational materials through the
lens of popular culture and media, which reflects the adaptability of the Don
Juan figure in various forms of art and literature. For example, the familiarity
and accessibility of film create an approachable backdrop for discussion. The
students comfortably navigate the medium and Don Juanism, taking their
analysis in a direction meaningful to them. As such, it becomes evident how
past preoccupations and themes remain relevant, as the different manifestations of the Don Juan figure persist. Each rendering of Don Juan and his male
and female counterparts continues to reflect societal and cultural anxieties
particular to the time and place of their creating as well as open discussions of
current cultural and societal conversations (and how to address them).

In this article, I propose a class activity that uses three twenty-first-century cinematic versions of the Don Juan legend to demonstrate how the figure continues to be a relevant cultural marker. The analysis of *Broken Flowers*
(2005), *John Tucker Must Die* (2006), and *Don Jon* (2013), proves invaluable
because each text relates traditional themes to a modern context. Without
a doubt, Don Juan still compels us to interrogate a number of issues in a
wide variety of contexts: honor, decadence, love, social class, gender roles,
and religion. Each film introduces a Donjuanesque figure at a different stage
of his life (in his youth, prime, or old age) and highlights the modern societal preoccupations embodied by the protagonist. As the final activity in
the course, this film exercise synthesizes a semester's worth of class materials. The learners use analytical thinking as they examine the universality of
Don Juan and explore connections between past and present versions of the
figure and their respective sociocultural contexts. By building a bridge of understanding that spans centuries of Don Juan works, the students have the
opportunity to expand their cultural understanding of the present and how
it is affected by the past. They recognize how Don Juan embodies change
but, at the same time, remains familiar. My ultimate goal as an instructor is
that students identify and engage problems in their own situations, reinforce
effective communication strategies and, in the case of the Spanish course,
practice the target language.

COURSE DETAILS

I have used this activity in two different courses, one taught in Spanish and the other in English. The first is a fourth-year Spanish literature course taught primarily to Spanish majors and minors. The second is part of the general education curriculum required for all undergraduate students. Though it may be taken at any time during the students' college career, most students are freshman or sophomores, and only a few have a background in Spanish. This activity is adaptable to both courses since the movies are in English; in the Spanish course, the students complete the other tasks and carry out discussions in the target language. Following Oscar Mandel's categorization of Don Juan, I divide the class material into three units: Classical, Romantic, and Molecular, which I will define shortly. This division, while not perfect, acceptably demarcates the figure into comprehensible and workable categories. The quintessential Classical Don Juan is the protagonist from Tirso de Molina's *Burlador de Sevilla*, which is one of the required texts for this unit. A libertine, this impulsive nobleman is brutal, handsome, and unscrupulous. He rejects social convention and religious beliefs and has an insatiable lust that drives him to trick both men and women without any remorse. He is always condemned to Hell after his death. The Romantic Don Juan is more complex than his predecessor. He is less impulsive, more meditative, and extremely charismatic. This Don Juan is also sensitive, emotional, and capable of love. He is commonly portrayed as a misunderstood outlier who is in a futile pursuit of the ideal. Don Juan is not always condemned to Hell: in fact, he is often saved by a woman. E.T.A. Hoffman's short story "Don Juan: A Fabulous Event that Befell a Music Enthusiast on His Travels" and José Zorrilla's *Don Juan Tenorio* are the cornerstones for this section of the course.

The Molecular Don Juan defies a specific definition. This modern version takes just about any form imaginable. Inspired by the turbulent times and significant crises of the twentieth century, Don Juan's innovative and often reflective characterization openly interrogates not only the Don Juan figure, but also society. In their reworking of conventional models, the Molecular versions underline the anachronistic nature of their predecessors. George Bernard Shaw goes so far as to write a pseudo-obituary for Don Juan in his preface to *Man and Superman*. Besides the obsolescence of the earlier Don Juan figures, another aspect that stands out in many modern Molecular versions is a self-awareness on the part of the protagonist that he is not *the* Don Juan, rather a Donjuanesque figure. The activity that I propose focuses on the Molecular Don Juan, though the Classical and Romantic versions are play an important role, underlining the continuity of the figure.

INTRODUCTORY STUDY OF TIRSO DE MOLINA'S *EL BURLADOR DE SEVILLA*
Tirso de Molina's *El burlador de Sevilla* is the cornerstone of the Don Juan legend, so an understanding of this foundational work is essential to ensure learners' success. Here I offer a brief study of the characters and principal themes as a point of departure for classroom discussion. The *Burlador* presents the prototype of the Classical Don Juan. He personifies societal preoccupations and problems of the Spanish Baroque period. During this second part of its "Golden Age," Spain had found itself in a state of extreme decadence. On the political front, inept kings and ambitious courtiers struggled to lead the faltering empire. The Church, emboldened by the fervor of the Counter-Reformation, took advantage of its great power as society reverted to the traditional institution and its belief systems following the anthropocentric Renaissance. Corruption abounded throughout society, exacerbating for most the hardships of everyday life. Indeed, Spain suffered from a multifaceted crisis that encompassed philosophical, moral, economic, political, and social spheres. A sense of disillusion (*desengaño*) prevailed, and Spaniards questioned the idealistic tendencies of the Renaissance. This sense of frustration and impotence drove a strong creative reaction to the dismal situation. Artistic expression strayed from previous norms, producing distorted, degenerate, and absurd views of Spanish society as it replicated a general feeling of *ennui*.

The *Burlador* dramatizes Spain's decadent state during the Baroque period. Though set in the fourteenth century to shield itself from censorship, the *comedia* offers a comprehensive and critical view of a corrupt seventeenth-century society fueled by the mundane vices of its characters, especially Don Juan, whose ubiquitous maxim "Tan largo me lo fiáis" vocalizes his disregard and abuse of free will. He feels there is always time to repent, so he does what he wants when he wants. Don Juan's destructive, uncontrollable, and manipulative nature shatters social norms and religious traditions. Simply put, this impudent nobleman breaks all the rules. Only God is capable of controlling Don Juan. Divine justice is meted out by Don Gonzalo—the only exemplary character in the play—who serves as a God's messenger and enforcer as a stone statue that returns from the dead. While not as diabolical as Don Juan, the rest of the play's cast is not his opposite, and Tirso highlights each one's character flaws. For example, the two kings do not live up to monarchical expectations in the play. The King of Naples is weak and obsessed with honor, which is fragile since he is unable to control what goes in his palace. The King of Castile proves more admirable, especially at the end of the play when he restores social order with the typical arrangement of marriages,[3] but before that, his attempts to exert power over Don Juan fall flat. The other noblemen prove no more virtuous. Don Pedro Tenorio, the ambassador to Naples, lies to the King and allows his nephew Don Juan to escape after being caught in Duchess Isabela's bedroom. The cuckolded Don Octavio is Don Juan's foil. He is weak and unassuming, concerned more with his own interests than anyone else's. Finally, the Marquis of Mota, Don Juan's long-time friend and accomplice, is fooled by Don Juan, who attempts to seduce the former's betrothed, Doña Ana, through false identity. In terms of the peasant class, the men are either powerless when confronted by Don Juan, or ridiculous, as seen with Gaseno, an overly ambitious social climber who essentially hands his newlywed daughter Aminta over to Don Juan. The female characters are not spared Tirso de Molina's disparagement either. He highlights their moral, ethical, and emotional deficiencies in the *Burlador*. The lascivious nature of Isabela leads to her downfall because she invites a man she believes to be her lover to her room at night, a clear violation of courtly protocol. Once discovered, her implication of an innocent Octavio reveals a self-serving side that recognizes the easiest way to erase the blemish of her transgression is their marriage. The beautiful fisherwoman Tisbea disdains love and her prideful demeanor challenges patriarchal standards, and established gender roles. Don Juan's arrival on the shore of Tarragon tests her steadfast rejection of love, which she deemed as frivolous and for the weakhearted. Eventually, she falls for Don Juan's fancy words and false promises. After he abandons her, Tisbea claims to be burning up with fury and walks into the sea, reflecting the baroque tendency toward contrast and tension: fire and water, as well as the emotional weight she bears after the encounter. Doña Ana, Don Gonzalo's daughter, is betrothed to two men, Don Juan and Don Octavio, but she is in love with the Marquis of Mota. Her desire to marry outside of her father's wishes subverts societal norms. Her encounter with Don Juan ends tragically with Don Gonzalo's death after attempting to protect his daughter's honor. The imposter escapes unscathed and puts the blame on the Marquis of Mota by returning the borrowed cape he wore to infiltrate Ana's house. Don

---

3   The King of Castile marries off the remaining characters, the stock ending in most *comedias*. A.A. Parker suggests that the case found in the *Burlador* is one of the clearest with regard to determining the severity of each character's shortcomings by their "frustration" felt throughout the play and in relation to their nuptials. None of the marriages is ideal in the sense of "happily ever after," but one could argue that social order is returned as honor is restored as are social class differences. A discussion of poetic justice is useful because it challenges the students to consider the severity of each character's transgression and to reinforce that no one is completely innocent in the play.

Juan's last conquest, the country girl Aminta, is the victim of social ambition. She is an absurd character who is easily fooled by Don Juan. Aminta does not realize that his promise of marriage was false, converting her into the laughing-stock. All in all, the characters in the play combine to form a self-indulgent, disorderly, and unethical cast. Catalinón, the *gracioso*, serves as his master's conscience, reminding him of what good comportment is and warning of the consequences of bad behavior. Don Juan's contemptuous reactions to this advice further reinforces his contempt for social and moral normalcy.

Tirso de Molina's exaggerated representations reinforce the play's three major themes: love,[4] honor, and religion, spinning a web that underlines the morally and ethically deficient character of Spanish society at the time. Love is carnal, passionate, and empty. There is no hint of the idealized notion of Neoplatonic love, which strove to mimic the divine love that God shared with his faithful. Instead, we see illicit encounters, fickle lovers, and insatiable appetites. Octavio's description of his love for Isabela in Act 1 satirizes the notion of courtly love, and Ripio's lascivious description of love with a washerwoman satirizes Octavio's absurd pining for Isabela (37-39).[5] Of course, Don Juan exemplifies these tendencies. A mere glance suffices to awaken his lust and initiate his predatory behavior.

In "Defining the *Comedia*: On Generalizations Once Widely Accepted That Are No Longer Accepted So Widely," Matthew Stroud notes that while life certainly inspired the arts, the exceptional was often distorted further, offering a skewed vision of society (293).[6] The honor code, thought to be so prevalent in early modern Spanish culture, appears frequently on the *comedia* stage and most often through hyperbole. It makes for good theater. Stroud asserts that due to so many variations of the honor code, it cannot be taken seriously (293). This is the case in the *Burlador*, where an obsession with honor looms over all social classes. Tirso de Molina ridicules the Neapolitan king's obsession with honor through his reaction to Isabela's transgressions:

---

4   The *Burlador* explores how the characters use love as an instrument of manipulation to satisfy their appetites stemming from acute self interest and extreme egotism; an ideal, neo-Platonic manifestation of love is missing from the text.

5   For undergraduate Spanish learners, John McCaw's edition is recommended. All citations come from McCaw's edition. A more academic critical edition is also included in the bibliography.

6   Stroud's article is a response to A.A. Parker's 1959 article "The Approach to the Spanish Drama of the Golden Age." I recommend that the articles be read in tandem as Stroud's piece dialogues with the earlier study.

¡Ah, pobre honor! Si eres alma
del hombre, ¿por qué te dejan
en la mujer inconstante,
si es la misma ligereza? (36)

A lack of honor characterizes Don Octavio, who chooses to abandon
Naples instead of protecting his reputation and that of his beloved (42-43).
A dishonored Don Gonzalo dies in a duel while protecting his family's reputation (85). Don Juan has no honor. In fact, he savors robbing women of their
virtue:

Sevilla a voces me llama
el Burlador, y el mayor
gusto que en mi puede haber
es burlar una mujer
y dejalla sin honor. (3.1309-13)

In the play, the honor code is an absurd social construct that Tirso de Molina
forcefully criticizes.[7]

The theme of religion is evident throughout the play, but most prevalent
in the third act. Up to that point, Don Juan has murdered Don Gonzalo,
falsely promised marriage, desecrated the sacrament of marriage, brushed
off the threat of divine judgement, and abused his God-given free will. Don
Juan's contempt for the dead comes to bear when he runs across Don Gonzalo's statue while taking refuge in a church in Seville, pulls his beard, and
invites him to dinner. Tirso de Molina's treatment of religion is definitive:
God is a punishing god, styled in a Christian understanding of the Old Testament tradition. Don Juan is startled for the first time in his life after Don
Gonzalo returns as the stone statue to deliver him a message of his imminent
demise. However, it is the next night, when the stone statue (Don Gonzalo)
refuses Don Juan's confession before dying, that the protagonist realizes that
there is not enough time to repent. Quite the contrary, and like everyone
else, he should have been prepared for divine judgement at any moment. This

---

7   In the case of Don Gonzalo's vengeance at the end of the play, his actions
are removed from a social context as he enforces divine justice upon Don Juan. His
actions are outside the realm of the human social milieu and are better understood as
the work of God. Poetic justice on the social level, however, is imposed by the King
of Castile in the *comedia*'s last scene.

reinforces how the abuse of freedom brings about detrimental consequences. The stone statue (Don Gonzalo) informs the title character:

> Las maravillas de Dios
> son, don Juan, investigables,
> y así quiere que tus culpas
> a manos de un muerto pagues.
> Y si pagas desta suerte,
> Ésta es justicia de Dios:
> «Quien tal hace, que tal pague» (3.2752-59)

Don Juan's condemnation to Hell demonstrates that only God could control him. Indeed, the strong and clear message aligns with the dogmatic tendencies of Counter-Reformation Spain. It would have been a reassuring reminder that no one was above divine law.

While some learners judge the seventeenth-century *Burlador* as irrelevant, quite the contrary is true. It is fundamental to an understanding of the Don Juan legend. When examining Tirso de Molina's portrayal of the contentious society of early modern Spain, conversations arise about modern conceptions of the play's three principal themes. For example, in discussions about love, the similarities in current dating practices (hooking up, online dating, catfishing, Tinder, etc.) begin to align with those described in the play. Another particularly lively conversation stems from describing the nature of Don Juan's amorous conquests: can they be categorized as seductions? Also, the honor code, or the obsession with one's reputation, is recognizable in modern society. Finally, the prevalence of religion in society has never disappeared and remains a topic of ideological interchange. In short, by introducing the *Burlador*, an instructor opens the door for conversations about the development of these topics in the different literary versions as well as the suppleness of the Don Juan character as seen throughout time and in many forms.

The Activity: "Popularity, Paternity, and Porn: The Molecular Don Juan in Twenty-First Century Films"

PRELIMINARY READINGS AND DISCUSSION:
As part of the introduction to the Molecular Don Juan, I assign the students to read Shaw's preface to *Man and Superman*: "Epistle Dedicatory to Arthur Bingham Walkley," and/or fragments of José Ortega y Gasset's "Introducción

a un Don Juan" to establish the early twentieth-century notion that Don Juan is an anachronism. At the same time, we look at numerous early twentieth-century versions of Don Juan to gauge the character's malleability and dynamic nature, emphasizing that he is a socio-cultural product of the times. In addition, we talk about how the changes can be formal and textual, and it is the former that I discuss in class, leaving the latter for the activity. Next, we begin a discussion of the relevance of film in current society, followed by an introduction to basic concepts of adaptation. Selected readings from Linda Hutcheon's *A Theory of Adaptation* and Julie Sanders's *Adaptation and Appropriation* offer a point of departure for a conversation about adapting other literary genres to film. Lectures emphasize that adaptations are not inferior to source materials, quite the contrary, and that such judgments are unjustified. As we know, adaptation is a ubiquitous process that recreates old material available for a new audience. Sanders notes that adaptation is constantly shifting and that the spectator has to be able to participate in the play of similarities and differences that are passed on in a transmuted and translated form over time (45). More specifically, one of my goals is for the students to recognize the need to engage with the text within a present context through the relationship with past Don Juan figures, a process that makes the new works recognizable. The Molecular Don Juan especially embodies the adaptation process, which, Hutcheon notes, involves (re)interpretation and (re)creation of earlier works as an announced and extensive transposition of a particular work (7-8). The students should also read the short section "Literary Adaptations" from Louis Gianetti's *Understanding Movies*, which discusses different degrees of cinematic adaptations (398-402), in order to put the discussion in the context of film. In addition to recognizing Don Juan's importance in popular culture, this idea of recreating previous works becomes especially clear after completing the film activity.

CLASSROOM ACTIVITY

This activity is one of the last assigned in the course. The goal of the exercise is for the students to apply the analytical skills they have learned during the semester, treating the films as literary texts. From there, the students identify how to utilize the Don Juan figure as a means to question their own situations. It is imperative to remind students that the movies portray Molecular Don Juans, but the protagonists still exhibit characteristics of their Classical and Romantic predecessors, which makes them recognizable as Donjuanesque figures.

The class is divided into three groups, and each will work with one film.[8] Initially, the students watch the movie and address the following prompts to prepare them for the subsequent group work. These questions help them focus on pertinent points that can guide the exchange of ideas that occurs later in the activity:

1. What is the title of the film? Where is it from? When was it released? Who are the major stars and the director? (see the IMDb website)

2. In your own words, BRIEFLY describe the plot of the movie.

3. Describe the Don Juan figure. Why is s/he to be considered a Molecular DJ? Explain.

4. How does this Don Juan figure embody societal preoccupation and criticism? Explain.

Their responses serve as a warm up for the next step, when the groups meet (either remotely or in person) to discuss each member's individual observations and prepare a collaborative multimedia presentation (i.e., more than a simple Powerpoint presentation) to upload to the course's learning platform. The guiding instructions for the group analysis of the films are broad:

1. Provide the socio-cultural context of the film.

2. Identify the Donjuanesque characteristics of the protagonist and the different categories represented.

3. Explain why this figure is ultimately a Molecular Don Juan.

4. Discuss the importance of the character(s) as a relevant social marker(s).

The presentations are posted online for review by the entire class. Next, each student writes a two-part reflection paper that describes how their assigned Don Juan relates to the others; here, I remind them to concentrate on the other groups' observations so that they do not simply rehash their own work. The second task asks them to reflect on how Don Juan leads them to comprehend their culture better. These papers are submitted before the class meets so that I can read them. In class, we discuss students' findings and ideas. This multi-step activity leads to an understanding of how the three

---

8   It would be ideal for them to see all three movies, but this is not realistic due to time constraints.

movies connect Don Juan and current-day issues by discussing the distinct portrayal of the Molecular Don Juan. The presentations and the essays are graded separately. Below, I include brief summaries of the films and points of departure for discussion for each one.

POPULARITY

John Tucker Must Die is a whimsical teen romantic comedy that presents four high school girls' attempts to exact revenge on John Tucker, who was dating three of them simultaneously and secretly. Their efforts fail, as John uncannily transforms any compromising situation into a positive opportunity to further heighten his popularity. After falling for the fourth girl, Kate Spencer, who was coached by his ex-girlfriends, Tucker does not change his dating habits, but he becomes forthright about them, signaling a change in his persona. The protagonist can be considered high-school nobility: he is captain of the basketball team, dates the popular girls, and has the admiration of both the student body and the faculty. He is also rich and handsome. He demonstrates some Classical Don Juan attributes because he is a philanderer who takes advantage of his status to trick and seduce any girl who catches his eye. Like Don Juan Tenorio, Tucker is able to discern his targets' interests and weaknesses and uses this knowledge to seduce them. He is also dishonest. For example, he claims that he cannot date during basketball season due to his father's orders, but this is simply a ruse to allow him to surreptitiously date various young women in different cliques. He is resourceful and escapes unsavory situations without problem: when falsely accused of having genital herpes, he turns this around by becoming an advocate for the prevention of sexually transmitted diseases in teens. He is driven by his passion and his ego. At one point, he demonstrates bravado in the locker room to maintain his reputation, promising that he will seduce Kate that night. He is unsuccessful, however, because she saw a recording of his audacious promise. Echoes of a Romantic Don Juan also resound in the movie. Tucker seems capable of love and he falls for Kate—or at least he claims to—who is ideal because she is the combination of all of his past girlfriends, who are her mentors. Their romance does not work out in the end, but Tucker is redeemed in the eyes of the school. We are reminded of the similarities of the movie and Zorrilla's *Don Juan Tenorio* in a number of scenes, but three stand out. The first is his attempted seduction of Kate on a boat, which is reminiscent of the "Sofa Scene" (I, 4, iii) in *DJT*. In the second one, Tucker actually climbs balconies to get to what he believes is Kate's room, bringing to life Tenorio's claim: "Yo a las cabañas bajé, / yo a los palacios subí, / yo los claustros escalé (I, 1, xii).

Finally, John's variety of girlfriends reminds viewers/us of Don Juan's claim to Don Luis de Mejía: "Desde una princesa real / a la hija de un pescador, / ¡oh! ha recorrido mi amor toda la escala social" (1.12.662-65). Using high school as a microcosmos, the film brings to light such themes as the importance of one's reputation and honor. It also interrogates social hierarchies and how those of certain privileged classes face few obstacles, including rules, in life. Lastly, it presents romantic relationships as shallow and deceitful, an eternal theme in Don Juan literature.

PORN

Don Jon tells the story of Jon Martello, an easily recognizable stereotype of a hyper-masculine Italian-American twentysomething made famous by the MTV series *Jersey Shore*. Martello describes the important things in his life as: "my body, my pad, my ride, my family, my church, my boys, my girls, my porn," but not necessarily in that order. He has a long "streak" of bringing home women from the bar when he goes out with his friends, but his true passion is internet pornography, the only means by which he is able to fully satisfy his sexual appetite. Physical relationships with real-life women do not provide him the same opportunity to "lose himself" as pornography does. One night, he meets Barbara Sugarman, whom he considers perfect, and falls for her immediately. She tries to change Martello, insisting that he take college courses, change jobs, and quit pornography, to no avail, and they eventually break up. In the meantime, he meets Esther, a middle-aged widow, at night school, and she eventually teaches him about reciprocal love and passion. They are able to "lose themselves" in one another, and they save each other emotionally. Jon kicks his addiction to pornography for her. They fall in love, but it is temporary, a fact that both acknowledge at the end of the film. Martello presents several parallels with the Romantic Don Juan. This character is odious at first, but he becomes more palatable as he falls in love and is saved by Esther. Barbara's mistreatment of him also evokes a certain degree of sympathy. As Martello struggles with Barbara's attempts at grooming him to her standards (cf. William Shakespeare's *Taming of the Shrew*), he reverts to his old ways of watching pornography, which ultimately causes the demise of the relationship. He cannot cope without it. Martello's search for the ideal, however, is not found in pornography or the "perfect" woman, Barbara, as neither can satisfy his needs. Instead, he cultivates a sublime relationship with Esther and is saved by her, and vice-versa. A parallel can be made to the ending of *Don Juan Tenorio*, as Don Juan and Doña Inés are also freed from suffering and ascend to Heaven. *Don Jon*'s ending is less exhilarating:

the couple does not marry or live happily ever after, but they do find themselves at a satisfying stage of shared intimacy. Other similarities to Zorrilla's text are detected. Jon's streak recalls Don Juan's list of conquests and duels that the latter revealed in the bet with Don Luis Mejía. Jon's friends also worship his escapades at the nightclubs, just like the reaction of Don Juan's admirers in Buttarelli's inn. The film is reminiscent of an earlier Molecular Don Juan: Jack Tanner from Shaw's *Man and Superman*. The Shavian notion of a woman taking a man's "life force" is reproduced in Barbara's efforts to change Martello. The movie brings to light a number of contemporary issues. Addiction and its effects on one's life is a fundamental one. Students also tend to note the "hook up" culture and how it affects interpersonal relationships. Escapism is also prevalent. Finally, religious practices are criticized as Martello, while a practicing Catholic, does not live a righteous lifestyle; rather, he depends on weekly confessions and mass in an attempt reconcile his narcissism with his faith.

PATERNITY

Broken Flowers stars Bill Murray as Don Johnston, an aging and apathetic single man who has made his fortune in the technology sector. After his current girlfriend, Sherry, leaves him, he receives a mysterious letter from an unnamed former girlfriend that informs him that he has a son. Johnston's indifference surprises his friend Winston, a modern-day *gracioso*, who convinces him to visit the women that chronologically could have written the letter and even plans the trip. Five women fit into the time frame, and he visits four of them; the other is deceased. As he visits his past lovers, each situation is worse than the previous. Laura, a widow, is needy and insecure. The couple sleep together the night of their reunion, and he leaves the next day. Dora, a former hippie, is now an uptight real estate agent that lives a suburban lifestyle. She is distant, and Johnston spends an uncomfortable afternoon with her and her husband. Carmen is an "animal communicator"—not an animal psychic—who has a relationship with her female assistant. She is dismissive of Johnston. His last visit is to Penny, who doesn't hesitate to express her dislike of him. After evoking her anger, one of the bikers that lives with Penny beats up Johnston, who wakes up in his car in an abandoned field. He visits the gravesite of the fifth woman, too. Finally, he returns home to find another letter in the same pink envelope, but this time it is from Sherry. Johnston and Winston wonder if this has been a cruel trick. The end of the movie resolves nothing; rather, Johnston's paternity conundrum becomes even more puzzling because of two seemingly casual encounters. First, he unexpectedly meets a young man that fits the profile of what he imagines his son to be, but the mysterious youth runs away due to Johnston's prying questions. Second, the last scene features another young man, dressed like Don and listening to the same music, who passes by and stares steadily into the camera. This version is the most recognizable as a Molecular DJ. Johnston is old and aloof, and lives a decadent lifestyle. There is no doubt that the protagonist is a Don Juan figure, the most obvious clue being his name. Additionally, he is called a Don Juan two times in the film: initially, by Sherry as she leaves him: "That's okay, you're never going to change, but I'm just not sure that I want to be with an over-the-hill Don Juan anymore," and subsequently, by his sidekick, Winston, who asserts: "You are the Don Juan." Also, at the beginning, Johnston is watching the 1934 movie *The Private Life of Don Juan*, which reminds us of his provenance. Furthermore, an aging Douglas Fairbanks plays the title character, but his pudgy physical appearance does not coincide with traditional notions of the earlier Don Juan Tenorio. This reference foreshadows Johnston's portrayal and misfortunes as a Don Juan figure. Students will inevitably draw parallels with Johnston and the aged Marqués de Bradomín in Ramón del Valle Inclán's *Sonata de invierno*, or with the title character of Don Juan de Carillana by Jacinto Grau, if these texts are assigned as previous readings. In all three cases, we see a once-illustrious figure who has lost his luster. In addition, the three men suffer indignities not common to their earlier analogs.

WRAP UP

Wright captures the essence of the class assignment with the following statement: "We need figures like Don Juan to restore our faith in the ability of culture to engage with social order, rather than merely to reflect on it" (194). Don Juan's innumerable forms and ubiquitous nature establish a mythical stature that is recognizable yet original; new versions of the figure constantly dialogue with those of the past. This activity benefits from the learners' familiarity with film and the inherent relevance of the protagonist as a means to interrogate cultural problems. Such conditions facilitate the examination of the films with a critical and analytical eye. There are numerous learning goals for the project. The review and application of course material are the most obvious, but the project does not end with a simple comparison; rather, it culminates with a reflection on how Don Juan affects their vision of contemporary society and—hopefully—instills the necessity to change it for the better. His infamous persona appeals to his modern audience just like he did in the past. Indeed, the Don Juan figure continues to challenge the public to take inventory of themselves and their circumstances.

Works Cited

Becerra Suárez, Carmen. *Mito y literature. (Estudio comparado de Don Juan)*. Vigo UP, 1997.

Broken Flowers. Directed by Jim Jarmusch, performances by Bill Murray, Jessica Lange, and Sharon Stone, Universal, 2005.

Brunel, Pierre. *Dictionnaire de Don Juan*. Laffont, 1999.

Dobry, Edgardo. *Historia universal de Don Juan. Creación y vigencia de un mito modern*. Arpa, 2017.

Don Jon. Directed by Joseph Gordon-Leavitt, performances by Joseph Gordon-Leavitt, Scarlett Johansson, and Julianne Moore, Relativity Media, 2013.

Fernández, Luis Miguel. *Don Juan en el cine español. Hacia una teoría de la recreación fílmica*. Santiago de Compostela UP, 2000.

Gianetti, Louis. *Understanding Movies*. 13 ed., Pearson, 2014, pp. 398-402.

Grau, Jacinto. *Don Juan de Carillana*. La editora, 1913.

———. *El burlador que no se burla*. Espasa Calpe, 1947, pp. 125-219.

Hoffman, E. T. A. "Don Juan. *A fabulous event that befell a music enthusiast on his travels.*" *The Worldview Annex, translated by Douglas Robertson, Aug. 1 2019*, https://sites.google.com/site/theworldviewannex/home/translations.

Hutcheon, Linda. *A Theory of Adaptation*. Routledge, 2006.

John Tucker Must Die. Directed by Betty Thomas, performances by Jesse Metcalfe, Brittany Snow, and Ashanti, 20th Century Fox, 2006.

Mandel, Oscar. *The Theatre of Don Juan. A Collection of Plays and Views, 1630-1963*. U of Nebraska P, 1986.

Molina, Tirso de. *El burlador de Sevilla*, edited by Alfredo Rodríguez López-Vásquez, Cátedra, 1994.

———. *El burlador de Sevilla*, edited by R. John McCaw, Cervantes & Co., 2003.

Ortega y Gasset, José. "Introducción a un Don Juan (1921)." *Obras Completas*, vol. 4, *Revista de Occidente*, 1961, pp. 121-37.

Parker, Alexander A. "The Approach to the Spanish Drama of the Golden Age." *The Tulane Drama Review*, vol. 4, no. 1, 1959, pp. 42-59.

Sanders, Julie. *Adaptation and Appropriation*. Routledge, 2006.

Shaw, George Bernard. *Man and Superman: A Comedy and a Philosophy*. Penguin, 1976.

Singer, Armand. *The Don Juan Theme. An Annotated Bibliography of Versions*. West Virginia UP, 1988.

Solís, Octavio. *Man of Flesh*. In *Plays from South Coast Repertory*, vol. 3, Broadway Play Pub, pp. 109-67.

Stroud, Matthew D. "Defining the *Comedia*: On Generalizations Once Widely Accepted That Are No Longer Accepted So Widely." *BCom*, vol. 5, no.2, 2006, pp. 285-306.

Valle-Inclán, Ramón del. *Las galas del difunto. Martes de Carnaval*, edited by Jesús Rubio Jiménez, Espasa-Calpe, 1968, pp. 10-61.

———. *Sonata de otoño. Sonata de invierno. Memorias del Marqués de Bradomín*, edited by Leda Shiavo. Austral, 1997, pp. 119-213.

Wright, Sarah. *Tales of Seduction. The Figure of Don Juan in Spanish Culture*. Tauris, 2007.

Zorrilla, José. *Don Juan Tenorio*, edited by Aniano Peña, Cátedra, 1994.

Teaching the *Mujer Varonil* as the Wonder Woman of Early Modern Spain

VALERIE HEGSTROM

Brigham Young University

THE JUNE 2, 2017 RELEASE of director Patty Jenkins' critically acclaimed movie *Wonder Woman*—starring Israeli actress and beauty pageant winner Gal Gadot—inspired almost immediate reactions from myriad commentators. On the Rotten Tomatoes website, the film has a 92% "certified fresh" score and is #2 on the list of "Best Superhero Movies of All Time."[1] However, in response to the film's premiere, a slew of reviews appeared on news outlets sporting titles like, "Wonder Woman, Feminist Icon or Bodacious Fantasy Figure?" questioning the sexual politics behind the movie's protagonist.[2] Such controversies surrounding the DC Comics' character are nothing new; feminists, comic book fans and creators, psychologists, and pro-censorship advocacy groups debated similar issues regarding the *Wonder Woman* television series (1975-1979), the use of Wonder Woman on the cover of *Ms.* magazine (1972), the loss of her super powers in the 1970s comics, and the associations of William Moulton Marston's original

---

1   *Wonder Woman* held the #1 position on the list until the release of *Black Panther* on February 16, 2018.

2   In Lewis Beale's *CNN* editorial by this title, he firmly answers "bodacious fantasy figure." Lina Abirafeh asks a similar question in her *Huffington Post* opinion piece, "Wonder Woman: Feminist Icon or Symbol of Oppression?" Abirafeh comes down on the side of oppression. Director James Cameron entered the fray with his own opinions about the topic (see Freeman, Breslin, and Nevins). Zoe Williams, on the other hand, who recognizes both sides of the argument, calls the film "a masterpiece of subversive feminism." All of these op-eds are easily readable and can lead to great classroom conversation.

1940s version of the heroine with sadomasochism and soft porn.[3] For all of these reasons and more, Wonder Woman is a complicated and contradictory figure and a character about whom many college students will have strong opinions.

Similarly, early modern Spain's *mujer varonil* appeals to audiences and readers for a number of contrasting reasons, and students will easily recognize the parallels between and controversies about the *Comedia* stock character and Wonder Woman. The *mujer varonil* pleases because she breaks traditional social and gender norms, moves in a man's world, and, at least temporarily, can accomplish things that the male characters around her cannot. In contrast, the perennial popularity of these characters may depend on their sexual objectification. When a *Comedia* heroine cross-dressed, she, like Wonder Woman, revealed more of her body, and, as Lope de Vega recognized in his *Arte nuevo*, "suele / el disfraz varonil agradar mucho" (282-83). The polemic surrounding the strong versus objectified woman can serve as an introductory exercise in reading Wonder Woman and the *mujer varonil* side by side and recognizing parallels between the two.[4] Students may feel more eager to engage in spirited classroom discussions about early modern Spanish texts because contemporary interest in superheroes can make the *mujer varonil* more appealing and relevant.

In addition to serving as a hook to interest 21st-century students in 17th-century texts, Wonder Woman can help them identify characteristics of the *mujer varonil* that might go unnoticed. In her 1974 book *Woman and Society in the Spanish Drama of the Golden Age: A Study of the mujer varonil*, Melveena McKendrick carefully classifies the several types of this stock character

---

3   In "How a Magazine Cover from the 1970s Helped Wonder Woman Win Over Feminists," Katie Kilkinney discusses the impact of the *Ms. Magazine* cover. Tim Hanley details many of the controversies surrounding the various versions of Wonder Woman in his *Wonder Woman Unbound*. For example, Hanley recognizes Marston's "bondage fixation" as "fetishistic" and Wonder Woman's ability to escape the "bondage scenarios" as "feminist, empowering, and redemptive" (71). See also Michael Cavna, "A Look Back" and Jill Lepore's *The Secret History of Wonder Woman*.

4   Countless beautiful and "manly" heroines cross-dress in early modern *comedias*, such as Lope de Vega's *La vengadora de las mujeres*, Tirso de Molina's *Don Gil de las calzas verdes*, Calderón's *La vida es sueño*, and Ana Caro's *Valor, agravio y mujer*. In her novella *El juez de su causa*, María de Zayas suggests that these characters could convince their audience of their physical prowess and leadership skills. Alternatively, Cervantes explores the erotic possibilities of female transvestism in his portrayal of Dorotea in *Don Quijote* (I.28).

and offers examples of each.[5] In her conclusion, McKendrick makes clear that in Spanish the word *varonil* always carries positive connotations:

> it is essential always to bear in mind that while the phrase masculine woman in English has strong derogatory overtones, *varonil* in the Golden Age was invariably a term of praise and admiration, as much when it was used of women as of men. (316)

The book, however, does not define *mujeres varoniles* beyond this notion: "women who, through inclination or through circumstance, departed from the feminine norm of the society in which they lived" (43). A course on the *mujer varonil* might seek answers to the following kinds of questions:

- What does it mean for a woman to be "manly"? What does that reveal about the ways we think about gender?

- What makes a *mujer varonil* a *mujer varonil*? What are her characteristics and how does she behave? How does she manifest her manliness?

- How do the early modern works portray gender roles and nature vs. nurture? What happens to the *mujer varonil* as a result of her "manliness"? Is she rewarded or punished?

- Do the works frame the manly behavior in positive or negative terms? Do they promote or criticize new roles for women?

- What do the works that include strong women characters reveal about other social issues: sexual assault, racism, classism, the context and consequences of war, etc.?

- Why so many *mujeres varoniles*? Why do authors return to them? Are they feminist icons or negative stereotypes?

Framing the class with a set of questions like these—introducing them at the beginning of the semester, reminding students about them throughout the course, and returning to them in final paper assignments and exami-

---

5 McKendrick groups *mujeres varoniles* into six broad categories: the *bandolera*; the *mujer esquiva*; the amazon, leader, or warrior; the scholar or career woman; the *bella cazadora*; and the avenger. Recognizing similarities between these Spanish characters and various versions of Wonder Woman can move the critical discourse about the *mujer varonil* beyond McKendrick's categories.

nations—can help make connections between what they read at home and what they might discuss in class. This facilitates closer and more meaningful reading, better analysis, and longer-term retention of the materials studied.[6] A course on early modern Spanish Wonder Women can expand and make more explicit the definition of *mujeres varoniles* by recognizing their super-powers and heroic deeds, their theme music, relationship issues, origin stories, secret identities and their costumes.

Such a course could focus on any of dozens of *mujeres varoniles,* almost all of whom McKendrick includes in her book. For example, Lope de Vega's *Las mujeres sin hombres* portrays several Amazons, including Hipólita, the latter of whom becomes Wonder Woman's mother in the comic book series. Although it might make sense to search for texts—like Lope's play—set in the ancient world, instead I have selected the works I discuss because they will introduce students to well known, easily accessible texts,[7] written by a variety of early modern authors, including Lope, Tirso, Vélez, Cervantes, Calderón, Caro, Zayas, and Azevedo. Because of this choice, the course will read frequently taught texts through a new (Wonder Woman) lens.

Laurencia Encounters the "World of Men" and Joins the Justice League

The setting matters in texts about Wonder Woman and early modern *mujeres varoniles.* Jenkins' film plays out against a backdrop of World War I, poetically allowing Wonder Woman to move across "no *man's* land" in slow motion. Marston, however, set the original 1940s Wonder Woman comic books in his own historical moment, during World War II. The wartime setting matters because the Amazon princess leaves Paradise Island, a place of peace and harmony, to save democracy and women's rights from the evil war god, Mars. In both comics and film, war is the defining characteristic of "Man's World." The opening line of the first Wonder Woman comic book story narrates, "At last, in a world torn by the hatreds and wars of men, appears a *woman* to whom the problems and feats of men are mere child's play" (Marston 11). Marston believed that all women should be wonder women and that the coming matriarchy would bring peace to a war-torn world (Hanley 48).

---

6   See James Lang's section on providing a framework in his chapter "Connecting" (103-04).

7   All but one of the texts is in print in easily accessible editions. That *comedia* and most of the others are available online at http://www.wordpress.comedias.org/play-texts/. Additionally, most of these works are now or will soon be available in English translation.

A course on Spanish "Golden Age"[8] wonder women could aptly begin with Lope de Vega's *Fuenteovejuna* (1612-14?), the fictionalized account of the town that took vengeance on their own abusive military commander. In this *comedia,* the story of the strong woman Laurencia interweaves with the events of a war waged by Isabel de Castilla and Fernando de Aragón on the Iberian Peninsula near the end of the fifteenth century, the Second War of Castilian Succession (1475-1479). Isabel and Fernando, as well as other historical figures, appear as characters in the play. *Fuenteovejuna* lays bare the position of women in the face of war: Laurencia and the other townswomen become more vulnerable to sexual exploitation and gender-based violence, and at the same time they rise to the occasion and fight as women warriors. Laurencia rallies her female troops by declaring, "torne / aquel siglo de amazonas" (3.1791-792). The squadron of women Laurencia leads are like the Amazon warriors fighting on the beach of Themyscira (Paradise Island) in the film or the Holliday Girls coming to Wonder Woman's aid in the 1940s comics; women rally behind strong women leaders.[9] Laurencia (and many another *mujer varonil*) wields a sword, just as the post-1987 rebooted Wonder Woman uses the "Flashing Blade" or "Godkiller" made for her by Hephaestus. Calling attention to the context of armed conflict in Wonder Woman and early modern Spanish texts can help students place greater value on the larger issues raised by the historical background portrayed in the Spanish works.

Before Laurencia gathers the women of Fuenteovejuna, she enters the town council meeting like Wonder Woman as the lone female member of the Justice League. Hanley describes Wonder Woman's situation: "During the Golden Age, Wonder Woman was a part of the Justice Society of America but was relegated to the role of the team's secretary. In the Justice League [which began in 1960], Wonder Woman was a full-fledged member. For almost the entire duration of the Silver Age, she was the sole woman alongside Superman, Batman, the Flash," and five other male superheroes (109).

---

8   The use of the term "Golden Age" to refer to sixteenth- and seventeenth-century Spanish literature and art (already problematic when discussing questions of gender, race, class, etc.) becomes even more troublesome in the context of Wonder Woman and superhero comic books, which have their own Golden Age (the 1940s-1956), Silver Age (1956-1970), Bronze Age (1970-1985), and Modern Age (1985-present).

9   The first issue of the 1987 reboot of Wonder Woman (Volume 2) renames Paradise Island Themyscira. Wonder Woman recruits Etta Candy and the Holliday Girls, "America's First Women's Expeditionary Force! One hundred beautiful, athletic girls," in *Sensation Comics* No. 2 (Marston 43-47).

Although the *Justice League* television cartoon series (2001-2004) includes other female heroes, the 2017 *Justice League* feature film once again locates Wonder Woman as the only female in the room. In *Fuenteovejuna*, Laurencia herself explains her unequal position: "Dexadme entrar, que bien puedo, / en consejo de los hombres; / que bien puede una mujer, / si no a dar voto, a dar vozes" (3.1712-715). Not only does she enter the male space and insult the men of the council, she claims the right to fight the commander's tyranny: "Dadme unas armas a mí" (3.1760). Her words and intentions have the same effect that Diana's movement across "No man's land" does in Jenkins' film; both the British soldiers and the men of Fuenteovejuna rise to the occasion and choose to enter the battle. Laurencia's speech to the men of the town becomes a turning point in the play worth highlighting in class and could lead to fruitful discussions about the representation of women and parity in government, making the *comedia* more meaningful to today's students.

Antona García and Gila Giralda: What Makes a *Mujer Varonil* a Superhero?

Like Wonder Woman, *mujeres varoniles* often have extraordinary strength and other capabilities that resemble superpowers, as well as their own theme music and relationship issues, and they accomplish heroic or larger-than-life deeds. When Charles Moulton (William Moulton Marston's pen name) introduced the new character Wonder Woman in *All Star Comics #8*, he began by describing her amazing abilities: "With a hundred times the agility and strength of our best male athletes and strongest wrestlers, she appears as though from nowhere to avenge an injustice or right a wrong! As lovely as Aphrodite—as wise as Athena—with the speed of Mercury and the strength of Hercules . . ." (Marston 11). For Marston, Wonder Woman's loveliness and wisdom are superpowers and as important to his character's ability to set the world right as her speed and strength. Similarly, in Luis Vélez de Guevara's *La serrana de la Vera* (1613), Gila possesses remarkable beauty, strength, and bravery. Her father explains that, in addition to her "presencia hermosa," Gila has such daring that she will compete with any man: "no hay labrador . . . que a correr no desafíe, / a saltar, luchar, tirar / la barra," and the men are all intimidated by her boldness: "no hay ninguno que porfíe / a mostrar valor mayor / en ninguna cosa de éstas" (1.133-42). Not only is Gila beautiful, her super abilities allow her to defeat any man. Likewise, in Tirso de Molina's *Antona García* (1622-25?), Don Antonio Fonseca characterizes the play's heroine as a "milagro / de las riberas del Duero": "Asombra con la hermosura / a cuantos la ven . . . Sus fuerzas son increíbles: / tira a la barra y al canto / con el labrador más diestro" (1.170-74, 185-87). Like Wonder Woman, Gila and Antona are remarkably beautiful, clever, and capable.

The early comic books repeatedly compare Wonder Woman's superpowers to those of ancient Greek and Roman gods and heroes: Aphrodite, Athena, Mercury, and Hercules. Early modern Spanish texts also make explicit comparisons between their heroines and mythological figures. This occurs most obviously in *La serrana,* when Captain Don Lucas calls Gila "dos Hércules" and recognizes her as braver than Achilles (1.355, 466-67). Further, the play compares both Gila and Queen Isabel to the legendary warrior queen Semiramis, Evadne (the wife of King Argos), and Pallas (Athena, the goddess of prudent warfare). Lucas seduces Gila by promising her these titles as she fights by his side as his wife in Isabel's campaign against Granada (2.1610-612). Rodrigo Girón uses these names to describe and honor Queen Isabel in her moment of distress (2.1927-30). Gila herself refers to the queen as "tan divina amazona" (1.884), and Fernando refers to his wife as "Católica Dïana, y vencedora / de tanto cuello alarbe belicoso" (1.1041-042). In *Antona García*, the Portuguese count of Penamacor calls the title character one of the Fates, measuring out and limiting his freedom (1.588-89), and also "Semíramis belicosa," emphasizing her daring and willingness to fight (2.858). Both Wonder Woman and the *mujeres varoniles* move in worlds colored by classical mythological and legendary references; making this link explicit could increase student interest in the allusions within early modern Spanish texts that often seem obscure and, therefore, irrelevant.

Some *mujeres varoniles,* like Wonder Woman and other superheroes, have their own theme music. Wonder Woman got her first theme song, along with her own television series, in 1975. Elana Levine describes the way the words to the piece initially supported the women's liberation movement: "All the world is waiting for you / And the power you possess / In your satin tights / Fighting for your rights," but by 1977 de-emphasized her powers and women's rights when key words and phrases shifted: "the power you possess" became "the *wonders* that you do," and "your rights" became "*our* rights" (139).[10] Wonder Woman acquired new theme music when she made her surprise entrance in *Batman v Superman: Dawn of Justice* (2016). Hans Zimmer composed the "Wonder Woman Main Theme," titled "Is She with You?" and Tina Guo performs the piece on an electric cello. Multiple versions of the piece exist on YouTube, and Dan Golding's video essay "How Wonder Woman's Theme Music Went from Bombastic to Smart," which describes the

---

10   All four versions of the TV series' introductory credits can be viewed on YouTube (ScreenBlaster13).

ways a four-note riff came to define an entire film score, deserves classroom time. These pieces can introduce the theme songs in *comedias*. In *La serrana*, for example, Gila enters the stage on horseback at the end of a procession of villagers who sing her theme music. The several verses focus on her great beauty:

> Su belleza y su donaire,
> la Serrana de la Vera,
> viene enamorando el aire
> la Serrana de la Vera . . .
> ¡Quién como ella,
> la Serrana de la Vera! (1.227-30, 243-44)

In the final act of the play, after Gila has sworn to kill all men who come near her until she can avenge the wrong the captain has done to her, the words to her theme song have changed. The singer, wandering in the mountains, positions himself as the victim of the Serrana's violence and beauty:

> Allá en Garganta la Olla,
> en la Vera de Plasencia,
> salteóme una serrana,
> blanca, rubia, ojimorena. . .
> al lado izquierdo un cuchillo,
> y en el hombro una escopeta.
> Si saltea con las armas,
> también con ojos saltea. (3.2202-205, 2222-223)

The wanderer tells Gila that her song and story are well known: "Agora / no solamente en la Vera, / sino en Castilla, no cantan / otra cosa" (3.2236-239). Antona García has her own theme song as well. The villagers sing it to celebrate her during her wedding:

> Más valéis vos, Antona.
> Sois ojiesmeralda,
> sois cariredonda,
> y en fin, sois de cuerpo
> la más gentilhombra.
> No hay quien vos semeje,
> reinas ni señoras,

porque sois más linda
que la corte toda. (1.232-240)

The song, sung just before Antona meets Queen Isabel, underscores her
beauty ("ojiesmeralda," "cariredonda"), her manly strength ("sois de cuerpo /
la más gentilhombra"), and her superiority to other women ("No hay quien
vos semeje"). Presenting these lyrics as superhero theme songs can help interest students in the form, function and meaning of ballads found within
these plays. Just as TV audiences in the 70s knew the words to the Wonder
Woman theme song prior to watching each new episode, *Comedia* audiences
came to plays about the Serrana de la Vera and Antona García, already knowing their stories and perhaps able to hum a few bars of their songs.

In spite of their beauty and superpowers, the early modern and modern women behind these theme songs struggle with relationship issues. They
tend to have greater strength, wit, and capabilities than the men around
them. Perhaps as a result, they also seem less inclined toward romantic relationships and marriage. Throughout the Golden and Silver Ages of comics,
Wonder Woman refused to marry her love interest, Steve Trevor. In the 40s,
the Amazon needed to protect and rescue the inept Air Force major. In *Wonder Woman Unbound,* Tim Hanley describes Trevor as Wonder Woman's
"own damsel in distress" (29). The early comics incorporate scores of bondage images, and the Amazon princess, who can easily break her own bonds,
must frequently free Steve from his. By the 50s, Wonder Woman had fallen
in love with Trevor, but, although she wanted to marry and settle down,
her "pesky superhero job" kept her from fully committing to her boyfriend
(Hanley 111). The Spanish wonder women find themselves in awkward love
relationships with their own weaker male counterparts. In *Fuenteovejuna,*
captured and bound, Frondoso becomes Laurencia's Steve Trevor. Although
ten soldiers hold Laurencia captive, she manages to escape and plans the rescue of Frondoso, her damsel in distress. The *serrana* Gila initially spurns both
the Captain Don Lucas and the *gracioso* Mingo. She humiliates Don Lucas
at gunpoint, forcing him to leave her town. When Mingo tries to hold her
hand, she squeezes his until he cries "uncle": "Que me matas, Gila. ¡Suelta!
... Afloja, Gila, por Dios" (2.1279, 1285). At first, Mingo serves as Gila's Steve
Trevor; she sees him as weak and tries to teach him strategies to succeed in
competitions. In the end, though, Mingo becomes one of Gila's potential
victims, and, rather than rescuing him, she becomes the captor who binds
him with a cord: "aquí / traigo guardada una cuerda, / con que algunos hombres ato / para echarlos de estas peñas" (3.2446-449). Antona García treats

the advances of the Count of Penamacor in much the same way as Gila responds to Mingo—by gripping his hand until it hurts: "Mi amor / no es más que quebrantahuesos" (1. 930-31). Later, Antona escapes the bondage in which the noblewoman María Sarmiento has placed her by setting fire to the locked door and fleeing through the flames. When two Castilian soldiers take Penamacor prisoner and chain him up on stage, he becomes Antona's Steve Trevor.[11] Overcoming the two soldiers, she frees the count from his chains. *Mujeres varoniles* are almost always *mujeres esquivas* who end up rescuing their love interests. They can escape from their bondage, but not from their relationship issues.

In every comic book adventure (at least until the 70s when she loses her superpowers), Wonder Woman accomplishes amazing deeds. The *mujeres varoniles* before her also carried out astonishing feats. When Gila comes on the stage during Act 1 of *La serrana*, her skills and achievements link her with the Wonder Woman of the 1950s and 60s. The Silver Age Wonder Woman fights "countless sea monsters and mythical beasts"; other foes include a "cannibal clam," "giants and massive birds," "pterodactyls, rocs, dimorphodons, and even a space eagle" (Hanley 110). For her part, Gila does battle with a wild boar, a wolf, and a bear, and she brings the trophies on stage to prove her accomplishment. She describes at length her hand-to-hand combat with the boar, then mentions the other animals, before asking her father's leave to attend a festival in Plasencia in the afternoon (1.273-335).[12] During the celebration, she overpowers a ferocious bull (1.925-28). When Gila becomes an antihero or a supervillain in the play's third act, still larger than life, she overpowers five men in fairly quick succession. She robs, woos, and hurls a wanderer from the mountainside (3.2224-262); captures Mingo and ties him to an oak tree (3.2400-455); confronts King Fernando with a weapon and then pardons his life (3.2529-580); guides Andrés, one of Don Lucas' servants, toward her hut and then flings him down the mountainside to the river (3.2813-853); and at last greets Lucas at the door of her shack with her shotgun, confronts him with the truth, and throws him to his death (3.2920-

---

11   Kathleen Regan explores the unequal relationship between Antona and Penamacor, as well as Penamacor's passive and ineffective nature in her study "Antona García: A *Mujer Varonil* for the 21st Century."

12   The Silver Age Wonder Woman overcomes several realistic wild beasts: cheetahs, lions, and bears, for example (Kanigher 263-64, 277-78, 326-27, 342). Campier examples that might prove more fun for classroom use include the episodes in which the Amazon fights Giganta the Gorilla Girl, the Crimson Centipede, or the Demon Man-Fish (Kanigher 157-65, 306-18, 354-67).

3075). In their own way, Antona's exploits also appear hyperbolic. Before the play begins, she has saved her cousin on his way to his execution by picking him and his donkey up and carrying them to a nearby church. Angry with six soldiers lodging in her house, she drove them into the corral by beating them with a burning stick from her fire. Locking them inside her grain silo, she left them there overnight for the weevils to chew on (1.193-214). During the course of the play, in battle against the Portuguese, Antona kills ten men and wounds ten more, without messing up her clothes (2.476-77). She can be strong and beautiful at the same time. Moreover, in the third act, she beats up four rude Portuguese men and rescues the count from two Castilian soldiers while in labor, giving birth to twin girls in between skirmishes. Without resting, she decides to wrap the babies, carry them on her back, and return to the battlefront. Reading these episodes in light of Wonder Woman's own amazing adventures underscores the comic-book-style, larger-than-life exploits of the *mujeres varoniles*. A discussion about the unrealistic nature of their achievements could lead to insights about impossible gendered expectations and perfectionism.

MARCELA: THE *MUJER ESQUIVA* WHO ESCAPES ENCLOSURE
In his article "Containing Wonder Woman: Fredric Wertham's Battle Against the Mighty Amazon," Craig This[13] describes the social, cultural, and political forces that sought to "contain" mid-twentieth-century American women, including Wonder Woman, within the domestic sphere. These forces led to the shift from Wonder Woman's 1940s Golden Age (authored by Marston) to the 1950s and '60s Silver Age (written by Robert Kanigher).

> Over and over again, Kanigher returned to [the] theme of struggle between career and marriage . . . . Although Wonder Woman was still single, independent, and focused on her career, these personal struggles and desires to become married gave the impression that she had become contained. (This 39)

Wonder Woman's inability to have it all—her career and a marriage to the man she loved—meant that she always felt disappointed with the choice she repeatedly made to work as a superhero.[14] Early modern Spanish plays, for

---

13   To avoid confusion, I explain that the surname of article's author is This.

14   An alternative reading of Kanigher's storylines might suggest that, although she seemed truly disappointed to postpone her marriage, Wonder Woman saw her future marriage to Steve Trevor as a kind of bondage that would keep her

their part, almost always end by containing their *mujeres varoniles*. *Fuenteovejuna*'s Laurencia's adventures as a public speaker and military leader end after Frondoso regains his freedom and the two characters return to their traditional gender roles. In the play's final scene, Laurencia gets to ask a single question, "¿Aquestos los Reyes son?" (3.2386). Her father Esteban, her husband Frondoso, and even the *gracioso* Mengo become the town's representatives who, in extended speeches, plead their case before the Catholic monarchs, and Frondoso gets the last word. *La serrana de la Vera* contains the tragic anti-hero Gila by executing her. The discovery space curtain opens to reveal her body, like a female Saint Sebastian, attached to a column and shot through with arrows. Antona García seems to escape containment, but only because her play ends abruptly, promising a second half. Both *Antona* and *La serrana* reinforce gender norms by insisting that women should give up their manly pursuits and accomplishments to stay at home and take care of their husbands. Students could complete an assignment in which they identify specific passages in these plays that reinforce gender norms and make efforts to contain their protagonists.

At least one Spanish *mujer varonil* does elude the marriage, death, or some other form of confinement and control that the restoration of order might call for at the end of a *comedia*. In chapters 12-15 of Part I of Miguel de Cervantes' *El ingenioso hidalgo Don Quijote de la Mancha* (1605), Marcela successfully avoids having to conform to the gender norms of her day. Cervantes' novel frames her episode within the much longer narrative of Don Quijote, the middle-aged gentleman whose comic view of himself as a knight errant reads very much like a Superman-style superhero: "me voy por estas soledades y despoblados buscando las aventuras, con ánimo deliberado de ofrecer mi brazo y mi persona a la más peligrosa que la suerte me deparare, en ayuda de los flacos y menesterosos" (Cervantes 183). For her part, Marcela has the beauty of Wonder Woman and the other *mujeres varoniles*, "Creció la niña con tanta belleza ... nadie la miraba que no bendecía a Dios, que tan hermosa la había creado" (178), but the interpolated story never compares her to a mythological goddess or even a female monster (Medusa, for example). Instead, Grisóstomo's friend Ambrosio calls Marcela a legendary male beast, "¡oh fiero basilisco," the king of serpents (195). In the "Canción de Grisóstomo," the feigned shepherd sings of Marcela's great deeds, but according to Grisóstomo, Marcela's "hazañas" amount to driving him to take his life (191).

from fulfilling her important work of battling crime and injustice. The "Strange Power of the Magic Lasso" episode could serve in the classroom as a basis for a discussion of this issue (Kanigher 270-80).

Within the context of the whole episode, though, her superpower is akin to Laurencia's and related to Wonder Woman's "wisdom of Athena"; Marcela has stage presence and outstanding public speaking skills. When she arrives at the funeral, every man in the crowd feels astonished and speechless: "Los que hasta entonces no la habían visto la miraban con admiración y silencio; y los que ya estaban acostumbrados a verla no quedaron menos suspensos que los que nunca la habían visto" (195). Marcela's looks, like Wonder Woman's "beauty of Aphrodite," give her power and control over her male spectators.

A *mujer esquiva,* like Wonder Woman and other *mujeres varoniles,* Marcela has relationship issues, or at least the men around her have issues. She rejects the advances of them all, and so they want to contain her. Pedro, the goatherd who first tells Don Quijote about shepherdess Marcela ends his tale with this somewhat aggressive statement, "todos los que la conocemos estamos esperando en qué ha de parar su altivez y quién ha de ser el dichoso que ha de venir a domeñar condición tan terrible y gozar de hermosura tan estremada" (180). Marcela, though, uses her superpowers to avoid domestication. She appears suddenly, like a "maravillosa visión," delivers her stirring speech, and disappears as quickly as she arrived (195). After defending her, Don Quijote tries to follow to offer his assistance, but she has vanished, escaped the enclosure imposed on most early modern Wonder Women. In the classroom, Wonder Woman and Marcela can become foils to spark a discussion about both gender and generic norms that enclose so many feisty *Comedia* heroines at the end of their plays.

MORE WONDER WOMEN: ORIGINS, IDENTITIES, CAREERS, AND MAKING HISTORY

A semester-length course on Wonder Woman and the *mujer varonil* could include several more texts and many other features and themes pertinent to both the early modern and modern superheroines. For example, like Wonder Woman, Spanish wonder women, such as Rosaura in Calderón de la Barca's *La vida es sueño* (1625) and Leonor in Ana Caro's *Valor, agravio y mujer* (1628-1653), have significant origin stories and disillusioning arrivals in "Man's World." Furthermore, just as Wonder Woman takes on the alter ego Diana Prince, Leonor confuses others and herself as Leonardo. Rosaura goes further, creating a new identity for herself in every act of her play. Over the decades, Diana Prince moves up in the world from nurse to secretary to government agent to curator at the Louvre museum. Zayas's Estela/Fernando, from the novella *El juez de su causa* (1637), similarly progresses from slave to soldier to captain of the cavalry to viceroy of Valencia, but Ângela de

Azevedo's Irene, from *La margarita del Tajo* (late 17th century), falls victim to gender-based violence and murder because of her love for learning.

Finally, during the Golden Age of comics, the Wonder Woman books always included a short strip called "Wonder Women of History." The *Historia de la monja alférez, Catalina de Erauso, escrita por ella misma* (first published in Paris in 1892) would fit well within that series. The story of Erauso's exploits in Spain, Latin America, and Italy reads like episodes from a comic book—one surprising adventure after another. These same kinds of parallels with Wonder Woman surface every time a *mujer varonil* appears.

Reading the early modern Spanish *mujer varonil* through the Wonder Woman lens can focus attention on several aspects of the characters and their circumstances, which students might otherwise find uninteresting and insignificant. The answer to the question, *Mujer varonil*, "Feminist Icon or Bodacious Fantasy Figure?" will become more nuanced and lead to more thoughtful classroom discussions and essays. For example, even when viewed as powerful champions, Wonder Woman and the *mujer varonil* may not turn out to be the kind of positive, healthy role models sought for by feminists. A discussion might mention that Wonder Woman and the *mujer varonil* set an impossible standard. Very few women can give birth to twins, strap them on their backs, and return to battle, as Antona García does, and no one should have to. Additionally, Wonder Woman texts will call attention to a *mujer varonil*'s amazing abilities and larger-than-life feats, and her costume, accessories, and multiple identities. The setting and background circumstances, especially as they relate to historic wars or individuals, will stand out as more important. A character's origin story or personal theme music will take on more meaning. Looking at all of these features of early modern wonder women will help to answer the questions suggested at the beginning of this essay and generate a much more developed definition of the term *mujer varonil*, a definition based on shared characteristics, in addition to distinguishing categories.

Works Cited

Abirafeh, Lina. "Wonder Woman: Feminist Icon or Symbol of Oppression?" *Huffpost*, 23 Jun. 2017. https://www.huffingtonpost.com/entry/wonder-woman-feminist-icon-or-symbol-of-oppression_us_594d30bbe4b0f078efd980e3.

Azevedo, Angela de. *La margarita del Tajo que dio nombre a Santarén. Women's Acts: Plays by Women Dramatists of Spain's Golden Age,* edited by Teresa Scott Soufas, U of Kentucky P, 1997, pp. 45-90.

Beale, Lewis. "Wonder Woman, Feminist Icon or Bodacious Fantasy Figure?" *CNN,* 2 Jun. 2017. http://www.cnn.com/2017/06/02/opinions/wonder-woman-you-call-this-feminism-beale/index.html.

"Best Superhero Movies of All Time." *Rotten Tomatoes. https://editorial.rottentomatoes.com/guide/best-superhero-movies-of-all-time/2/.*

Bravo-Villasante, Carmen. *La mujer vestida de hombre en el teatro español: Siglos XVI-XVII.* Mayo de Oro, 1988.

Breslin, Susannah. "What James Cameron Gets Right about the 'Wonder Woman' Feminism Debate." *Forbes,* 26 Aug. 2017. https://www.forbes.com/sites/susannahbreslin/2017/08/26/james-cameron-wonder-woman/#b8959a740aab.

Calderón de la Barca, Pedro. *La vida es sueño,* edited by Ciriaco Morón, Cátedra, 2000.

Caro, Ana. *Valor, agravio y mujer. Women's Acts: Plays by Women Dramatists of Spain's Golden Age,* edited by Teresa Scott Soufas, U of Kentucky P, 1997, pp. 163-94.

Cavna, Michael. "A Look Back at Wonder Woman's Feminist (and Not-So-Feminist) History." *The Washington Post,* 26 May 2017. https://www.washingtonpost.com/news/comic-riffs/wp/2017/05/26/a-dive-into-wonder-womans-feminist-and-not-so-feminist-history/?utm_term=.974d32f6f309.

Cervantes, Miguel de. *Don Quijote de la Mancha I,* edited by John Jay Allen, Cátedra, 1994.

Finn, Michelle R. "William Marston's Feminist Agenda." *The Ages of Wonder Woman: Essays on the Amazon Princess in Changing Times,* edited by Joseph J. Darowski, McFarland, 2014, pp. 7-21.

Freeman, Hadley. "James Cameron: 'The downside of being attracted to independent women is that they don't need you.'" *The Guardian,* 24 Aug. 2017. https://www.theguardian.com/film/2017/aug/24/james-cameron-well-never-be-able-to-reproduce-the-shock-of-terminator-2.

Golding, Dan. "How Wonder Woman's Theme Music Went from Bombastic to Smart." *YouTube,* 17 Sep. 2017, https://www.youtube.com/watch?v=CTXVY9bDtVY.

Hanley, Tim. *Wonder Woman Unbound: The Curious History of the World's Most Famous Heroine.* Chicago Review P, 2014.

Historia de la Monja Alférez, Catalina de Erauso, escrita por ella misma, edited by Ángel Esteban, Cátedra, 2002.

Kanigher, Robert. *Showcase Presents Wonder Woman.* vol. 4, DC Comics, 2011.

Kilkenny, Katie. "How a Magazine Cover from the 1970s Helped Wonder Woman Win Over Feminists." *Pacific Standard Magazine,* 21 Jun. 2017. https://psmag.com/social-justice/ms-magazine-helped-make-wonder-woman-a-feminist-icon.

Lang, James M. *Small Teaching: Everyday Lessons from the Science of Learning.* Jossey-Bass, 2016.

Lepore, Jill. *The Secret History of Wonder Woman.* Vintage, 2015.

Levine, Elana. *Wallowing in Sex: The New Sexual Culture of 1970s American Television.* Duke UP, 2007.

Marston, William Moulton. *The Golden Age Wonder Woman Omnibus Volume 1.* DC Comics, 2016.

McKendrick, Melveena. *Woman and Society in the Spanish Drama of the Golden Age: A Study of the Mujer Varonil.* Cambridge UP, 1974.

McMillan, Graeme. "Wonder Woman Overcame Her Origin Story to Become a Feminist Icon." *Wired,* 5 Jun. 2017. https://www.wired.com/2017/06/wonder-woman-origin-story/.

Nevins, Jake. "James Cameron Repeats Wonder Woman Criticism: 'That's Not Breaking Ground.'" *The Guardian,* 27 Sep. 2017. https://www.theguardian.com/film/2017/sep/27/james-cameron-defends-wonder-woman-criticism.

Regan, Kathleen. "Antona García: A *Mujer Varonil* for the 21st Century." *Prismatic Reflections on Spanish Golden Age Theater: Essays in Honor of Matthew D. Stroud,* edited by Gwyn E. Campbell and Amy R. Williamsen, Peter Lang, 2016, pp. 193-203.

ScreenBlaster13. "Wonder Woman TV Series Intros." *YouTube,* 18 Aug. 2012, https://www.youtube.com/watch?v=nx2JdJhAL94.

Tirso de Molina. *Antona García,* edited by Margaret Wilson, Manchester UP, 1957.

Vega, Lope de. *Arte Nuevo de hacer comedias,* edited by Enrique García Santo-Tomás. Cátedra, 2006.

———. *Fuente Ovejuna,* edited by Juan María Marín, Cátedra, 1987.

Vélez de Guevara, Luis. *La serrana de la Vera,* edited by William R. Manson and C. George Peale. Juan de la Cuesta, 2002.

Williams, Zoe. "Why Wonder Woman is a Masterpiece of Subversive Feminism." *The Guardian,* 5 Jun. 2017. https://www.theguardian.com/lifeandstyle/2017/jun/05/why-wonder-woman-is-a-masterpiece-of-subversive-feminism.

Wonder Woman, directed by Patty Jenkins, Warner Bros. Pictures, 2 Jun. 2017 [United States].

Zayas y Sotomayor, María de. *El juez de su causa. Novelas amorosas y ejemplares,* edited by Julián Olivares. Cátedra, 2000, pp. 487-513.

The Fastest Lance in the West: Don Quijote, High Plains Drifter

Margaret Marek
Illinois College

THE PAST TWENTY YEARS have witnessed remakes of *High Noon* (2000), *3:10 To Yuma* (2007), *True Grit* (2010), and *The Magnificent Seven* (2016), and a movie version of *The Lone Ranger* (2013). The HBO series *West World* is now in its third season.[1] These events lead me to two trifling, yet fascinating, details. First, the intervening 115 years between *West World* and *The Great Train Robbery* (1903)—a silent, black and white, twelve-minute dramatization of its title, directed by Edwin S. Porter, widely considered to be the first Western movie—replicate the lapse between the first volume of the *Quijote* and *Tirant lo Blanc* (1490). Secondly, like Cervantes, who was shot in the chest and arm in the Battle of Lepanto, John Ford—arguably the most famous maker of Westerns— "took a shoulderful of shrapnel" while filming his WWII documentary, (1942) *The Battle of Midway* (Eric Mills).[2]

Don Quijote and the Western drifter traverse the same arid terrain. Like the *Quijote*, the Western undertakes issues of national identity, violence, race,

---

1   The influence of the *Quijote* is immeasurable, but that of the Western may be analogous: "The Spaghetti Western may have burned out 40 years ago, but you can still see its children in multiplexes around the world" (Jason Bailey 8). The terms "Spaghetti Western," "Italian Western," and "European Western" are more or less interchangeable and refer to the low-budget Westerns filmed in Europe, especially Italy and Spain, but also West Germany and France. "Zapata" Westerns are a subgroup of Spaghetti Westerns that focus on the U.S.-Mexican border.

2   See Bruce Burningham's nuanced analysis of Lope's *Las famosas asturianas* and Ford's *Stagecoach*, which elucidates extensive points of contact between the early modern Spanish *comedia histórica* and the Western.

gender, and even religion, points of intersection that, together, make this genre an ideal form of pop culture for the teaching of the *Quijote* to today's undergraduate students.[3]

WHERE'S THE BEEF?[4]: DEMAND, GENRE, AND COMMONLANDS

My initial motivation for teaching the *Quijote* by way of the Western was to introduce to readers new to Cervantes all-important questions of genre, for as Howard Mancing highlights: "[*Don Quijote*] exists because of *Amadís de Gaula, Belianís de Gercia*, and others of the same genre" (*Encyclopedia*; "Chivalric Themes" 144).[5] It is essential that students apprehend its longevity.[6] Before reading the *Quijote*, students analyze the frontispieces of the *Amadís*, the *Palmerín*, the *Belianís*, and others,[7] which anticipate the extremely for-

---

3   I teach this text regularly using the approach outlined in this essay, both in Spanish and, as part of a first-year or transfer-student seminar, in English. Some of these strategies are tried and tested; others are more recent developments, which I will adopt when I am next slated to teach the *Quijote*. When teaching the novel in English, I recommend Edith Grossman's translation.

4   This question became the famous and comical slogan for the Wendy's fast food chain in 1984.

5   Cervantine critical sources cited are deliberately overarching and more universal, and therefore especially useful for students new to Cervantes. Moreover, given that my chief aim is to offer insight about the specific pairing of the *Quijote* and the Western, these pages devote substantially more attention to the latter, reckoning that the present reader, having consulted a volume focused on the teaching of Golden Age Spanish literature, will already be well-versed in Cervantes scholarship and thoroughly acquainted with our ingenious gentleman.

6   A. D. Deyermond situates the earliest Spanish reference to the Arthuriad in the 12th c. and attests to its widespread popularity by the 14th c. (156). For Kathryn C. Esselman: "The knight, the quest, Camelot and, to a lesser degree, Courtly Love bear directly and indirectly on the history of the Western. The modern cowboy here became defined through a process of wedding the traditional frontiersman to the knight while visually defining him according to the conventions set by Buffalo Bill's Wild West Show and the Western melodramas" (9-10). See also John G. Cawelti (*Mystique* 86-87) and Holly George-Warren (6). Burningham draws the parallel between El Cid and the cowboy but argues that the latter bears even greater resemblance to the Arthurian knight errant or to Amadís and don Quijote (22). Diana De Armas Wilson notes that knights and cowboys share some common ground: "an ideology of good and evil, a respect for formulaic behavior, and ease with violence, a proclivity to idealization, and a salvific complex ('cavalry to the rescue')" (145).

7   For example, I pose questions such as "What do these images depict?" and "What elements do they have in common?"

mulaic nature of the *libro de caballerías*.[8] I screen the opening and closing credits to the *Lone Ranger* television series and trailers from various Western films,[9] whose contents are sufficiently embedded in contemporary U.S. culture that the material provides a touchstone for students, even if they are not fans.[10] This juxtaposition of the Western and the *Quijote* helps to corroborate the relative quickness and ease with which certain of Cervantes' characters—such as the priest, the innkeeper, and Dorotea, and—on a more protracted scale—Sansón Carrasco, and the household of the duke and the duchess, readily jump into the world of knight errantry and improvise accordingly.

While the *libro de caballerías* dominates the early modern Spanish landscape, it is difficult to elaborate a clear picture of its consumers or its exact rate of consumption. R. O. Jones counts about thirty editions of the *Amadís* between 1508 and 1587.[11] This statistic, impressive in its own right, is but a drop in the bucket when compared to the total number of chivalric books published in early modern Spain (53).[12] In the twentieth-century U.S., the

---

8   Another effective entrée is to screen "Thug Notes Don Quixote." This 12-minute YouTube video is uproariously funny and—for its type—fairly thorough.

9   Outside of *High Plains Drifter*, the films chosen for this analysis are somewhat arbitrary and by no means prescriptive, though it is helpful to include early and later films, as well as both American and Italian Westerns. Another useful strategy may be to assign students to view and summarize *The Great Train Robbery*, an exercise that models the practice of close reading, in which they become increasingly adept as they proceed through Cervantes' novel.

10   A confession: This non-*connaisseuse* grudgingly became an *aficionada* late in life.

11   De Armas Wilson cuts to the chase, calling the *libro de caballerías* "the first wave in the history of mass media and the entertainment industry" (143).

12   Jones cites Henry Thomas' reckoning: "During the hundred years following the publication of the *Amadís de Gaula*, some fifty new chivalresque romances appeared in Spain and Portugal. They were published at an average rate of almost one a year between 1508 and 1550; nine were added between 1550 and the year of the Armada; only three more came out before the publication of *Don Quixote*" (53). Keith Whinnom cautions against such tallies: "In the early part of the sixteenth century the average edition seems to have been somewhere between two hundred and two hundred and fifty copies; but the *Cancionero general* of 1511, a lavishly produced and extremely expensive book had—contrary, one might think, to all expectations—a first edition of 1,000 copies. . . . An unverifiable variable of this magnitude cannot be lightly dismissed. Moreover, while the early Spanish printers found it hard to compete with the mass-production of books in centres such as Lyon or Venice, in the second half of the sixteenth century they were better able to hold their own, and sizes of editions accordingly steadily increased. In spite of all this, the only realistic

Western movie holds the reins: "For more than one hundred years, moviegoers have sat on the edge of their seats, mesmerized by great train robberies, Indian attacks, cavalry charges, and shootouts at high noon. Yet, they have never grown tired of watching cowboys and Indians gallop across Big Sky country" (Richard Aquila 4). The Western's sheer numbers are staggering. Aquila estimates that about 2,000 silent Westerns were made prior to 1929, and more than 3,700 talkies between 1930 and 1959 (7-8). To this total we must add the 500 or so European Westerns, produced between 1964 and 1973 (Jason Bailey par. 1). Stephen Prince adds the extraordinary number of B films: "From 1941 to 1945, the B studios produced 645 features, of which half were Westerns" (247). Cawelti factors in books—most of the films were based on novels—and television series:

> Westerns constituted 10.76% of the works of fiction published in 1958 and 1.76% of all books published. In 1959 eight of the top ten shows on television, as measured by Neilson ratings, were Westerns and thirty of the prime-time shows were horse operas. At least 54 Western feature films were made in 1958. (*Sequel* 1)

These two genres cornered their respective markets, but neither is monolithic. When faced with two exemplary models in I.25, should don Quijote follow the prudent, long-suffering Amadís or the tree-uprooting, stream-soiling Roland? To frame this dilemma another way, who is the better Western hero, John Wayne or Clint Eastwood?[13] We shall revisit this question presently.

A NATIONAL BRANDING (IRON): AMBITIONS OF EMPIRE AND EXPANSION
Ubiquitous, elastic, and thematically appealing (from the perspective of the colonizer), the creation of empire inevitably infuses the arts. Hence, both the *Quijote* and the Western, disparate temporally and geographically, dexterously exemplify nationhood and expansion. Yet, the cowboy is—at least

---

criterion which we can usefully employ in defining our best-sellers is the number of editions through which they passed" (191).

13   Robert Warshow's description of the Western hero, be it either type, forcibly reminds us of don Quijote's discussion with the innkeeper in I.3: "The Westerner is *par excellence* a man of leisure. Even when he wears the badge of a marshal or, more rarely, owns a ranch, he appears to be unemployed. We . . . are not actually aware that he owns anything except his horse, his guns, and the one worn suit of clothing, which is likely to remain unchanged all through the movie. It comes as a surprise to see him take money from his pocket or an extra shirt from his saddlebags" (46-47).

in part—a Spanish creation, for during the period the term *vaquero* was applied to the cattle herders of colonial Mexico.[14] More to the point, the same systems of oppression that operate in the *Quijote* continue to proliferate in the Western. Critics of the latter wax hyperbolic. Michael T. Marsden conceives of a "Sagebrush Savior who is kind, yet strong; who is just, yet firm . . . The hero must be superhuman, and he must, above all, be invulnerable to the human weakness shared by those whom he must defend and protect" (99-100).[15] John Calvin Batchelor contends: "And the cowboy? He is the Declaration of Independence, the Constitution, and the Bill of Rights all at once . . ." (16). Alternatively, James Folsom suggests that "the Western mirrors a persistent nagging doubt in American life about whether the choice which America made to become a great, capitalist, industrial power was indeed a wise one" (81). Whatever view one might adopt towards the Western, Ralph Brauer correctly concludes that "Westerns are our fables of identity, our national 'epics' in which we express the complexities and ambiguities of our own existence" (119-120).

Knighthood is a direct expression of empire. Don Quijote's famous discourse on Arms and Letters in I.37 has its complement in John Ford's *The Man Who Shot Liberty Valance* (1962). At the funeral for rancher Tom Doniphon, the now-successful Senator Ransom Stoddard flashes back to his initial arrival to the town of Shinbone, where the new law school graduate from the East is terrorized by the powerful Liberty Valance. Symbolically, the outlaw rips fistfuls of pages from Stoddard's lawbooks, beats him to within an inch of his life, and leaves him for dead. The film equivocates, privileging letters and arms in turn. Stoddard establishes a school but in the end must duel against Valance. The shooting propels Stoddard into immediate political and romantic success, but the identity of the shooter is later called into question, and Hallie Stoddard continues to harbor feelings for Doniphon. Unless it is enforced by the gun, the film seems to imply, the law is of little use.

The violence, racism, and oppression inherent to the Western parallels the thematic presence of the figure of the Moor throughout early Spanish lit-

---

14   As Burningham observes: "It is far from incidental, for instance, that in some sectors of U.S. society John Wayne has become a kind of patron saint, similar in many ways to Spain's medieval Santiago Matamorros" (10). He goes on to note that Bartolomé de las Casas attests to the use of the battle cry "¡Santiago!" in the conquest of Mexico (10).

15   Marsden's assessment bears keeping in mind. Is this, then, our yardstick against which to measure the Stranger of *High Plains Drifter*?

erature.[16] The colonists' persecution, removal, and genocide of Native Americans in the U.S. provides a useful backdrop to Philip III's expulsion of the *Moriscos* from the Iberian Peninsula in 1609, which the *Quijote* references in II.54. Films such as *Stagecoach* (1939) and *Fort Apache* (1948) present the Apache as bloodthirsty and shrewd.[17] In *Stagecoach*, Doc Boone and banker Henry Gateway respectively warn of Apache "butchers," who "strike like rattlesnakes." The violent and unstable Lieutenant Colonel Thursday, who landed in Fort Apache after having been demoted, seeks to restore his former glory by vanquishing the Apache. Despite this largely unilateral portrayal, as is the case with Cervantes, these sentiments do, at least occasionally, originate from the mouths of characters who are themselves problematic—Doc Boone is a drunk; Gateway is a ruthless tycoon; Thursday is unhinged and despotic.

A second—but still problematic—possibility, for both the Native American and the Moorish outlaw, is a romanticized portrayal. Such individuals have proven themselves demonstrably noble or trustworthy. For example, Lightfoot—who is half Comanche—helps the title character to hunt down the bank robbers in *Cahill, U.S. Marshal* (1973), and the Native American doctor of *True Grit* (1969) treats Mattie Ross' snakebite, saving her life against improbable odds. Cervantes' portrait of *Morisco* Ricote, too, is in many ways quite sympathetic. These figures, however, are truly exceptional. In contrast, the more average Cide Hamete Benengeli, judged to be a liar by default, is perennially accused of taking liberties with don Quijote's history.

If the Western "is always about America rewriting and interpreting her own past, however honestly or dishonestly" (Philip French 24), it is no surprise that the homogenized cinematic hero does not accurately reflect the real-life cowherd, who "came from a variety of backgrounds: Easterners seeking adventure, Texans, European immigrants, Mexicans, and ex-slaves, with roughly two-thirds being white and one-third black or Mexican" (George-

---

16   See Burningham's analysis of the respective treatment of these figures (*caballero*/cowboy, Moor/Indian) in the *comedia* and the Western.

17   Other Westerns, such as *My Darling Clementine* (1946), Ted Post's *Hang 'Em High* (1968), and Leone's *Dollars Trilogy*, do not contain an explicit Native American presence, relying instead on the white outlaw antagonist. Even still, the objective of the Western is to extol the expansion of territory, whether or not the film contains Native American characters. When they do so, it is consistently in opposition to the white cowboy hero. Cawelti conflates both Indian and outlaw as "savage": "The role of savage is more or less interchangeable between Indians or outlaws, since both groups are associated with lawlessness, a love of violence, and rejection of the town's settled way of life" (*Sequel* 35).

Warren 13). For Cawelti, this refashioning stems from the vision of prominent white eastern aristocrats such as Theodore Roosevelt, Owen Wister,
and Frederic Remington, who traveled west and brought back a hero created
in their own image (*Sequel* 37-38).[18] As a result, endemic to the Western is the
assimilation, removal and slaughter of Native Americans; the institution of
slavery; and the misappropriation of Mexican lands. This process transposes
that of Alonso Quijano, who has fashioned himself in the image of the protagonists of the *libro de caballerías*. However, don Quijote pledges in II.6
to bolster His Majesty's fleet in Naples, Sicily, and Malta. Even as his vision
conflates literary knights errant and early modern soldiers, don Quijote em-
braces his king's expansionist tendencies.

GRASS-FED NOTIONS: «*LA VERDADERA HISTORIA*»
In the same way that the Spanish Golden Age is unprecedented in terms of its
hegemony and literary output, historical events (and history as a discipline)
crafted the West and the Western. The frontier thesis, which predominated
for nearly a century, was first presented by Frederick Jackson Turner's paper
"The Significance of the Frontier in American History" at the 1893 meeting
of the American Historical Association in Chicago. In sum, the westward
progression of the frontier forged the democratic and individualistic nature
unique to the United States (i.e., as differentiated from Europe), thereby
establishing (white) America's signature identity. Jack Nachbar clarifies its
implications for the Western:

> [T]he primal American experience was over; as of 1890, census reports
> showed that the frontier was officially closed. Western movies, with their
> historical time customarily fixed between 1860 and 1890 and their loca-
> tion in the sparsely settled areas West of the Mississippi, are thus a per-
> petual re-enactment of the last moments of the white man's settlement
> of the wild American landscape. (3-4)

Simultaneously, historic frontiersman, buffalo hunter, Pony Express
rider, and military scout William Frederick, aka Buffalo Bill, starred in Wild
West shows. These traveling vaudeville performances, popular in the U.S. and
in Europe from the 1870 to the 1920s, showcased reenactments, shooting,

---

18   Wister authored *The Virginian* (1902), considered to be the first Western
novel; Remington was a well-known painter, illustrator, and journalist. De Armas
Wilson traces Wister's somewhat romanticized comparison in "The Course of Empire" between Sir Lancelot and the Texas cowboy (145).

and rodeo skills. As George-Warren notes, "Sitting Bull (Tatanka-Iyotanka), chief of Hunkpapa Lakota, joined the Wild West show for four months in 1885; he rode once around the arena every performance for $50 a week" (38). Many of the scenes from Buffalo Bill later became integrated in early Western movies (Richard Etulain 23). The historian coincides alongside and within the historical figure/celebrity entertainer. As Aquila, citing Louis S. Warren, observes: "Ironically, just a few miles away from where Turner was analyzing the end of the frontier at a gathering of historians, Buffalo Bill Cody's Wild West show was doing banner business right next door to the World's Columbian Exposition. Cody's colorful company of cowboys, Indians, and other frontier types attracted more than three million customers eager to experience the American West" (13).[19]

A mishmash of historical and literary figures inhabits don Quijote's "verdadera historia." In I.32, the priest attempts to disabuse the innkeeper's notion that *Don Cirongilio de Tracia* and *Felixmarte de Hircania* are factual accounts: "se consiente imprimir y que haya tales libros, creyendo, como es verdad, que no ha de haber alguno tan ignorante, que tenga por historia verdadera ninguna de estos libros" (325).[20] The Western deposits historical figures—including lawmen James Butler Hickok, "Wild Bill" (1837-1876); Wyatt Earp (1848-1929); and Bartholomew William "Bat" Masterson; as well as outlaws Jesse James (1847-1882); Henry McCarty, aka, William H. Bonney, "Billy the Kid" (1859-1881); and Robert Leroy Parker, "Butch Cassidy" (1866-1908)—onto the fictional plane. At times, characters themselves create fictions. Bat Masterson and Wyatt Earp worked as consultants on various Western films (George-Warren 22). In I.22, freed galley slave Ginés de Pasamonte proclaims himself author of the forthcoming and (ostensibly) highly acclaimed *La vida de Ginés de Pasamonte*. Inspiration for this character likely comes from an autobiographer known to Cervantes (Mancing *Encyclopedia*; "Ginés de Pasamonte" 334-35).

«DEL DONOSO Y GRANDE ESCRUTINIO»: THE SPANISH INQUISITION
AND THE MOTION PICTURE PRODUCTION CODE
The Inquisition published its Índice de libros prohibidos in 1551. Jones outlines the stringent procedures for a text to be licensed and approved for pub-

---

19   Furthermore, quick on the heels of the novel's publication and exportation to the Americas, don Quijote and Sancho are incarnated on both continents in spectacles such as processions and masquerades (Mancing *Encyclopedia*; "Reception History of *Don Quixote*" 603).

20   All citations to the *Quijote* come from Francisco Rico's edition.

lication under the reign of Philip II. Beginning in 1558, books had to contain the *aprobación*, indicating that it had passed censors' approval. The importation of unlicensed books was a capital offense (76-77).[21] In I.6 the priest and the barber, along with the housekeeper and the niece, burn the more than a hundred pricey, "muy bien encuadernados" volumes comprising don Quijote's library (60). The reader laughs right along with the priest at the housekeeper's superstitious sprinkling of holy water on the offending volumes, but the licentiate's hasty, uninformed, and reckless evaluation of these texts proves every bit as quixotic as don Quijote's believing their every word.

The Western experienced its own brush with the law, and with priestly sanction.[22] At first, censorship of the motion picture industry was enacted at the state or even municipal level, beginning with Chicago in 1907. In the following year, the licenses of more than 500 theaters were revoked in New York (John Hess).[23] In the attempt to stave off federally-mandated censorship, Hollywood created the New York Board of Motion Picture Censorship,[24] but increasing scandals, such as the implication of comedic silent film star Roscoe Arbuckle in the death of actress Virginia Rappe, spurred additional backlash. The industry responded by creating the Motion Pictures Producers and Distributors of America (MPPDA) in 1922. The MPPDA paid William Hays, former U.S. Postmaster General under the Harding administration, a yearly salary of $150,000 "to relieve the pressure between Hollywood and Washington and lobby for the interests of the studios" (Hess). In 1927 Hays, "an upright teetotaling elder of the Presbyterian Church," drafted a set of guidelines entitled "Don'ts or Be Carefuls" (Doherty 2). The Production code, authored in 1929 by Hollywood insider Martin Quigley and Jesuit priest Daniel Lord, specifically prohibits nudity, sexual intercourse, profane and obscene language, torture, and disrespectful use of the flag. Films must distinguish unequivocally between Good and Evil and may not ridicule religion or include religious fig-

---

21   Mancing's *Reference Guide* provides succinct historical context for the Inquisition, pp. 60-62. Monty Python's Spanish Inquisition sketches do not go amiss here; nor does the "Sam Peckinpah's 'Salad Days'" sketch, which satirizes the extreme violence for which Peckinpah was well known.

22   Thomas Doherty asserts that "though the Code was a deeply Catholic document in tone and temper, the Jesuit theology was concealed for tactical reasons under a broader, Judeo-Christian blanket" (3).

23   Hess's concise, informative, and entertaining overview of the topic, beginning with the first prohibitions in Maine in 1897 to today's rating system, would work well as an assigned class text.

24   This body later became the National Review Board.

ures as comic characters or villains. Adultery is permitted, provided that it is neither explicit nor central to the plot (Motion Picture Production Code).

In 1933, when the Code remained unenforced, the Catholic Church founded the Legion of Decency to identify objectionable content and to urge boycott of offending films. Hays presided over the Production Code Administration (PCA), which reviewed scripts pre-production and then evaluated the film once cut. Certified films received "a Code Seal printed on the title card of each Hollywood film, an emblem that would be the motion picture equivalent of the imprimatur the Vatican stamped on approved books" (Doherty 5).[25] Hays appointed Joseph Breen, himself a devout Catholic, to oversee this process. Breen sent the following communiqué in 1947 regarding *David and Bathsheba*, which was not released until 1951:

> We direct your particular attention to the need for the greatest possible care in the selection and photographing of the costumes and dresses of your women. The Production Code makes it mandatory that the intimate parts of the body—specifically, the breasts of the women—to be fully covered at all times. Any compromise with this regulation will compel us to withhold approval of your picture. (Doherty 7-8)

The Breen Office had rejected Howard Hughes' *The Outlaw* (1941), whose initial release was delayed until 1943, for this same reason.[26] However, with WWII, the increased importation of foreign films, and the ending of the Hollywood studio system, the Code underwent change. In 1968 the industry adopted letter classification system, a form of which is still in use today.

"THEY DIDN'T KNOW HIM WHEN HE DRIFTED INTO TOWN. NOW THEY'LL NEVER FORGET HIM."[27]

Amongst Westerns, like the *Quijote* amongst chivalric books, *High Plains Drifter* (1973) deserves special recognition. At the time of its premiere, Eastwood's dark film, if not exactly parodic, departs from the traditional American Western. These two iconic texts coincide in remarkable ways. By default, both are set in depopulated lands, accessible only by horseback and administered—at least provisionally—by frontier justice. Also, both contain the

---

25   As Doherty goes on to note: "Studio-affiliated theaters that dared to screen a film without a Code Seal would be fined $25,000" (5).

26   At this point the class might view the promotional materials for this Western, along with a short clip.

27   So boasts the narrator in the official trailer to *High Plains Drifter*.

same set of stock characters: priest/preacher, barber, innkeeper, muleteer/
freighter. Like don Quijote, the Stranger commissions a short, coarse, comedic sidekick. Like Sancho, the timorous and loquacious Mordecai is fond of
drink and material goods yet loyal, made of strong moral fiber. Governorship
is thrust upon Mordecai when the Stranger instates him as sheriff and mayor
of Lago. Improbably, like Sancho, he governs effectively.

The choleric don Quijote is no Stranger. In the first volume he readily
declares himself before going into battle. In the second, accurately if wrong-
headedly, he expects those he meets to have read his history. In contrast, the
comparatively phlegmatic Stranger steadfastly refuses to disclose his identity.
The Stranger's unmatched aptitude as a gunslinger provides an antithesis to
don Quijote's adventitious victories, such as against the Biscayan.[28] While the
havoc wreaked by don Quijote is incidental—importantly, he never wounds
fatally—the depraved Stranger starts off by shooting the town's hitmen and
raping townswoman Callie Travers. He then exacts extravagant payment for
his protection, in the form of two pairs of hand-tooled boots, a decorated
saddle, as well as firearms and a round of drinks for all of Lago. In the end,
the Stranger bullwhips Cole Carlin, reenacting Lago's initial killing of the
federal marshal. If the film's vision is at all quixotic in the romantic sense,
it is only because the Stranger and Mordecai have avenged the voiceless Jim
Duncan, whose soul may finally rest in peace.

Despite these differences, the two heroes resemble each other in striking
ways. Don Quijote sallies forth "para defender las doncellas, amparar las viu-
das y socorrer a los huérfanos y a los menesterosos" (I.11; 98-99). The Stranger
appears seemingly out of nowhere as if riding through the mist, in order to
set Lago to rights. Don Quijote, from "un lugar de la Mancha cuyo nombre
no quiero acordarme," abides by the rules of knight errantry. The Stranger,
too, adheres to a strict moral code, albeit an unconventional one. Like don
Quijote, the Stranger advocates for the underdog, supplying blankets and
candy from the general store to a Native American family and attempting
to teach the townspeople to defend themselves. Both the cowboy and the
knight demand restitution from wrongdoers. The latter commands that his
defeated subjects appear before Dulcinea. The former demands 35 sheets,
200 gallons of red paint, and a barbecued steer and obliges corrupt hotelier
Lewis Belding to dismantle his own barn to build picnic tables.[29]

---

28   Outlaw Cole Carlin, like don Quijote (as well as the servant Malchus in
the four Gospel accounts, and much more recently, J. K. Rowling's George Weasley),
suffers the loss of an ear in battle.

29   Along with Camacho's wedding, this sight brings to mind an opening
scene of Leone's *Once Upon a Time in the West* (1968). The whole town has been

Don Quijote and the Stranger leave considerable material destruction in the wake of their battles. When the Stranger first rides into Lago, the viewer can almost smell the newly cut lumber used to create the pristine town, flush with the ill begotten fruits of the illegally placed mine. Paradoxically, the graveyard not only survives intact, but experiences growth and renewal. If the Stranger vanquishes real villains to don Quijote's imaginary ones, both are, for a time, deluded. Not until the full depth of Lago's treachery has been revealed, in part through the supernatural or fantastic visions experienced by the Stranger, does he—along with the viewer—conclude that no one in the town is worthy of redemption, excepting Mordecai and Sarah Belding, its citizens having colluded with the very outlaws from whom they have sought his protection.

Triumphantly riding out of Lago's ashes, the Stranger composes the negative image to don Quijote's. In the final scene he reveals himself to Mordecai, who carves a tombstone for Marshal Duncan.[30] Conversely, after his irrevocable defeat at the hands of Sansón Carrasco, Alonso Quijano recants on his deathbed. His tombstone, too, is carved: "Déjanse de poner aquí los llantos de Sancho, sobrina y ama de don Quiote, los nuevos epitafios de su sepultura" (1104). Don Quijote returns to the annals of La Mancha: "Este fin tuvo el ingenioso hidalgo de la Mancha, cuyo lugar no quiso poner Cide Hamete puntualmente, por dejar que todas las villas y lugares de la Mancha contendiesen entre sí por ahijársele y tenérsele por suyo. . ." (1104). The Stranger disappears back into the mist.

THE GOOD, THE BAD AND THE UGLY: SHOWDOWN AT THE CORRAL (*DE COMEDIAS*)

As happens with celebrity feuds, the sordid details elude us. And so the complicated relationship between Cervantes and Lope: "Lo cierto, sin embargo, es que las causas nunca han quedado del todo esclarecidas" (César Vidal 35).[31] In part, we are dealing with a simple matter of professional opinion.[32] Just as Cervantes reproached the *comedias* produced by the so-nicknamed *Fé-*

---

invited to a wedding reception that will never take place. Tables are lavishly set outdoors with red-checked tablecloths.

30   The viewer is meant to equate the Stranger with the marshal, played by Buddy Van Horn, Eastwood's stunt double. In addition, the Stranger dreams about Duncan's murder, lying in a posture that mimics that of the dying marshal.

31   See Vidal, who despite this assertion, provides a painstakingly detailed and comprehensive account of the information that does exist.

32   When teaching the *Quijote* in Spanish, of course, one may assign excerpts from the *Arte nuevo* to further contextualize this rivalry.

nix, some fans of the American Western take issue with the newer Spaghetti Western. The two types of Western heroes referenced early on in this essay, embodied in the protagonists played by John Wayne and Clint Eastwood, correspond respectively to these two competing visions.

While the American and the Spaghetti Western overlap a great deal, immediate differences stand out. The latter purports a more realistic portrayal. Unlike his classically handsome, clean-cut, brightly lit counterpart in the American Western, the sexy "Man with No Name" is weather-beaten, gritty, and irritated. For George-Warren, the protagonist of the Spaghetti Western is "more gunman than cattleman" (199). Accordingly, in the *Dollars Trilogy*, nary a bovine meanders onto the set. Produced abroad, Spaghetti Westerns were cost-effective as well as creatively appealing. They cast heretofore unknown or less successful actors, names who later became industry giants, such as Clint Eastwood, Burt Reynolds, Lee Van Cleef, Charles Bronson, and others (Howard Hughes xvi). Spain was prized "for its deserts, palm trees, agaves and decaying whitewashed villages," and many films were set in Almería (xii).[33]

Spaghetti Westerns additionally "brought to the genre raw violence, vulgar language and attention to details that the American Westerns did not have up to this point. Weapons and shootouts were usually represented more accurately" (Jeff Lawson 2). The staple conventions of the Western were upended.[34] For example, Hughes observes that in *The Savage Guns* (1962), directed by Michael Carreras, "the good guy (Baseheart) wore black and the bad guy (Nicol) wore white, a reversal of normal western conventions, while Baseheart had both his hands crushed by wagon wheels, in a bloody precursor of later spaghettis" (xii). The Spaghetti Western acted as a gateway to American films, such as Sam Peckinpah's notoriously violent *The Wild Bunch* (1969).

Sergio Leone's *A Fistful of Dollars*, *A Few Dollars More*, and *The Good, the Bad, and the Ugly* (collectively known as the *Dollars Trilogy*, which was

---

33   See Hughes (not to be confused with the director of the same name) for a meticulous accounting of film locations throughout Spain, which include Andalusia, Madrid, Aragon, and Catalonia.

34   As George-Warren explains: "In Italy, violence wasn't subjected to the same scrutiny by film censors as in the States. The Hays Commission had traditionally restricted American productions from showing in a single frame the act of a gun being fired and the bullet striking a victim" (201). She cites Christopher Frayling's conversation with Eastwood, who compares the filming of the *Dollars Trilogy* to that of the popular U.S. TV series *Rawhide* (1965-1966): "You had to shoot separately, and then show the person fall.... And that was always thought sort of stupid. But on television we always did it that way... And you see, Sergio never knew that" (201).

released in the U.S. in 1967) were applauded by the public, but vilified in the press and by directors John Ford, Anthony Mann, and Bud Boetticher. Mann argues that in *For a Few Dollars More* "the true spirit of a Western is lacking. We tell the story of simple men pushed to violence by circumstances. . .not of professional assassins. In a good Western, the characters have a starting and a finishing line; they follow a trajectory in the course of which they clash with life" (qtd. in George-Warren 204). This new vision, however, remained standing. Clint Eastwood gained favor with *The Outlaw Josey Wales* (1976), and "in the 1990s he would be fêted for his artistic vision of the West. . ." (George-Warren 211).

Just as the Spaghetti Western incites controversy, the conflict between Cervantes and Lope becomes increasingly heated. Vidal implicates Lope in the publication of the pseudonymous Alonso Fernández de Avellaneda's un-authorized continuation and argues that the work trashes not only Cervantes, but also his wife (38). Cervantes fires back, excoriating the unauthorized con-tinuer, to whom he ostensibly declines to refer as "asno," "mentecato," and "atrevido" in the Prologue to the second volume of the *Quijote* (543).[35] The Old West features similar scripted skirmishes. Sergio Leone's *Dollars Trilogy* is considered the prototype for the Spaghetti Western. However, Leone takes the plot of the first directly from Akira Kurosawa's *Yojimbo* (1961). As Hughes explains, "Though *Fistful* was released in West Germany and Spain in 1965, legal problems concerning *Yojimbo* ensured that it didn't make it to the US until January 1967. Kurosawa claimed copyright infringement on his original story and was allowed distribution rights in Japan as a compensation" (15).

The ongoing interpersonal tensions between Cervantes and Lope are additionally reproduced in Hollywood lore, which posits a feud between John Wayne and Clint Eastwood. In an interview with the latter, James Lip-ton asserts: "Your character was, I think, the first movie character, really, who didn't wait for the other guy to draw his gun." Eastwood's baffled response reflects changes to the genre: "It doesn't make sense . . . I never could under-stand that." This newer type of Western does not adhere to the antiquated moral code that is modeled on chivalric ideals and so vital to the Ameri-can Western. Eastwood goes on to relate an anecdote about *The Shootist*, in which director Don Siegel suggested that the reportedly apoplectic Wayne shoot a character in the back, in the manner of Eastwood: "I don't care what that kid would have done I don't shoot in the back."

---

35   At this point, one may wish to highlight the previous round fired at Lope's *La Arcadia* from the Prologue of the first volume, where the author's friend advises him to simply make up the desired "acotaciones al fin del libro" (11).

The making of *High Plains Drifter* created additional hype for this supposed dispute:

> Shortly after the film's release, Clint Eastwood wrote to John Wayne, suggesting that they make a Western together. Wayne sent back an angry letter in reply, in which he denounced this film for its violence and revisionist portrayal of the Old West. Eastwood did not bother to answer his criticisms, and consequently they did not work together. (IMDb)[36]

Mark Boardman concurs:

> Two iconic Western stars almost got together for a movie in the mid-1970s. Almost. The story goes that Clint Eastwood wanted to work with John Wayne, so he sent him a script. Wayne would star; Eastwood would act and direct. But the Duke wasn't so eager. Wayne sent Clint a letter, complaining about Eastwood's 1973 revisionist Western *High Plains Drifter*, in which a town of cowards backs the murder of their own marshal. That wasn't how the Old West really was, Wayne said—and not how a real Western should go.[37]

A different blogger attributes the following appraisal to Wayne: "[The West] was not a cesspool for murderers and immoral jerks, but full of honest people struggling to settle a wide-open country" (Falcon). In response, "Clint Eastwood told Wayne to lighten up, because *High Plains Drifter* was really just an allegory" (Falcon). The sentiment is humorously encapsulated by two side-by-side stills of Clint Eastwood and John Wayne. The former, in a thought bubble, proclaims 'This is Deep,' to which the latter responds 'No, this is

---

36   This text appears elsewhere: https://dukewayne.com/index.php?thread/4903-high-plains-drifter-1973/.

37   The townspeople of *High Plains Drifter* stand in sharp relief to the characters populating the American Western, where even the villains are governed by a rigid and traditional moral code. In *True Grit*, for example, even the outlaw, hired hand Tom Chaney, on whom the young heroine Mattie Ross seeks revenge for the murder of her father, acts virtuously. Their face-off is Mattie's first time firing a gun. In the interest of a fair fight—and in part because he does not believe that she will really shoot—Chaney instructs her on how to cock and fire the pistol. An additionally interesting aspect of this film in relation to the *Quijote* is Mattie's *catabasis* in the snake pit, which reminds the viewer of the adventure of the Cave of Montesinos in II.23 and Sancho's accidental spelunking experience in II.55.

crap'" (Falcon). However apocryphal, this alleged metaphorical shootout between Wayne and Eastwood enriches a present-day conception of relations between Cervantes and Lope, and of portions of the novel that might otherwise fall flat for readers new to the *Quijote*.

The Western—or at least, John Wayne, its most familiar face—delivers a helpful corollary to the death of don Quijote. In the words of the actor himself, which Pat Stacy recounts in her 1983 memoir, *Duke: A Love Story*: "As long as a man has a project—something to look forward to—there'll always be something important to him. He'll never really get old. If I had nothing to look forward to, I might as well be dead" (qtd. in Jeremy Roberts). The proposed pastoral agenda is not sufficiently invigorating a prophylactic against the disappointing return of Alonso Quijano. John Wayne, "the Duke," and the Knight of the Sad Countenance, then, are extremely compatible. As we have seen, when faced with the Sisyphean task of teaching the *Quijote* to undergraduates, we may call upon the Western to provide scaffolding for first-time readers. Cervantes' satirical *libro de caballerías* becomes visible and accessible to today's students, more than four hundred years after and a continent away from its initial publication.

Works Cited

Aquila, Richard. *The Sagebrush Trail: Western Movies and Twentieth-Century America.* U of Arizona P, 2015.

Bailey, Jason. "A Beginner's Guide to Spaghetti Westerns." *Flavorwire*, 9 Apr. 2013, flavorwire.com/383336/a-beginners-guide-to-spaghetti-westerns/4.

Brauer, Ralph. "Who Are Those Guys?: The Movie Western During the TV Era." Nachbar, pp. 118-28.

Burningham, Bruce R. *Tilting Cervantes: Baroque Reflections on Postmodern Culture.* Vanderbilt UP, 2008.

Cahill, U.S. Marshal, directed by Andrew V. McLaglen, Batjac Productions, 1973.

Cascardi, Anthony J. "Don Quixote and the invention of the novel." *The Cambridge Companion to Cervantes*, edited by Anthony J. Cascardi, Cambridge UP, 2002, pp. 58-79.

Cawelti, John G. *The Six-Gun Mystique.* 2nd ed., Bowling Green State University Popular P, 1984.

———. *The Six-Gun Mystique Sequel.* Bowling Green State University Popular P, 1999.

Cervantes Saavedra, Miguel de. *El ingenioso hidalgo don Quijote de la Mancha* (1605 and 1615). Edited by Francisco Rico, Ed. del IV Centenario, Madrid, RAE, 2005.

De Armas Wilson, Diana. "Knights and Cowboys: The Quixotic Course of Empire." *Cervantes and/on/in the New World*, edited by Julio Vélez-Sainz and Nieves Romero-Díaz, Juan de la Cuesta, 2007, pp. 139-50.

Deyermond, A. D. *The Middle Ages*. Ernest Benn, 1971.

Doherty, Thomas. "Hollywood, Censorship, and the Motion Picture Production Code." *Archives Unbound*, www.gale.com/binaries/content/assets/gale-us-en/primary-sources/archives-unbound/primary-sources_archives-unbound_hollywood-censorship-and-the-motion-picture-production-code-1927-1968.pdf, pp. 1-14.

Esselman, Kathryn C. "From Camelot to Monument Valley: Dramatic Origins of the Western Film." Nachbar, pp. 9-18.

Etulain, Richard. "Cultural Origins of the Western." Nachbar, pp. 19-24.

Falcon at the Movies. "John Wayne Hates *High Plains Drifter*." *Falcon at the Movies*, 31 Aug. 2015, www.falconmovies.wordpress.com/2015/08/31/john-wayne-hates-high-plains-drifter-1973/.

Fistful of Dollars, directed by Sergio Leone, Jolly, 1964.

Folsom, James. "Westerns as Social and Political Alternatives." Nachbar, pp. 81-83.

For a Few Dollars More, directed by Sergio Leone, Produzioni Europee Associati, 1965.

Fort Apache, directed by John Ford, Argosy, 1948.

French, Philip. *Westerns: Aspects of a Movie Genre*. Viking, 1973.

George-Warren, Holly. *How Hollywood Invented the Wild West*. Reader's Digest Association, 2002.

The Good, the Bad and the Ugly, directed by Sergio Leone, Produzioni Europee Associati, 1966.

The Great Train Robbery, directed by Edwin S. Porter, Edison, 1903.

Grossman, Edith, translator. *Don Quixote*. By Miguel de Cervantes, HarperCollins, 2003.

Hang 'Em High, directed by Ted Post, Malpaso, 1968.

Hess, John. "The History of Hollywood Censorship and the Ratings System." *YouTube*, uploaded by Filmmaker IQ, 27 November 2013, www.youtube.com/watch?v=Ynf8BmfgPtM.

High Plains Drifter, directed by Clint Eastwood, Malpaso, 1973.

Hughes, Howard. *Once Upon a Time in the Italian West*. I.B. Taurus, 2004.

Ife, B.W. "The historical and social context." *The Cambridge Companion to Cervantes*, edited by Anthony J. Cascardi, Cambridge UP, 2002, pp. 11-31.

Jones, R. O. *The Golden Age: Prose and Poetry*. Ernest Benn, 1971.

Lawson, Jeff. "The Italian Western and the American Western." *Audioholics* 14 Apr. 2007, www.audioholics.com/editorials/the-italian-western-and-the-american-western.

Lipton, James. Excerpt from "Inside the Actors Studio." *YouTube*, uploaded by Paul Riet, 11 November, 2011. www.youtube.com/watch?v=h_ncnLoiejo.

The Man Who Shot Liberty Valance, directed by John Ford, Paramount, 1962.

Mancing, Howard. *The Cervantes Encyclopedia*. 2 vols. Greenwood P, 2004.

———. *Cervantes' Don Quixote: A Reference Guide*. Greenwood, 2006.

Marsden, Michael T. "Savior in the Saddle: The Sagebrush Testament." Nachbar, pp. 93-100.

Mills, Eric. "John Ford, USN." *Naval History Magazine*, vol. 27, no. 2, 2013, www. usni.org/magazines/navalhistory/2013-03/john-ford-usn.

The Motion Picture Production Code. www.asu.edu/courses/fms200s/total-read-ings/MotionPictureProductionCode.pdf.

My Darling Clementine, directed by John Ford, 20th Century Fox, 1946.

Nachbar, Jack, editor. *Focus on the Western*. Prentice-Hall, 1974.

———. "Introduction." Nachbar, pp. 1-8.

———. "Riding Shotgun: The Scattered Formula in Contemporary Western Mov-ies." Nachbar, pp. 101-12.

"Official Trailer." *High Plains Drifter*, directed by Clint Eastwood, Malpaso, 1973. *Youtube*, uploaded by WilliamBillMunny, 31 July 2012, www.youtube.com/ watch?v=Ek9CwmjisLE.

Once Upon a Time in the West, directed by Sergio Leone, Rafran Cinematografica, 1968.

Prince, Stephen. "The Western." *An Introduction to Film Genres*, edited by Lester Friedman et al. N. W. Norton, 2014, pp. 242-77.

Roberts, Jeremy. "'Beau John'—The untold story of John Wayne's last film project." *Medium*,

27 Oct. 2016, www.medium.com/@jeremylr/beau-john-the-untold-story-of-john-wayne-s-last-film-project-9fd1f479e61f.

"Sam Peckinpah's 'Salad Days.'" *Monty Python's Flying Circus*, Series 3, Episode 33, written by Graham Chapman *et al.*, directed by Ian MacNaughton, BBC, 30 November, 1972.

"The Spanish Inquisition." *Monty Python's Flying Circus*, Series 2, Episode 2, written by Graham Chapman *et al.*, directed by Ian MacNaughton, BBC, 22 Septem-ber, 1970.

Stagecoach, directed by John Ford, Walter Wanger, 1939.

"Thug Notes Don Quixote." *Youtube*, uploaded by Wisecrack Unofficial Fan-Club, 29 October 2017, www.youtube.com/watch?v=wf8xqVx8nY8.

Trendel, George W. and Fran Striker, creators. *The Lone Ranger*. Apex Film and Wrather Productions, 1949-1956.

True Grit, directed by Henry Hathaway, Paramount, 1969.

Vega Carpio, Lope Félix de. *Arte nuevo de hacer comedias en este tiempo*. Edited by Juan Manuel Rozas. *Biblioteca Virtual Miguel de Cervantes*, 2003, www.cervantesvirtual.com/obra-visor/arte-nuevo-de-hacer-comedias-en-este-tiempo--0/html/ffb1e6c0-82b1-11df-acc7-002185ce6064_4.html.

Vidal, César. *Enciclopedia del* Quijote. Madrid, Planeta, 1999.

Warshow, Robert. "Movie Chronicle: The Westerner." Nachbar, pp. 45-56.

Whinnom, Keith. "The problem of the 'best-seller' in Spanish Golden Age litera-ture." *Bulletin of Hispanic Studies*, vol. LVII, 1980, pp. 189-98.

The Wild Bunch, directed by Sam Peckinpah, Warner Bros.-Seven Arts, 1969

PART III
Classroom as Case Study/Popping Pedagogy

From the *Epopeya* to the *Narcocorrido*: The Hero in Hispanic Literature and Popular Culture

LORI A. BERNARD

State University of New York, College at Geneseo

TEACHING MEDIEVAL AND EARLY modern peninsular literature to undergraduates can be challenging on many levels, but one of the main difficulties is helping them identify the connections that exist between two disparate worlds, pre-modern/early modern Iberia and the contemporary U.S. An effective way to facilitate a conversation about the literary production of pre-17th Century Iberia and its continued relevance today is through the use of popular culture. When instructors incorporate familiar, pop culture references, students are able to quickly grasp key concepts that allow them to begin to recognize the connections between the literary texts of the past and their lives in the present. Medieval and early modern literature courses study a wide variety of topics that relate well to contemporary society, but my article will focus on only one—the hero.

Through this thematic approach, the class delves into the essential characteristics of a hero and how these evolve during three distinct eras (medieval, early modern, contemporary) and two different spaces (Spain, North America). As a springboard, we begin by discussing the characteristics of the modern superheroes, like Superman and Wonder Woman, a familiar topic to many students. Once a baseline has been established, we can move into identifying the characteristics of the antagonists that are ever-present in these movies. As a point of comparison, the protagonist of the narco(corrido) is introduced as he allows for a lively discussion about whether a criminal is a hero or an anti-hero. Finally, the medieval hero is analyzed and the discussion continues about how these defining characteristics have changed over time. While the epic poem is traditionally considered canonical and is routinely taught in undergraduate classrooms, the *romance* and *corridos* are not; however, I would argue that all three styles pertain to the area of popular culture, connected by means of their varied representations of the hero, and that, when introduced as such, are more accessible and engaging for students.

When we connect the familiar theme of the hero in contemporary movies and music to manifestations of the hero in unfamiliar genres (epic and lyric poetry), students are better able to grasp chronologically remote material and discuss the relevance of the "old" texts in today's society. Further, by bringing in examples from an additional ballad tradition, Mexican and Mexican-American *corridos* and *narcocorridos*, students gain perspective about how heroes are defined across time and cultures, the role that they play in society, and the importance that they have to us on a personal level. In sum, they ponder the hero's evolution and what the future implications of such transformations might be.

Although traditionally considered unorthodox for the classroom, pop culture has become a more acceptable pedagogical method for teaching difficult material, and my approach to teaching the hero reflects this shift. As Irina Reta explains: "materials on popular culture make the classes more student-centered, the end result of which is a more responsive and active involvement of the students in the education process" (Luo and Rowsell qtd. in Reta). My own classroom experiences, while anecdotal, affirm these assertions; indeed, I have found that connecting the unfamiliar with the familiar allows students to gain confidence and to demonstrate a level of expertise that may not have been possible if we had begun our discussion without any contemporary contextualization. The use of popular culture also allows us to meet the students where they are, creating a bridge between them and us as well as between the medieval/early modern texts and contemporary representations. Various researchers, such as Chi-Kim Cheung and William Clapton, among others, have studied this idea. According to Clapton, incorporating references to popular culture can lead to more interactive lectures, more active student learning and participation as the source is more engaging to them. Clapton continues by saying that popular culture examples should be used carefully as they can sometimes be distracting or become the focus in place of the texts. For this reason, such examples should only be incorporated into the class when they add value; overuse or using them as fillers may negatively impact the goals that the educator is trying to achieve. In my own classes, I choose short examples that explicitly demonstrate the key points that we are analyzing and that are stimulating to the students. Additionally,

I typically use the popular culture examples at the beginning of a unit as a tool that allows students to connect more easily with the texts that we are studying.

When reading the *epopeya*, students are often intimidated by the strange looking words and grammatical structures, the unusual poetic meter, and the unfamiliar characters and scenes. On this point, Greg Wegner observes (and I agree with him to a degree): "Allowing students to absorb some of the strangeness of the medieval period, without trying to immediately dispel that strangeness, does help to illustrate the importance of concepts like diversity, historical perspective, and empathy." Nevertheless, I think that it is important to limit this "absorption" period so that students do not tune out entirely. For this reason, I usually incorporate relevant popular culture references into their assignments to aid understanding while also helping to generate discussion. For example, early on in the semester, when students are struggling to understand the medieval period, I might include links to websites[1] or have them view a short clip from the 1961 film *El Cid* (the latter being especially effective in both visualizing what certain scenes might have looked like while simultaneously allowing us to dispute inaccurate representations). In addition to incorporating modern pop culture, we discuss the idea of Medieval "popular culture" and its implications in Spain. At this point we examine theories surrounding the creation of the epic poem—whether it was the work of many authors, in essence, the *pueblo*, or if it was the work of just one, an educated monk— and why it is important to think about how and why a text was created. Pop culture is easily incorporated here through the example of sampling in music where one artist creates an original song while another artist uses part of the first artist's song to create an entirely new song.

After these initial discussions of the Middle Ages, students delve into the *Cantar de Mio Cid*, and we start with the basics of the hero unit— defining the general characteristics of a hero.[2] By talking about themes that they already understand (the definition of a hero), they are able to draw conclusions about how the Cid fits (or does not fit) the mold set by the earlier Greco-

---

1　　Online videos range from the highly sophisticated to the downright silly (for example, Lego reenactments). Here are two representative examples: https://www.youtube.com/watch?v=aeWVSt5Jm6U, https://www.youtube.com/watch?v=jQXI4uEG8Sw&t=11s.

2　　While no one definition of a hero is accepted by all, I often begin with a traditional dictionary definition, followed by Northrop Frye's ideas about heroes, and end with a student generated definition of what a hero is to them. This exercise allows students to see from the very beginning how difficult it is to define the term.

Roman (or even contemporary[3]) traditions. Once a set of characteristics has been determined, we are able to explore the evolution of the Spanish hero through time and space by analyzing how public opinion affected the original story, its subsequent fragmentation / recreation in prose texts and ballads from the medieval to the early modern period, and how the modern hero is represented throughout the Spanish-speaking world in pop culture.[4] Finally, the class delves deeper into what roles the text, religion, societal norms, and power played in the creation of both the hero and Castilian identity.

With respect to specific classroom exercises that I use when teaching the *Cantar de Mio Cid*, I like to start with activities that allow students to work with the text in the target language in a low-stress environment and to organize their ideas for the larger class discussion. This can be done individually, in pairs/small groups, or as a class. *The Pocket Instructor: Literature: 101 Exercises for the College Classroom* includes a plethora of activities that advance this unit. Depending upon the class and the time allotted for the warm up, any one of the following three examples (found in the aforementioned edition) could be utilized. "Explode the Poem"[5] (whole class activity) consists of the professor reading a selection of one of the poems multiple times while the students choose one verse to comment upon at the end. After the recitation, the class reflects upon what they heard, any patterns they noticed, or if there were any surprises. Additionally, we think about which verses were the most popular and why. The most popular verse in my class is normally the first, *in medias res* line of the poem: "De los sos ojos / tan fuerte mientre lorando." Some students are affected by imagery and are intrigued to know more (suspense), others are surprised that when we first meet the hero he is sobbing (an atypical behavior, especially for a male hero), and a few are just curious about the linguistic elements. By focusing on the one line that appeals to the them, the students listen closely first to understand the words and, subsequently, to form an opinion. In addition to whole group activities, there are also small groups ones such as "Form and Content"[6] or "The Six-Word

---

3   Some examples include: https://www.huffingtonpost.com/susie-lee/who-are-our-21st-century-heroes_b_9585206.html, https://digitaldreamdoor.com/pages/movie-pages/movie_hero.html, https://www.esquire.com/entertainment/movies/a29702/action-hero-types/.

4   In some classes, I also include the Romantic and Nationalist portrayals of the Cid in the nineteenth and twentieth centuries.

5   The author of this activity is Jennifer Minnen.

6   The author of this activity is Andrew Benjamin Bricker.

Story."[7] The first focuses on the form, while the second encourages students to think about content. In both, the students analyze selections of the poem and then reflect upon how the form and content change (or stay the same) in the different versions that they read prior to class. By working in groups, they are able to try out ideas and find support from their peers before having to interact with the whole class and/or the professor. Once the warm up has ended, the answers from the group work activities are shared with the whole class as they relate to the topics that will be discussed later. Alternatively, the work could be collected to evaluate how well the students are interacting with the texts and writing in Spanish.

Overall, the students tend to prefer the first two activities, as they are more text based and "easier," whereas the last activity requires a higher level of comprehension and creativity (i.e. "not easy"). Each of the activities allow the students to engage actively with the text. On the most basic level, students identified and had to justify the one line that they liked (due to its rhythm or its meaning, for example). The students found it more challenging to spot the variations between texts, but nonetheless, they were able to do so. For instance, they noticed that sometimes the characters had a given name while other times only a title or nickname was used, and they wondered if that was significant or not. Some students felt that it was (not using a person's name might imply that they are not that important), while others did not because the nickname identified the person. These types of slow, deliberate exercises and conversations lay the groundwork for students' solid footing as we proceed to storm the text.

After the warm up, the remainder of the class is dedicated to textual analysis. In small groups or as a class (depending upon the comprehension level), we compare and contrast five different texts/videos that feature the character of the Cid. The texts come from different centuries, different poetic or musical traditions, and portray the main characters and the story in different ways, yet there are clear connections between them.

The first passage students examine is a selection from the *Cantar de Mio Cid*, which they have already seen in the warm-up. The thirteenth-century epic poem is the most complete written text due to the fact that a learned monk carefully documented the text in manuscript form. The passages that historically have generated the most discussion have been underlined and marked with a section number (x) in the complete texts (or sections) that

---

7   The author of this activity is Jacquelyn Ardam.

appear in the appendix.[8] The first section of the first text (A.1) deals with the use of oral techniques and descriptions that allow for visual recreations of the battlefield:

> De sus tiendas les arrojan y persiguiéndoles van:
> Vierais allí tantos brazos con sus lorigas cortar,
> tantas cabezas con yelmo por aquel campo rodar
> y los caballos sin amo correr de aquí para allá.
> Aquella persecución siete millas fue a durar.

In this version, the Cid is identified by his epithet, My Cid, and the Moor King by his given name, Búcar: *"Mío Cid a aquel rey Búcar a los alcances le va"* (A.2). The climax of this fragment (A.3) is the final battle on the shore, where the Cid tries to deceive Búcar by promising to put aside their differences and become friends. Búcar, doubting his sincerity, chooses to flee:

> "Vuélvete, Búcar, decía, viniste de allende el mar
> y al Cid de la barba grande cara a cara has de mirar,
> los dos, hemos de besarnos, pactaremos amistad."
> Repuso Búcar: "¡Que Dios confunda a un amigo tal!
> Espada tienes en mano y te veo espolear,
> se me figura que quieres en mí tu espada ensayar.

Both the dialogue and the narrator's words show the bravery and valor of both combatants—the Cid's victory would not be as successful if they weren't—but ultimately the Cid defeats Búcar, an event that is described in hyperbolic detail (A.4):

> Buen caballo tiene Búcar, grandes saltos le hace dar,
> pero Babieca el del Cid a los alcances le va.
> Mío Cid alcanza a Búcar a tres brazas de la mar,
> alza su espada Colada, un fuerte golpe le da,
> los carbunclos de su yelmo todos se los fue a arrancar,
> luego el yelmo y la cabeza le parte por la mitad,
> hasta la misma cintura la espada fue a penetrar.

---

8   To avoid confusion, I use letters (A-E) to refer to the texts that appear in the appendix and numbers to refer to the specific sections that I discuss in my essay. Thus, a reference to the first section of the first text would appear as: A.1.

Victory and honor go to the Cid as summarized in the last lines (A.5):

Batalla maravillosa y grande supo ganar.
Aquí se honró Mío Cid y cuantos con él están.

Moving to early modern manifestations of the hero, we next discuss the
romance. *Romance*s are an ideal place to start studying Golden Age poetry
because in my experience, students connect with them immediately. These
short poems that tell compelling stories through the use of dramatic elements
and dialogues are more easily understood, as opposed to Italianate sonnets
or mystical *liras* that often include figurative language or poetic tropes that
need to be deciphered. Additionally, the subject and characters are familiar
to our modern students (hero, villain, fathers and daughters, among others).
What also interests our students is that the *romances* were and continue to
be sung in Spain and around the world (music is typically an important part
of many students' lives). However, to truly understand the hero that appears
in the *romance*, we must understand the origins of the literary style. For this
reason, the unit begins with the origins of the Castilian hero.

I explain to students that the *romancero* tradition had many phases and
most likely evolved from the loose-leaf, *pliegos sueltos* that were immensely
popular in the late fifteenth and the early sixteenth century and included
fragments of earlier epic poetry forms. In its essence, the *romance* is the product of popular culture. Generations of singers created and recreated the songs
of their ancestors and adapted them to the prevailing tastes of each era. As
many investigators have noted, the ballad tradition both inherits many characteristics of the earlier traditions while simultaneously innovating said traditions (Chicote 5). They are especially useful as a bridge between the earliest
testimonies (epic poetry) and the more contemporary examples (*corridos*).

The product of court poets and musicians dedicated to the dissemination of the new-style ballads from the sixteenth century that glorified the
Moors long after their final defeat in 1492, *Helo, helo, por do viene / el moro
por la calzada,* is a more polished work. This text differs from the passages
from the *Cantar de Mio Cid* in that it moves away from the battle scenes to
focus on character development, dialogue, and a new plot twist between Urraca (the Cid's daughter, more commonly known by other names) and the
Moor King. The imagery focuses on the characters' appearance and actions
through an abundance of adjectives used to describe them and the emotions
that they are feeling (B.1 and B.2), perhaps reflecting the humanist spirit of
the time in which the text was created:

Helo, helo, por do viene el moro por la calzada
caballero a la jineta   encima una yegua baya;
borceguíes marroquíes   y espuela de oro calzada,
una adarga ante los pechos y en su mano una zagaya.
Mirando estaba Valencia   cómo está tan bien cercada.
-Oh, Valencia, oh, Valencia, de mal fuego seas quemada.
Primero fuiste de moros   que de cristianos ganada;
si la lanza no me miente   a moros serás tornado.
Aquel perro de aquel   Cid prenderélo por la barba,
su mujer doña Jimena   será de mí captivada,
su hija Urraca Hernando   será mi enamorada,
después de yo harto d'ella   la entregaré a mi compaña.

In this version, the Cid is mentioned by name, while Búcar becomes into an unnamed Moor; however, in spite of this, the Moorish king more actively participates in this version with an introductory monologue that laments the loss of Valencia to the Christians and vows to reclaim it (B.2). Whereas the first text portrays the main characters as worthy opponents, Búcar's harsh words towards the Cid and his family (B.2) set a more combative and negative tone in the second one. While this version retains some of the oral formulas included in the original poem (B.3): "El buen Cid," "mientras yo ensillo a Babieca y me ciño la mi espada," there is a new twist, Urraca's "seduction" of the Moor King (B.4):

La doncella muy hermosa se paró a una ventana;
el moro desque la vido desta suerte le hablara:
-Alá te guarde, señora, mi señora doña Urraca
-Así haga a vos, señor, buena sea vuestra llegada.
Siete años ha, rey, siete que soy vuestra enamorada.
-Otros tantos ha, señora, que os tengo dentro en mi alma.

Additionally, the final battle scene on the shore (B.5) was completely altered—it ends with the Moor King escaping and leaving the Cid without a moral victory:

El moro desque la vido con ella bien se holgaba.
Grandes gritos da al barquero que le allegase la barca;
el barquero es diligente, túvosela aparejada.
Embarcó muy presto en ella, que no se detuvo nada.

Estando el moro embarcado el buen Cid que llegó al agua
y por ver al moro en salvo   de tristeza reventaba,
mas con la furia que tiene   una lanza le arrojaba
y dijo: -Recoged, mi yerno, arrecogédme esa lanza
que quizá tiempo verná que os será bien demandada.

Since the students have already read this part of the *Cantar de Mio Cid,* many of them question these two plot changes, which often leads to a robust discussion about why these alterations were made and how the audience might have reacted to them. As a result, we are able to spend more time discussing reception theory, poetic license, and the use of textual variation by the singers. For example, as noted above, the sixteenth-century *romance* focuses more on the personalities and emotions of the characters, while the original version described the intense battles and the valor and bravery of the combatants. The changes were most certainly the result of the changing tastes of the public, upon whose charity the *juglar* or the court poet/musician relied.

My third example, *Moro alcalde, moro alcalde, / el de la veyuda barba* is the least polished and coherent of the texts due to its suspected creation and preservation throughout the centuries via oral transmission among Sephardic families who were expelled from Spain in the fifteenth century. While this version maintains many of the same themes identified in the previous examples, the singer, producing the text from memory, tends to jump around while the Judeo-Spanish language sometimes impedes a clear comprehension of the story (C.1).

A eso de la mediodía, al Sidi se presentara,
en un cabayo montado con muchas marcas marcado.
El moro que en eya viene, parese de grande estrado.
- ¡Ay, Valensia! y ¡ay, Valensia!
¡Valensia la bien tomada!
Primero, fuitis del moro que de cristiano tomada.
Si Alá me ayudara, y al moro serís tornada.
A ese perro de ese Sidi, yo le pelaré sus barba[s].
Su mujer la Shelimena será la mi cosinera.
La de lo[s] rubios cabeyo[s], esa me hará la cama.
La má[s] chiquita de eya[s], esa me ensende la[s] tuayas. . .
Su hija la Urraca, esa se mi namorada.

Although this version does help to clarify some parts described in other texts, it seems incomplete, including an abrupt ending. This text tends to focus more on the Cid and Urraca's relationship than previous versions; one example is when we see how the Cid teaches his seemingly innocent daughter to seduce the Moor King in order to buy himself more time to prepare for battle (C.2):

[. . .] asómate a esa ventana.
Por ahí, pasará el buen reye y entreténele en palabra[s].
Las palabras sean cortas y en amor sean tomadas.
-¿Cómo lo haré, mi padre, que de amor no entiendo y nada?
-Yo te enseñaré, mi hija, como si fueradh uzzada.
-Ya se levanta la Urraca, se levanta de mañana.
Se quita paño[s] de siempre, se pone los de la Pascua.
Se arrebolara su cara como espada relumbrada.
Por ahí pasara ese Sidi, de esta manera le habla:
- ¿Quién edh ese o cuál edh ese que se pasa y no me habla?

The climax of this version is chaotic, as the singer does not seem to remember all the verses and ends abruptly with the Cid cutting off the Moor King's head (C.3):

Esto que yegara [e]l Sidi, la cabesa le cortara.
Otro día en la mañana, el Sidi que ya reinaba. Le mató.

This ending seems to deprive the audience of the moral victory seen in the original version (but also absent in the *romance* when the Moor King escapes). Of the three examples, students are most confused by this version, perhaps due to the aforementioned linguistic difficulties. Although both *romances* are similar in content, the presentation of the story varies greatly, which causes the students to question why these variations exist.[9] The Judeo-Spanish ballad tradition is an excellent example of how literature is cre-

---

9   It is impossible to study the Spanish ballad without discussing the ideas of variants, *estado latente*, and orality. When we discuss these ideas, I like to reference the practice of sampling in contemporary music as this helps to clearly demonstrate what often happened during the early modern period (as previously mentioned). One text that could be used in this discussion (although most students have a solid understanding of what sampling is) might be: https://www.npr.org/2011/01/28/133306353/Digital-Music-Sampling-Creativity-Or-Criminality.

ated and preserved by the *pueblo*. Although we may never be able to establish beyond any doubt whether the texts were sung orally first and then written down or vice versa, the fact remains that centuries after their creation, the exiled descendants of the Iberian Peninsula have enjoyed singing and sharing these songs. An easy comparison here would be how a popular song can be recorded and reworked over generations. One example is Leonard Cohen's "Hallelujah," released in 1984, which appears regularly in films and on television.[10]

After reviewing the similarities and differences concerning the content in the poems about the Cid, we focus on the hero and how he appears in each of the texts. We talk about the motifs of the origin story, the hero as a role model, and his role in helping forge a national identity. Finally, we think about how the hero and his relationships with the other major characters evolve over time as we ponder the relevance of these "old" texts and reflect upon how many of the themes are still popular in contemporary literature, television, and film (themes such as family dynamics, territorial disputes, and emotions, among others). These comparative exercises allow the class to explore more meaningfully what it means to be a hero today and reflect upon whether or not the Cid was really a hero as per their twenty-first century understanding of the term . At this point, we return to the idea presented in the *Cantar de Mio Cid* when the Cid lies to the Moor King in order to trick him into surrendering or when it seems that the Cid is trying to use his daughter to seduce his enemy. Many of the students find these and some of his other actions to be morally corrupt and question the Cid's status as a role model or hero. This discussion ends with a note about cultural relativism and the difficulties of trying to understand authors and texts that are far removed from our own time.

The final two texts examine how the idea of a hero is portrayed in modern music[11]— the Mexican/Mexican-American *corridos* and *narcocorridos*. While these texts do not use the Cid as the hero, they do connect in a va-

---

10   A quick internet search finds at least 60 covers: https://www.newsweek.com/60-versions-leonard-cohens-hallelujah-ranked-303580.

11   This is a good time to reiterate the lyric nature of medieval and early modern poetry and how music has replaced poetry's historical role in creating heroes and myths. Additionally, I like to make the connection between music and literature. According to a recent blog post by Ana María Ferreira where she explores the controversy surrounding Bob Dylan being awarded the Nobel Prize for Literature: ". . .la relación entre música y literatura es larga e indisoluble" (4). This connection is especially strong in the medieval and early modern poetic traditions.

riety of ways to the other three texts. Just as many scholars posit that epic poetry created the Castilian identity, many *corrido* scholars believe that these compositions enabled Mexicans or Mexican-Americans to create an identity separate from the United States. There are other commonalities. Samuel Armistead discusses the three crucial features of epic narratives: "Each poem involves ethnic or religious conflict, each involves armed confrontation along a disputed frontier (today we would say a border) and each narrative, too, has at its beginnings, a more or less distant historical nucleus, a core of historical fact, that, over the years, usually centuries, may have acquired a dense overlay of legendary elaborations" (96). Armistead continues by drawing the connections between the epic and the *corrido*: "the *corrido* highlights the essential role of borders and border conflicts as an ideal seed-bed for epic and epic-lyric adventures recreated in narrative verse" (96-97). Obviously, the subgenre of the *corrido*, the *narcocorrido*, meets these criteria as well. Although the epic poem, the *romance*, and the *corrido* show clear connections, we find that the *corrido* and the *narcocorrido* focus on a very different type of hero. While our students often question the Cid's moral character, many of his actions were socially acceptable at the time. In contrast, as the heroes of the *corrido* ballads tend to be bandits or drug traffickers, detractors find them unsavory and have tried to ban them from airplay,[12] despite their enormous popularity and commercial success. This is perhaps because, as Sarah Berry comments: "There is something very compelling about men who make their own rules. Though their actions are not always laudable, their self-generated freedom supersedes moral reservations" (8). However, Berry lists another convincing reason for the continued success of the *narcocorrido* as a "narrative attempt to reconcile complex and often contradictory elements of life" (1). In effect, she seems to imply that these songs explore the class stratifications and lack of economic opportunity that, for reasons understood by the people implicated, force some members of society to adopt alternative morals (2).

For the last section of class, I show two videos instead of using written texts, as this allows students a unique experience— both visual and auditory. This incorporation of visual narratives through the use of video enhances the learner's experience. According to Thyra Knapp, visual representations can be effective and rewarding: "For twenty-first century students brought up in a society dominated by visuality, paintings provide an immediate connection, inviting them to explore linguistic structures, literary texts, and cultural constructs in new and memorable ways" (26). While Knapp is referring spe-

---

12   This could be compared to the crusade against music with explicit lyrics launched by Tipper Gore in the 80s and 90s.

cifically to paintings, videos play a similar role in their ability to tap into the visuality that permeates our students' lives as, I would submit, does music. By starting with the familiar (music videos), the students become more comfortable with the "texts." The two representative examples from each genre are *El Corrido de César Chávez* y *El más buscado (Chapo Guzmán)* (texts D and E of the appendix). I chose this *corrido* because César Chávez really did embody heroic qualities, as opposed to some of the other heroes that appear in the epic poems, *romances*, and *narcocorridos*.[13] Additionally, the history of the Chicano Movement (along with earlier struggles) and its role in the creation and ongoing popularity of the *corridos* (Paredes 35) is unknown to many students in New York. For the *narcocorrido* text, I chose one of the more recent ones about El Chapo as many students are familiar with him due to his recent arrest and trial in New York. Although not seen as a traditional hero at first, both Sarah Berry (see above) and Juan Carlos Ramírez-Pimienta support the view that: "*Narcocorridos* give voice to a phenomenon that runs against the goals of the state and against cultural norms" (11). In addition to a different type of hero, the circumstances surrounding the creation of these texts is also unique, although similar to those that forged the *epopeya*.

Through these videos, the class is able to examine how different societies create their own ideas about what constitutes a hero, and about what it means to be a hero during different historical periods and in different geographical locations. We also reflect upon how someone might be considered a hero due to his or her positive impact (such as César Chávez) or how one who may not fit the accepted definitions might still be considered heroic (El Chapo). This last discussion point connects well with the earlier one that raised the question about whether or not the Cid was a hero and allows the students to talk about moral ambiguity and how heroes may not always behave "heroically."

Overall, this is one of the more powerful lessons for both my students and me. The mixture of written texts and audiovisual musical interpretations clearly demonstrates a continuation of the purpose and the role of epic-lyric poetry in the subsequent *romancero* and *corrido/narcocorrido* traditions. To

---

13   It is important to note the main difference between folk culture and popular culture. The former are cultural traditions shared by small, homogeneous groups, while the later are those traditions found in large, heterogeneous societies that are normally more economically developed. While *corridos* are traditionally considered part of folk culture, the explosion of the *narcocorrido* tradition should be considered part of both folk and popular culture in certain regions of Mexico and the United States.

conclude the unit, I assign an essay for which students select a poem (or a fragment) from the readings to compare with a song from the twentieth or twenty-first centuries that includes similar themes. While the song may be in English or Spanish, I find that the students benefit more from choosing a song in their own language as it makes the activity more relevant to them. In the past, students have really found this activity to be interesting as it has allowed them to connect what they are learning in class with what they are doing outside of it. Jerome Evans discusses a similar assignment in which he gives his students a list of nine prominent and persistent themes in American Literature and then shows how each song develops several of these themes. He states: "Students find it pretty easy to provide specific evidentiary support from the text of the song, at least in part because they have better familiarity with popular songs (even ones they haven't heard before) than they do with poetry or fiction or drama" (33). The assignment, a synthesis of what they have been studying during the unit, allows students to demonstrate what they have learned in an academic, yet non-traditional, fashion. The homework assignment allows me to evaluate their grasp of the key concepts discussed in a more open-ended and creative format than a written exam.

In a blog post from 2015, Mary Jane Kelley asked: "What can one gain from reading the *mester de clerecía*?" While her question referred to a less commonly studied medieval poetic form that many find too difficult or cumbersome to teach, these are some of the same complaints I have heard about teaching medieval and early modern poetry in general; thus, her answer helps to explain why we should study the *mester de juglaría* texts as well. We read these texts in order to learn how to read critically, as well as how to deal with ambiguity, a multiplicity of perspectives, and the instability of meaning (to mention some of Kelly's ideas). I would argue that this applies to all types of traditions, both literary and popular. Although some may still question the value of using popular culture in the college classroom, exposing students to a wide variety of texts and styles from the "classic" to the popular opens up a realm of possibilities that allow students to not only acquire practical skills but to also actively interact with the themes. In other words, not only do they analyze the typical medieval hero, they also learn to think critically about what a hero represents to a specific society and how a drug trafficker could possibly be considered a hero. By bringing popular culture into the academic classroom, students are able to delve much deeper into the material and the culture that produced it— not only do they learn about medieval traditions in Spain, but also about the interconnected traditions of the exiled Sephardic Jews, the Chicano Movement in California, and the drug cartels in Mexico.

In my experience, the connections made in this type of class are deeper and more enduring than merely reading about one seemingly perfect hero who lived many centuries ago in a far-away land.

Works Cited

Ardam, Jacquelyn. "The Six-Word Story." *The Pocket Instructor: Literature: 101 Exercises for the College Classroom*, edited by Diana Fuss and William A. Gleason, Princeton UP, 2016, pp. 47-49.

Armistead, Samuel G. "Spanish Epic and Hispanic Ballad: The Medieval Origins of the Corrido." *Western Folklore*, vol. 64, No. 1/2, Winter - Spring, 2005, pp. 93-108.

Berry, Sarah. "Heroes or Villains: Placing Narcocorridos in the Mexican Corrido Tradition." Western Oregon University Digital Commons @WOU, https://digitalcommons.wou.edu/pat/3/. Accessed August 1, 2018.

Bricker, Andrew Benjamin. "Form and Content." *The Pocket Instructor: Literature: 101 Exercises for the College Classroom*, edited by Diana Fuss and William A. Gleason, Princeton UP, 2016, pp. 105-109.

Cheung, Chi-Kim. "The use of popular culture as a stimulus to motivate secondary students' English learning in Hong Kong." *ELT Journal*, vol., 55/1, Jan. 2001, pp. 55-61.

Chicote, Gloria Beatriz. "Cultura popular y poesía narrativa medieval: contactos productivos." *Orbis Tertius,* vol. 11(12), 2006, pp. 1-6.

Clapton, William. "Pedagogy and Pop Culture: Pop Culture as Teaching Tool and Assessment Practice." (Excerpt). E-International Relations, https://www.e-ir.info/2015/06/23/pedagogy-and-pop-culture-pop-culture-as-teaching-tool-and-assessment-practice/. Accessed May 15, 2018.

Davies, Rhian. "New ways of teaching literature." Centre for Languages, Linguistics, and Area Studies, https://www.llas.ac.uk/resources/gpg/2593. Accessed May 1, 2018.

Evans, Jerome. "From Sheryl Crow to Homer Simpson: Literature and Composition through Pop Culture." *The English Journal*, vol. 93, no. 3, Jan., 2004, pp. 32-38.

Ferreira, Ana María. "De Bob Dylan a Maluma: la música como literatura y los límites del arte." Razón Pública, https://www.razonpublica.com/index.php/cultura/9979-de-bob-dylan-a-maluma-la-m%C3%BAsica-como-literatura-y-los-l%C3%ADmites-del-arte.html. Accessed May 1, 2018.

Fuss, Diana, and William A. Gleason, editors. *The Pocket Instructor: Literature: 101 Exercises for the College Classroom*. Princeton UP, 2016.

Kelley, Mary Jane. "Why Study the Literature of the *mester de clerecía*?" La corónica Commons, http://lcc.ku.edu/articles/kelley-mary-jane-why-study-the-literature-of-the-mester-de-clerecia/. Accessed May 28, 2018.

Knapp, Thyra E. "Picturing German: Teaching Language and Literature through Visual Art." *Die Unterrichtspraxis / Teaching German*, vol. 45, no. 1, Spring 2012, pp. 20-27.

Minnen, Jennifer. "Explode the Poem." *The Pocket Instructor: Literature: 101 Exercises for the College Classroom*, edited by Diana Fuss and William A. Gleason, Princeton UP, 2016, pp. 130-132.

Morrell, Ernest. "Integrating Pop Culture in the Classroom." *University of Notre Dame, Alliance for Catholic Education*, https://ace.nd.edu/blog/integrating-pop-culture-in-the-classroom, May 27, 2018.

Mujica, Barbara. *Milenio: Mil años de literatura española*, Wiley, 2002.

Paredes, Américo, and María Herrera-Sobek. "The Corrido: An invited Lecture at the 'Music in Culture' Public lecture Series." *The Journal of American Folklore*, vol. 125, no. 495, Winter 2012, pp. 23-44.

Ramírez-Pimienta, Juan Carlos. "Narcocultura a Ritmo Norteño El narcocorrido ante el nuevo milenio." *Latin American Research Review*, vol. 42, no. 2, 2007, pp. 253-261.

Rets, Irina. "Teachers' Perceptions on Using Popular Culture when Teaching and Learning English." *International Conference on Teaching and Learning English as an Additional Language, GlobELT 2016, 14-17 April 2016, Antalya, Turkey. Procedia, Social and Behavioral Sciences 232 (2016)*, 154 – 160.

Wegner, Greg. "The Risks and Rewards of Teaching Pop Culture." Amity Reading, Department of English, DePauw University, http://glcateachlearn.org/2018/03/29/the-risks-and rewards-of-teaching-pop-culture/, May 29, 2018.

Appendix

Text A: *Poema de Mio Cid* (selection): Cantar Tercero, Tirada 118
http://ciudadseva.com/texto/poema-de-mio-cid-cantar-tercero/

De sus tiendas les arrojan y persiguiéndoles van:
Vierais allí tantos brazos con sus lorigas cortar,
tantas cabezas con yelmo por aquel campo rodar
y los caballos sin amo correr de aquí para allá.
Aquella persecución siete millas fue a durar. (1)
Mío Cid a aquel rey Búcar a los alcances le va: (2)
"Vuélvete, Búcar, decía, viniste de allende el mar
y al Cid de la barba grande cara a cara has de mirar,
los dos, hemos de besarnos, pactaremos amistad."
Repuso Búcar: "¡Que Dios confunda a un amigo tal!
Espada tienes en mano y te veo espolear,

se me figura que quieres en mí tu espada ensayar. (3)
Mas si no cae mi caballo y ningún tropiezo da,
no te juntarás conmigo como no sea en el mar."
Responde entonces el Cid: "Esto no será verdad."
Buen caballo tiene Búcar, grandes saltos le hace dar,
pero Babieca el del Cid a los alcances le va.
Mío Cid alcanza a Búcar a tres brazas de la mar,
alza su espada Colada, un fuerte golpe le da,
los carbunclos de su yelmo todos se los fue a arrancar,
luego el yelmo y la cabeza le parte por la mitad,
hasta la misma cintura la espada fue a penetrar. (4)
El Cid ha matado a Búcar aquel rey de allende el mar,
ganó la espada Tizona, mil marcos de oro valdrá.
Batalla maravillosa y grande supo ganar.
Aquí se honró Mío Cid y cuantos con él están. (5)

Text B: *El rey moro que reta a Valencia* (versión del *Cancionero de romances, sin año* [1548]): Versos 1-41
https://faculty.washington.edu/petersen/591rom/helo1548.htm

Helo, helo, por do viene el moro por la calzada
caballero a la jineta   encima una yegua baya;
borceguíes marroquíes   y espuela de oro calzada,
una adarga ante los pechos y en su mano una zagaya.
Mirando estaba Valencia   cómo está tan bien cercada. (1)
-Oh, Valencia, oh, Valencia, de mal fuego seas quemada.
Primero fuiste de moros   que de cristianos ganada;
si la lanza no me miente   a moros serás tornado.
Aquel perro de aquel   Cid prenderélo por la barba,
su mujer doña Jimena   será de mí captivada,
su hija Urraca Hernando   será mi enamorada,
después de yo harto d'ella   la entregaré a mi compaña.- (2)
El buen Cid no está tan lejos   que toda bien lo escuchaba. (3)
--Venid vos acá, mi hija, mi hija dona Urraca.
Dejad las ropas continas   y vestid ropas de Pascua
aquel moro hi de perro   detenémelo en palabras
mientras yo ensillo a Babieca   y me ciño la mi espada. (3)
La doncella muy hermosa se paró a una ventana;

el moro desque la vido   desta suerte le hablara:
-Alá te guarde, señora,   mi señora doña Urraca
-Así haga a vos, señor,   buena sea vuestra llegada.
Siete años ha, rey, siete   que soy vuestra enamorada.
-Otros tantos ha, señora,   que os tengo dentro en mi alma.- (4)
Ellos estando en aquesto   el buen Cid que asomaba.
-Adiós, adiós, mi señora,   la mi linda enamorada
que del caballo Babieca yo   bien oigo la patada.
Do la yegua pone el pie   Babieca pone la pata
allí hablara el caballo,   bien oiréis lo que hablaba:
-Reventar debía la madre   que a su hijo no esperaba.
Siete vueltas la rodea   alderredor de una jara;
la yegua, que era ligera,   muy adelante pasaba
fasta llegar cabe un río   adonde una barca estaba.
El moro desque la vido   con ella bien se holgaba.
Grandes gritos da al barquero   que le allegase la barca;
el barquero es diligente,   túvosela aparejada.
Embarcó muy presto en ella,   que no se detuvo nada.
Estando el moro embarcado   el buen Cid que llegó al agua
y por ver al moro en salvo   de tristeza reventaba,
mas con la furia que tiene   una lanza le arrojaba
y dijo: -Recoged, mi yerno,   arrecogédme esa lanza
que quizá tiempo verná   que os será bien demandada. (5)

Text C: *Búcar sobre Valencia: Moro alcalde, moro alcalde, /el de la veyuda barba* cantada por Luna Elaluf Farache, Tetuán, Morocco (1962): http://www.sephardifolklit.org/FLSJ/TranscriptionDetails/7

Moro arcalde, moro alcalde, el de la veyuda barba . . .
Moro alcalde, el de la veyuda barba.
El rey le mandó a prender por la pérdi[da] de Holanda.
A eso de la mediodía, al Sidi se presentara,
en un cabayo montado con muchas marcas marcado.
 El moro que en eya viene, parese de grande estrado.
- ¡Ay, Valensia! y ¡ay, Valensia!
¡Valensia la bien tomada!
Primero, fuitis del moro que de cristiano tomada.
Si Alá me ayudara, y al moro serís tornada.
A ese perro de ese Sidi, yo le pelaré sus barba[s].

Su mujer la Shelimena será la mi cosinera.
La de lo[s] rubios cabeyo[s], esa me hará la cama.
La má[s] chiquita de eya[s], esa me ensende la[s] tuayas . . .
Su hija la Urraca, esa se mi namorada. (1)
- Oyido l[o] había ese Sidi desde su salón de estare . . . .
Los dados tiene en la mano, al suelo lodh arronzhara.
Fuérase pa los palasio[s] dónde la Urraca asentaba.
-En buena hora estés, la Urraca, espejo donde yo me miro.
-En eyadh venga, mi padre, la estreya ande yo resmiro.
-Levántate tú, la Urraca, levántate de mañana.
Quítate paños de siempre y ponte los de la Pascua.
Con agua de esa redoma, arrebólate tu cara,
hasta que saquedh el rostro como espada relumbrada.
[. . .] asómate a esa ventana.
Por ahí, pasará el buen reye y entrétenele en palabra[s].
Las palabras sean cortas y en amor sean tomadas.
-¿Cómo lo haré, mi padre, que de amor no entiendo y nada?
-Yo te enseñaré, mi hija, como si fueradh uzzada.
-Ya se levanta la Urraca, se levanta de mañana.
Se quita paño[s] de siempre, se pone los de la Pascua.
Se arrebolara su cara como espada relumbrada.
Por ahí pasara ese Sidi, de esta manera le habla: (2)
- ¿Quién edh ese o cuál edh ese que se pasa y no me habla?
Siete añodh hase, siete, que estoy por esta ventana.
-Otros siete yo tengo, la Urraca, que por ti penando estaba.
- De tudh amoredh, el Sidi, tirarme po[r] esa ventana.
-Si te tiraredh, mi vida, te resiberé en mis brasos. –
- Eyodh en estas palabra[s], los cabayo[s] regusnara[n].
-- ¿Qué ezz eso tú, la Urraca?
Gran s . . . traisión traedh armada.
-- No es traisión, el mi señor rey, ni mi linaje d[e] uzzada.
Los cabayodh de mi padre lo[s] están dando sebada.
- Esto que yegara [e]l Sidi, la cabesa le cortara.
Otro día en la mañana, el Sidi que ya reinaba. Le mató. (3)

Text D: *Corrido de César Chávez.* Loa Perros del Pueblo Nuevo (Miguel Gabriel Vázquez, Lorenzo Martínez, David Maestas) From ¡Viva César Chávez!, cassette, 1994.

• Video: https://www.youtube.com/watch?v=H_6e9WAtfqs

- Letra: *Rolas de Aztlán: Songs of the Chicano Movement*

https://media.smithsonianfolkways.org/liner_notes/smithsonian_
folkways/SFW40516_additional.pdf

Text E: *El más buscado (Chapo Guzmán)*, sin autor y fecha.
- Video con letra en inglés por Ariel Nuño:

https://www.youtube.com/watch?v=rFCTQESd-bA

The Loves and Follies of Teaching Non-canonical Texts that "Pop": Morales' *Comedia de los amores y locuras del conde loco*

SIDNEY DONNELL

Lafayette College

I N THIS ESSAY, I shine a light on my quixotic efforts to teach early modern studies to second-language learners at the advanced undergraduate level. Among the many cultural artifacts that students explore in class, I include selections of sixteenth-century Spanish drama. Plays that were produced for mass audiences are particularly helpful in discovering the ways in which popular culture and fine arts converged into a genre that today is associated with Spain's "national theater." In this essay, I examine some of the curricular ins and outs (based, in part, on some of my own successes and failures) of programming and scaffolding assignments based on these and other early modern texts. At the same time, I reflect on the advantages and disadvantages of adhering to or straying from the literary canon. In so doing, I contrast the little-known play *Comedia de los amores y locuras del conde loco* [*Comedy of the Loves and Follies of the Mad Count*] by the mostly forgotten sixteenth-century dramatist Alonso de Morales with works by more canonical authors in order to reflect upon an academic discipline that celebrates "Golden Age" icons (e.g., Lope de Vega) and that overlooks "one-hit wonders" (e.g., Morales).[1] In my view, uncritical adherence to the canon underestimates the abilities of students (as subjects of a consumer society) to grasp the ephemeral merits of works (or bodies of work) that constitute a genre or subgenre. In this respect, the fame of sixteenth-century dramatists and the plays they authored was often as fleeting as that of today's pop artists whose

---

1   It is possible that Morales also authored *Comedia de los naufragios de Leopoldo* (Baratella 19-30).

songs chart on the *Billboard* Top 40 or Hot 100. This dynamic is worthy of students' consideration to help them track shifting attitudes about what constitutes mass culture or pop culture over time.

My contribution to this volume is told, in part, in the confessional mode. Like many professors of my generation, graduate school prepared me for the language classroom and literary scholarship, but I needed to become an autodidact in order to teach literary and cultural studies at the undergraduate level. Early in my teaching career, I discovered that even the briefest pop-culture reference used as an analogy can motivate second-language learners to discover the meanings of words and concepts that otherwise might have taken hours for me to explain or for them to comprehend. In fact, this strategy helped me land a job offer. As part of the on-campus interview, I was asked to teach an undergraduate seminar on *Don Quixote*. During class, I described a writing assignment in which students compare the relationship between Molina and Valentín in Hector Babenco's feature-length film *Kiss of the Spider Woman* (1985) with the relationship between Quixote and Sancho in Cervantes' novel. Having viewed the movie or having read the novel *El beso de la mujer araña* by Manuel Puig, most faculty in attendance immediately recognized the reference. Students, in contrast, needed to see a short film clip in order to be brought up to speed. In this moment, both groups understood and enjoyed the point I was trying to make: Comparative analysis produces deeper understanding of the main subject of study, and the deployment of mass media and tropes found in pop culture can expedite this process throughout a student's educational journey.

It almost has become a pedagogical imperative in today's classrooms to reference mass or pop culture to help communicate the significance of elite texts from the early modern period to students. Can the same be said about teaching non-elite or popular artifacts of old?[2] Whether a particular artifact was perceived as a sample of "high" or "low" culture in its day, the stated learning outcomes of courses in early modern studies are often more difficult to achieve than those of courses in modern or contemporary studies because most students at the undergraduate level think of the past as "a foreign coun-

---

2   From the point of view of contemporary students who are new to cultural studies or the early modern period, all literary texts may appear at first glance to be "elite" or privileged reading. In order to locate this specific text in its original context and to generate conversation about how literary critics have treated this and other popular texts, it is important to distinguish between canonical and non-canonical literary texts and, at the same time, between early modern texts whose intended audience were either the court or the masses.

try" (Swaffar and Arens 178). Apart from a general lack of familiarity with a given cultural artifact's historical context, students in a second-language acquisition program often feel overwhelmed by the vocabulary, grammatical structures, rhetorical devices, discourses and genres inherent in the Renaissance or the Baroque—even when their textual roots are in mass or pop culture. In other words, almost anything in the target language that reads "old" to undergraduates is likely to appear more distant, more remote and, therefore, more elite than texts from the modern or contemporary periods.[3] Moreover, instructors have to be keenly aware of when to introduce second-language learners to the challenges of studying drama because students easily lose their way when tasked with reading a play from *any* time period. Dramatic dialogue lacks most of the contextual markers they need in order to make sense of what they are reading. Therefore, drama studies are often placed at the end of a second-language acquisition program designed for undergraduates. According to Janet Swaffar and Katherine Arens,

> Drama appears . . . last . . . because it is often a more consciously elite genre, lacking the additional descriptions and explanatory aids often associated with nonelite forms. Learners must be taught to read between the lines of a dialogue on the basis of what they know about time, place, staging conventions, and presumed audience for a piece; drama gives them fewer clues than does the more realistic world of a film. (170)

The above citation is part of a multiple literacies approach to second-language acquisition that treats genres as distinct communicative acts. Genres, therefore, should be taught in sequence according to the level of difficulty they present to language learners. If a particularly challenging genre or subgenre also happens to be written in an older form of the target language, then second-language learners will experience an inevitable breakdown in communication (that is, an author's written message will not signify much

---

3   In addition to selecting materials and preparing classes, professors of early modern studies have to be proactive about collaborating with faculty across disciplines, with academic advisers, and with college administrators so that students have positive, informed impressions about every aspect of their home department's curriculum. Potential majors and minors need to know before registering for classes why they are required or expected to take a subject that focuses on an age that predates the lives of their (and our) great grandparents by hundreds of years. For more information, please see my contribution to a recent volume on approaches to teaching *Don Quijote* (Donnell 2015).

or anything to this particular set of recipients). Though regrettable, it is perfectly reasonable in such instances for a department to choose either to offer
such material in translation or to postpone instruction by assigning it to classrooms or reading lists at the postgraduate level. In fact, some very successful
undergraduate programs in German over the past twenty years have elected
not to teach any texts written prior to their target language's standardization
in the mid-1700s. It may not be as difficult for Spanish-language students
to navigate early modern texts as doing so is for their counterparts in German, and Spanish departments do not find themselves in the dire straits of
many departments in the Humanities. There is, nevertheless, a similar sense
of urgency in sixteenth- and seventeenth-century studies in Spanish, and this
chapter is dedicated to pedagogical renovation and renewal in response to
dwindling enrollment throughout the North American Academy.

Professors of medieval, early modern, or colonial literature are likely to
identify with the above challenges whenever they have the urge to teach a
Spanish-language text for which there is no modern edition. Those who feel
sufficiently compelled to bring the contents of an unedited artifact into the
classroom are faced then with transcribing the document themselves (which
may be of interest if they are working on a critical edition) or teaching students how to read sixteenth- or seventeenth-century handwriting or typeset
(which may fascinate a precocious major headed to graduate school, but acquisition of these skills is time consuming and not a goal commonly shared
by most undergraduates). As for Morales' *Comedia de los amores y locuras
del conde loco* (herein, *El conde loco*), which is the focus of much of this essay, there is exactly one modern edition. Morales' Spanish-language text has
undergone minimal modernization, and the critic's introduction and notes
are in French.[4] Taken as a case in point, most would agree that it is too much
trouble to adopt this category of text because, without direct intervention
on the part of the instructor, second-language learners at the undergraduate level would find it mostly unintelligible. It is much easier to stay on the
beaten path by choosing more canonical texts. Professors and students of
Don Quijote, for example, can take advantage of a wide selection of critical editions (including student-friendly publications), translations, reading
guides and film adaptations. Such abundance, however, creates a different
challenge: How much of Cervantes' original text do language learners truly
read in the target language?

---

4   All references to Morales' play come from Canavaggio's edition of *Comedia
de los amores y locuras del conde loco* (1969). The source document is a manuscript
housed by the Hispanic Society of America.

At my home institution the current sequence of courses in the Spanish-language curriculum rarely affords me the opportunity to offer an under-graduate seminar that focuses exclusively on early modern drama. Before they graduate, most Spanish majors take at least one subject in early modern or colonial literature. However, by the time they are sufficiently prepared to enter a seminar on early modern drama, they already have received their di-plomas and moved on. This reality is somewhat frustrating, but I also recog-nize—as stated above—that gaps in literacy grow exponentially when stu-dents are faced with dramatic works written during the early modern period. Based on past classroom experience, I still believe, nevertheless, that early modern theater has the potential to resonate with advanced second-language learners. To achieve the quixotic goal of teaching the *comedia*, every assign-ment has to be carefully scaffolded. In particular, the thoughtful enhance-ment of lessons through mass and pop culture can inspire students to dis-cover meaning in genres and historical periods that otherwise might be lost to them, even in translation.

About twelve years into my full-time teaching career, I was in rotation to offer a writing-intensive seminar to Spanish majors that conforms to depart-mental and college-wide guidelines on process writing. Until that moment, I had taught *comedia* upon occasion but had much more experience guid-ing students through novels like *Don Quijote*. Having recently published a gender-bending book about sixteenth- and seventeenth-century theater in Imperial Spain, I decided to introduce a small group of college juniors and se-niors to what I hoped would be a fun-filled, semester-long adventure in queer interpretations of early modern drama. Results were mixed. Student output (e.g., discussions, presentations, formal essays) was sometimes muddled, and I came to the realization that the theme of a revised seminar would need to deal more explicitly with concepts of "high" and "low" culture in early modern Spain as compared with what students experience today. It is not enough for a professor to contrast entertainment for the masses (e.g., *Com-media dell'arte*) with more elite forms for courtesans (e.g., early opera). Even though the subject of classroom examination may be the text from a play's performance for sixteenth-century masses, its mere inclusion on a course syl-labus elevates it—at least at first glance—to elite status from the perspective of today's undergraduates. This "revelation" (though obvious) is in itself wor-thy of academic discussion in a seminar that deals directly with manifesta-tions of mass and pop culture from faraway times and places.

Although advanced undergraduates can and should read secondary sources to achieve an intellectual understanding of literary history, criticism and theory, these readings are not an effective substitute for other types of support that second-language learners need in order to read, fully comprehend, and write about primary texts in the target language. For several participants in the first iteration of my seminar on the early modern stage, the expenditure of time and energy reading and discussing some of the secondary sources resulted in an accumulation of too many abstract thoughts, a sense of greater distance from the course's primary texts, and feelings of alienation in relation to their chosen area of specialization. Although this particular seminar was far from an "epic fail," these inadvertently negative outcomes revealed that I had allowed my authority as a scholar to undermine my skills (and common sense) as an experienced docent in what is predominantly a second-language acquisition program. Lest courses in our particular subfield disappear like those in other areas of the Humanities, professors have to remember to prepare second-language learners for the many linguistic and conceptual trapdoors they will encounter in subjects devoted entirely to something as seemingly remote, from their point of view, as the early modern stage.

If you are reading these words, you already are familiar with the importance of careful selection and preparation of literary texts before their debut in the classroom. In addition, you probably have a strong sense as to why you would consider adding an exemplary novel by Cervantes or a selection of poems by Sor Juana Inés de la Cruz to a syllabus that devotes at least one course unit to studying literary production in the early modern period. But what if you are inspired, like me, to teach a non-canonical work by an unknown author from the 1500s or 1600s? There are specific risks involved, and you will have to weigh the advantages and disadvantages—including the time commitment—when preparing this and other course readings and activities. To this end, I will discuss my choice of *El conde loco* in order to spotlight some of the rewards and challenges of trying to make this rare dramatic text part of an enjoyable learning experience for second-language learners.

There are very good reasons for including lesser-known cultural artifacts like *El conde loco* in courses that examine mass culture or popular culture (as well as gender and genre). Historically speaking, for example, Morales' play can be positioned as sort of a "missing link" in the evolution of the *comedia*. Even though the play is a comedy in four acts, the total number of verses is about half the average length of a typical three-act *comedia nueva* by Lope de Vega or one of his followers. In this regard, students can *see* the difference between *El conde loco* and easily recognizable "classics" of the Spanish stage. The work also invites scrutiny of questions related to authorship, ownership and dissemination of scripts in the early modern period. For example, the playwright's name does not appear on the single extant manuscript copy of *El conde loco*, and little is known about the work's author, exact date of composition, or staging. Scholars rely on specific references in the "Loa de la comedia" [Play's Prologue] from Agustín de Rojas' *Viaje entretenido* [Entertaining Voyage] (1603) in order to attribute authorship of *El conde loco* to either Alonso de Morales or Pedro de Morales. After careful research, Jean Canavaggio concludes that Morales' work pertains to the generation of dramatists who wrote between 1579 and 1588 (Morales et al. 22). For those interested in pop culture or gender identity, the question of when *El conde loco* was written has as much bearing as who wrote the play because this information tells us something about its staging and the ephemerality of its mass appeal, as we shall see in a moment.

As regards the sequencing of course materials in my seminar's first iteration, *El conde loco* appeared relatively early in the semester. Texts were presented mostly in chronological order, and I took a multiple-literacies approach to the overall subject by starting with sixteenth-century pop culture (e.g., sketches, songs, dances) and ending with seventeenth-century court theater (e.g., *comedia cantada*). Students began the semester by reading brief histories of sixteenth-century Spanish theater, and we focused on professional touring companies (e.g., *commedia dell'arte* players), which included the overlapping roles of troupe directors, actors, singers and dancers. By the start of week 2, students had read Lope de Rueda's *Comedia Medora*, which is a more familiar work to many scholars and teachers than *El conde loco*. In class, we reread passages from Rueda's comedy out loud, viewed and listened to scenes of the play in performance, and discussed the work's basic structure and themes. By week 3, students had read literary criticism about *Comedia Medora* and had started reading *El conde loco*.

One has to look beyond plot to gain a better understanding of the gender dynamics embedded in the dialogue of these plays, thereby revealing certain heteronormative assumptions and biases on the part of modern-day readers about sixteenth-century mass culture. In this instance, familiarity with staging practices is of paramount importance. Because *Comedia Medora* was published posthumously in 1567, we can assume that boys and men performed the roles of male and female characters because women were customarily prohibited from acting on the Spanish stage throughout much of the sixteenth century (Donnell, *Feminizing* 110). This fact is not spelled out in playscripts because male-to-female transformations on stage were, by and large, expected. This sudden insight (or satisfying "aha" moment) motivated my students to reread passages of *Comedia Medora* and to continue reading Morales' play. As for *El conde loco* (c. 1585), "[t]he Count's beloved Doña Alda, in all likelihood, would have been played by a boy if [the play's] staging occurred prior to the simultaneous legalization of married women actors and prohibition on drag performance in 1587" (Donnell , *Feminizing* 105). Furthermore, the plots of *Comedia Medora* and *El conde loco* require their protagonists to cross-dress, although the respective causes and effects of these actions are quite different. While *Comedia Medora*'s main characters attempt to *pass* for one gender or another, *El conde loco*'s mad hero undergoes a male-to-female transition that results in what some spectators today might call "butch drag."[5]

Still, seeing is believing. In order for a play from another time and place to convey meaning, readers, especially second-language learners, need to *experience* the text in performance. Using class time to have students rehearse and recite certain passages out loud is a tried-and-true method to boost their comprehension, but the significance of certain scenes (whether restrained or raucous) may elude some second-language learners unless they view or hear performers interpret the actions and utterances of a play's characters on stage or on screen.

In contrast with *Comedia Medora*, I am unaware of any modern-day revivals or adaptations of *El conde loco*; therefore, to my knowledge, there are no recordings of performances of this play to show in class. In addition, the author's muse (textually based or otherwise) is indeterminate. Perhaps Morales' play "was inspired by the spirit if not a precise episode of *Orlando Furioso*," but this genealogy is based on a heteronormative tendency to classify *El conde loco* as a "comic work" (Thacker 20). Certainly, references to Ludovico Ariosto's epic poem are helpful in establishing a degree of thematic continuity between *Comedia Medora* and *El conde loco*, but in truth, it is difficult to refer to a concrete predecessor of the Count that students find satisfying or memorable. To this end, discovering an adequate audiovisual representation of the serious mental condition depicted in *El conde loco* was a crucial factor in my decision to include it on my course syllabus. This, I believe, is where imaginative applications of pop culture (broadly defined) can provide necessary tools and resources that are a help to students in bridging the gap between past and present, and between signifier and signified.

Mental illness has fascinated audiences of comedy and tragedy for millennia. Moreover, since the late nineteenth century, psychoanalytic case

---

5   The Count's agency and subjectivity require in-class discussion. If the Count is insane, is he concerned with societal norms and the intricacies of performing a masculine or feminine gender identity? Or does self-awareness even matter?

studies (whose authors have been known to borrow from Greek tragedy to describe and name certain conditions) are a frequent source of inspiration for stories and characters in contemporary forms of entertainment. It is here that I found a modern-day fictional representation of a psychotic episode similar to the one experienced by Morales' mad count. Rene Gallimard, the protagonist of David Henry Hwang's tragedy *M. Butterfly*, self-identifies as "a man who loved a woman created by a man. Everything else—simply falls short" (Hwang 80). In order to gain insight into the mental state in which the Count transforms himself into his beloved Doña Alda (Morales, vv. 1191-1433), I assigned Gallimard's monologue at the end of *M. Butterfly*. Then we viewed Jeremy Irons' interpretation of Gallimard's metamorphosis into Butterfly during the climatic conclusion of David Cronenberg's 1993 feature-length screen adaptation of the play.

It is difficult to understand the mad count's breakdown because it defies personal experience, and Morales' text does not provide sufficient context to explain this phenomenon to modern-day readers. Therefore, viewing the above film sequence supplies relevant data that informs the interpretative process and influences readings of scholarly debate. In his introduction and notes to the critical edition of *El conde loco* published in 1969, Canavaggio cannot find a precedent for the Count's madness beyond Ariosto, and he concludes that the play is mere buffoonery. Instead of rewarding Morales' play for its uniqueness, the critic thinks it crass and utterly lacking in literary merit. To the contrary, as I have argued, "The play is simply too over the top for Canavaggio's taste, [which is] influenced by a twentieth-century popular imaginary that reduces [insanity, transvestism and homosexuality] into one indistinguishable taboo" (Donnell, *Feminizing* 108).

Although most Spanish-language students in North America will require translation of Canavaggio's words from the original French, the renowned critic's response to *El conde loco* will help instructors guide discussion towards modern-day notions of high and low culture and, furthermore, towards categorization of Morales' play as a sixteenth-century example of pop culture. Classroom conversation can expand at the metalevel to find out if the inclusion of the closing sequence from *M. Butterfly* (a film adaptation of a Broadway play inspired by a Puccini opera) is a useful point of comparison. Generationally, most students will not recognize the film's star, Jeremy Irons, and will not categorize him as a pop-culture icon. Arguably, much of the artist's stage, film and television career is too highbrow for mass appeal, and memories of *M. Butterfly*'s success as a 1988 Tony-winning play have faded. (In fact, its Broadway revival in 2017 flopped and closed early.)

But this is part of the overall point. As fame fades so does context. In his *loa* to the *Viaje entretenido*, Rojas pays explicit homage to Morales and implicit respect to aging or deceased audience members who were excited to see his play decades earlier. Put another way, *El conde loco* was all the rage once upon a time. Pop culture has a shelf life, and it takes familiarity with the historical context of a cultural artifact to even begin to appreciate what a generation shared and took for granted at a specific moment in space and time. In order to be fashionable, "hip," or in the know, one needs both context and a comparison group with which to compare—that is, people who are not fashionable, "hip," or in the know. In this respect, pop culture can serve as its own commercialized form of elitism.

Curiously, twenty-first-century institutions of higher learning might have something to say (directly or indirectly) about *El conde loco*'s generic classification. Morales' work is technically a comedy inasmuch as there are many humorous scenes and a happy resolution to the play's conflict; however, the *El conde loco* also can be read as an early tragicomedy if the Count's story is taken with any degree of seriousness (Canavaggio 29-37). As with Gallimard's monologue near the end of *M. Butterfly*, explicitly violent representations of the Count's psychotic break and attempted suicide may prompt instructors to provide a disclaimer (or "trigger warning") so that they are in compliance with college or university policies about teaching violent content that may be offensive or disturbing to some audiences.

The combination of *El conde loco* and *M. Butterfly* appeared to intrigue my students, but I confess to having rushed them in the seminar's debut because I was too eager about moving on to the next exciting topic (early seventeenth-century drama) and too rigid about having students fulfill the writing component of the course. In general, students need time to explore the myriad facts and concepts that intersect with course readings and viewings, and they need additional time to express their abstract thoughts in writing. In response to the prompt for a short essay,[6] most demonstrated basic knowledge of outside readings about the history of drama, cultural history, or femi-

---

6   I assigned several brief exploratory essays with the expectation that one (or more) of these would serve as the foundation for a longer essay at the end of the term. Four pages was the maximum length of each draft, which students later revised. The wording of the assignment based on *El conde loco* is as follows:

El conde loco es un documento que requiere gran esfuerzo interpretativo por diferentes razones. Dentro del mundo académico (específicamente, el campo de la crítica literaria), hay varias escuelas de pensamiento sobre cómo hacer esto aunque, en general, se puede distinguir dos extremos contrarios:

nist theory (e.g., as applied to phallic references throughout *El conde loco* to a missing key). The most proficient draft was that of a dual major in English and Spanish who, due to her background in literary and cultural studies, had started the semester with a strong sense of what would be expected of her in a course on gender and genre. The least proficient drafts were aimless plot summaries of *El conde loco* in broken Spanish.

Although my hope had been to spark a nascent interest in psychoanalysis or queer theory (e.g., by asking and answering questions related to subjectivity, homosociality or gender performativity), students were much more pragmatic. Some had posed smart questions and made intelligent observations during film screenings, class discussions and office visits, but the thoughts behind their questions and comments did not necessarily translate on paper into a deeper understanding of the texts they had read, viewed or discussed. I also had overestimated the linguistic skills and cultural literacy of several second-language learners in my seminar. As evidenced in their drafts, some were still trying to understand the plot.

At present, I am putting together a seminar on mass and pop culture in the early modern period. Within this framework, the next time I teach *El conde loco*, I will approach it differently by moving beyond early-modern constructions of gender roles in the play's text and performance in order to focus more on modern-day constructions of genre, especially in light of recent attempts to categorize Morales' composition as a comic work. Generic categorization depends on context in the here and now, and, in this respect, *El conde*

---

(1) Algunos académicos dicen que no importa si sabemos quién es el autor, cuándo se escribió el documento, cuál es el momento histórico, etc. Lo importante es explicar el mundo literario creado a través de las palabras empleadas dentro de la obra. Para hacer esto, sí, se puede emplear teorías que provienen de otras disciplinas (por ej., psicoanálisis, lingüística, antropología cultural, etc.).

(2) Al otro lado, hay académicos que dicen que sólo podemos entender un texto escrito si lo situamos dentro de una corriente literaria o un movimiento artístico de una época concreta. Otra característica de esta escuela es su creencia en la posibilidad de explicar el propósito del autor (lo que estaba pensando) cuando escribió su obra; otra es su general rechazo de aplicaciones teóricas que provienen de otras disciplinas (por ej., psicoanálisis, lingüística, antropología cultural, etc.).

Ahora bien, el tema de tu ensayo es el siguiente: Identifica los problemas que *El conde loco* te puede dar como intérprete (crítico literario) de la obra. ¿Cuál de las dos aproximaciones mencionadas arriba emplearías para hablar de *El conde loco*? ¿Por qué emplearías una y no la otra? ¿O irías por otro camino completamente? Desarrolla tu ensayo, empleando buenos ejemplos y citas de la obra misma para explicar por qué es difícil el trabajo interpretativo.

loco's awkward position vis-à-vis the literary canon is due, in some part, to mis-guided assumptions about the meaning of the protagonist's male-to-female gender transformation in the plot. The play, therefore, is caught in a sort of generic limbo between its status as a popular performance piece for sixteenth-century consumption to an elite (and somewhat exoticized) cultural artifact for the consideration of modern-day students and a handful of researchers.

The thematic reframing of *El conde loco* for the classroom will require further pedagogical adjustments. First, looking back at my seminar on gen-der and the *comedia*, I was too conservative in my estimation of what con-stitutes process writing, especially for second-language learners. Since that time, I have come to rely more heavily on the modalities of today's mass culture—which translate into computer-assisted language learning—when I ask students to write. For example, in my seminar on *Don Quijote*, students use storyboard applications to retell one of their favorite scenes from the two novels.[7] Far from a one-off exercise, this creative writing project (which students like to share with one another) is the second part of a three-step process. The first is a take-home quiz in which students have to identify three different diegetic levels in Cervantes' novels, provide quotations and page numbers, and apply narratological terms to help them explain and categorize the passages they have selected. The last step is to write a discourse analysis of their own writing, that is to say, a narratological study of the comic book they produced for step two.

The reasons for storyboarding scenes from an early modern play are rela-tively obvious from the perspective of second-language acquisition. Again, in the words of Swaffar and Arens, "Learners must be taught to read between

---

7   Unless your students are graphic artists or cartoonists (which is possible), most will appreciate using the storyboard settings in MS Word or the application ComicLife. Hundreds of illustrations from volumes of *Don Quijote* are readily avail-able on-line, but students also can use other iconic images (e.g., Batman and Robin in lieu of Cervantes' heroes). Some choose to write their own text, but I encour-age them to take advantage of on-line versions of *Don Quijote*. To do so requires more skill than cutting and pasting. Transferring scenes from a novel to a storyboard requires thoughtful editing on the part of the author. The use of on-line text also reduces the number of typographical or grammatical errors on the part of students. Basic instructions for this creative writing project are as follows:
La meta de este proyecto es pensar en la relación entre personajes y narradores a través del empleo de narración, descripciones y diálogo. Necesitas crear un tebeo o "comic" basado en un episodio de *Don Quijote*. Tienes que producir como mínimo una (1) página con imágenes y texto en la cual incluyas un título original, tu nombre, narración, descripciones y diálogo.

the lines of a dialogue" (170). Students can learn that narration is often embedded in the direct speech of a play's characters, but many lose sight of the story because they cannot visualize what is happening by simply reading and rereading the script. Therefore, if students literally cannot see a work performed (either live or recorded), then storyboarding becomes an effective way of bringing to life the many words (and worlds) that have eluded them. Once learners have completed this task successfully, they can perform the very same scenes (or others of their choosing) live in class or record their performances on video. By redoubling efforts to study drama as an act of communication, storyboarding can help students unlock the genre's unique approach to storytelling.[8]

Second, as part of a course on mass culture that includes *El conde loco* or a similarly rare dramatic work, it is important to sample what contemporary pop culture has to offer in the way of exciting, up-to-date parallels with specific lines of inquiry into the cultural production of the early modern period. *El conde loco* is about a man who is so obsessed with his object of desire that he *becomes* her. The pilot episode of Noah Hawley's twenty-first-century sci-fi action thriller *Legion* (2017) takes this transformation in a maddeningly different direction. When the heterosexual protagonists of this series first kiss, their respective consciousnesses switch bodies (one male, one female). In both instances, early modern and modern day, conventional gender categories are disrupted, identities are blurred, and all reason appears to fly out the window.

Finally, in keeping with the theme of this essay, I have attempted to demonstrate that applications of mass and popular culture in both form (i.e., video, storyboards, comic books) and content (i.e., stories) can assist second-language learners in acquiring the information they need to make comparisons, both linguistic and cultural, and connections between the diverse perspectives they encounter in the early modern period and their own lives. This approach is not a cure-all, but its purposeful deployment in the North American Academy can assist instructors in blazing trails around the many pitfalls inherent in teaching elite genres (e.g., drama) from remote times (e.g., the early modern period) and far-away places (e.g., the Iberian Peninsula). In other words, focused applications of mass culture and pop culture can supply us with useful tools to make rarefied cultural artifacts more accessible and immediate to the lives of our students. Moreover, as long as we recognize and take all of the necessary steps involved as teachers, we should not fear straying from the literary canon. In this light, I hope to have shown that the inclusion of an unorthodox dramatic text

---

8   Edward Friedman demonstrates how narratology has influenced (or has the potential to influence) our theoretical understanding of the *comedia* (1998).

like Morales' *El conde loco* can stimulate healthy debate among undergraduates (and scholars), which in turn can lead to further research with an eye towards cultural and historical specificity, in this case, the growth of the *comedia* and Spain's theater industry, changes in staging practices related to the performance of masculine and feminine roles, and generic classification based on shifting perceptions of gender identity during the early modern period and today.

Works Cited

Ariosto, Lodovico, and Guido Waldman. *Orlando Furioso*. Oxford UP, 1974.

Babenco, Hector, and Manuel Puig. *Kiss of the Spiderwoman*. United States: Charter Entertainment, 1985.

Baratella, Claudio. *Comedia de los naufragios de Leopoldo: Edición y estudio*. MA Thesis. Unversità Ca'Foscari Venezia, 2012, dspace.unive.it/bitstream/handle/10579/2472/831087-1154961.pdf;sequence=2. Accessed Aug. 2018.

Cronenberg, David, David H. Hwang, et al. *M. Butterfly*. Burbank, CA: Warner Home Video, 2009.

Donnell, Sidney. *Feminizing the Enemy: Imperial Spain, Transvestite Drama, and the Crisis of Masculinity*. Bucknell UP, 2003.

———. "*Don Quixote* in the Balance: Early Modern Studies and the Undergraduate Curriculum." *Approaches to Teaching Cervantes's* Don Quixote, edited by James A. Parr and Lisa Vollendorf, Modern Language Association of America, 2015, 197–205.

Friedman, Edward H. "Theorizing the *Comedia*: The Impact of Narratology." *A Society on Stage: Essays on Spanish Golden Age Drama*, edited by Edward H. Friedman, H. J. Manzari, and Donald D. Miller, University Press of the South, 1998, pp. 73–87.

Hawley, Noah, Brian L. Parker, et al. *Legion: The Complete Season One*. United States: 20th Century Fox Home Entertainment, 2018.

Hwang, David H. *M. Butterfly*. Penguin, 1989.

Morales., Pedro de. *Comedia de los amores y locuras del conde loco*, edited by Jean Canavaggio, Centre de recherches hispaniques, Institut d'études hispaniques, 1969.

Puig, Manuel. *El beso de la mujer araña*. Seix Barral, 1976.

Rojas, Villandrando A., and Jean P. Ressot. *El viaje entretenido*. Castalia, 1972.

Rueda, Lope de, and Alfredo Hermenegildo. *Las cuatro comedias*. Cátedra, 2001.

Swaffar, Janet K., and Katherine Arens. *Remapping the Foreign Language Curriculum: An Approach Through Multiple Literacies*. Teaching languages, literatures, and cultures. MLA, 2005.

Thacker, Jonathan. *A Companion to Golden Age Theatre*. Tamesis, 2007.

Enrique Iglesias, Madonna and ¿San Juan de la Cruz?: Using Pop Music to Teach Spanish Mystic Poetry

BONNIE L. GASIOR

California State University, Long Beach

O FTEN RECOUNTED FROM A first-person perspective detailing the soul's journey toward and ultimate communion with God, as well as the harmony established after this arduous voyage as a blissful reward, mystic poetry originates from a place of exclusivity. As a result, the interior, clandestine and intimate nature of sixteenth-century mystic experiences recounted in early modern Spanish mystical poetry often perplexes—if not wearies and alienates—the twenty-first century student. As Alison Weber affirms, most find these poems "arcane, archaic or simply bizarre" (2). Because supposedly only mystics themselves could understand what this sort of transcendental experience entailed, and because articulating this experience textually added yet another layer of incomprehensibility, reading mystic poetry demands an informed, patient and determined reader.[1] Assuming that said reader, does, in fact, *read*—humanities scholars regrettably report that on average only 30% of students admit to regularly fulfilling reading assignments at the university level—teaching mystic poetry proves additionally challenging, even the most seasoned professor.[2] What can instructors do,

---

1   Elizabeth Rhodes maintains that "[b]y all accounts, the direct experience of God cannot be captured by human language with anything close to high fidelity" (47). Note the choice to use an auditory term to describe the mystical experience.

2   Clump, Bower and Bradley found that 27.46% of psychology students complete assigned class readings; Eric H. Hobson cites a similar number (70% non-compliance for any given day); and Mary E. Hoeft concluded that in a comparison between a large and small section of the same freshman course, students surprisingly

then, to ensure that students not only read (purposefully) but also in a way demystifies mysticism?[3]

One strategy that I have relied on to diminish the anxiety students sometimes feel when confronting challenging texts is to bring the reading to a place of familiarity in which their personal, cultural and/or academic backgrounds and course content subtly interact. As education scholar Rose-Marie Cipriani Sklar asserts, "Students need to connect with literature on three basic levels: text to text, text to self, and self to the world." Although my experience is purely anecdotal, I have found that after nearly two decades of teaching Hispanic literature this integrative approach boosts confidence, enhances learning and even—I suspect—puts everyone in a better frame of mind for subsequent readings.[4] Surely we have all noticed how a student, even the most disengaged one, will eagerly volunteer to answer a reading question when you associate it with something meaningful, comfortable and/or familiar in his or her own life. This is where, when handled appropriately, popular culture becomes a strategic pedagogical tool, one we often omit because we overlook, undervalue or simply fear its power to captivate our students. So, why not harness that energy and redirect it toward the text on behalf of our unsuspecting students, who, as William Clapton asserts, are "already steeped and well-versed in popular culture, much more so than the disciplinary knowledge that we seek to impart on them?"

In this case, such an endeavor begins with Howard Mancing's double reading of "Noche oscura," in which he argues that mystic writers convey spiritual activities by invoking amorous imagery—what Bernard McGinn calls "illicit sexuality" (205)— and ends with two well-known, contemporary pop songs, "Experiencia Religiosa" (1995; Spain) and "Like a Prayer" (1989;

---

read for class at the same rate (46%), while only 55% were able to demonstrate comprehension (10), which furthermore suggests basic discrepancies in the definition of the verb "to read." Couple these statistics with the fact that Spanish may not be the native tongue of many students, and the numbers invariably nosedive.

3   Search engines become the life preservers of students adrift in a sea of words and ideas as they attempt to propel themselves toward a land mass of understanding. A recent Google search—out of sheer curiosity on my part—did little, however, to explain mysticism. A Google Image search did even less, providing visuals (e.g., an illuminated dove, a figure walking toward a keyhole along the galaxy, a horned deity and abstract expressions of heaven) that when considered collectively, render a confusing, synesthetic cacophony.

4   See Kristina Robertson's article, particularly the Sheltered Instruction Observation Protocol model (SIOP). Although she writes in the context of youth ELL language learners, the methodology could apply to any reader.

U.S.A.).[5] In order to communicate the sensory overload inherent to the divine mystic union reserved only for mystics, their poems, as scholars have contended, suggest metaphors of corporeal ecstasy in a familiarizing move. This idea aligns with the claim that mystic poets favor emotion over erudition, as Herbert Moller points out: "Almost all the Spanish mystics were of the affective type, not speculative thinkers" (316).[6] Just as poets describe this reserved experience between the soul and God in terms similar to a spiritual catharsis, Iglesias and Madonna describe carnal passion in terms of a climactic divine contemplation, an analogy that ultimately renders the mystic encounter less metaphysical and more concrete and therefore, more reader friendly. Popular music's ability to bridge generational gaps and historical expanses thus incites an appreciation for the past vis a vis the present as these sorts of artistic expressions decussate in rich, creative ways. Although these songs, now in their third decade of existence, are probably not well known by the envisioned audience of this book, they are both still closer to twenty-first century students than San Juan de la Cruz, and so their style and images are more likely to resonate with them. Pop culture references have the potential, among other things, to disencumber the enigmatic nature of Spanish mysticism, and perhaps, in the process, to fortuitously dispel any preconceived notions about poetry in general.

Due to poetry's formal peculiarities, students are already more apprehensive about it than other literary genres, according to Hirvela and Boyle (180), despite—or perhaps due to—its myriad interpretive possibilities.[7] We as instructors, then, owe it to our students to think about new ways of study-

---

5   Michelle Dunaway offers a pedagogical selling point to students and teachers alike: "Lyricists and musicians are like novelists and poets in that their creations often come from the heart and reflect the world around them. As teachers, we need to connect these things to our students' lives so that they begin to see cause/effect relationships and so they begin to see the lines of connection. Doing so creates relevance and interest, and continues to nurture their desire for learning and exploration, something that often gets lost in the tediousness of the test-based classroom environments currently being foisted on us."

6   Dana Bultman asserts that "John's poems affirm that spiritual understanding is progressive and that experience of the divine can be achieved not through the intellect's powers of reason but only through direct intervention by the forces of God's grace" (233).

7   In a world where students seek out the elusive "correct" answer, often culminating with the vexing (for us), frustration-fraught (for them) question—"What are you looking for?"—pop culture parallels might help students think outside the box.

ing and connecting to and with poetry since we are the ones responsible for guiding them through those daunting verses and stanzas in the first place. If, as playwright William Congreve wrote, music soothes the savage breast, could it not work in the same way to lessen students' anxiety?[8] Even Sancho Panza, Cervantes' delightful squire in *Don Quijote* reassures the nervous Duchess in II.34 that "Donde hay música no puede haber cosa mala."[9] Nicholas Ferroni advocates for the music-infused classroom due to its ability to stand the test of time and transcend trends: "in a day when activities and education methods get replaced year after year with the 'next big thing,' music will remain a constant to which every student (year after year) will form a connection and association." Repurposing pop music for the classroom has the potential to revolutionize how we teach as well as how students learn and retain knowledge. Pop music pedagogy advantageously, and perhaps logically, circles back to our enigmatic mystic poets, who in a way are stimulating our senses by relaying a mystic experience in earthly terms so that we, as readers, "live" vicariously through them. Popular music not only has the ability to shape the way students perceive and respond to literature but also to render its study more personally significant, since melodies persist in our minds despite the passage of time (think about a song you have not heard in a decade yet whose lyrics you recall verbatim). Indeed, music encourages connection making during students' educational careers and throughout their lives, including the sort that they make when reading sixteenth-century mystic poems.

San Juan de la Cruz's late sixteenth-century poem "Noche oscura" figures as the quintessential mystic poem of the Spanish tradition. When I first read it as a master's student more than twenty years ago—before the Google revolution—my professor (coincidentally, Howard Mancing) presented it to us as a handout to read for homework. He suppressed the poem's title to encourage a formalist, context-limited reading to see how we would interpret those mysterious verses by a certain "Juan de Yepes." Everyone returned to the next class meeting with a similar summary: a woman slips away from her home late at night to rendezvous with her lover; we all assumed—as Mancing probably hoped—this was an example of romantic rather than religious-inspired poetry. When he finally provided more historical and cultural back-

---

8   See *The Mourning Bride*, Act I, Scene I, 1697: "Music hath charms to soothe a savage breast, / to soften rocks, or bend a knotted oak."

9   See Chad Gasta's "Music, Poetry, and Orality in *Don Quijote*" for an overview of the importance of music in the novel as well as Golden Age Spain in general. Weber's volume *Aids to Teaching* also lists several titles of musical interpretations of mystic poetry (25-26).

ground, we read the poem a second time, and gauging by my peers' perplexed faces, only then did we begin to appreciate his strategy, although the missing contextual links sparked more questions than they answered. For example, how could a priest, of all people, manage to invoke such sensual imagery, particularly under Counterreformation Spain's watchful eye? Despite establishing communion with God as its ultimate goal, we gained an understanding that mystics were highly suspect during the period, which in turn will signal that religiosity did not necessarily imply orthodoxy, what María del Pilar Ryan qualifies as "lives of both defiance and obedience" (142), a detail that comes into focus through the juxtaposition of text and song.[10]

Mancing's argument becomes relevant when he proposes that mystic poets invoke metaphors of stealth, enigma and ensuing ecstasy to better connect with all readers, on one hand to appeal to their ecclesiastic counterparts, and on the other, to engage secular, material-oriented human beings. Because a poem requires a different sort of reading than, say, a prose text, and because the mystic experience was confidential, mystic poets often employed images and invoked emotions that their lay counterparts could more easily comprehend. In other words, the allegory—Mancing's reading of the poem "twice"—was a means to an end that facilitated an approximation of what the mystical experience *might* be like.

Popular music's catchiness is inescapable, and repurposing it for pedagogical aims is something that a diverse, Southern Californian classroom like mine has historically welcomed.[11] I regularly have my students, at both the graduate and undergraduate level, read "Noche oscura" with Enrique Iglesias in mind after we analyze the poem (since Mancing's approach—thanks, Google!—obviously would not work in 2017).[12] I introduce Iglesias' song in two phases. In

---

10   See Lisa Vollendorf's article for a succinct overview of the reception of mystic writing in light of their reform activities. Judith Pace's discussion of "multicultural democratic learning," which "can produce critical thinking, deeper understanding of complex problems, and the ability to participate in civil discourse across differences," can help frame these religious tensions pedagogically.

11   Coincidentally, both songs featured in this essay contain four-chord loops, which, according to musicologist Nate Sloan, have "hit" power: "I think four-chord loops are one of the most surefire ways to see your song get some traction . . . A four-chord loop usually includes some combination of major and minor triads is something listeners seem to really gravitate toward."

12   There are, in fact, multiple ways to incorporate the songs, including following Mancing's lead by having students promise to forego any electronic resources while reading, either at home or in class. As for the incorporation of the song, students could listen to the song first to ensure engagement and then read the poem to

the first, students contemplate melody, instrumentation, and tempo during a two-minute selection. I encourage them to close their eyes to focus more on the "feel" of the music than the words. Afterward, we talk in general terms about what they sensed as they listened: the slow and ceremonious rhythm; the piano and organ music; and the increasingly celebratory if not climactic tone, including the culminating, ecstasy-echoing choral backup. In the most general terms, they sense the solemnity of the melody, which conveys a churchlike ambience. For phase two of the listening exercise, I project the lyrics so that students couple affect with meaning. The words they most often identify as tangentially mystical—because by this point they begin to realize the exercise's objective—include: "noche," "éxtasis," "infinidad," "temblar," "iluminar," "harmonía," "rescucito," "subir al cielo," and "aleluyah." I usually ask them why those words were of particular interest, to which they have historically responded, "Iglesias ha descrito, a través de su relación amorosa, una experiencia religiosa, o sea, una experiencia mística."[13] My follow up is something like "¿Sí? ¿Como la de San Juan?" After a few more rounds of prodding, some student will finally understand the essence of my activity: *Similar a como San Juan intenta relatar una experiencia mística a través de imágenes sensuales, Enrique Iglesias describe su deseo sexual en términos místicos.* The (humanizing) comparison reminds students that feelings and emotions—such as love—are, as we know, often indescribable and are better understood through metaphor. It also demonstrates, in a serendipitous upshot, that Iglesias may well have been familiar with the mystic tradition in order to write "Experiencia religiosa": students realize that even famous singers read literature (and that maybe more students should, too).[14]

While I have not used Madonna's "Like a Prayer" in the classroom, it could perhaps be more relatable and less daunting for L2 learners. In addition to being more linguistically lenient, it also boasts additional pedagogical advantages. Like Iglesias, Madonna employs similar religiously oriented expressions: mystery, solitude, prayer, midnight, power, journey, angels, flying, God, Heaven, dreams. What makes Madonna's song more compelling than Iglesias', however, is its accompanying, unconventional music video. This groundbreaking and to-this-day controversial spectacle—which suggests

---

see if they make any connections on their own, or they could consider all three at once as part of a one-page reaction paper for the next class period.

13   Here, I am paraphrasing student responses.

14   Gian Lorenzo Bernini's "El éxtasis de Santa Teresa" helps reinforce those ties between mystic poets and the songs of contemporary crooners like those of Iglesias and serves as a way for text, sound and image to coalesce.

her character's physical relationship with a black, sixteenth-century Peruvian saint, Martín de Porres Velázquez, as part of her salvation—more closely parallels/exemplifies the sensuality/sanctity paradox expressed in San Juan's poem.[15] Steven E. Young refers to Madonna's visual narrative, which probes and dismantles the sex/religion dichotomy, as a "blurring of distinctions" (66). Likewise, it also invites a deeper discussion, should one have the time and be so inclined, to talk about intersectionality, in what Young describes as a commingling of sex, religion and race throughout the music video (64-65).

Although recounted non-sequentially, the MTV classic begins as Madonna, in character, witnesses an injustice: a black man, who we soon learn bears a striking resemblance to Porres Velázquez, is wrongly arrested for an assault.[16] A conflicted Madonna—Should she go to the authorities with the information? Will they believe her? What about the scene-fleeing perpetrator's intimidating glare?—enters a church to seek spiritual guidance and quickly discovers it in the form of an effigy of the black saint. She approaches an enclosure behind which this effigy stands among relics, and her gaze triggers the sculpture's anthropomorphism. Soon thereafter, she effortlessly unlocks the gate and enters a dream-like state in which, among other things, she intimates a sexual consummation with the statue-turned-human. Similar to the choir's climactic performance in Iglesias's song, the chorus' crescendo implies sexual pleasure as she reclines to receive her lover. This alternative "religious" experience ultimately compels her to denounce the incarceration of the innocent man, signaling the climax of the story as good triumphs over evil.

The video of "Like a Prayer" has the potential to take the discussion of mysticism to a whole new level and place, one that includes the doubling of the male protagonist as well as the dagger used in the crime, which Madonna later cradles in her hand causing stigmata; the theme of imprisonment as both a social repercussion and mystic phenomenon; the implications of a kiss on the forehead as opposed to one on the mouth; the burning of crosses not as an act of desecration but rather the ultimate signifier of religious fervor; and even social justice issues, such as systemic racism and Black Lives Matter. Together, the transgressive elements of the song vis à vis the video promote a more nuanced reading of "Noche oscura." The music video also offers an interesting parallel that will speak to students' common interest in themes

---

15   Iglesias's video, in contrast, mostly strays from the literalness of the song's lyrics, opting instead to recount the end of an amorous relationship he later illicitly revives, which, for all intents and purposes, does not enhance our pop culture approach.

16   This detail figures as an additional point of connectivity to students' lives given the recent Black Lives Matter movement.

of self-expression, censorship, and the law: just as Madonna contended with critics, such as when the release of her video immediately prompted Pepsi Cola to cancel her endorsement deal with them as a way to condemn her artistic boundary pushing, mystic poets, whose direct relationship with God threatened the Catholic church (and smacked of Protestantism) also dealt with their own persecutors in Inquisitional Spain. McGinn succinctly summarizes mystic poetry's appeal as one of resistance and intrigue, which we as instructors should capitalize on in the classroom as yet another way to bridge the past with the present: "mysticism's fundamental attraction to the postmodern mentality is its subversive character: it has always been a protest against dogmatic theology and more often than not it has also served as a female critique of male-dominated religion" (200).[17] Because both "Experiencia religiosa" and "Like a Prayer" hold iconic stature in the English- and Spanish-speaking music realm, their familiarity has the potential to put students in the right—or at least a better— frame of mind as they bilocate, as many mystics professedly did, between the world of Early modern Spanish mystic poetry and our current one.[18]

Given that Western pop culture figures as part of what Stacey Goodman calls students' "universe ecosystem," we can—and she would argue *should*—use it as part of the larger framework to create "rich and meaningful content" in our classrooms and more importantly, "make connections between the sometimes seemingly superficial controversies and the bigger questions and themes of which we want [students] to gain critical understanding." Moreover, by introducing mystic poetry, which often details (human) relationships, through popular music, we can make the former more manageable by focusing on its main idea, as James B. Anderson asserts:

> One trait that subsumes even the mystical experience is the motive of love. Love provides the motivation for the arduous process of preparation. It becomes a unifying substitute for the pursuit of abstract truth. It

---

17   According to Bultman, "Since the study of theology was prohibited to women in sixteenth-century Spain, "La noche oscura" can potentially be seen as an indirect way of encouraging the dissemination of such knowledge to readers who did not have access to it" (236).

18   Perhaps the two songs in tandem would provide a unique experience for students at any level when teaching "Noche oscura." If something a bit more esoteric is desired, Peter Gabriel's "In Your Eyes" is also a sort of mystic inversion. Instructors may even want to have students identify additional songs that have mystic influences to deepen their understanding and reinforce their connective networks of knowledge.

also gives tone and color to the symbols of mystical poetry. It is important to recognize it as the basic feature of Christian mysticism because it is linked to the ontological quest, and emerges as the unifying link to all aspects of the poems of St. John of the Cross (116).

Now, I recognize that some purists might find this approach dangerous, superficial, or misguided, but the pop culture allusions used to elucidate more complex concepts in my courses more often flourish than fail. The argument that pop culture has no place in the classroom collapses in light of my own experiences and of what we now know about how students learn. We must come to terms with the fact that it is up to instructors to overcome our own fear-driven pedagogical prejudices to which Mindy Badia and I allude in the introduction. This undertaking—make no mistake—does require work on our part (e.g., not allowing the discussion to veer off course, channeling creativity into energy-consuming activities that often challenge or compromise long-standing lesson plans, becoming pop culture savvy ourselves, for example), but most worthwhile endeavors by default do. Additionally, a pop culture approach to teaching Spanish mystic poetry may well spark other innovative teaching strategies for similarly complex notions from the early modern period in Spain, from explaining blood purity to gender violence, as many of my colleagues eloquently and persuasively have argued throughout this volume. Indeed, the inclusion and integration of pop culture into our lesson plans should not be about "dumbing down" the curriculum, nor should it exclude or preclude the text; rather, these outside, recognizable references serve to enhance the way(s) we teach it. A pop culture approach vis à vis contemporary music is simply another way to relate to our students who, with each passing generation, are increasingly removed from sixteenth-century Spain (as we, in similar fashion, become more and more distanced from their social realities). I say, in response, let us meet them where they are, just as Mancing implies the mystics do, and in the process, we also might learn something about the way students think, their motivations, and alternative ways of learning and teaching for both us and them.

Works Cited

Anderson, James B. "The Spanish Mystical Aesthetic." *Mystics Quarterly*, vol. 19, no. 3, 1993, pp. 115-122.

Bultman, Dana. "Comparing Humanist and Mystical Understanding in Luis de Leon's "Noche serena'" and John of the Cross's 'La noche oscura.'" Weber, pp. 232-39.

Carlson, James R. "Songs that Teach." *The English Journal*, vol. 99, No. 4, 2010, pp. 65-71.

Cipriani-Sklar, Rose-Marie. "Gnerating Enriched Literacy Experiences for Older English Language Learners." *RHI: Reaching Reluctant Readers*. Random House, Inc. 31 Jul 2018, www.randomhouse.com/highschool/RHI_magazine/reluctantreaders/cipriani -sklar.html.

Clapton, William. "Pedagogy and Pop Culture: Pop Culture as Teaching Tool and Assessment Practice." *E-International Relations*. 23 Jun. 2015, www.e-ir.info/2015/06/23/pedagogy-and-pop-culture-pop-culture-as-teaching-tool-and-assessment-practice/.

Clump, Michael A.; Bauer, Heather; Bradley, Catherine. "The Extent to Which Psychology Students Read Textbooks: A Multiple Class Analysis of Reading across the Psychology Curriculum." *Journal of Instructional Psychology*, vol. 31, no. 3, 2004, pp. 227-32.

Dunaway, Michele. "Using Music to Connect to Literature." *Teachers at Work: A Column About Teaching*. 24 May 2012, www.visualthesaurus.com/cm/teachersatwork/using-music-to-connect-literature/.

Ferroni, Nicholas. "Using Music in the Classroom to Educate, Engage and Promote Understanding." *Huffington Post THE BLOG* 8 Nov 2012, www.huffingtonpost.com/nicholas-ferroni/music-in-the-classroom_b_2072777.html.

Gasta, Chad. "'Señora, donde hay música no puede haber cosa mala': Music, Poetry, and Orality in *Don Quijote*." *Hispania,* vol. 93, no. 3, 2010, pp. 357-67.

Goodman, Stacey. "Who Is Taylor Swift? Using Pop Culture for Deeper Learning." George Lucas Educational Foundation. *Edutopia*, 18 Sept. 2015, www.edutopia.org/blog/who-taylor-swift-using-pop-culture-deeper-learning-stacey-goodman.

Hoeft, Mary E.. "Why University Students Don't Read: What Professors Can Do To Increase Compliance." *International Journal for the Scholarship of Teaching and Learning*, vol. 6, no. 2, 2012, digitalcommons.georgiasouthern.edu/cgi/viewcontent.cgi?article=1343&context=ij-sotl.

Hirvela A. & Boyle J. (1988). "Literature courses and student attitudes."*ELT Journal*, vol. 42, no. 3, 1988, pp. 179-84.

Hobson, Eric H. "Getting Students to Read: Fourteen Tips." *Idea Paper 40*. The Idea Center. 31 Jul 2018, 10:06 a.m., ideaedu.org/Portals/o/Uploads/Documents/IDEA%20Papers/IDEA%20Papers/Idea_Paper_40.pdf.

Jenkins, A., R. Breen & R. Lindsay. *Reshaping Teaching in Higher Education. Linking Teaching with Research*, Routledge, 2007.

Leonard, Augustin and Erwing W. Geissman. "Phenomenological Inquiries into Mystical Experience." *CrossCurrents*, vol. 3, no. 3, 1953, pp. 231-50.

Mancing, Howard. "Reading 'Noche oscura' Twice." Weber, pp. 202-07.

McGinn, Bernard. "Evil-Sounding, Rash, and Suspect of Heresy": Tensions between Mysticism and Magisterium in the History of the Church." *The Catholic Historical Review*, vol. 90, no. 2, 2004, pp. 193-212.

Moller, Herbert. "The Social Causation of Affective Mysticism." *Journal of Social History*, vol. 4, no. 4, 1971, pp. 305-38.

Pace, Judith. "The benefits of bringing controversial issues into the classroom." *EdSource: Highlighting Strategies for Student Success.* July 27, 2016, edsource. org/2016/bringing-controversial-issues-into-the-classroom/567439.

Pilar Ryan, María del. "Defiance and Obedience: Reading the Spanish Mystics in Historical Context." Weber, pp. 142-47.

Rhodes, Elizabeth. "Mysticism in History: The Case of Spain's Golden Age." Weber, pp. 47-56.

Robertson, Kristina. "Connect Students' Background Knowledge to Content in the ELL Classroom." ¡Colorín Colorado!: A Bilingual Site for Educators and Families of English Language Learners. 31 Jul 2018, http://www.colorincolo-rado.org/article/connect-students-background-knowledge-content-ell-class-room.

Sitomer, A, and M Cirelli. *Hip-Hop Poetry and the Classics*, Milk Mug Publishing, 2004.

Sloan, Nate. "How a Song Captures the Zeitgeist." *Spotify for Artists*, July 28, 2020, https://artists.spotify.com/blog/how-a-song-captures-the-zeitgeist

Taylor, A.E. "St John of the Cross and John Wesley." *The Journal of Theological Studies*, vol. 46, nos. 181 and 182, January/April 1945, pp. 30-38.

Vollendorf, Lisa. "Making Mysticism Accessible to Undergraduates." Weber, pp. 114-22.

Weber, Alison, ed. *Approaches to Teaching Teresa of Ávila and the Spanish Mystics*, MLA, 2009.

———. "Introduction." Weber, pp. 1-14.

Stephen E. Young. "Like a critique: A postmodern essay on Madonna's Postmodern Video *Like a Prayer.*" *Popular Music and Society*, vol. 15, no.1, 1991, pp. 59-68.

Drugs, Magic, Coercion, and Consent: From María de Zayas to the "World's Scariest Drug"

JOHN SLATER

Colorado State University

IN EURIPIDES *BACCHAE*, A Dionysian messenger declares that "If we didn't have our wine, there wouldn't be sexual love" (48); Bill Cosby may have been telling himself something similar when he urged women to "relax" with what appear to have been Quaaludes before he raped them. Cosby generally means little to my students, but they know the creepy type. They are painfully aware of the dangers of drug-facilitated sexual assault. My students uniformly take two things as fact: they believe in their own free will, and they also believe, especially if they are women, that someone may try to treat their free will as a surmountable obstacle to sexual conquest. Even the students who take most seriously Nick Bostrom's suggestion that we are living in a computer simulation—that we are Segismundo's virtual ghosts in a machine of illusion—reject Martin Luther's argument "On the Bondage of the Will." They also know that they are vulnerable to date-rape drugs such as Rohypnol or roofies (flunitrazepam), GHB or scoop (gamma hydroxybutyric acid), and Ketamine. My students do not need a philosophical or theological justification to believe that if their ability to make decisions can be involuntarily stripped from them, then it is possible that someone will try to do so. They train for these terrible eventualities every weekend.

However, they are often surprised to learn that long before the existence of Rohypnol and GHB, people wondered whether there might not be natural substances or magical practices that could strip resistant would-be lovers of their volition. In other words, they are surprised to learn that their knowledge of drug-facilitated assault can help them understand early modern Spanish literature and culture. Because students live in a world in which their free will can be treated as superfluous or dispensable, they are perfectly prepared to understand issues related to the subjugation of free will in early modern literature about witchcraft, as well as the lore associated with medicinal plants and magic. Across many genres of early modern Spanish writing, frustrated would-be lovers summon natural and supernatural powers to coerce the will of another, in what was euphemistically called the "conciliation" of desire. Both magic and science are utilized to this conciliatory end, drawing on shadowy powers or the occult virtues of plants. In the historical documents and literary texts of early modern Spain, students find a world of dark fantasies of domination in which the body of another can be made available by recourse to powerful drug plants (i.e. chemical submission), incantations, and pacts with the devil.

Although there are broad comedies about date rape drugs, such as Todd Philipps' *The Hangover* of 2009, using popular culture to discuss ideologies of domination and the erotic bondage of another's will generally leads students to grim, but important analysis.[1]

This chapter explores the representation of the magical and medical techniques used to rob another person of his or her free will, frequently for the purposes of sexual exploitation and assault. I begin with early modern Spanish literature (*La Celestina, El mágico prodigioso,* the *Desengaños amorosos,* and *Don Quijote*) in order to examine how authors represented the possibility that magic and medicine could be used to force an unwilling subject to yield. I then lay out a short unit composed of historical documents and studies of witchcraft and plant lore that I have used in my teaching. I end by describing how I have utilized a recent YouTube sensation about the natural substances that render victims suggestible zombies in order to provide popular cultural context and opportunities for comparison.

The object of these comparisons is three-fold: first, to provide historical context for understanding the accounts of perpetrators and survivors of the subjugation of free will; second, to provide a philosophical framework for understanding what it means to use drugs in order to violate another person's ability to make choices freely; and third, to help students understand with greater clarity early modern representations of rape, domination, and control. Coming to terms with these representations both in early modern and contemporary cultures is, I believe, essential, because it allows students to understand the transhistorical relatedness of cultures of domination and technologies of coercion that encompass phenomena as disparate as, on the

---

1   On the dubious sexual politics of *The Hangover,* see Terri Carney's "Still Hungover: Todd Phillips and Rape Culture."

one hand, the genesis of the global slave trade and, on the other, campus sexual assault.

The texts and materials I discuss in this paper form part of a topics course I teach regularly on witchcraft and magic that includes readings from the Bible (on the witch of Endor, from Samuel I), *La clavícula de Salomón* and the *Picatrix*, Julio Caro Baroja's account of the witch Juana Núñez, historical studies by María Tausiet and Angélica Morales Sarabia, *La Celestina*, María de Zayas's *La inocencia castigada*, *El caballero de Olmedo*, and *El mágico prodigioso*.[2] The way I approach these materials has as much to do with my students' identities as with my goal of teaching students about the literature and cultures of early modern Spain.

I have been teaching upper-division courses about early modern Spanish literature for fifteen years, and during that time my classrooms have overwhelmingly been populated by women. At the University of California, Davis,[3] at least a plurality of my students identify as Chicana. UC Davis was recently ranked third in the United States by the New York times among "Top Colleges Doing the Most for the American Dream," which means many of my students are also low income and first generation. At the same time, these are extraordinary students; the average high school grade point average for the middle 25%-75% of incoming first-year students ranges from 3.95 to 4.25 ("UC Davis freshman admission profile") These are students for whom, despite the odds, the system has worked. Their efforts have paid off. They have been recognized for their accomplishments and been able to take advantage of the opportunities extended to them. However, in the state of California, Chicana women face an enormous pay gap; they earn 43 cents "for every dollar paid to white, non-Hispanic men" ("Latinas and the Wage Gap"). So, while the education system has worked so far for my students, they face a labor marketplace that continues to discriminate against them egregiously. I mention these facts because having classrooms full of bright, successful women who belong to groups that have been historically underserved by higher education changes the way that I teach. The fact that the

---

    2   For the *Clavícula de Salomón,* the *Picatrix,* Caro Baroja's *Vidas mágicas e Inquisición,* Tausiet's *Abracadabra omnipotens,* and Zayas's *Desengaños amorosos,* I transcribe selections of the texts and annotate them with a reading guide. They tend to be too difficult for students to read without giving them considerable aids and context. The results are worth it, however, because student interest in witchcraft is very high.

    3   Since writing this article, the author has moved to the Colorado State University. [*Ed.*]

system has worked, at least in some measure, for the women who make it to my classroom, but may ultimately fail them when they graduate, makes questions of domination, sex discrimination, and inequity enormously pressing.

Early modern Spanish literature provides students with a complex taxonomy of domination and exploitation. David Castillo and others have examined the erotics of cadavers in the *Desengaños amorosos*. Lope de Vega has a number of plays that explore the relationship between desire, domination, and degradation in his plays about voluntary or feigned slavery (*Los melindres de Belisa, La esclava de su galán*, and so on). However, I have found the most productive conversations with students arise when discussing characters who are either robbed of their free will or rendered unconscious through magic or drugs. It is when we discuss the persistence of the image of a woman's living body entirely subjected to the malevolent desires of another that students are best able to historicize issues related to campus sexual assault. There is no better place to begin talking about a system that devalues women's work and counts their lives and desires as little than Fernando de Rojas' *La Celestina*.

LITERARY REPRESENTATIONS OF MAGIC AND DOMINATION

Rojas' masterpiece brings together occult powers and unwanted sex in ways that serve as a template for further readings. Students take readily to debates regarding whether Melibea and Calisto are really in love, whether Celestina's magic makes Melibea have sex with Calisto (or if Melibea falls in love of her own accord), and whether the characters' sexual encounters are consensual, unwanted sex, or rape.[4] Unless prompted, students do not tend to linger over the passages in which Melibea expresses her own desires. Melibea, however, says "no" many times in her first face-to-face encounter with Calisto: "no quieras perderme por tan breve deliete," "no pidas ni tomes aquello que, tomado, no será en tu mano volver," "Guarte, señor, de dañar lo que con todos los tesoros del mundo no se restaura," "no obren las manos cuanto pueden," "Está quedo," "Bástete, pues ya soy tuya," "no me quieras robar el mayor don..." (174-75). She could not be clearer. Bewitched or not, Melibea does not give her consent. Resigning herself to her fate, she says bitterly, "Si pensara que tan desmesuradamente te habías de haber conmigo, no fiara mi persona de tu cruel conversación" (175).

---

4   Students are frequently more comfortable talking about Melibea's experiences as unwanted sex, rather than rape. The term "unwanted sex" can open up space to discuss Melibea's conflicted feelings and can help students think about the importance of consent, especially if they are reluctant to identify Calisto's actions as rape.

When Melibea laments that she has lost her virginity, the reaction of Calisto's servant Sosia throws Melibea's despair into higher relief: "Todas sabés esa oración después que no puede dejar de ser hecho" (176). Sosia says, in effect, that women's regret and shame are a routine part of any sexual encounter. Despite the fact that Celestina's conjuring of demonic forces in the third "auto" is the culminating passage of the book's first chapters, my students are remarkably willing to agree with Sosia, at least at first. They know that Celestina tried to bewitch Melibea, but is this not, after all, a tragic love story? Wasn't Melibea's prudery just an artifact of living in a society that was not sex-positive, something she just needed to get over in order to have what she secretly really wanted? Frequently, my students' expectations about "old" literature and their willingness to believe that *La Celestina* is perhaps lusty, but is at heart a romance, makes them deaf to Melibea's repeated pleas. Their expectations of the genre and period make Melibea's resistance invisible.

Calisto is clearly a cad; no more base and insensitive words have been imagined than Calisto's statement, upon ripping off Melibea's clothing, that "el que quiere comer el ave, quita primero las plumas" (208).[5] I do not ask students to agree with me about Calisto's caddishness, but I do ask that they acknowledge two things: first, that Celestina attempts to summon forces that can overpower Melibea's will; and second, that Calisto disregards Melibea's very clear and repeated statements that she does not want to have sex with him. Over the course of an academic term, students come to see that magic provides a rhetorical matrix of domination in which Melibea's consent, and that of other characters, can systematically be disregarded.

La Celestina is far from unique in coupling magic and unwanted sex. Readers of early modern texts find themselves confronted with fantasies about witches, plants, and supernatural forces able to "sujetar la voluntad" or bind the will with depressing regularity. Sometimes, as in Pedro Calderón de la Barca's *El mágico prodigioso*, the desired woman is delivered into the hands of her suitor in the form of a lifeless effigy. In Calderón's play, Cipriano, overcome by lust, sells his soul to the Devil to possess Justina: "por gozar a esta mujer / diera el alma" (70). Although Cipriano thinks he has conquered Justina through magic – "ya es trofeo tu belleza / de mis mágicos estudios" – what Cipriano gets is a "Figura" who only appears to be Justina (116). The "Figura," dressed as Justina delivers herself into Cipriano's arms "forzada," but

---

5   One assignment that changes the conversation is to ask that students create a digital illustration of the scene with thought bubbles that graphically represent Melibea and Calisto's thinking. They tend to place a plucked chicken in Calisto's thought bubble.

quickly reveals herself to be a cadaverous substitute (114). *El mágico prodigioso* invokes the erotics of a woman's lifeless body delivered unwillingly into the hands of a lascivious man, but turns the story into a warning. However, not all female characters are able to resist the power of magic and satanic influence.

María de Zayas's *La inocencia castigada*, the fifth of the ten novellas that compose the *Desengaños amorosos*, tells the story of Inés, who was unwillingly subjected to the thrall of a desiring man through magic. The narrator of the tale, Laura, begins by complicating notions not of possession but of exchange. Inés's father was deceased, but her brother served as a substitute: "en cuanto a la obediencia y amor reverencial le tuviese en lugar de padre..." (265). Her brother's desires were her own: "no tenía más voluntad que la suya" (265). But the possibility that one might substitute a brother for a father or exchange a brother's wishes for one's own is quickly problematized by Laura: "qué moneda tan falsa es ya la voluntad, que no pasa ni vale sino el primer día" (266). There is no reciprocity or reliability when women deal with men.

A neighbor, Diego, sees Inés and falls in love with her. When another neighbor, a woman, learns of Diego's love for Inés, this "tercera" offers to arrange a tryst. Recalling the *figura* that Cipriano gets instead of Justina, what Diego gets from the procuress is not Inés at all but a substitute: a more willing woman dressed in Inés' clothing. When Inés learns of the ruse, she calls the authorities who punish the tricksters. But Diego harbors the mistaken suspicion that there was no switch, no trick at all, and that Inés had simply slept with him and then repented of it. Diego, like Sosia, thinks that women's shame is a sham. With this conviction, Diego seeks the help of "un moro, gran hechicero y nigromántico" (276). The sorcerer creates a doll in Inés' image, another substitute, "copiado al natural" (276). This copy so delights Diego that, as Laura remarks, if it were as tall as Inés, "con [la figura] olvidara el natural original de doña Inés" (277). The lifeless simulacrum is very nearly as good as the real thing. When Diego lights a candle sitting atop the figure, Inés, unconscious, rises from her bed and is magically compelled to walk to Diego's house where he rapes her night after night. He would have preferred her to be conscious and is aware that "todo aquello era violento," but this does not cool Diego's desire (278).

The extraordinary conclusion to this first part of the novella is that, once again, the authorities gain knowledge of Diego's misdeeds. The enchantment is tested and proven repeatedly, "averiguando el caso" and confirming "muchas veces" that she had been reduced to Diego's plaything "sin su voluntad" (281). And once again, someone, this time Inés's sister-in-law, refuses to believe the results of the judicial process: "decía que doña Inés debía de fingir el embelesamiento" (281-82). The codes of patriarchy trump the tests and findings of the judicial system. Inés's family concludes that she asked for it. They wall her into a tiny prison where she suffers horrifically for six years in darkness.

Several elements of Inés's story are painfully familiar to students. Diego understands that Inés is unconscious when he rapes her, and it causes his conscience the slightest twinge. Even when the authorities prove Inés' innocence, she is not believed by her family members. Women's desires and their will is of no real importance at all in this malevolent system of exchange and possession. Their words and their innocence are of no account. Women, in these stories, are always already objectified by a licentious man; women have no desires worthy of consideration and they are often only marginally preferable to the objects and effigies that represent them. Elsa of Arendelle, of *Frozen* fame, has taught a generation that magic is about selfless love and self-actualization. Inés begs to differ. Early modern literature uses witchcraft and sorcery to underscore differentials of power, and the lessons are more mundane than magical: the "magic" of a patriarchal society makes women's volition disappear. Poof.

LITERARY, RELIGIOUS, AND SCIENTIFIC SKEPTICISM ABOUT MAGIC

In a volume I co-edited, *Medical Cultures of the Early Modern Spanish Empire*, both Angélica Morales Sarabia and Tayra Lanuza, respectively, explore the scientific, medical, and theological debates about the freedom of the will and the ability of natural agents, such as plants, to curtail or direct love and desire. Morales Sarabia, drawing on Inquisitorial documents related to Mexico, explains that even when magic is used by women, it is frequently employed "to pacify violent husbands" (22). María Tausiet, drawing on Inquisitorial processes in Zaragoza, echoes this idea: "la insistencia en someter a los hombres a través de la magia femenina representaba en el fondo una forma de revancha, o al menos de compensación frente a la violencia masculina" (88). Magic is still about power differentials, but women use it to build solidarity and to give ritualized voice to suffering (Tausiet 88).[6]

The power of magical rituals and incantations to build solidarity among women and express suffering was far more important than the actual effec-

---

6　Among all of the texts I cite in this article, only Tausiet's has proven too difficult for my students, even when they are provided with a detailed reading guide. The anecdotes she provides, however, including the wording of spells, are so delicious that I abstract sections for students.

tiveness of spells. As Tausiet explains, "La eficacia de la magia no radicaba en el éxito de sus conjuros" (88). Women who were questioned by the Inquisition routinely denied that they believed in the power of the magic they performed. Even the Inquisitors were reluctant to believe that the women who practiced magic believed in its power. For this reason, it is not surprising that literary sources so often cast doubt on the power of magic.

Lanuza notes that in Tirso de Molina's *Amazonas en las Indias* the possibility that physical properties might move the will is firmly rejected: "el alma, espíritu puro / ni a las yerbas, ni al conjuro / como el cuerpo se sugeta . . . " (Molina 102). The most famous example of a literary rejection of the power of plants to force the will is probably from *Don Quijote*: "Aunque bien sé que no hay hechizos en el mundo que puedan mover y forzar la voluntad, como algunos simples piensan; que es libre nuestro albedrío, y no hay yerba ni encanto que le fuerce" (I:22). Curiously, a physician born a generation after Cervantes, Bernardo de Cienfuegos, nearly paraphrases this Cervantine locution in a grudging acknowledgement of the possibility that plants or "yerbas" actually can force the will: "Aunque entiendo y creo que no ay hierba que haga tal efecto [i.e. el de conciliar amor] contare aquí lo que he visto escrito y auténtico . . . "

Cienfuegos was the author of a massive manuscript entitled *Historia de las plantas*, completed around 1630.[7] Totaling some 5000 pages, the *Historia de las plantas* is divided into seven volumes.[8] Cienfuegos locution—"Aunque entiendo y creo que no hay yerba que haga tal efecto"—echoes Cervantes' passage quite directly: "Aunque bien sé que no hay . . . yerba ni encanto que le fuerce." Although there is no evidence to suggest that Cienfuegos was alluding to the *Quijote*, the story he tells recalls the literary texts I have discussed to this point. It involves the subjugation of another's will, an accusation of witchcraft, a test, and an uncertain vindication.

Cienfuegos' true history has four characters and it takes place in Cuba in 1613, just about the time that Cervantes was enjoying his most fecund period. The first character is known only as "cierto español," and the second is called only "una negra." When Bernardo de Cienfuegos recorded the account over a decade later, sometime during the 1620s, he reported that the Spaniard and the woman, who was probably of African descent, shared an "amistad torpe,"

---

7   Cienfuegos' manuscript, *Historia de las plantas*, is digitized on the website of the Biblioteca Nacional de España. It is written in such a fair and legible hand that with some training, students can read selections of the digitized manuscript themselves.

8   On Cienfuegos, see: Blanco Castro, Morales Valverde, and Sánchez Moreno.

meaning that they were lovers. This Spaniard "había dado mucha hacienda en confianza sin escrituras" to the governor of Cuba. Desiring to return to Spain, the Spaniard "acudió a el [gobernador] a que confesase la deuda y pagase o asegurase," which the governor refused to do. Despairing, the Spaniard asked his lover for help and she reassured him, saying "yo haré que haga cuentas contigo, te pague y satisfaga." She gave him an herb and instructed the Spaniard to touch the governor with it. When the Spaniard did so, the governor did as the Spaniard requested: "confesó la deuda y le dio satisfacción." The entire story is as follows:

> . . . una negra, la cual tenia amistad torpe con cierto Español que a este Gobernador había dado mucha hacienda en confianza sin escrituras y tratando de venirse a España, acudió a el a que confesase la deuda y pagase o asegurase, no lo quiso hacer negándolo todo; el acreedor afligido y perdido acudió a contar a la negra, la cual le dijo "yo hare que haga cuentas contigo te pague y satisfaga." Diole una yerba y díjole, "vete a hablar y tócale con ella." Hízolo ansí al tiempo que estaba ya a caballo para embarcarse y luego en tocándole se aposentó a cuentas, confesó la deuda y le dio satisfacción. Hecho esto conociendo ansí que esto había sido algún hechizo de los que usan los Indios, [el gobernador] hizo prender al hombre por hechicero y luego confesó que la negra le había dado aquella yerba y mostróla. Quiso castigarle y el obispo pareciendo que le tocaba a él la causa como ordinario prendió la negra que así mesmo confesó de plano y dio mucha más yerba diciendo y asegurando que era natural y no obra diabólica; y se hicieron diversas experiencias, pidiendo cosas que otros habían negado y en tocándoles con ella, la concedían: visto esto el obispo absolvió al hombre y negra con muy poco castigo, creyendo que era natural. (VII: 460-1)

This fascinating story unfolds in a marvelous narrative, replete with details from the "acreedor afligido y perdido" to the reassuring words of his lover, to the surprising proofs or "experiencias" of the efficacy of the plant. As in Zayas's story of Inés and Diego, the governor is forced to do something against his will.[9] Through the mere touch of a plant, he is subjected to the desires of his creditor. Morales Sarabia notes that it was never clear

---

9   Readers of seventeenth-century literature will notice familiar turns of phrase in Cienfuegos' account, such as "amistad torpe." This phrase that was commonly used to describe sexual acts considered unnatural. The word "torpe" is used similarly in Zayas's *Desengaños amorosos*, in which Blanca's husband and a servant,

to Inquisitors whether the use of hallucinogenic plants was properly magic or medicine (21-22). Something similar is at stake in Cienfuegos' account: what appears to be magic turns out to be a natural effect of a mysterious plant. Once again, however, despite these reported proofs conducted by no less an authority than the bishop of the archdiocese of Santiago de Cuba, Cienfuegos finds the story incredible.

Knowing that Cienfuegos' anecdote takes place in 1613, students have little difficulty ferreting out the identities of the bishop, Alonso Orozco Enriquez de Armendáriz, and the governor: Gaspar Ruiz de Pereda. It takes very little research for students to discover that the bishop and the governor were bitter rivals. Cienfuegos' story, when coupled with the historical analyses of Morales Sarabia and Tausiet, alongside Zayas's *La inocencia castigada*, creates a short but rich unit to consider the ways in which early modern Spanish writers considered the possibility that powerful forces existed in the cosmos that could reduce people to automata with no desires of their own.

CHEMICAL SUBMISSION AND POPULAR CULTURE: THE "WORLD'S SCARIEST DRUG"

A number of the texts that I have discussed to this point deal with the judicial mechanisms for determining whether or not a person has given his or her consent. There are productive discussions to have with students about the Obama administration's "dear colleague letter" and its guidance on adjudicating sexual assault, as well as the rescinding of this guidance by Education Secretary Betsy DeVos; students quickly see that the burden of proof is a moving target. In terms of popular culture, Laura L. Finley's *Domestic Abuse and Sexual Assault in Popular Culture* provides helpful points of departure. Mostly, however, I take my direction from student interests and suggestions.

The simple reason that I let students be the classroom experts on popular culture is that their interests constantly surprise and often delight me. A few years ago, my students became fascinated with, of all things, scopolamine. It was a drug I knew quite well because my father-in-law loves to sail, and I suffer from seasickness with fairly embarrassing regularity; family outings involve, for me, the application of a transdermal patch that delivers a steady dose of scopolamine to stave off nausea. My students were familiar with the drug in a less innocuous and more sensational context: as a zombifying tincture known popularly as "devil's breath" or burundanga, featured in a popular YouTube video.

Arnesto, are found "en delietes tan torpes y y abominables, que es bajeza, no solo decirlo, mas pensarlo" (360).

The half-hour video, billed as a documentary by its makers, Vice Media LLC, carries two titles: "World's Scariest Drug" and "Colombian Devil's Breath." The video's narrator, Ryan Duffy, calls burndanga or scopolamine "the worst roofie you can imagine times a million." He explains that the most terrifying aspect of this drug is that victims remain "completely conscious and articulate." Outwardly, victims seem altogether normal, but they are at the whim of a thieving, South American sexual predator. "The deal with burundanga," intones Duffy, "is that it pretty much eliminates your free will." At the opening of the video, slow-motion Steadicam shots of Bogotá, set against brooding music, intensify the sense of danger. In a brief article framing the "World's Scariest Drug" video, Duffy writes that "idea of a substance that renders a person incapable of exercising free will seemed liked a recipe for hilarity and the YouTube hall of fame." He was right about one thing: the YouTube video has been viewed more than thirty million times.

Videos, including news pieces with titles such as "Burundanga o Escopolamina: anula la voluntad," abound on YouTube. Many of the top hits that turn up in a Google search for burndanga fact-check the extraordinary claims about the drug. However, the reach of the Vice's "World's Scariest Drug" in particular was amplified by unquestioning online articles in outlets from the *Huffington Post*, which "hailed" scopolamine as "World's Scariest Drug" (Cotroneo), to *El Mundo*, which warned that gangs of South American women were forcing victims into chemical submission using scopolamine (G.C.) and *El País*, which promised that "more cases will emerge" (Domínguez). These stories either repeated Duffy's claims explicitly, or reproduced anxieties identical to those found in the "World's Scariest Drug" video.[10] Despite widespread debunking of scopolamine rumors, it is easy to see why the lurid Vice video captured my students' imagination. It plays on a number of fears and exoticizing beliefs: that deep in the jungles of South America there grow mysterious plants whose powers are nearly beyond our comprehension; that there are drugs that strip victims of their will and make them almost infinitely suggestible; and that malevolent, shamanic villains who know the mysterious ways of these plants use the drug-induced pliancy of their marks to empty their victims' bank accounts and rape them. These fears are related to those that we find in early modern Spanish letters and center on the same concern: to what extent is our free will our own, and can it be taken from us?

"World's Scariest Drug" is an especially helpful counterpoint to the texts of Zayas and Cienfuegos. The video contains a dash of scientific inquiry,

---

10   *The Huffington Post* article carried a rather bizarre reference to Marcy Playground's 1997 song "Sex and Candy."

which consists of a visit to Bogota's botanical gardens to see a living specimen of the plant, and an interview with a toxicologist, Miriam González, who confirms the physiological effects of scopolamine. Duffy shows an interest in the ways in which the legal system handles claims about the drug, with a visit to a police station and an interview with a police officer named Romero Mendoza. Duffy even recounts the supposedly ancient, indigenous uses of burundanga (e.g. the mass murder of concubines). Mostly, his interest is in first-person testimonies of victims who were robbed under the influence of scopolamine. There is a lengthy testimonial of a prostitute who used scopolamine to rob for the first time at age 15, causing her elderly victim to have a heart attack. There is also the account of a gangster who, as revenge for being drugged with scopolamine and robbed, raped and killed the perpetrators. The following is a typical anecdote:

A guy was taken back to his apartment, woke up the next morning in the empty apartment completely confused as to what happened, went down and said to his doorman, you know, "why is my apartment empty, what happened?" and the doorman said, "well you brought it out last night with two of your friends, all your stuff, you loaded it into a van" and the guy was like, "why in the hell would you let me do that," and he was like, "because you told me to." So that's kind of the stuff were dealing with, complete elimination of free will, while still acting, which is pretty much the scariest shit I can imagine.

Mostly, "World's Scariest Drug" is about sex, violence, and tired stereotypes about Colombia. One man, who procures a dose of scopolamine for Duffy, claims that just an ounce can kill 10 or 15 people. Scenes shot from inside a bordello explain in a voiceover that scopolamine has "always been kind of inextricably linked to sex in one form or another." (Lingering shots of exotic dancers underscore the point.) Duffy concludes, "It seems quite Colombian, all in all; very beautiful and very dangerous." He chuckles. "This is pretty much the symbol of Colombia, isn't it?"

Duffy's vision of the brothels and bars of Bogotá, in which inhibition and peril comingle, recall the Las Vegas of the date-rape-drug farce *The Hangover*. Both cities are lawless, hedonistic, sensual, and dangerous. Why ask students to take this journey into the heart of the imaginary of the "bromagnon" (Carney)? I wondered this myself, and initially tried to steer students back to more sober subjects by giving them articles such as De Feo's "The Ritual Use of Brugmansia Species in Traditional Andean Medicine in

Northern Peru." But academic histories could not compete with the juiciness of the tidbits Duffy fed them. (He records, for example, that scopolamine is called Devil's Breath or "el soplo del diablo" because "te roba el alma.") I quickly figured out that, because students were the ones who introduced me to "World's Scariest Drug," they should develop tools to analyze the video in light of the texts we had read, focusing on those by Cienfuegos and Zayas.

Students started by listing the commonalities between Zayas's *La inocencia castigada*, Cienfuegos' *Historia de las plantas* and Duffy's "World's Scariest Drug." All three describe techniques for producing submission, or effects of drugs that are hard to believe. Cienfuegos and Duffy describe mechanisms of intoxication that are nearly identical: with just a swipe of a piece of paper covered in scopolamine or the mere touch of a plant, both a gangster and the governor of Cuba could be reduced to zombies. This did not make either story more credible, but it did attest to the persistence of a very specific anxiety: that our hold on our own free will is tenuous. Knowing this, Zayas' *La inocencia castigada* became more comprehensible as the expression of a related fear, rather than a dubious story about magic. This was the first of the satisfying achievements of using popular culture in the classroom: students shifted from a position of doubt—a doubt that uncomfortably reproduced the incredulity they associated with Sosia, Diego, and Inés's sister-in-law—to one of comprehension and compassion. In other words, students stopped wondering whether Ines' story could be true, whether magic could really have caused the effects described in the story, and considered the extent to which *La inocencia castigada* expressed fears about forced submission that people continue to face. It was a small step from there to talking about roofies and other date-rape drugs.

The profoundly problematic politics of "World's Scariest Drug" also helped students think about the colonial gaze. The possibility that white men from the United States might travel to Colombia and determine that scopolamine "is pretty much the symbol of Colombia" helped students consider the ways in which even Cienfuegos' skepticism exoticizes Afro-Cubans and American nature. Paradoxically, this also helped students analyze the ways in which the Black Legend shapes the ways in which we consume early modern Spanish cultural production. After analyzing the ongoing effects of cultural imperialism—and the extent to which our current political climate continues to denigrate Hispanic cultures—Zayas seemed less the exponent of a brutal, fanatical, Inquisitorial Spanish society, and more human. (Using "World's Scariest Drug" as a foil to *La inocencia castigada* actually makes Zayas' work seem reserved in comparison.)

Some of the most productive student discussions had to do with what is not in the video, namely any analysis of race, class, and gender. This became especially clear when they compared "World's Scariest Drug" to Morales Sarabia's study of the cultures of hallucinogens in New Spain. Drawing on analyses of gender and power, Morales Sarabia, like Tausiet, explains why people turned to powerful drugs and magic. Duffy, for his part, never comments on the social context of the use of the drug that so fascinates him; he never examines the dynamics of power that led the prostitute he interviews to drug her johns and steal, and never considers the codes that lead the gangster to rape and kill the people who drugged him.

Also missing from Duffy's video is any first-hand evidence of the drug's efficacy. He buys a dose of scopolamine on the street but does not have the sample tested. Some of the stories about the drug that he collects are simply not credible. (One interviewee, for example, claims to have "tripped" for 17 days after ingesting some of the drug.) In the end, Duffy's fear of scopolamine's power serves in lieu of any analysis. He is afraid to even look at the white powder he says is scopolamine without wearing latex gloves and a hospital mask. He treats the supposed prevalence of the drug as a natural outgrowth of Colombian kidnapping epidemic, but no one he interviews claims to have held a victim for ransom. In the final scenes of the video, Duffy flushes the drug down the toilet.

Students were initially fascinated by Duffy's sensational claims and the lurid qualities of his video. They ended up better able to analyze the ways in which human beings have long considered that their ability to make choices can be subjected to the malevolent desires of another. This helped provide a historical axis to our discussions of rape culture. Without question, the techniques used to produce chemical submission on campuses today are relatively new. The fears, however, are old. My hope is that these considerations helped students forge a sense of solidarity with Melibea and Inés, making their stories not simply dusty tales of women who were dominated by dubious magic, but icons of a long struggle for self-determination and freedom.

When I consider whether or not to use popular culture in my classroom, I focus on the yield. If a video or song just entertains my students or grants me a fleeting illusion of hipness, then it is a waste of my students' time. Popular culture must deliver some measurable outcome: better reading comprehension, more understanding, notably higher engagement. What I do not worry about when choosing whether to use popular culture in the classroom is anachronism. I do not worry about it because I do not believe that the relevance of literature is described by the historical circumstances of its production. If a reader can use popular culture as a means to apprehend more clearly what is transcendent in literature, if she can enact literature's magic, violate the laws of time, and through this conjuring make present the voices of authors long dead, then I am all for it. If popular culture lets my student read the words "desocupado lector" and know that they are spoken to her, then even a sophomoric expression of ancient dread in the form of "World's Scariest Drug" is welcome in my classroom.

Works Cited

Blanco Castro, Emilio, Ramón Morales Valverde and Pedro M. Sánchez Moreno. "Bernardo Cienfuegos y su aportación a la botánica en el siglo XVII." *Asclepio,* vol. 46, no. 1, 1994, pp. 37-123.

Bostrom, Nick. "Are You Living in a Computer Simulation?" *Philosophical Quarterly,* vol. 53, no, 211, 2003, pp. 243-255.

Calderón de la Barca, Pedro. *El mágico prodigioso.* Ed. Michael J. McGrath. European Masterpieces, 2003.

Carney, Terri. "Still Hungover: Todd Phillips and Rape Culture." *Bright Lights Film Journal,* July 31, 2011, http://brightlightsfilm.com/still-hungover-todd-phillips-and-rape-culture/#.W1OSW9gzqZY

Castillo, David R. *Baroque Horrors: Roots of the Fantastic in the Age of Curiosities.* University of Michigan Press, 2010.

Cervantes Saavedra, Miguel de. *Don Quijote,* edited by Luis Andrés Murillo. Castalia, 1978.

Cienfuegos, Bernardo. *Historia de las plantas.* [c. 1627]. Biblioteca Nacional de España, http://bdh.bne.es/bnesearch/CompleteSearch.do?numfields=1&fieldi=autor&showYearItems=&visor=&field1val=%22Cienfuegos%2c+Bernardo+de%22&advanced=true&field1Op=AND&exact=on&textH=&completeText=&text=&pageSize=1&pageSizeAbrv=30&pageNumber=1

Cotroneo, Christian. "Devil's Breath: Scopolamine, AKA Burundanga, Hailed As 'World's Scariest Drug'." *The Huffington Post Canada,* Verizon Communications, Sept. 3, 2013, https://www.huffingtonpost.ca/2013/09/03/devils-breath-scopolamine_n_3860318.html

De Feo, Vincenzo. "The Ritual Use of Brugmansia Species in Traditional Andean Medicine in Northern Peru." *Economic Botany,* vol. 58, 2004, pp. 221-229.

Domínguez, Íñigo. "Burundanga: The Stealth Drug that Cancels the Victim's Willpower." *El País,* PRISA, July 25, 2016, https://elpais.com/elpais/2016/07/25/inenglish/1469445136_776085.html

Duffy, Ryan. "Colombian Devil's Breath." *Vice,* Vice Media LLC, July 22, 2007, https://www.vice.com/en_us/article/kw3kam/colombian-devil-s-breath-1-of-2

———. "World's Scariest Drug." *YouTube*, Vice Media LLC, May 11, 2012, https://www.youtube.com/watch?v=ToQ8PWYnuo4

Euripides. *The Bacchae of Euripides*. Translated by C. K. Williams, Farrar, Straus and Giroux, 1990.

Finley, Laura L. *Domestic Abuse and Sexual Assault in Popular Culture*. ABC-CLIO, 2016.

G.C. "Los robos con 'burundanga' se extienden por Alicante." *El Mundo*, Unidad Editorial, Nov. 8, 2013, http://www.elmundo.es/elmundo/2013/08/11/alicante/1376221891.html

Lanuza Navarro, Tayra M.C. "The Dramatic Culture of Astrological Medicine in Early Modern Spain." *Medical Cultures of the Early Modern Spanish Empire*, edited by John Slater, Maríaluz López-Terrada, and José Pardo Tomás, Ashgate, 2014, pp. 189-212.

"Latinas and the Wage Gap." National Partnership for Women and Families, April 2018, http://www.nationalpartnership.org/research-library/workplace-fairness/fair-pay/latinas-wage-gap.pdf

Molina, Tirso de. *Trilogía de los Pizarros: Amazonas en las Indias*. Edited by Miguel Zugasti, Reichenberger, 1993.

Morales Sarabia, Angélica. "The Culture of Peyote: Between Divination and Disease in Early Modern New Spain." *Medical Cultures of the Early Modern Spanish Empire*, edited by John Slater, Maríaluz López-Terrada, and José Pardo Tomás, Ashgate, 2014, pp. 21-39.

Rojas, Fernando de. *La Celestina*. Edited by Patricia S. Finch, European Masterpieces, 2003.

Tausiet, María. *Abracadabra omnipotens. Magia urbana en Zaragoza en la Edad Moderna*. Siglo XXI, 2007.

"Top Colleges Doing the Most for the American Dream." *New York Times*, May 25, 2017, https://www.nytimes.com/interactive/2017/05/25/sunday-review/opinion-pell-table.html

"UC Davis Freshman Admission Profile." University of California, Davis, 2017, http://admission.universityofcalifornia.edu/campuses/davis/freshman-profile/index.html

Zayas y Sotomayor, María de. *Desengaños amorosos*. Cátedra, 2006.

Students as Co-Architects at Hispanic Serving Institutions: Latinx Students Building Knowledge in *Siglo* Studies

Darci L. Strother

California State University, San Marcos

ACCORDING TO THE 2017 Annual Report of the Hispanic Association of Colleges and Universities (HACU), there are 416 Hispanic Serving Institutions (HSIs) spread across 38 of the United States, and in the District of Colombia and Puerto Rico (22-26). These are institutions where Latinx students constitute a minimum of 25% of the total student headcount. Nationwide, Latinx students accounted for approximately 19% of the total student body in higher education in 2016. Moreover, the

> growth in college enrollment among Hispanics has been especially pronounced in the last decade. After growing by 0.7 million from 1996 to 2006, the college enrollment of Hispanics went up by 1.7 million from 2006 to 2016. The result has been an overall tripling of college enrollment by Hispanics over the past two decades. (Bauman)

This threefold increase in student enrollment has outpaced the hiring of Latinx faculty, resulting in a growing deficit in the Latinx student-to-Latinx faculty ratio: "Between 2003 and 2014, the percentage of Latinos among all faculty members grew from 2 to 4 percent, moving the ratio of Latino students to Latino faculty from 80:1 to 90:1 over the same period" (Morris). With a 90:1 Latinx student to Latinx faculty ratio generally, it seems fair to posit that at both HSIs and non-HSIs, Latinx students are introduced to *Siglo* studies, if at all, by faculty who only occasionally look like them or come from similar cultural backgrounds. Even if we allow for the likelihood that

Siglo de Oristas may account for a larger-than-average share of that dismal Latinx faculty number of just 4%, our discipline still has an undeniable demographic imbalance between those who learn and those who teach it. This matters for all sorts of reasons, and the benefits of faculty diversity have been discussed widely. For example, Josh Young states: "by creating a diverse faculty, your school can encourage increased success among groups that have been traditionally underrepresented on campus. When students see themselves reflected in the makeup of your staff, they are often encouraged to reach for higher standards of performance." Additionally, "a diverse faculty can help improve retention rates among minority student populations" (Young).

Anytime our institutions experience significant changes in student populations, such as increases in enrollment of veterans, non-traditionally-aged students, first-generation college students, formerly incarcerated students, etc., it behooves us to pause and consider whether new types of pedagogies can aid us in better addressing the needs of the students we serve, and enhancing their success. Given the aforementioned demographic statistics relating to the increase in Latinx enrollment in many of our institutions, this pause-and-consider moment has most certainly arrived. As the focus of this volume affirms, embracing the incorporation of pop culture into our pedagogy can be fruitful in numerous ways when working with all of our 21st century college students. There may be even more reasons to give pop culture our careful consideration when teaching Siglo de Oro texts to Latinx students, and this chapter aims to explore why pop culture may be particularly valuable in HSI settings. At the same time, we should be mindful not only of our demographic imbalance between learners and teachers of Siglo de Oro literature, but also of our growing generational divide: "The share of people older than 65 teaching full time at American colleges and universities nearly doubled between 2000 and 2010. College professors are now among the oldest Americans in the workforce" (Rodríguez Campbell). With each year we remain in the classroom, we add another year to that generational divide that can potentially distance us from our students. How, then, might we achieve successful integration into our classroom of popular culture, arguably skewed towards the young, despite divergent teacher/learner demographics? And why might we want to in the first place?

Henry Giroux offers a clue:

Pedagogy is about the creation of a public sphere, one that brings people together in a variety of sites to talk, exchange information, listen, feel their desires, and expand their capacities for joy, love, solidarity, and struggle. Though I do not wish to romanticize popular culture, it is precisely in its diverse spaces and spheres that most of the education that matters today is taking place on a global scale. (x)

Certainly, anyone who has wielded a piece of chalk or a whiteboard marker would wish to provide "education that matters," and a growing number of faculty in the Humanities are coming to view popular culture as a bridge to that destination. Richard Keller Simon, for example, discusses his innovative and successful use of the TV series *Friends* as a way to help students approach Shakespeare. Simon argues:

> Because the entertainments that Americans love, and the great books that their professors know how to teach, are often similar in this fashion, popular culture can be the salvation rather than the nemesis of traditional humanities disciplines, particularly English. We need more, not less, of such materials in our classrooms, and not isolated from the rest of the curriculum in courses set aside for them—as is typically the case—but carefully integrated into core requirements. (B4)

For their part, Maxwell A. Fink and Deborah C. Foote describe how their Gen X and Gen Y students' analytical skills and participation have been catalyzed thanks to their inclusion of *The Simpsons* in their Humanities classes. Foote notes:

> Unlike other Humanities courses that I've taught, this course elicits so much participation that I cannot keep up with the raised hands and the voices of students who have something to say. Furthermore, student preparation for class seems significantly higher in this course than in others, and I receive homework assignments in a more timely manner and with a generally higher level of thought and analysis. (51)

Kathleen Forni has discussed the pedagogical and critical value of Chaucer's reproduction in popular culture, citing Brian Helgeland's 2001 film *A Knight's Tale* as but one among a sizable group of useful tools drawn from popular culture, to help students engage meaningfully with these medieval texts.

Each of these aforementioned examples represents instances in which faculty select the primary text (works by Chaucer, Shakespeare, etc.), and faculty also select the manifestation(s) of popular culture they deem most suited to analogizing with the primary text. Apart from benefits such as stimulating student conversation and critical thinking, our selection of popular music, films, TV programs, YouTube clips, comics, memes, etc., offers the added benefit of the *coolness factor,* (partially) dismantling students' image of us as stuffy professors of classical literature cloistered in our ivory towers. The fact that we do live and breathe in the real world, and even have Netflix accounts, can be a revelation to some students, and can make us more relatable figures. (As an aside, I remember vividly the day a scandalized student came to my office to relay her concern to me that she had seen one of my faculty colleagues gambling at a local casino and drinking whiskey on a Saturday night. Yes, we do that too, when we're off the clock!). And while Elaine Showalter doesn't mention whisky drinking in casinos, in her thought-provoking work *Teaching Literature*, she does urge the following: "Teachers should read contemporary literature, go to the theatre and movies, watch television, write in all forms, and reflect on how all these activities contribute to what we do in class" (viii). As someone whose academic life has been centered primarily on the study of centuries-old literature, I find refreshing Showalter's encouragement to engage meaningfully with popular culture, and the validity she ascribes to it.

Those among us who live under the same roof as teenagers or college-aged kids might fancy ourselves even more attuned than average to the cultural reference points of today's students. Yet no matter how "in the know" we might purport to be, we should proceed with caution. For if our aim in using pop culture in the classroom is to build a bridge between *Siglo* texts and the lives of our 21st century students, we may unintentionally impose a sort of double-marginalization on those students for whom our faculty-selected examples of popular culture do not form a part of their shared experience. And given the phenomenon of the graying of the American professoriate coupled with the statistical unlikelihood that many of us come from the same ethnic and cultural backgrounds as our growing numbers of Latinx students, we need to check ourselves before assuming that we know which sorts of pop culture they will connect with. It's one thing for a twenty-something student in an introductory college literature class never to have read Chaucer, or Góngora, or Balzac. It's likely that many fellow classmates would be in the same situation, resulting in no particular social stigma. But it may be quite different if the faculty member has chosen *Friends, Sex and the City,* or *The Simpsons* as that bridge to Chaucer, Góngora, or Balzac, if a student's points of reference tack more towards TV shows such as *Mi marido tiene familia, Marimar,* or *El Chavo del Ocho.* A professor's gleeful announcement that "now we're going to watch something I know you'll all be familiar with" as a preface to screening a clip from *The Office* or *Game of Thrones,* may have an effect on an already-vulnerable subset of our students akin to being present when the "in group" tells an inside joke, and they are left to chuckle awkwardly from the sidelines, while actually having no idea what's so funny. In the case of our Latinx students—a group that is already more likely than average to drop out of college—(see Tate), creating classroom learning environments that further accentuate their potential otherness, or don't recognize the critical and connective value of the popular culture that might be most relevant to them, could come with a cost.

This is not to say, of course, that Latinx college students are a homogeneous group, nor that there might not be plenty of Latinx *Game of Thrones* fans. In fact, Alejandra C. Elenes has pointed out:

> the history of colonialism, augmented with a globalization of communication technologies, has resulted in global mestizaje where most groups adopt different cultural, intellectual, and political practices from different milieus. The ability to embrace this ambiguity is the hallmark of mestiza consciousness. (162)

Still, she cautions,

> The knowledge produced by white males is more likely to be considered universal, while the knowledge produced by those on the bottom of the hierarchy is viewed as local and not capable of being generalized to the population as a whole" (160)

As we work towards creating learning environments that provide the type of support that makes it possible for students of all backgrounds to connect with *Siglo* texts and to attain (and sometimes surpass) their own educational goals, how might we adapt our discipline's pedagogy to make it more inclusive of all students, and honor what they each bring to the classroom?

I would argue that if one of the aims of our use of popular culture is to construct a bridge to our students and their experiences, then our students should in fact be co-architects and join us on the construction crew of that bridge. In their introduction to the provocatively titled *Students as Colleagues,* Edward Zlotkowski et al affirm "Clearly one of the most difficult hurdles for students in becoming both academically and civically empowered is the more or less exclusive control that faculty members have over the curriculum" (7). In his study of motivation in the college classroom, Wilbert J. McKeachie observes: "Most individuals want to be in charge of their own behavior and value a sense of control over their environment. We can enhance students' sense of control by offering choices and supporting their autonomy, which in turn enhances motivation" (119). Apart from motivating students and giving them a measure of autonomy, we can help build their self-confidence as learners approaching literary studies. Thomas C. Foster's *How to Read Literature Like a Professor* recounts the following:

> When I suggest to students that they use their past reading experiences, their response is on the order of, 'We don't have any.' Which, as we have seen, is untrue. And here's what I say in reply: You know more than you think you do. No, you have not read everything. But you have probably read enough —enough novels, memoirs, poems, news stories, movies, television shows, plays, songs, enough everything when it's all added up. The real problem is that 'inexperienced' readers tend to deny themselves credit for the experience they do have. Get over it! Focus on all that you do know, not all that you don't. And use it. (249)

I'd like to share an illustration of my own pedagogical evolution in which I came to relinquish my teacher-centered approach to the integration of pop culture, and instead fostered learners' autonomy, something I've found particularly useful with Latinx students. My first foray into the use of pop culture to teach a *Siglo* text occurred in the mid 1990s and was admittedly a faculty-controlled lesson. On the first day of an upper-division, prerequisite-free, general education, literature in translation class, I gave students Góngora's Sonnet CLXVI ("Mientras por competir con tu cabello") with no introduction and asked that they read and try to interpret it in pairs. Most students sat in awkward silence, had little to say, or used the time to chat with their classmates about something else, which was exactly what I'd hoped they would do. Some wondered aloud which other general education classes might still have open seats, since they were sure this class was not going to be their cup of tea, if such an indecipherable sonnet was any indication of coming attractions. Then, I played two songs for them from the 1970s, a time period which may have seemed nearly as distant to them as the sonnet's 1582 composition. The songs I selected were Rod Stewart's "Tonight's the Night" and Billy Joel's "Only the Good Die Young." Students were then instructed to confer again in pairs, this time about the meaning of the two songs, and what they had in common with each other. This, it turns out, the students could do with ease. Persuasion, seduction, religious imagery, pressure to give up one's virginity, a prioritizing of present pleasures over future consequences; all were identified quickly and confidently by the students. They discussed whether or not the issues that surfaced in these two "old" songs still had relevance in their 1990s lives, and sure enough, they did! With this in mind, I then asked the students to return to Góngora's sonnet, letting them know that he was around their age, just 21, when he wrote it. I asked that they re-read the sonnet, and this time, that they look for connections between the two songs and Sonnet CLXVI. It was as if the songs were a key to unlocking not only their ability to decipher the text, but also their motivation for wanting to do so. As I steered the class conversation towards a deeper analysis of the poem, they were already hooked.

However, as someone who is decidedly on the musical anhedonia spectrum, I didn't (and don't) have a wealth of musical examples at the ready for future classes. And this particular class activity did not provide students with any autonomy over either the primary text or the pop culture with which they were supposed to identify parallels. I had given them a dot-to-dot book and they had dutifully (albeit enthusiastically) connected the dots. When students asked hopefully if we would be doing the same for all the texts we'd be reading that semester, they were disappointed to learn that the Góngora/ Stewart/Joel triad was all I had. And then a hand from the back of the class went up. "Can *we* help you find more?"

Fast-forward to today, and an integral part of the same course involves students working in groups outside of class, reading several steps ahead of their classmates, sharing and discussing numerous songs with their group-mates, and working to come up with just the right one for their classmates to analyze. I still give them the first "dot," but they come up with the second "dot," and their classmates draw the connective line via their analyses. At first, students tiptoed cautiously into their newly constructed zone of autonomy, bringing in musical examples that were more mirrors of my own background and generation than of theirs. Jim Croce's "Bad, Bad Leroy Brown" was brought in to help us through *Fuenteovejuna*, and Bonnie Tyler's "Holding Out for a Hero" (reintroduced to later generations thanks to *Shrek*), served as a springboard for discussions of *Don Quixote*. When one of my Latino students asked me if his group could select a song in Spanish, I could see his eyes light up when I consented and in fact wholeheartedly endorsed the idea (with the caveat that they also bring an English-language translation for those in the class who didn't understand Spanish). Now, songs in Spanish are frequently selected, and those who can understand them without the

English translation have their home language and culture validated. Even though they might not know any more about Golden Age Spanish literature than other classmates, their connection to the Spanish-speaking world often results in other students seeking them out as experts when discussing the songs. Interestingly, although I have been doing this now for over 20 years using many of the same core literary works on my reading list, there has never been a song repetition from one semester to the next. Each group of students who bring their own unique combination of backgrounds, musical tastes, and literary focus has always found a song that forges new territory. Each group offers something that is much more likely to speak to them and to their classmates than what I might have found even after many hours of searching. My students and I have all discovered new music and new artists along the way, which without exception have helped us approach our texts usefully. Something that has been particularly rewarding and eye opening for me has been when students select a song that I'd encountered before but did not understand, or found rather obnoxious. In their presentations to the class, the "Aha!" moments are just as likely to be mine as theirs, and I have been truly moved, on a number of occasions, with my students' passionate and convincing avowal of the beauty and literary relevance of songs that, had I happened upon them on the radio, would frankly have made me immediately turn the dial.

Parker Palmer, in *The Courage to Teach*, writes eloquently about the many fears we educators carry with us and how they impact our teaching. He suggests that one such fear involves our relationship to knowledge.

> If we regard truth as emerging from a complex process of mutual inquiry, the classroom will look like a resourceful and interdependent community. Our assumption about knowing can open up, or shut down, the capacity for connectedness on which good teaching depends. (51)

Giving up part of our monopoly on the content explored in our classrooms, and allowing students to bring in their own musical examples as valid subjects of analysis, may induce some initial trepidation, or concern that we will not cover all we would like to by taking time out to listen to 21st century tunes. Still, I have found the tradeoff to be well worth it, and the co-architects of this learning experience, my students, seem to agree.

A recent graduate-level course in *Literatura del Siglo de Oro* for our Spanish M.A. students presented another opportunity to see where the combination of popular culture and student autonomy might take us. This class

was made up exclusively of Latinx students, some recently immigrated to
the U.S., bringing with them a rich exposure to non-U.S.-based popular culture. Many of these students were serving as Graduate Teaching Associates
(GTAs) in our department and/or were preparing for careers in teaching.
The GTA population, typically closer in age to our undergraduate students
than to us, can serve as a particularly valuable resource, since they often have
their finger more on the pulse of our undergraduates' life experiences, while
working at the same time to develop their own pedagogical skill set. In this
particular class, the M.A. students felt empowered by me giving them options. They could either write a more traditional end-of-semester research
paper or propose research and develop lessons for teaching one or more of
the works we would read, integrating pop culture into their lessons. Perhaps
unsurprisingly, the lion's share of the class selected the lesson plan project,
even though these were typically lengthier and required research in several
different fields. The table below indicates examples of both the *Siglo* selections and the works of pop culture that my students selected as being profit-
able avenues into these texts:

TABLE 1:[1]

Siglo de Oro	Pop Culture for Lesson Plan
La Celestina – Fernando de Rojas	TV program "Como dice el dicho" Song "La granja" – Los Tigres del Norte
El burlador de Sevilla – Tirso de Molina	TV program "El Chespirito"
"La inocencia castigada" – María de Zayas	Song "Aún estás en mis sueños" – Rata Blanca Illustrated story "La Cenicienta que no quería comer perdices" – Myriam Cameros Sierra & Nunila López Salamero
Lazarillo de Tormes - Anonymous	Film "Los olvidados" – Luis Buñuel
"Rinconete y Cortadillo" – Miguel de Cervantes	Several *narcocorridos* and the life story of El Chapo
Life and Works of Sor Juana Inés de la Cruz	Film "Coco" – Disney/Pixar

1   Special thanks go to my students, Ana F., Raymundo R., Rodrigo V., and
Yesenia C. for these examples.

With the possible exception of the film *Coco*, none of the pop culture references are ones I myself, as a 50-something white woman, might have thought to include had I been the one creating these lessons. This table is not meant to suggest that these are *the* recommended linkages between *Siglo de Oro* texts and 20th-21st century pop culture, although there are certainly some innovative and thought-provoking choices listed. Rather, my point is that there is merit in allowing our students to propose, justify, and analyze what they themselves discover as linkages between the two, as we aim to deepen their understanding of and appreciation for our field. When we do so, students of all backgrounds have the opportunity to select what is most relevant to them, their work becomes more personally meaningful, they go about it with more enthusiasm and dedication, and they teach *us* symbiotically. In my state of California, typically ranked in the top 2 most diverse states nationwide, there still exists great student/faculty racial disparity: "About 70 percent of UC students are nonwhite, while more than 70 percent of tenured faculty and people in leadership positions are white" (Wu), and state-wide across all of our public higher education systems "more than two thirds of students enrolled in the 2016-2017 school year identified as nonwhite, while more than two thirds of faculty and leadership are white" (Wu). And if, as Elenes has suggested, knowledge produced by groups other than white males is typically viewed as "not capable of being generalized to the population as a whole," we have an opportunity to refute this as we bring our students of color onto our content-creation teams. While we can't change our own age or race, we can certainly make strides to ford the generational and racial divides in our own classrooms. Having students take the lead in the choice of pop culture content is one step towards that. I am inspired by the words of Parker Palmer, addressed to students: "There are great gaps between us. But no matter how wide and perilous they may be, I am committed to bridging them—not only because you need me to help you on your way but also because I need your insight and energy to help renew my own life" (49). And if Wilbert McKeachie's message to students was "You know more than you think you do," perhaps his message to the professoriate should be "They know more than we think they know." Let us harness the power of pop culture as we build a bridge alongside our students, to empower them to demonstrate it.

Works Cited

Bauman, Kurt. "School Enrollment of the Hispanic Population: Two Decades of Growth." *Census Blogs*, United States Census Bureau, 28 Aug. 2017, www.census.

gov/newsroom/blogs/random-samplings/2017/08/school_enrollmentof.
html.

Elenes, C. Alejandra. *Transforming Borders: Chicana-o Popular Culture and Pedagogy.* Lexington Books, 2011.

Fernández Campbell, Alexia. "The Workforce That Won't Retire." *The Atlantic,* Atlantic Media Company, 17 June 2016, www.theatlantic.com/business/archive/2016/06/colleges-offer-retirement-buyouts-to-professors/487400/.

Fink, Maxwell A., and Deborah C. Foote. "Using *The Simpsons* to Teach Humanities with Gen X and Gen Y Adult Students." *New Directions for Adult and Continuing Education,* vol. 115, 2007, pp. 45–54., doi:10.1002/(issn)1536-0717.

Forni, Kathleen. "Teaching Chaucer and Popular Culture: A Prolegomena." *The Chaucer Review,* vol. 48, no. 2, 2013, pp. 190–204.

Foster, Thomas Campbell. *How to Read Literature like a Professor: a Lively and Entertaining Guide to Reading between the Lines.* Harper, 2014.

Giroux, Henry A. *Disturbing Pleasures - Learning Popular Culture.* Routledge, 1994.

HACU. "Annual Reports." *Hispanic Association of Colleges and Universities - Home,* 2017, www.hacu.net/hacu/Annual_Report.asp.

McKeachie, Wilbert James, and Barbara Hofer. *Teaching Tips: Strategies, Research, and Theory for College and University Teachers.* Houghton Mifflin Company, 2002.

Morris, Catherine. "Experts Say Latino Student Enrollment Outpacing Faculty Growth." *Diverse Issues in Higher Education,* 6 Oct. 2016, diverseeducation.com/article/87181/.

Palmer, Parker J. *The Courage to Teach: Exploring the Inner Landscape of a Teacher's Life.* Jossey-Bass, 1998.

Showalter, Elaine. *Teaching Literature.* Blackwell, 2003.

Simon, Richard Keller. "Much Ado about 'Friends': What Pop Culture Offers Literature." *Chronicle of Higher Education,* vol. 46, no. 41, 16 June 2000, p. B4. EBSCO*host,* ezproxy.csusm.edu/login?url=https://search.ebscohost.com/login.aspx?direct=true&db=aph&AN=3203297&site=ehost-live.

Tate, Emily. "College Completion Rates Vary by Race and Ethnicity, Report Finds." *Inside Higher Ed,* 26 Apr. 2017, www.insidehighered.com/news/2017/04/26/college-completion-rates-vary-race-and-ethnicity-report-finds.

Williams, James R., et al. *Students as Colleagues: Expanding the Circle of Service-Learning Leadership.* Campus Compact, 2006.

Wu, Qiaozhen. "Study Shows Discrepancy between Diversity in College Faculty, Students." *Daily Bruin,* 9 Mar. 2018, dailybruin.com/2018/03/09/study-shows-discrepancy-between-diversity-in-college-faculty-students/.

Young, Josh. "The 3 Most Powerful Benefits of a Diverse Faculty." *Campus Answers,* 9 Feb. 2017, www.campusanswers.com/the-3-most-powerful-benefits-of-a-diverse-faculty/.

AFTERWORD
The Faces of Relevance

EDWARD FRIEDMAN
Vanderbilt University

LITERARY ANALYSIS, BY DEFINITION, involves acts of interpretation. In its most basic form, commentary depends on a critic, one who offers an opinion, an assessment, a "reading" of a text. On opposite ends of the spectrum lie the creator and the consumer of the work of art, with the text itself in the center. The text might seem to be the object of scrutiny, but that object also may be the author or the reader, as well as a series of focal points that may seem to place context above text. The boom in theory of the final decades of the twentieth century has made the critical act more self-referential, more broadly based, and more intricate. The object of study, in turn, has become—if not more elusive—less transparent. Changes in theoretical and critical approaches have, logically, affected models of teaching. We are far removed from literature classes purely built around a professor's lectures, as perceptive (and often pleasantly anecdotal) as they may have been. In general, the classroom is interactive, especially since classes taught in Spanish, for example, will have linguistic goals along with the analysis of literature and culture. For those instructors who are, shall we say, seasoned, a key difference between the past and the present is the extent to which student satisfaction is a factor in course development. This hardly means that our predecessors were not gifted and inspiring teachers, but rather that the system, as it were, more conspicuously demanded that the students please the teacher than that the teacher please the students. This would seem to be a change for the better, although one needs to have a strong sense of proportion and avoid tilting the scales into unconstructive imbalance. In sum, the learning curve should never have an adversarial tenor when a spirit of cooperation and goodwill can rule the day. The unifying element in this case could be creativity: a creative course design, creative activities, and creative responses.

We necessarily are preoccupied with questions of relevance, since we can teach only those students who register for our courses. Succinctly stated, we need to grab and keep students, to capture and maintain their interest in an age of high technology and (at times, at least) short attention spans. We need to be aware of the difference between complementary and intrusive materials; that is, the new subject matter should not intrude upon or overwhelm the early modern treasures, be they canonical or newly discovered, nor should associations be forced. Course objectives will vary, but an instructor will want to cover key texts of a given period, genre, or thematic foundation. The contributors to this collection of essays consider early modern Spanish texts in relation to contemporary popular culture in the U.S. and beyond. The approach is comparative and aimed at highlighting works of one period and one nation—cultural artifacts—with current works, trends, and media. Comparative studies are valid when they advance insights on both sides, when they allow for one element to illuminate the other(s). Each of the essayists faces the challenge of demonstrating the value of the proposed correlations and how the particular technique enhances our knowledge of the target texts. The contributors are trained in early modern Spanish literature, history, and culture. Their admiration of and enthusiasm for the texts chosen for analysis are obvious, yet they recognize the benefit of combining the teaching of sixteenth- and seventeenth-century works with contemporary points of contact. Time is a precious commodity in the classroom, and thus the added materials must "earn" their place in the order of things. This is a joint venture, and the crux—the juncture of each frame of reference—is as significant, or arguably more significant, than the sets in isolation. Within this equation, what has been called the literary imagination comes into play on multiple levels. The instructor, bearing in mind the sensibility of the audience, or the collaborators, posits a second field through which to access and clarify a specific text or group of texts. The students use the familiar to address the unfamiliar, and every stage of this dialectical relationship enriches the process of comprehension and examination.

In decades past, advanced undergraduate Spanish courses seem to have been geared to providing a solid background to students who might be doing further work in the field. Survey courses routinely started with the *jarchas* and with indigenous Latin American texts and ended with contemporary works from Spain and Latin America. A lecture format and manuals of literature frequently accompanied selections from the respective canons. Students did not always have to delve into the selected passages because the instructor would submit critiques, in essence, analyses to be replicated on tests, along with names, titles, dates, movements, and so forth. Modifications in pedagogical methods and, in the case of Spanish, the practicality of knowing the language for a number of purposes led to a paradigm shift. The thought was that rather than preparing students for graduate studies in Spanish, courses should focus on a wider and more compelling range of topics that would, at the same time, increase critical and analytical skills. The field of cultural studies in itself expands the parameters of literary studies and invites instructors to be innovative in their presentation of materials and resourceful in engaging student participation. Study of an individual text can motivate students (1) to analyze and evaluate formal elements, (2) to note the distinctive style of an author, (3) to pursue major themes and messages, and (4) to explore significant contexts for comparisons and contrasts. The instructor's explanation of the value and relevance of a determined text—in a word, *telling*—cedes to assisting students in investigating on their own, by supplying interpretive tools and by guiding as opposed to decreeing. In this way, students will be better equipped to tackle new texts and to deal with confront literary and cultural encounters. Learning, as a collaborative experience, takes on new dimensions. There is a preconceived plan of instruction that permits adjustments due to individual appraisals and group dynamics. The openness of the enterprise is never cast into doubt.

The rise of theory—notably structuralism and poststructuralism—has made practically everything about the critical endeavor more self-conscious. Accordingly, and justly, we do not want students to be in the dark about course content, requirements, expectations, or criteria for evaluation. We want to define and explain connections and to show students their crucial role in the undertaking. A move away from the instructor who stands at the head of the class and lectures to those assembled—somewhat akin to delivering a sermon—is hardly a downward move. Using a theatrical analogue, one might contend that the instructor is a director with a partially written script who relies on the actors for a discerning form of improvisation. The students must "come through" for the design to be functional. Therefore, the instructor must shape the details to conform to and to honor, to the extent possible in a difficult task to measure, the students' priorities and aspirations. The search will be on for connecting threads that can facilitate the reading, analysis, and discussion of early modern texts. Naturally, instructors have to frame the use of materials from popular culture as part of a serious investigation, so that the project cannot be seen, even remotely, as "Spanish lite," just as a film course should not be seen as equivalent to going to the movies. The juxtapositions made in this collection of essays illustrate careful, judicious, and persuasive selection of supporting materials on the part of the contributors. Their choices are diverse, as are the primary texts with which they are matched. Each phase broadens horizons, and each group—the instructors and the students—can help to increase the knowledge and the analytical skills of the other, together with judging the advantages of comparative methodologies. The Horatian dichotomy *dulce et utile* would seem to apply; coursework and class dialogue can be intellectually stimulating and entertaining if there is a meeting of minds and if the proverbial stars are aligned. The prospects seem endless, but positive results cannot be guaranteed. Still, the formulation of an inventive course design per se would seem to indicate a sincere effort on the part of the instructor, something that students will appreciate and, perchance, acknowledge.

The essays reveal distinct approaches to teaching early modern Spanish texts, but at the heart of each essay is a dual commitment to literature and culture and to education and inspiration. I believe that teachers of literature in a language other than English learn quickly that one must become a bit of an actor—and more of an extrovert—in order to garner student participation and to establish a comfort level in the classroom. If literature, as the Russian Formalists propose, *defamiliarizes* language, instructors can work to "refamiliarize" or recontextualize. Popular culture can suggest what might be termed bouncing-off places from which to process texts, traditions, and milieus, and, of course, to comment on them. How to write commentary in a convincing manner—without aspiring to make definitive statements—is always a test, and perhaps an ordeal, but instructors can serve as guides and as examples. This volume is about creative stages, seen as steps and as platforms. Underscoring the pedagogical mission is respect for the objects of study and for a public that one hopes will not see itself as captive. Instructors pick texts and approaches for a reason, and their personal tastes will tend to fit prominently into the selection. Likely—and I surmise that this is true among the contributors—talented instructors will want to experiment with both texts and approaches on a regular basis. The essays substantiate the notion that conscientious course design stems from practice and, not surprisingly, from some trial and error. They are models and testaments. I find several "clusters" or shared focal points among the essays: gender issues, music, film, and the classic of all classics, *Don Quijote*. The names of writers and characters—María de Zayas and Don Juan Tenorio stand out—appear repeatedly, and, as would be expected, the current political scene and current political discourse are consistently cited. Those of us who are drawn to rhetorical analysis, and to semiology, are not lacking in points of reference or "unversed" in the far-reaching observations and interpretations of pundits and spin doctors. Discourse analysis in today's world is, as they say, a whole new ballgame, and an exciting (albeit depressing) one at that. This is a propitious time to add new ingredients to the mix.

Let me begin on an upbeat note. Valerie Hegstrom focuses on the representation and characterization of women in early modern Spanish texts, with special regard to the *mujer varonil*, a ubiquitous type with numerous manifestations. The category of "manly woman" can be deemed laudatory or demeaning, but those classified as such are, with few exceptions, assertive, resilient, gifted, and self-protective. The contemporary analogue is Wonder Woman, portrayed in Patty Jenkins's 2017 film by the Israeli actress Gal Gadot. Wonder Woman and others of her ilk "embody" a blend of strength and beauty, and their complex nature (and openness to interpretation) can allow us to reflect on their Iberian counterparts in a new context. Hegstrom's essay looks at female characters in plays by Lope, Tirso, Calderón, Luis Vélez de Guevara, Ana Caro, and Ángela de Acevedo. María de Zayas, Catalina de Erauso, and the independent and disdainful ("esquiva") Marcela of *Don Quijote* come into the picture. Hegstrom poses the important question of whether the Wonder Woman archetype is a feminist icon or a fantasy figure. Is physical prowess or physical presence—power or voluptuousness—the salient feature? How are femininity and masculinity proportioned? Hegstrom makes a case for studying the origin stories of the characters as backdrops to their actions, social status, and degrees of success or failure.

Robert Bayliss, seeking to "historicize feminism," stresses that readings of texts such as Tirso de Molina's *El burlador de Sevilla* in the present political climate are different than they would have been if Hillary Clinton had been elected president. Patriarchal structures are firmly in place then and now, and consequently one can unite the two periods, with, for instance, "Tan largo me lo fiáis" in dialogue with the #TimesUp and #Metoo movements. An inquiry into inequalities in the twenty-first century can assist in identifying and accentuating the power structures operative in early modern Spain, where male aggression and the suppression of justice were the norm. Don Juan's story may be a hyperbolic—baroque—exemplum, but he is scarcely a male figure in isolation. In an essay that concentrates on the novellas of María de Zayas, the honor plays, Francisco López de Úbeda's *La pícara Justina*, and the writings of Sor Juana Inés de la Cruz (including the *Respuesta a Sor Filotea*), David Castillo likewise employs the concept of historicizing to emphasize the continuity of misogyny, abuse, and discrimination. Castillo's essay encourages the contextualization of discourse and social practice by elucidating the theme of victimization from various angles of vision. Zayas and Sor Juana clearly are precocious feminist standard-bearers. As an extraordinary polemicist, Zayas uses Cervantes' model of exemplarity to make her narratives a warning to women to be mindful of male hypocrisy, duplicity, and cruelty, which is to say, to beware of what marriage has in store for the "perfect brides" of her generation. Sor Juana is discreetly subtle yet extravagantly eloquent in her defense of women. The intelligence, wit, and devotion to justice of Zayas and Sor Juana should make them role models for readers of all persuasions. Castillo begins and ends by expounding on the ways in which writers and readers construct reality, and the early modern Spanish texts fit effectively—and affectively—into the scheme. In a similar vein, Bradley Nelson links Tirso and Zayas with contemporary feminism and legal struggles.

Nelson connects early modern texts and society to the present through the practice of scapegoating. Probing the institutions of marriage and criminal justice, he finds points of contact among Tirso's *El burlador de Sevilla*, María de Zayas's *El jardín engañoso*, and the television programs *Criminal Minds* (paired with Tirso) and *Orange Is the New Black* (paired with Zayas). The guiding trope of his essay is irony, an irony that assumes many guises but that unfailingly inverts the premises by which those in authority abuse those ranked below them. The intended solution may be the root of the problem. Nelson wants to animate students to put justice—and poetic justice—at the core of reading and discussion, and the events of every day (alas, no exaggeration) give fuel to the fire. Sonia Pérez-Villanueva treats the theme of violence against women, in the past and in the present, by starting with the testimony of a seventeenth-century Spanish rape victim, Anna Ramírez. In these circumstances, women had few rights, for speaking out jeopardized a family's honor, and hence complaints largely remained private. Then, as now, there was a tendency to blame the victim. Pérez-Villanueva consults legal documents and treatises, and she praises María de Zayas for embedding the injustice into her narratives, which display an unfortunate reality rather than an idealization of women or of the legal system. Zayas depicts violation within each sphere. Breaking silence was a clear act of courage, a sign of feminism. Pérez-Villanueva introduces a parallel topic: pictorial versions of rape. Her chief examples are *Danae* and *The Rape of Europa* by Titian, whose most celebrated patron was Philip II of Spain. The paintings of this kind were typically kept in private rooms for the "pleasure" of men. Gender-inflected aesthetic judgment was and is a debatable matter, as are distinctions between public and private spaces. Men as subjects and women as objects are constants, and so are the criteria by which society determines, negotiates, and responds to beauty. That beauty and rape stand side by side is certainly telling.

John Slater associates our current drug culture with a motif found in Spanish texts from the late fifteenth to the seventeenth centuries (among them, *La Celestina*, *El mágico prodigioso*, *Don Quijote*, and *La inocencia castigada*): the use of magic and medicine to force an unwilling subject to comply with an aggressor's wishes. An obvious example is Doña Inés, the married protagonist of Zayas's novella. Inés resists the pursuit of the infatuated and relentless Don Diego, who finally employs a necromancer to draw the unconscious victim to his house and to his bed. Slater relates the literary renderings to the mammoth volume *Historia de las plantas* (c. 1630) by the physician Bernardo de Cienfuegos, some exempla of which have an uncanny resemblance to the fiction that involves subjugation of the will, accusations of witchcraft, a test, and what Slater calls "an uncertain vindication." The contextualization in Slater's essay revolves around the drug scopolamine, billed as "the world's scariest drug" and featured in newspaper articles and much-viewed videos by Ryan Duffy and others. The interplay of fiction and science can serve to update the early modern texts and to satisfy Slater's personal and pedagogical interest in literature and medicine.

Don Juan Tenorio as a figure of engagement inspires Anthony Grubbs to go from Tirso to the cinema of the new millennium, with mediating commentators and theorists (George Bernard Shaw, José Ortega y Gasset, Sarah Wright, Linda Hutcheon, et al.). The films examined are *Broken Flowers* (dir. Jim Jarmusch, 2005), *John Tucker Must Die* (dir. Betty Thomas, 2006), and *Don Jon* (dir. Joseph Gordon-Levitt, 2013). Grubbs's exercise not only validates the universality of Don Juan, but it gives a sense of continuity to readings of literature, society, and their interdependence. The plot of *El burlador de Sevilla* is at once about sex, theology, and the power of words, and that list is incomplete. As with Cervantes, Zayas, and significant others, Tirso takes a pre-Freudian mindset to staggering heights. The scriptwriters and directors do the same in a post-Freudian world.

As one walks around any college or university campus and observes headphones as accessories, or appendages, it is indisputable that students are "into" music. Some of the essayists punctuate the study of poetry with music. Following a technique that "demystifies mysticism," Bonnie Gasior teaches Spanish mystic poetry through pop music. Noting that the poets of spirituality themselves take recourse to the images and figurations of love poetry to evoke the union of the soul with God—this is amorous verse "a lo divino"—Gasior sees in contemporary love lyrics a religious tie-in, as in her principal examples, Madonna's "Like a Prayer" and Enrique Iglesias's "Experiencia religiosa" in dialectical play with San Juan de la Cruz's "Noche oscura." The approach yields rewards on the secular and spiritual levels. Iglesias and Madonna take the imagery and symbols of religion to communicate love, whereas San Juan appropriates the lexicon of love to convey spirituality in its ultimate form. On both levels, the imagery becomes mixed, confusing, transgressive. The inner workings of mystic poetry and contemporary lyrics can be direct or indirect, obscure, and sophisticated. Gasior's method does demystify mysticism, but quite possibly, and unpredictably, it "mystifies" pop music and, by extension, pop culture.

Mindy Badía frames her essay around the theme of "performing blackness." Her focal text is a *letrilla* by Luis de Góngora, who attempts to recreate the speech of those of African origin (*bozal*). The poem is complicated by virtue of its linguistic and socio-cultural bases, and biases. The tone is not complimentary, and the poem exposes the strong sense of difference—alterity, otherness—that pervades the hierarchies of early modern Spain. Badía chooses the critique of two commentators, Nelson González-Ortega and Nick Jones, to cast the work in opposing lights. González-Ortega sees the poem as a poorly wrought and demeaning caricature—a sign of white superiority—while Jones views Góngora, whether consciously or subconsciously, elevating the speech patterns of blacks through links with *culteranismo*. For Jones, giving the black presence a poetic space is meaningful in itself. Badía presents Góngora's poem in the context of debates that Gerald Graff has labeled the "culture wars," and she relates the racial content to African-American English: its use by African-Americans and its appropriation by others. Her examples include minstrel shows and blackface, the movie *Airplane!* (1980), the current television series *Atlanta*, and, more broadly, the hip-hop movement and its values. The intimate relation between language (and literature) and culture permits a consideration of two multifaceted (if not byzantine) social structures. What we say, what we poeticize, and what we sing never take place in a vacuum, and a single composition can become a social document and a stimulus for dialogue.

Centering on the depiction of heroes and heroism and popular culture through the centuries, Lori Bernard moves from epic poetry and traditional ballads to *corridos* and *narcocorridos*. She notes that the characterization of El Cid in the ballads can vary from that of the *Cantar de mio Cid*, and she asks students to consider topics such as variations, reception, and poetic license.

In historical terms, she discusses how literature is crafted and preserved by the public (*el pueblo*) over time and, correspondingly, how different periods and places offer different modes of defining heroes and assessing their deeds. The variations that Bernard finds in medieval and Renaissance texts provides an approach to the themes of heroism and identity in the Mexican and Mexican-American *corridos* and *narcocorridos*. Popular culture and popular music (and videos) connect with the past to foreground the criteria for—and the ironies of—representing the hero. Readings are dependent on context, and the social status quo can cede to new norms and to the dominance of the antisocial. Bernard's lessons are lessons in multiperspectivism and an acknowledgment of writing as a reflection of times and circumstances.

The essay by Darci Strother considers the teaching of the Spanish classics at a designated Hispanic-Serving Institution (HSI). Her major goal is to set popular culture as a bridge to literary studies, by bearing in mind the backgrounds, interests, and experiences of students. The instructor can design a course while counting on students as "co-architects," an idea that can boost enthusiasm. Strother's examples include pairing Góngora's sonnet "Mientras por competir con tu cabello" with Rod Stewart's "Tonight's the Night" and Billy Joel's "Only the Good Die Young"; Lope's *Fuenteovejuna* with Jim Croce's "Bad, Bad Leroy Brown"; *Don Quijote* with Bonnie Tyler's "Holding out for a Hero" (reintroduced in the film *Shrek*). Strother gives a sample of the collaborative exercise: a table that links Spanish texts from *La Celestina* to the works of Sor Juana Inés de la Cruz. Examples: *Lazarillo de Tormes* with Luis Buñuel's film *Los olvidados* and Cervantes' *Rinconete y Cortadillo* with a selection of *narcocorridos* and the life story of El Chapo. The plan accelerates the learning process and amplifies the literary heritage of her students.

Sidney Donnell's essay deals with a little-known sixteenth-century play, the *Comedia de los amores y locuras del conde loco*, by a writer named Morales (of whose first name scholars are not sure). As he addresses approaches to comparative analysis, with an emphasis on the need to fit the examples to the audience, Donnell associates Morales's non-canonical work with "one-hit wonders" in an array of media and seeks ties with contemporary popular culture. The study of Morales's play lends itself to the examination of madness, of gender-bending, of classifications, of distinctions between high and low culture and, not coincidentally, of the ups and downs of fame and popularity for writers and artists. A moral of the story presented by Donnell is that success can be fleeting and publics can be shortsighted and somewhat capricious. What manuals and commentators say may be valid, but no one really has the last word.

The curious but on-target correlation of the statutes of blood purity (*limpieza de sangre*) and the Harry Potter novels and films informs the essay by Bruce Burningham. For Burningham, J. K. Rowling's representation of ethnicity in the Harry Potter series has been scrutinized in the context of twentieth-century German anti-Semitism and postcolonial theory, but rarely explored with respect to connections with early modern Spain. Burningham takes his lead from a 2011 essay by Ruth Abrams, who compares Rowling's "pureblood" wizards with the Iberian *cristianos viejos*, the "Muggle-Born Registration Commission" with the Spanish Inquisition, and the "specter of hidden identities" with crypto-Judaism. The essay demonstrates that Burningham is well-versed, or fluent, as are few researchers, in both the intricacies of the Potterverse and the ideological, socio-political, and cultural dialectics of sixteenth- and seventeenth-century Spain.

Three of the essays approach the most revered and one of the most iconic of novels. Yolanda Gamboa observes the presence of *Don Quijote* in all media and in culture high and low, from ballet to restaurant names to candy. The brief windmill episode, for example, has made its mark on language, on infinite works of art, and on attitudes toward idealism. People who have never read a page of Cervantes' narrative "know" Don Quijote and Sancho Panza. The knight and the squire come to mind in binaries in literature, film, television, and the plastic arts: Stan Laurel and Oliver Hardy, Batman and Robin, Jerry Seinfeld and George Costanza, and the list goes on and on, the world over. Gamboa highlights *The Big Bang Theory*, which premiered on television in 2007 and is in its final season (2018-2019), but with a spinoff, *Young Sheldon*. She sees the two leading characters, the physicists Sheldon Cooper (Jim Parsons) and Leonard Hofstader (Johnny Galecki) as figures of Don Quijote and Sancho, respectively. The star of the show is Sheldon Cooper, who resembles Don Quijote "in myriad ways." Gamboa submits that "Sheldon seems to be aware of his chivalric nature," and this instance of "quixotic emulation" is one of many correspondences between the early modern narrative and the contemporary series. Sheldon often misreads reality and speaks without a filter. He has trouble—appreciably more than most men—understanding women. *The Big Bang Theory* tests boundaries and features "journeys of discovery" that transform the characters, "all the while making the viewers question the nature of their own reality." Fans of the show can relate to Sheldon's world, and the parameters of that world can help one to understand the literary world of Don Quijote and its references to the Spain of his time.

Margaret Marek uses the impact of chivalric romance on *Don Quijote* as key to a reading of the text. She stresses the ties between the romances of chivalry and the Western tradition, in film and television, which may have begun in 1903 with *The Great Train Robbery* (dir. Edwin C. Porter) and continues in the present. Questions of genre are vital to both categories, as are variations on themes. *Don Quijote* is, after all, an imitation and a rejection, satirical and profound, of *Amadís de Gaula* and its brethren. One can speak of formulas and deep structures in both cases, yet similitude will give way to difference. Matters of nationhood and expansion come into the two frames, as do persecution, violence, racism, and questions of truthful and false representations of reality. Marek notes the role of censorship in Inquisitional Spain and in Hollywood's Motion Picture Production Code, and she sees a reflection of baroque rivalry in the American Westerns versus the "Spaghetti" Westerns (e.g., John Wayne vs. Clint Eastwood). The Western genre can serve as "scaffolding" for first-time readers of *Don Quijote* and the labyrinthine journeys contained within the text.

William Childers ingeniously uses the ideology of the Broadway musical *Man of La Mancha* (1965) to weigh the political force of Cervantes' *Don Quijote*. Based on a 1959 teleplay by Dale Wasserman, *Man of La Mancha* has Cervantes in prison, acting the role of the knight errant as entertainment for his fellow inmates. This play within a play projects a truly idealistic protagonist, whose greatest moment of glory comes in the song "The Impossible Dream," a paean to virtue and blind idealism, sung by the knight and, at the end of the play, by Aldonza and the full cast assembled at Don Quixote's deathbed. Childers's thesis is that Wasserman and his collaborators manage to "depoliticize" *Don Quijote* in order to win the approval of a mass audience. The edginess and subversive thrust of the original are sacrificed so that theatergoers will be absorbed emotionally rather than intellectually. Wasserman seeks to inspire, to encourage goodness, but not to provoke or foster debate. If *Don Quijote* is a magical gesture to irony and profundity of thought, *Man of La Mancha* is a superb balancing act, aimed at pleasing, mutually and across the board, those who personify the dominant culture and the counterculture. A riveting aspect of Childers's essay is the commentary on the shift in librettists for the musical. The first choice was the British poet W. H. Auden, who wrote some sixteen songs, only to have them rejected. Auden was replaced by Joe Darien, whose lyrics conform to the idealism and sentimentality of Wasserman's vision. Auden accepts Alonso Quijano's disil-

lusionment at the conclusion of the narrative; Wasserman does not. Auden
wants to spice up the proceedings; Wasserman does not. The disagreement
between Auden and Wasserman leads Childers to muse on other adaptations
of *Don Quijote* and to delve further into the implied political stance of Cervantes' masterwork. Wasserman strives for an "absence of controversy," while
Cervantes relishes openness and polemics. As he argues his point, Childers
cannot help but notice the conflictive atmosphere of the early seventeenth
century in Spain and of the late 1960s in the U.S.

One of my favorite courses bears the title "*Don Quijote* and Metafiction,"
a graduate seminar. The class begins with preliminary readings as a means of
setting the stage: a selection of short stories and essays on narrative theory
and on the baroque, supplemented by an introduction to metafiction, intertextuality, and aspects of early modern Spain. The centerpiece is, needless to
say, *Don Quijote*, with a healthy dose of criticism. The additional selections,
in the latest offering of the seminar, included Miguel de Unamuno's *Niebla,*
Javier Cercas's *Soldados de Salamina*, Paul Auster's *City of Glass*, and *The
Purple Rose of Cairo* (dir. Woody Allen). The discussion of each work begins
with "resonancias cervantinas" and with how the authors and the director
put their unique signature on the intertext, on borrowings from the past,
newly inscribed. I have talked, slightly in jest, about ordering the readings in
reverse chronology, and I may have the opportunity (and the audacity) to do
so in the near future.

In sum, the coeditors have put together a fascinating and varied collection of essays, all of which present ways of engaging students in the reading
and analysis of early modern Spanish texts. Contemporary popular culture
becomes a means of access and a stimulus for comparative inquiry. The past
can help to explain the present, and vice versa. The suggested approaches can
aid in course design and can embolden instructors to experiment and to find
ways of presenting the classics. The early modern texts need not be seen as un-
solvable mysteries or as less than brilliant or appealing. The essays prove that,
as teachers, the writers are thoughtful, versatile, and dedicated to their field
of specialization and to their students. One of the attractions of the collection for me is my position on the other side of the equation, or the counter-
premise. To a degree, I know more about sixteenth- and seventeenth-century
Spanish literature than about current U.S. popular culture. For example, I
knew next to nothing about the Potterverse, and now I am primed to read
the novels and to watch the films. I thought I knew everything about *Man
of La Mancha* (which I saw on Broadway in 1968 with Hal Holbrook in the
lead, and later in productions with John Cullum, Brian Stokes Mitchell, and

others), but I was wrong, and now I know almost everything. (I had never read of the Auden connection and other details.) Although I am totally out of touch with hip-hop and rap, I will think about music—and, I must say, about diversity—in a different way. The act of reading and contemplating the essays has taught and moved me. I have rethought the question of relevance, to my benefit. Influenced by these essays, I am inspired to try the reverse-order version of my seminar and to ponder other pedagogical *novedades*. A final lesson of the collection is that the texts of the past and the creative spirit are alive and well.

Notes on Contributors

MINDY BADÍA is Professor of Spanish and International Studies at Indiana University Southeast. She specializes in early modern Spanish theater, in particular contemporary productions of the *Comedia*. She has published essays in journals such as *Gestos, Comedia Performance, and On-Stage Studies*. She and Bonnie Gasior co-edited the book *Crosscurrents: Transatlantic Perspectives on Early Modern Hispanic Drama* (Bucknell, 2006) and co-wrote *Redes literarias*, a literary anthology (McFarland 2018). She is a member of the board of directors of the Association for Hispanic Classical Theater.

ROBERT BAYLISS is Associate Professor of Spanish at the University of Kansas and author of *The Discourse of Courtly Love in Seventeenth-Century Spanish Theater* (Bucknell UP). He has published articles in a number of edited volumes and journals, including *Comparative Literature, Comparative Drama, Hispanic Review, Hispania, Comedia Performance*, and *Bulletin of the Comediantes*. He is also the co-editor of *Peculiar Lives in Early Modern Spain: Essays in Honor of Amy Williamsen* (UP of the South). His forthcoming book, *The Currency of Cultural Patrimony: The Spanish Golden Age*, addresses the continual re-use of Spanish literary classics in contemporary Spain.

LORI A. BERNARD is Associate Professor of Spanish at the State University of New York (SUNY), College at Geneseo where she teaches primarily courses in Peninsular literature and civilization. Her specialization is Medieval and early modern Spanish literature with a focus on poetry, specifically, *poesía de tipo tradicional / popular, cancioneros de poesías varias*, oral traditions, and other forms historically excluded from the canon. Her current research interests include the origins of Spanish secular drama and theater; connections between early drama and poetry; and the literary-musical/dramatic courts in Valencia and Toledo.

BRUCE R. BURNINGHAM is Professor of Hispanic Studies and Theatre at Illinois State University. He specializes in medieval and early modern Spanish and Latin American literature, Hispanic theater, and performance theory. His publications include *Millennial Cervantes: New Currents in Cervantes Studies* (U of Nebraska P, 2020), *Tilting Cervantes: Baroque Reflections on Postmodern Culture* (Vanderbilt UP, 2008), and *Radical Theatricality: Jongleuresque Performance on the Early Spanish Stage* (Purdue UP, 2007). He is Editor of *Cervantes*, the journal of the Cervantes Society of America. He is also President of the Association for Hispanic Classical Theater.

DAVID R. CASTILLO is Director of the Humanities Institute and Professor of Spanish at State University of New York (SUNY) Buffalo. He has authored *Awry Views: Anamorphosis, Cervantes, and the Early Picaresque* (Purdue UP, 2001) and *Baroque Horrors: Roots of the Fantastic in the Age of Curiosities* (Michigan UP, 2010) and co-authored *Zombie Talk: Culture, History, Politics* (Palgrave, 2016) and *Medialogies: Reading Reality in the Age of Inflationary Media* (Bloomsbury, 2016). Castillo has also co-edited *Reason and Its Others* (Vanderbilt UP, 2006), *Spectacle and Topophilia* (Vanderbilt UP, 2012), and *Writing in the End Times* (HIOL, 2019). He is working on a new book entitled *Alt-Realities*.

WILLIAM CHILDERS is Associate Professor of Spanish at Brooklyn College and the City University of New York (CUNY) Graduate Center. He is the author of *Transnational Cervantes* (Toronto, 2006), and some three dozen articles on Cervantes, Moriscos, the Inquisition, and other topics related to early modern Spanish cultural history. His current research project, *Countercultural Quixotes*, focuses on the reception of *Don Quixote* in the United States during the Cold War.

SIDNEY DONNELL is Professor of Spanish at Lafayette College in Easton, Pennsylvania. Together with *Feminizing the Enemy: Imperial Spain, Transvestite Drama, and the Crisis of Masculinity* (Bucknell University Press, 2003), Prof. Donnell has published a critical edition of the seventeenth-century crossdressing play *El caballero dama* by Sevillian dramatist Cristóbal de Monroy y Silva (Juan de la Cuesta, 2019) and scholarly articles and book chapters about a number of topics including films inspired by *Don Quixote* and the Cervantine tradition.

YOLANDA GAMBOA TUSQUETS is Associate Professor of Spanish at the Department of Languages, Linguistics, and Comparative Literature at Florida Atlantic University. Her research interests within early modern cultural studies center on the lives and cultural production of early modern women. She has authored a book on María de Zayas (*Cartografía social en la narrativa de María de Zayas*, Biblioteca Nueva, 2009), published articles on chocolate and Naples as part of the seventeenth-century Spanish imaginary, and she is also a literary translator. Her co-edited *Making Sense of the Senses: Current Approaches in Spanish Comedia Criticism* (Juan de la Cuesta, 2017) with Bonnie Gasior, was awarded the Vern Williamsen prize from the AHCT this year. Her latest publications are "Translating Alejandro Céspedes with Ezra Pound" (*Translation Review*, 2019), and, co-written with Bonnie Gasior, "From Houses to Humilladeros: Violence, Fear, and Zayas's Female Monster Victims" (University Press of the South, 2020). She is working on a book project tentatively titled *Spanish Women and Culture in Early Modern St. Augustine*.

BONNIE GASIOR is Professor of Spanish and the Interim Director of the University Honors Program at California State University, Long Beach. She has published a textbook, *Redes Literarias: La literatura hispánica en su contexto socio-histórico* (with Badia), and two edited volumes: *Crosscurrents: Transatlantic Perspectives on Early Modern Hispanic Drama* (also with Badia) and *Making Sense of the Senses in the Spanish Comedia* (with Gamboa). In addition, she has authored numerous articles that appear in journals such as *Hispania, Hispanic Issues Online, Laberinto Journal, Chasqui*, and *Bulletin of the Comediantes*. Her current book project focuses on developing and understanding internship programs, particularly as they relate to equity and social justice issues.

TONY GRUBBS is Associate Professor of early modern Spanish literature and culture in the Department of Romance and Classical Studies at Michigan State University where he also serves as chairperson. His publications focus on Golden Age Spanish theater, hagiography, and performance theory. His transcription and scholarly edition of *Vida y muerte de San Cristóbal (c. 1600)*, published by the Arizona Center for Medieval and Renaissance Studies, comes out in 2021.

VALERIE HEGSTROM is Professor of Spanish Literature and Coordinator of Global Women's Studies at Brigham Young University. Her research focuses on early modern Spanish theater and the recovery of forgotten women writers. Her edition of Ângela de Azevedo's *El muerto disimulado* (translated by Catherine Larson) appeared with Liverpool UP in 2018. She has published on the works of Guillén de Castro, Bernarda Ferreira de Lacerda, Marcela de San Félix, Maria do Céu, Leonor de Almeida Portugal, Tirso de Molina, and María de Zayas. In 2019, she taught a course on "Wonder Woman and the *mujer varonil*" to advanced undergraduate and graduate students of Spanish literature.

MARGARET MAREK is Professor of Spanish at Illinois College in Jacksonville, IL. She has published on the *libro de pastores*, on Cervantes, and on the teaching of medieval and early modern literature. She is particularly interested in the intersection of the Spanish pastoral book and the booming Merino wool trade, the latter of which drove the early modern Spanish economy. She studies herding practices, both early modern and present-day, and has spent time with Merino flock owners in León and Extremadura.

BRADLEY J. NELSON is Professor of Spanish and Associate Dean, Academic Programs and Development in the School of Graduate Studies at Concordia University. He is the author of *The Persistence of Presence: Emblem and Ritual in Baroque Spain* (UToronto, 2010), and co-editor (with David Castillo) of *Spectatorship and Topophilia in Early Modern and Postmodern Hispanic Cultures* (Vanderbilt UP, 2012); and *Writing in the End Times: Apocalyptic Imagination in Hispanic Cultures* (Hispanic Issues Online, 2019). His most recent publication is "Religion and Sex Crimes in Baroque Spain: The *Ave Maria* as Alibi in *His Wife's Executioner*, by María de Zayas" published in *Théologiques*, a special cluster edited by Éric Bellavance and Vivek Venkatesh.

SONIA PÉREZ VILLANUEVA is Associate Professor of Spanish Studies at Lesley University, in Cambridge, MA. Her research interests are women's and gender studies, particularly cultural, visual and media representations of violence against women in Spain. Her latest research project focuses on the persecution of Crypto-Jewish women in Spain by the Inquisition. She is a research member of the project "Women against the Inquisition," funded by the Spanish government and led by Dr. María Jesús Zamora Calvo from the Universidad Autónoma in Madrid, Spain. She is the founding editor, with Leyla Rouhi and Irene Mizrahi, of *ConSecuencias: A Journal of Spanish Criticism*.

JOHN SLATER is Associate Professor of Spanish at Colorado State University. He is the author of *Todos son hojas: literatura e historia natural en el barroco español* (CSIC, 2010), and co-editor of *Medical Cultures of the Early Modern Spanish Empire* (Routledge, 2014; with Maríaluz López-Terrada, and José Pardo-Tomás) and Calderón de la Barca's *En la vida todo es verdad y todo mentira,* and *Sueños hay que verdad son* (European Masterpieces, 2016; with Harrison Meadows). His articles have appeared in *MLN, Bulletin of the Comediantes, History of Science, Social History of Medicine,* and elsewhere.

DARCI L. STROTHER is Professor of Spanish and former Department Chair at California State University San Marcos. She lived and worked in Chile as a U.S. Fulbright Scholar in 2007. Dr. Strother is currently the Vice President of the California State University World Language Council and Vice President of the Association for Hispanic Classical Theatre. She is the author of numerous scholarly publications including *Family Matters: A Study of On- and Off-Stage Marriage and Family Relations in Seventeenth-Century Spain* (Ibérica/Peter Lang Press, 1999). She is also a certified instructor of Mental Health First Aid courses and regularly offers training on college campuses.

Index

"A su retrato", 60-62

abandonment, 93, 110, 120

abuse
  freedom, 180-184; cycle, 126; male abusers, 87, 112-113, 116, 146, 150; personal histories, 53, 306; physical, 77, 112; sexual, 54, 61, 102, 112-121, 146, 151-152, 155-157; victims, 59, 150-151; violent, 111

academia, 24-25, 28

acceptance, 107-108, 126

accessibility
  film, 178; popular culture, 22; of texts, 22-23, 27; undergraduate students, 143

accountability, 150, 155

accusers, 56, 59-60, 95, 110

accusations
  false, 109, 281, 307; rape, 87-88, 101-103, 108-117

Acker, Kathy
  Don Quixote (1986), 78, 114

activism
  feminist, 103, 151-152, 157; political, 62, 71; self-ironic, 78

activities
  appropriate to gender, 60; brainstorming, 177; group, 232; multistep, 186; online, 149; small group, 232-233; text-based, 254; warm up, 232; whole class, 178-179, 185-186, 190, 232-233, 242, 266-268, 271, 296

acts
  of belonging, 141; communicative, 251; criminal, 93, 101; desecration, 269; identity, 133, 136, 141; unnatural sexual, 282; violent, 50-51, 102, 117, 150

adaptations
  appropriation, 72, 185; film, 33, 51, 178, 185, 252, 257; ideologically conservative, 71; of the Don Juan legend, 153, 176-178; popular, 66, 75, 235; problematic; Quixote, 65-66, 70-77, 81, 252, 312; satirical, 70

addiction, 94, 188-189

adultery, 107, 218

adventure, 15, 161, 168, 202-206, 214, 223, 240

advertisements, 61, 125

advocate, 26, 102, 117, 187, 219, 266

aesthetic
    beauty, 107, 120, 124; con-
    temporary, 87; empathy, 124;
    frameworks, 53, 102; modes, 103;
    pleasure, 97, 117, 119; representa-
    tion, 27-28, 107; sexual violence,
    87-89, 97, 103, 107, 111, 117-118,
    124; tropes, 89
African-Americans, 36, 133, 136-138,
    141-143, 308
African American Vernacular Eng-
    lish (AAVE)
    aka African American English
    (AAE), 133-135, 308
Africanized Spanish, 132, 139, 141,
    308
    also sayagués or Black Spanish
Afro-Cubans, 286
Age of Discovery, 173
agency, 149-150, 152, 156
agenda
    change, 77; pastoral, 224; the-
    matic, 212-213
agents, 153-154, 157, 280
aggression
    gender-based, 106; male, 155-157,
    305
aging, 61, 189-190, 258
airbrushing, 60-62
    see also Photoshop
Airplane!, 134-138
El alcalde de Zalamea, 48, 51
Alemán, Mateo
    Guzmán de Alfarache, 55
Alfonso X, 114
Alias Grace, 57-59

alibi, 102
alienation, 254, 263
allegory, 119, 223, 267
Allen, Woody, 102, 312
Allies (WWII), 40
allusion, 199, 271
Alonso Quijano, 73, 76, 215, 220,
    224, 311
    see also Don Quixote
alter ego, 205
Althusser, Louis
Althusserian, 50
Amadís de Gaula, 210-211, 311
"Amar sólo por vencer", 52
Amazons, 196
Amazonas en las Indias, 281
ambiguity, 62, 213, 241-242, 294
America
    mainstream, 69-70, 102, 176;
    white, 134-138, 141-142, 151, 215,
    276, 286, 299
    see also United States
American West, 216
American Western, 221-223, 311
Americana, 135
amistad torpe, 281-282
An Enemy of the People, 66
anachronism, 71, 87, 179, 185
analysis
    comparative, 38, 87, 147-148, 154,
    232, 250, 267, 283, 309; critical,
    22, 148, 190; discourse, 22, 260,
    305; film, 178, 186, 190, 211, 216;
    race, class, and gender, 88, 107,
    286-287; student, 26, 178, 185-

186, 196, 210, 230, 233, 242, 275, 286, 292, 297-299, 303, 312; textual, 23, 53, 27, 101, 229, 233, 296, 302-304

anarchism, 78

anecdotes, 27, 222, 230, 264, 280-285, 301

anger, 164, 189

Anthony, Susan B., 151

Anthropologists, 103

Anthropomorphism, 269

anti-converso laws, 41-42

anti-feminism, 54, 57

antihero, 54, 202, 204, 229

anti-Semitism, 35-38, 45, 310

antithesis, 219

Antona García, 198-206

anxieties
social, 42, 178, 284, 286; student, 264, 266

aphrodisiacs, 119

Aphrodite, 198-199, 205

appearances
coded, 125; physical, 38, 61, 120, 164, 190, 235; youthful, 61

approaches
counterculture, 74-76; critical, 73, 77, 87-88, 150, 162, 301-302, 309; integrative, 24, 178, 229, 264, 295; multiple literacies, 251; pop culture, 269-271, 292, 308; Romantic, 67, 71; teaching, 22-28, 77, 87-88, 131-132, 142, 153-154, 157, 160-162, 178, 182, 210, 229-230, 251, 259, 261, 264, 269-271,

276, 295, 297-298; theoretical, 27-28, 131

appropriation
countercultural, 76, 79; linguistic, 133, 141; speech, 133, 140-142, 308

aprobación, 217

archetypes, 51, 161, 305

Ariosto, Ludovico
Orlando furioso, 169, 256-257

aristocracy 52-53, 87-92, 97, 100-102, 115, 121, 123, 215
see also nobility

Armendáriz, Alonso Orozco Enriquez de, 283

art
and the artist, 102; *arte nuevo*, 194, 220; Baroque, 119; boundary pushing, 270; commissioning, 117, 119-121, 138; conventional, 61, 75; of conversation, 165; depictions of rape, 117-121; expression, 81, 180, 265; high, 125; leaders, 126; nudes, 117-20, 122-123; Renaissance, 119; rights, 81, 222; Spain, 27, 108; vision, 53, 182, 219-222, 311; visual, 123; Western, 119

Arthuriad, 210

artifacts
cultural, 87, 249-261, 302; discursive, 153; non-elite and popular, 250

Aryan, 38

Ashkenazi, 39

Asia, 37

assimilation, 215

assumptions
    challenged, 25, 140, 297; cultural,
    112; of guilt, 39; heteronormative,
    255, 260; unexamined, 78, 94,
    148, 255, 260
Atlanta (television show), 136-138
attraction, 121, 124
Atwood, Margaret, 57-62
Auden, W.H., 14, 72-77
audiences
    appealing to, 72, 77-78, 81, 167-
    169, 190, 194, 212, 221, 232, 255-
    257, 267, 270, 312; confronting,
    74; contemporary, 173; external,
    58; heterogeneous, 50; identifica-
    tion, 67, 73-76; imagination, 284,
    302; mass, 167, 249, 311; North
    American, 165; passive, 161; pre-
    sumed, 251
Augustine *see* St. Augustine
authors
    anonymous, 48, 254, 298; con-
    trol, 94; female, 60, 82, 318;
    intervention, 54-55; male, 59;
    misogynist, 54, 93; surrounding
    reality of, 169
authority
    civil, 40, 96, 269, 279-280; cul-
    tural, 56, 59; male, 50, 54-58;
    moral, 59, 283; paternal, 89, 156;
    position, 35, 154, 254, 306
auto-da-fé, 39
autonomy, 295-297
avant-garde, 71
avant-la-lettre, 143
Avellaneda, Alonso Fernández de,
    222

awareness, 45, 73, 77, 107, 111, 143,
    147, 154, 157, 169, 172, 179, 256
Axis powers, 40
Azalea, Iggy, 137
Azevedo, Ángela de, 196
    La margarita del Tajo, 206
    El muerto disimulado, 318

B films, 212
Babenco, Héctor, 250
Baby Boom, 69
backgrounds
    cultural, 214, 264, 290, 293-294;
    ethnic, 38, 116, 141, 240, 293;
    historical, 197; interaction, 297,
    299, 309
Baillie, Bruce, 70, 72
Balanchine, George, 71
Baldwin, James, 93-94
ballad, 50, 201, 230-232, 235-242, 308
ballet, 71, 159, 310
Balzac, Honoré de, 293
Baroque
    art, 118-119, 131-132; culture, 50-
    51; plays, 51; rhetoric, 99, 251;
    Spanish, 89, 180, 318; style, 60,
    305, 312; tales, 52; tendency, 60,
    181; tropes, 311
barriers, 152
Batman, 169, 197, 260, 310
    *Batman v Superman: Dawn of
    Justice,* 199; *Justice League,* 198
The Battle of Midway, 209
Beats (Beatniks), 67-69, 76

beauty, 60-61, 93, 97, 107, 118-120, 124, 140, 143, 168, 193, 198, 200-201, 204-205, 297

behavior
aristocratic, 89; criminal, 102; cultural interpretations, 113; formulaic, 210; male, 195; model, 49-50; patterns, 49, 295; predatory, 182; problematic or questionable, 9, 22; protagonist, 165, 172, 232; towards women, 54, 102; victim, 112, 155

Belianís de Gercia, 210

beliefs, 38, 45, 80, 157, 179-180, 284

Benjamin, Walter, 77, 160

El beso de la mujer araña (novel), 250

biases, 87, 107, 109, 255, 308

Bible, 12, 276

The Big Bang Theory, 159-173

binaries, 27, 35, 140, 167, 310

Black
culture, 102, 132-142; English *see also* African American Vernacular English, 8, 132-135, 141, 308; men, 143; people, 133, 142; saint, 269; Spanish (*sayagués*), 138, 140; speech, 132; women, 138-139, 143

Black Legend, 286

Black Lives Matter movement, 57, 269

blackface, 134, 138, 308

blood purity *see limpieza de sangre* and *pureza de sangre* statutes, and purity

body

female, 53, 120-121, 124-126, 194, 204, 277, 279; functions, 165; image, 61; intimate parts, 124, 218; social, 55, 112, 166

Boetticher, Bud, 222

bondage, 194, 202-203, 274-275

books
approved, 216, 218; burning, 67, 217; censorship, 123, 180, 193, 311; gender-bending, 253; mass-production, 211; prohibited, 123; unlicensed, 217

borders, 37, 209, 240

boundaries, 66, 143, 161-162, 169-172, 270, 310

Brecht, Bertolt, 75

Breen, Joseph, 218

Broadway, 72, 76, 257, 311-312

Broken Flowers, 178, 189, 307

brothers, 50, 52, 97, 99, 279

Búcar sobre Valencia: moro alcalde, moro alcalde, / el de la veyuda barba, 246-247

"El buen Cid" *see Cantar de mio Cid*

burden of proof, 283

buried self, 33, 42-45

Burke, Tarana, 106,
see also #MeToo movement

El burlador de Sevilla, 48, 88-97, 102, 146-157
see also Don Juan

burlesque, 54, 56

butch drag, 256

El caballero de Olmedo, 276

Cahill, U.S. Marshal, 214

Calderón de la Barca, Pedro, 90, 107, 111, 196, 305
   El alcalde de Zalamea, 48-51; *El mágico prodigioso*, 275, 278, 307; *El médico de su honra*, 51-52, 62; *La vida es sueño*, 194, 205; Segismundo, 274
campaigns
   hashtag, 149; political, 96; social media, 101
Cancionero de romances, sin año, 245
Cancionero general, 211
Cannes Film Festival, 79
canon
   figures, 70-73, 163, 176-179, 185-186, 190-191, 213-216, 229-243, 305, 310; literary, 75, 249, 260-262; masterpieces, 118; texts, 51, 147, 157, 230, 249-254
Cantar de mio Cid, 236-237
   see also El Cid
capitalism, 23, 71, 77
career
   damage, 126; and marriage, 203; teaching, 298; women, 195, 205
caricature, 69, 140, 308
Carnestolendas, 109, 111
Caro, Ana
   Valor, agravio y mujer, 194, 205, 305
caste, 91
catharsis, 265
Catholicism
   Catholic Church, 217-218, 270; conversion, 39, 41-42; monarch, 39, 204; practicing, 189

cautionary tale, 126
celebrity, 150, 216, 220
La Celestina, 275-278, 298, 307, 309
La Cenicienta que no quería comer perdices, 298
censors, 217, 221
censorship
   advocacy groups, 193; *aprobación*, 217; books, 180; federally-mandated, 217; *Índice de libros prohibidos*, 216; Joseph Breen, 218; motion picture industry, 217, 221, 311; theme, 270
Central America, 79, 81
Cervantes, Miguel de, 107, 111, 204
   comedic duos, 160-169; contemporary readers, 169, 311; dialogue, 173; feud with Lope de Vega, 27, 66, 220, 222, 224; "Rinconete y Cortadillo", 298; satire, 67, 69; scholarship, 162, 210; story, 161
   see also Don Quixote
change
   positive, 95, 241; resistance, 170; social, 70
El Chapo *aka* Joaquín Guzmán, 241, 298, 309
characters
   chivalric, 172, 310; comedic, 218, 140, 160-169; comic book, 163-165, 169, 193-206; complex, 168, 179; contrasting, 160; delusional, 75, 161, 220; development, 166, 170, 235; discussions, 35, 167, 180, 198, 206, 229, 231, 241; female, 57, 92, 94-95, 101-102, 154-155, 181, 195, 255, 279, 305, 307; Indian,

167; instructive, 95; main, *also* protagonist, 42, 54, 57, 136, 155, 163, 165, 168, 172, 176, 179, 183, 185-190, 193, 204, 221, 229, 233, 236, 256-257, 260-261, 269, 307, 311; male, 255, 269; mythical, 120; Native American, 212-216; problematic, 214; quixotesque, 160-169, 172-173; stock, 194, 219; transformation, 166-167, 170, 230, 255, 260-261; two-dimensional, 165

Charles I, 116

Charles V, 118

chastity, 110, 115

Chaucer, Geoffrey, 292-293

Chávez, César, 241, 247

Chicano movement, 241-242, 248

chivalry
Don Quixote, 73, 75, 162-173, 218; ideals, 170, 222, 310; renunciation, 73, 75; romance, 67, 76, 311; tales, 168, 211

Christian
conversion, 39, 41-42; *cristianos viejos*, 39, 236-237, 245, 310; -Jewish relations, 39, 42, 217; mysticism, 271; outwardly, 42

church
Spanish, 40; and state, 89
see also Catholicism

CIA, 71

El Cid, 210, 229-243, 308
see also Cantar de mio Cid

El Cid (1961), 231

Cienfuegos, Bernardo de, 281-286, 307

cinema *see* film

Civil Rights movement, 135

civilization-building, 91

class
analysis, 287; difference, 181, 195; dominant, 94; lower, 109, 111; middle, 94, 133, 135; social, 94, 181; stratification, 36, 240; upper, 18, 115

classics, 23, 28, 160, 254, 304, 312

classroom discussion, 28, 35, 49, 61-62, 76, 88, 97, 99, 133, 139, 142-143, 156, 178-181, 184-187, 194, 198, 203, 206, 229-233, 237-241, 253, 256-259, 269, 271, 283, 287, 296, 303-306

La clavícula de Salomón, 276

climate
political, 157, 286, 305; sexual, 99

climax, 44, 99, 234, 238, 269

Clinton, Hillary, 146, 305

close reading, 131, 156, 211

Coco, 298-99

codes
antiquated, 222; Counter-Reformation, 115-117, 121; honor *also código de honor*, 49-52, 147, 182-184; legal, 16, 91, 102, 114; moral, 219, 222-223; Motion Picture Production Code, 216-218, 311

code switching, 37

coercion *see also* consent, 274-288

cognitive science, 160

Cohen, Leonard, 239

Cold War, 70-71, 77, 149, 316

college
administrators, 252; classroom, 242, 295; curricula, 21, 179, 253, 271, 292, 295; enrollment among Hispanics, 290-291; fraternities, 155

Colombia, 284-287

colonialism
history, 294-295; Spanish, 153; British, 37; Western, 212-214, 286

comedia, 147, 157, 180-183, 196-204, 214, 220, 253, 260-262, *cantada*, 200-201, 255; *de capa y espada*, 157; evolution, 254; heroines, 194, 197-198, 204; *histórica*, 209; *nueva*, 50-51, 254; stock character, 91, 194, 214; three-act

Comedia de los amores y locuras del conde loco
see *El conde loco*

Comedia de los naufragios de Leopoldo, 249

Comedia Medora, 255

commedia dell'arte, 255

comedies
American, 159-173, 187; about date rape drugs, 275; Don Quixote, 160-164, 167; Shakespeare, 50, 164, 188; situational, 163; Spanish, see *comedia*

comic books, 159-173, 193-206, 260-261, 293, 310

Comic-Con, 171-72

common sense, 254

communication

act, 261; breakdown, 251; revolution, 15, 173; strategies, 178

communion, 73, 263, 267

Communism, 66, 70, 75
see also Cold War

communities
building, 133, 149; Jewish, 38-39, 43

comparisons, 14, 67, 90, 153-157, 159, 164, 189, 199, 215, 229, 239, 257, 261, 267, 275, 303

comprehension, 26, 132, 140, 233, 302

computer-assisted language learning, 260

concealment, 42
see also buried self

conceptistas, 27, 143
see also Quevedo

concubines, 285

El conde loco, 249-262, 309

condemnation
Don Juan, 179, 184; Madonna, 270; of rape, 107, 113-114; of sexual violence, 126; Sor Juana Inés de la Cruz, 60; of victims, 116

confession, 58-59, 62, 183, 189

conflict, 77, 197, 240

conformity, 44, 66, 68, 70, 161, 204

congress, 66, 116, 151

Congress for Cultural Freedom, 71

connections
contemporary, 159; emotional, 160; identifying, 10, 147-148, 155, 178, 185, 229, 296, 305; immediate, 81, 235, 240, 261; meaning-

ful and personal, 26, 160, 178, 198, 239, 264, 270, 292-293, 299; onomastic, 41-42; real-world, 82; Spanish, 38

conquest, 153, 182, 184, 189, 213, 274

consent, 89, 112-114, 274-288

consequences
offending fans, 150; private, 125; for rape, 112-113; social, 132, 142, 152, 155, 182-184, 296

conservatism, 66, 71-72, 77

conspiracy, 52, 57, 102

constructs, 49, 183, 240

consumers, 148-150, 154, 157, 211, 249, 301

consumerism, 67-71

content
objectionable, 218; rich and meaningful, 270; political, 78; satirical, 72; violent, 258

contexts
of armed conflict, 197; burlesque, 56; classroom, 23; contemporary, 177, 230; cultural, 132, 147, 173, 178, 186, 275; discursive, 146, 153; familiar, 23, 132; historical, 48, 131, 140, 143, 217, 251, 258, 275; institutional, 96; marriage, 50; #MeToo and #Time'sUp movements, 48-62, 87-103, 106-126, 146, 156, 305; of mid-1960s turmoil, 78; political, 147, 153; of reception, 75; social, 117, 179, 183, 287; unfamiliar, 22-23, 152, 230-231; useful, 154

continuity, 49, 65, 179, 256

contradictions, 66-67, 76-78, 94, 124, 148, 150-151, 194, 240

control, 50, 91, 94, 149-150, 152, 181, 204-205, 275, 295

controversy, 77, 81, 222, 239, 312

conventions
literary, 61, 75, 171; social, 146, 165, 169-173, 179, 261; Western, 219-221

conversations *see* classroom discussion

conversion *also converses*, 39, 41-42

coolness factor, 293

copyright, 81, 222

Corpus Christi, 138-139

corridos, 229-248
see also narcocorridos

El Corrido de César Chávez, 241

corruption, 54-55, 74, 153, 180

Cosby, Bill, 16, 88-90, 101-102

Council of Trent, 90, 123,

Counter Reformation, 88, 94, 97, 101, 108, 116-117, 121, 180, 184, 267

counterculture, 65-72, 76-79, 311

court
musicians, 235, 237; of law, 80, 101, 107, 110, 113, 116, 118, 171; poets, 235, 237; protocol, 181; Spanish, 122, 155, 180; theater, 9, 182, 250, 253, 255

courtly love, 27, 90, 97, 99, 165, 182, 210, 315

cowboys
in film Westerns, 209-224; hero, 214, 219; and Indians, 216; *vaqueros*, 213; Woody (*Toy Story*), 161

crime
  legal, 91, 96, 107, 114-116, 154;
  meaningless, 96; of passion, 98;
  sex, 52, 88-92, 97, 102-103, 110-
  116; shows, 74, 87-103
criminal justice system, 88, 94-95,
  101-103
Criminal Minds, 88, 92-94, 103, 306
crisis, 57, 73, 78, 152, 180
cristianos viejos, 39, 236-237, 245, 310
critical
analysis, 22, 87, 132-133, 141, 148,
  150, 153, 173, 180, 190, 195, 301;
  distance, 154, 157; issues, 136,
  141, 149; media literacy, 26, 294;
  thinking, 22, 25-27, 103, 147, 154,
  267, 270, 293, 303; vision, 70;
  writing, 73, 210, 252, 257
criticism, 22, 223, 255, 312
critiques
  contemporary society, 80, 138,
  157; cultural, 23, 77; female, 87,
  270; ironic, 102; patriarchy, 152,
  154; U.S. foreign policy, 81
Cronenberg, David, 257
cross-dressing, 194, 256
crowdsourcing, 149
cruelty, 52, 112, 306
crypto-identities, 42-45
crypto-Judaism, 42, 310
cryptonomy, 33, 44
culteranismo, 141, 308
  see also Góngora
cultistas vs. *conceptistas*, 27, 143
culto style, 140

cultural circumstances, 151, 156, 206,
  241, 309
cultural exchange, 141
cultural studies, 102, 148-149, 250,
  259, 303
cultural products, 77-78, 142, 148-
  150, 154, 157, 185, 261, 286
culture
  Black, 102, 131-143; celebrity,
  150; commodification, 136, 142;
  constructs, 240, 294; contemporary, 24, 69, 159-162, 168, 177,
  275; continuity, 49, 65, 179, 256,
  306-307; counterculture, 65-72,
  76-79, 311; crisis, 78, 180; distinction between high and popular,
  27, 74, 169; folk, 241; Hispanic,
  286; hook-up, 184, 189; industry,
  75, 77, 90, 121, 125, 149-150, 211,
  217-218; literary, 93; and male
  power, 117; mass, 22-24, 27-28;
  oppressive, 107; participatory,
  152; *see* pop culture; postmodern, 160-161; rape, 155, 287; role,
  78-79; Spanish, 131, 154, 157, 182,
  286; U.S., 131, 150, 168; wars, 131;
  white, 138
curriculum, 107, 179, 249, 253, 271,
  292, 295
customs, 91, 100, 102

Dal Pozzo, Cassiano, 120
damsel in distress, 161, 168, 170, 201
Danae, 117, 119-121, 124
Darion, Joe, 72-79
date-rape drugs, 102, 274-275, 285-
  286

dating, 184, 187

daughters

and fathers, 50, 52, 94-95, 102, 123, 176, 181, 235, 239; obedient, 97; unmarried, 181

David and Bathsheba, 218

DC Comics, 163, 194

De las excelencias de la virtud de la castidad, 113

death

Don Juan, 90, 98-102, 156, 179, 181; Don Quixote, 70, 74-76, 220, 224, 311; *mujer varonil*, 202, 204; penalty, 115-116; Sor Juana, 60-61; violent, 52, 100

Deathly Hallows see Harry Potter series

debates

current, 22, 157, 193; healthy, 262; larger, 77; Miller-Wasserman, 66, 311; rhetorical, 89, 97, 100, 102; scholarly, 24, 79, 81, 131, 135, 257, 277, 280, 308

decadence, 178

deceit *see* dishonesty

deconstruction, 156

deeds, 196, 198, 202, 204, 309

defamation, 109, 112

defeat, 38-39, 45, 176, 198, 219-220, 234-235

Del rey abajo, ninguno, 48

delusions, 75, 161, 220

denouement, 98-99

depoliticization, 65-83

desengaño, 54, 146, 151, 180

Desengaños amorosos, 48, 51-54, 111-112, 275, 277, 282, *Amar sólo por vencer*, 53; *Estragos que causa el vicio*, 53; *El verdugo de su esposa*, 51

desire, 57, 77, 92, 98-100, 119-120, 123, 125, 157, 168, 171, 203, 261, 275-283, 287

destiny, 54, 91, 97

deviancy, 88

devil, 72, 98-102, 176, 275, 278-279, 283-284, 286

devocalization, 137

DeVos, Betsy, 283

The Dharma Bums, 69, 72

dialect, 76, 133-136

dialectic, 88, 302, 308, 310

dialogue, 87, 135, 137, 147, 154, 160, 166, 173, 182, 190, 234-235, 251, 255, 261

Diarios de la motocicleta (film), 48

dictatorships, 34, 40, 82

didactic, 50, 54

digital age, 148-150, 152

disclaimer, 59, 80, 258

discourse

analysis, 22, 260, 305; misogynist, 61; religious, 157; self-reflexive, 162

discovery, 95, 172-173, 310

discrimination, 152, 276-277, 306

discussions

critically-informed, 87; philosophical, 169; taste, 97; transcultural, 49

see also classroom discussion

Disenchantments of Love

see Desengaños amorosos

dishonor, 89, 156, 183,

dishonesty, 52, 90, 99-100, 181, 187-188, 214, 239

disillusionment, 73-76, 180, 205

diversity, 37, 142, 231, 261, 267, 291-292, 299, 313

divides

cultural, 102, 155-156; economic, 77; generational, 77, 291, 299; historical, 62, 87, 147, 155-156, 160, 241, 251, 265; linguistic, 137, 147; racial, 38-39, 43, 143, 299

divine

contemplation, 265; intervention, 150, 265; judgement, 180, 183-184; love, 182, 308; mystic union, 263-271; patriarchy, 156; providence, 156; punishment, 90-91, 180; redemption, 99-100

documentary, 209, 284

domestic sphere, 52-54, 110, 203

domestic violence, 48-62, 283

domination, 275-278

Don Cirongilio de Tracia, 216

Don Jon (2013), 179, 188-189

Don Juan,

adaptations, 176-191; anachronistic, 179, 185; changing with the times, 176; character, 146-157, 177, 184; death, 90, 98-102, 156, 179, 181; Don Juanism, 178; figure, 178-179, 185-186, 190-191; in film; legend, 153-154, 178, 180, 184; pervasiveness, 177; punishment, 156; treatment of women,

153; universality, 177-178; victims, 88-91

see also El burlador de Sevilla, Don Juan Tenorio

Don Juan de Carillana, 190

Don Juan Manuel, 49-50

Don Juan Tenorio, 91, 146-147, 153, 176-178, 187-188, 190, 304, 307

Don Quixote de la Mancha,

archetype in Western tradition, 161; Arms and Letters, 213; Biscayan, 219; *The Big Bang Theory*, 159-173; Buzz Lightyear, 161, 165; contemporary culture, 69, 159-162; delusions, 75, 161, 220; depoliticization, 65-83; diegetic levels, 260; Dorotea, 157, 168, 194, 211; dreams, 65, 75, 165; Dulcinea, 71, 165, 168, 219; effects, 160, 172; elements, 160-164; "I, Don Quixote," 65-69; *Man of La Mancha* (1965), 65-82; *Quixote* (film), 72; *Quixote* (magazine), 71; Sancho Panza, 160, 165-168, 170, 216, 219-220; Sheldon Cooper; the Stranger, 218-220, 223, 266, 310; timelessness, 70-72; Woody, 161

see also Cervantes, chivalry

Don Quixote (1986), 70

Don Quixote (ballet), 71

double standards, 89, 181, 206

The Dozens, 143

drag, 256

drama, 50, 180, 182, 194, 235, 242, 249, 251, 253-254, 258-259, 261

dreams, 48, 53, 65, 68, 75, 162, 165, 220

drugs, 95, 102, 274-288

duos, 160, 162, 167-168, 172

Dylan, Bob, 21-22, 239

early modern
authors, 107, 196, 283; cultural production, 28, 286; drama, 253; feminism, 53; Iberia, 33, 42, 45, 132, 229; literature, 178, 280; medicine, 51, 55, 275, 280; novel, 164; patriarchy, 157; peninsular literature, 229; poetry, 242; representations of rape, domination, and control, 275; society, 146; studies, 250; texts, 23, 143, 230, 249-250, 252, 278, 303, 306-307, 312; theater, 253; Vizcaya, 110

early modern period, 107-108, 114, 116, 126, 131, 155, 232, 238, 250, 253-255, 259-262, 271

early modern Spain, 22-23, 28, 35, 90, 106-110, 113, 116-117, 142-143, 156-157, 184, 193-194, 211, 253, 275-276, 308-312

early modern Spanish
conception of divine providence, 156; cultural production, 22, 27-28, 286; culture, 131, 134, 157, 182; literature, 178, 229, 280; plays, 260; social and legal institutions, 88, 101; society, 154; studies, 153; texts, 45, 150, 197, 199, 302-306, 312; writing, 275

Eastwood, Clint, 212, 220-224
feud with John Wayne, 222-23

Easy Rider, 48

economics, 38, 54, 87, 102, 133, 138, 143, 180, 240

ecstasy, 124, 265, 267-268

education, 23, 25, 49, 95, 106, 108, 133, 147, 157, 169, 179, 230, 264, 266, 276, 290-295, 299

educators, 26 28, 148, 157, 230, 297

ego, 44, 57, 182, 187

ejemplares see exemplary

La esclava de su galán, 277

El Escorial, 121

election (2016), 117, 146, 151

emotions, 99, 112, 160, 164, 166, 180-181, 188, 235, 237, 239, 265, 267-268

empathy, 124, 165-166, 231

empire, 37, 153, 180, 212-213

empowerment
consumer, 149-150; divine, 156; female, 56, 194; victim, 156; student, 24, 154, 298-299

"En la fiesta del santísimo sacramento," 132, 138

The Enchanted Garden see El jardín encantado

endings, 61, 73, 181, 258

enemies, 66, 77, 239

engagement
critical, 147; with injustices, 150, 190; with the horrors of life, 81; meaningful, 60, 162; political, 72; student, 22, 26-28, 87, 131-132, 143, 148-150, 153-154, 159, 178, 185, 194, 233, 264, 267, 287, 292-293

engaño, 60-61, 151

English, 135, 138, 146, 297

see also African American Vernacular English

entertainment industry, 90, 121, 125, 149-150, 211, 217-218, 221

environments

cultural, 23, 49, 134; digital, 149; domestic, 110, 117, 124; dynamic; learning, 265, 294-295; low-stress, 24, 232; polarized, 150

epic poetry *also epopeya*, 27, 213, 229-231, 233, 235, 240-241, 256, 308

equality, 101, 117, 141, 146-147, 152, 157

eroticism, 107-108, 117-125, 194, 275-279

escapism, 75, 189

La Estrella de Sevilla, 48

ethnic cleansing, 38, 214

ethnicity, 35-37, 39, 94

ethnolect, 133

evidence, 96, 112-115, 287

evil, 34, 45, 100, 196, 210, 217, 269

exemplary *also ejemplares*, exemplum, 49-50, 100, 180, 212, 254, 305

exercises, 28, 229-299

expectations

culturally determined, 49-50; gendered, 203; genre, 278; unrealistic, 61, 161, 180

experience

active, 161; affirmation, 161; American, 215; historical, 38-39; journey, 161-162, 166, 170-172; mystical, 263, 267, 270; parallel, 39, 155; shared, 293; of time and space, 173; unique, 240, 270

"Experiencia Religiosa," 264, 268

see also Iglesias

exploitation, 197, 275, 277

expulsion

Moriscos, 214; non-converted Jews, 39

ex-slaves, 205, 214, 216

faculty, 25-28, 40, 250-251, 290-295, 299

failure, 62, 72-73, 77, 99-100, 155, 176, 187, 249, 254, 271, 277

faith, 73, 112, 182, 189

fake news, 173

falsehoods, 89-90, 114, 181, 311

family

dynamics, 239; honor, 50-53, 91, 97-98, 114-115, 147, 157, 180-183; legislation, 115; loyalties, 44; matter, 115

fan fiction, 149

fantasy, 125, 162, 173, 193

Farrow, Ronan, 101

fate, 199, 278

see also destiny

fathers, 50, 89-91, 100, 115, 181, 187, 198, 202, 204, 223, 235, 279, 283

fear, 37, 57, 68, 93, 109, 111-112, 119, 126, 261, 264, 271, 284-287, 297

fecundity, 121

Felixmarte de Hircania, 216

female characters, 57, 92, 94-95, 101-102, 154-155, 181, 195, 255, 279, 305, 307 femicide, 53, 97

feminism

activists, 103, 111, 151-152, 157; antifeminism, 54, 57, 146; contemporary, 102, 151; hashtag, 152-153, 156-157; history, 102, 151-157; icons, 193, 195, 206; ostensible, 154; proto-feminist writing, 53, 62, 102; subversive, 193-194; theory, 151

Fernando de Aragón, 197, 199, 202

feuds

celebrity, 220; Eastwood and Wayne, 212, 222-224; Cervantes and Vega, 27, 66, 220, 222, 224; Góngora and Quevedo, 27, 143

figurative language, 235

figures

authority, 35, 40, 96, 154, 254, 269, 279-280 306; canonical, 10-11, 70-73, 163, 176-179, 185-186, 190-191, 213-216, 229-243, 305, 310; comedic, 140, 160, 162, 167-168, 172; contradictory, 194; doctor; Don Juan, 177-179, 185-186, 190-191; Donjuanesque, 178-179, 185; Don Quixote, 70-73, 178; female, 118-119, 125, 193, 206; historical, 197, 216; literary, 216; male; Moor, 231-214; mythological, 199; religious, 73, 264; traditional, 163; Western, 270

film

adaptations, 33, 51, 178, 185, 252, 257; B, 212; censorship; 216-218; depicting male sexual fantasy, 125; directors, 78, 99, 186, 193, 221-222; foreign, 218; Hollywood,

70-71, 121, 125, 217-218, 222; independent, 102; score, 200; silent, 217; Western, 209-224

First Nation peoples, 37, 214-215, 219

first-person perspective, 54-55, 110, 263

The Fisher King, 79

flattery, 61, 114

flesh, 52, 61, 120, 125

foil, 146, 156-157, 181, 205, 286

The Force of Blood see *La fuerza de la sangre*

Ford, John, 209, 213, 222

foreshadowing, 94, 190

formalist, 266, 304

Foucault, Michel, 42

fourth wall, 74

frame story, 53, 93

frameworks, 82, 88-89, 94, 148, 195-196, 270, 275

Franco, Francisco, 40, 82

free will, 50, 77, 88, 90-91, 109, 117, 180, 183, 199, 274-275, 278-282, 284-286

free speech, 55, 71

freedom, 66, 69, 82, 111, 184, 204, 240, 287

Freud, Sigmund, 91, 307

friendship, 138, 166-169, 172

Friedan, Betty, 151

frontier, 210, 215-218, 240

Frozen, 280

Fuenteovejuna, 48, 89, 196-198, 201-205, 296, 309

Fuero Real, 126

La fuerza de la sangre, 110, 157

Gallego, Juan, 109-113
Game of Thrones, 294
gaps
    bridging, 134, 156, 256, 299;
    generational, 265; ironic, 67;
    unbreachable, 73; literacy, 253;
    pay, 276
gaze
    anamorphic, 61; colonial, 286;
    female, 54-55, 57, 269; male, 120-
    121, 125
gender
    appropriate activities, 60; bend-
    ing, 253, 256, 260; categories, 261;
    conflict, 54; construct, 49, 62;
    discrimination, 152; equality, 101,
    117, 146, 157; hierarchy, 50, 157,
    287; identity, 195, 254-256, 262;
    ideology, 50; perspective, 60;
    inequality, 53-54, 102, 147, 152;
    nature, 82; norms, 194, 204-205;
    performativity, 203, 259; rela-
    tions, 50, 54, 92; values, 97, 157,
    210
gender roles, 48-49, 54, 61-62, 178,
    181, 195, 197, 204, 259
gender-based violence, 106-108, 111-
    113, 125-126, 206, 271
generation
    Baby Boom, 69; divide, 77, 156,
    258, 265, 271, 291, 299; first,
    276, 291; Millennial, 159; multi-
    tasking, 159; new, 235, 239; older,
    152-153, 170, 250, 296; selfie, 154;

students, 150, 153; X; Y; younger,
    169, 257, 280; Gen Z, 159
genocide, 214
genres
    action-hero, 51; elite, 261; expec-
    tation, 259, 278; influence of Don
    Quixote, 159, 210, 311; literary,
    23, 28, 178, 185, 249, 251, 265, 275;
    modern day constructions, 259;
    musical, 132, 142-143, 240-241;
    popular, 160, 163, 210, 212, 254;
    subgenre, 240, 249, 251; teaching,
    261, 265, 302; unfamiliar, 80, 230,
    253; Western, 221-222, 311
Germany, 35, 38, 40, 76, 209, 222,
    252
Gilliam, Terry, 78-79, 173
The Girl with the Dragon Tattoo,
    53-54
glass ceiling, 146
globalization, 173, 294
God, 15, 156, 180, 182-184, 263-270,
    308
gods, 117, 121, 124, 196-197, 199, 204
The Godfather saga, 48, 51
Golden Age
    classroom, 22, 49, 62, 154, 197,
    210; comics, 197, 203, 206; critics,
    160; culture,143; Hispanic, 157;
    icons, 249; literature, 138, 210,
    215, 297; narratives, 147; poetry,
    131-132, 142, 235; postmodern
    reading, 161-162, 270; Spain, 23-
    24, 48, 90, 101, 132, 140, 180, 215,
    266; texts, 22, 24, 27-28, 48, 51,
    101, 132, 147, 153, 182, 291, 297-299
Góngora, Luis de

culteranismo, 141, 308; feud with Francisco de Quevedo, 27, 143; "Mientras por competir con tu cabello," 61, 296, 309; Sonnet CLXVI, 295-296

good
and evil, 34, 210, 217, 269; family name, 56; feeling, 81; guy, 221; taste, 97

El gordo y la flaca, 160

gracioso, 182, 189, 201, 204

graduate school, 153, 250, 252, 267, 297-298

Grail legend, 79

grammar, 50, 98, 231, 251, 260

Grau, Jacinto, 176
Don Juan de Carillana, 190

The Great Train Robbery (1903), 209, 211-212, 311

Grisóstomo, 204

guilt, 39, 58, 88, 100-101, 171

Guzmán, Joaquín *see* El Chapo

Guzmán de Alfarache, 55, 241

hallucinogens, 283, 287

Hang 'Em High, 214

The Hangover, 275, 285

harassment

Harding administration, 217

Harry Potter series, 33-45, 310

hashtags 149-157

hate, 36, 93-94, 53

The Hate U Give, 57

Hayek, Salma, 107, 126

Hays Commission, 221

Hays, William, 217-18

hazañas see deeds

heaven, 188, 264, 268

heirs, 97, 100-102
see also inheritance

hell, 179, 184

Helo, helo, por do viene / el moro por la calzada, 235-236, 245

heresy, 44

heroes
action, 162; Castilian, 232, 235; cinematic, 214; characteristics, 229-232, 241; chivalric, 165, 171-172; comic, 163-164, 169; different historical periods, 241; evolution, 230, 232; female, 193-206; identification, 97; imitation, 165; male, 97, 99, 197, 232; modern, 36, 240; past, 199; Spanish, 232; superheroes, 194, 197, 199, 229; teaching, 230, 260; unbridgeable separation, 76; Western, 215, 219, 221
see also Don Quixote

heroine, 54, 194, 199, 205, 223

he-said/she-said, 110

hierarchies
gender, 50, 157; prison, 95; racial, 35, 143; social, 188, 294

high culture, 27, 74

High Plains Drifter, 209, 211, 213, 218, 223
see also The Stranger

hip-hop, 131-143

hippies, 21, 189

Hispanic Association of Colleges and Universities (HACU), 290,

Hispanic-Serving Institutions (HSIs), 12, 290-291

Historia de la monja alférez, Catalina de Erauso escrita por ella misma, 206,

Historia de las plantas, 281, 286

Historia universal de Don Juan, 177

Hitler, Adolf, 38, 40
    see also Nazis

Hollywood, 70, 72

Holy Trinity, 89

homosexuality, 167, 258

homosociality, 167, 259

honor
    code, 49-52, 147, 182-184; concept, 115; damaged, 51, 110; essential value, 51; husbands, 51-52, 98, 115; killing, 51; mandate, 51; plays, 48, 50; principle, 91; preserving, 98; putting a price on, 100; sacrificial dimension, 51; sexual virtue, 50; symbolic weight, 51; system, 52

hooks, bell, 151

Hughes, Howard, 218, 221

humanities, 21, 24, 26, 252, 254, 263, 292,

humanity, 68, 81, 160, 177

Humes, Harold L. 'Doc', 72

humiliation, 201

humor, 160, 162-167, 173

husbands, 50-52, 92, 96, 98-100, 115, 156, 189, 204, 280, 282

Hwang, David Henry, 257

hyperbole, 182, 203, 213, 234

hypermasculinity, 188

hypnotism, 57-59

hypocrisy, 52, 55-57, 59-60, 74

"I, Don Quixote," 65-69

Iberia, 33, 38-40, 42, 45, 132, 134, 141, 197, 214, 229, 239, 261

Ibsen, Henrik, 66

icons, 135, 193, 195, 206, 218, 223, 249, 257, 260, 270, 287

ideals
    gender equality, 157; higher, 77; professed, 67; social caste, 91; unattainable, 61

idealism, 70, 72-73, 77-79, 176, 180, 310-311

idealization, 76, 82, 111, 154, 165, 210, 306

identity
    acts, 133, 136, 141; Castilian, 232, 240; creation, 167, 240; crisis, 57; crypto, 42-45; false, 181, 205; formation, 133-134, 149; gender, 255-256, 261-262; hidden, 42, 111, 196, 219; LGBTQ, 151; local, 133; multiple, 206; national, 209, 213, 215, 239-240; political, 47; racial, 94, 132-133, 136; secure, 169; self-invented, 43; shared, 132-133; signature; student, 276; submersion; true, 43-44

ideology
    Communist, 75; conservative, 66, 71; good and evil, 210; insular, 68; interpellation, 50; Nazi, 40, 45; patriarchal, 153, 275; racist,

38, 40, 43; tension, 67, 72, 76-77,
147, 184; unconscious, 76; underpinnings, 62, 82
idols, 164-166
Iglesias, Enrique, 263-271
illusions, 65, 112, 161, 171, 274
images
    airbrushing, 60-62; amorous,
    264; anachronistic, 71; bondage,
    194, 201; character, 235; Don
    Quixote, 159, 215, 220; familiar,
    49; iconic, 135, 260; key, 49; mas-
    culine, 51; negative, 220; positive,
    71; powerful, 232, 265; religious,
    296; sensual, 123, 264, 267, 296;
    women, 52, 125, 138, 140, 277
imagination, 79, 172, 178, 284, 302
immigrants, 37, 57, 214, 298
immorality, 68, 94, 96, 223
imperialism, 70, 253, 286
impersonation, 50, 155
implications
    cultural; 132, 141, 215, 231; future,
    56, 230; ideological, 76, 150; rac-
    ist, 142; sociocultural, 157; theo-
    logical, 156, 269
imprisonment, 38, 52, 69, 93, 96, 155,
269
impunity, 117, 151
incarceration, 195, 269, 291
inclusion, 24, 151
incomprehensibility, 263
incredulity, 286
Índice de libros prohibidos, 216
Indigenous peoples, 37, 285
individualism, 215

inequality, 53-54, 71, 102, 132, 147,
152
El ingenioso hidalgo Don Quijote de
la Mancha, 205
    see Don Quixote
inheritance, 99-100, 115
injustice, 87, 92, 100, 150, 154, 156,
198, 204, 269
inmates, 95-96
innocence, 52, 58, 280
La inocencia castigada, 52, 276, 279,
283, 286, 298
Inquisition, 216, 281, 286
Inquisitors, 39-40, 42, 44, 55, 281,
283
insanity, 67, 163, 256-257
institutions, 40, 54-55, 87-88, 90, 92,
94, 96, 100-103, 132, 138, 148-153,
180, 215, 258, 290-291
insularity, 68, 81,
Internet Movie Database (IMDb),
163, 186, 223
interpellation, 50, 57
intersectionality, 151, 269
intertextuality, 160, 312
intervention
    author, 54-55; direct, 252; divine,
    150, 265
Invasion of the Body Snatchers, 68
Irons, Jeremy, 257
irony, 25, 36, 44, 67, 73, 78, 82, 87,
92, 94-95, 99, 102, 160, 216, 306,
311
Isabel de Castilla, 197, 199, 201
Isabel of Portugal, 117
issues

accessibility, 27; contemporary, 67, 76-77, 187, 189, 296; cultural, 154, 193, 221; gender violence, 97, 101, 106, 116, 125, 275, 277; health, 61; LGBTQ, 151; national identity, 209; race and ethnicity, 35-39, 136, 143, 269; within feminist politics and theory, 150-151; political, 39; private, 126, 163; relationship, 196, 198, 201-202, 205; social, 42, 87, 97, 131, 178, 195, 197
ivory tower, 293

jail, 113, 171
El jardín encantado, 88, 97, 101
jealousy, 99
Jenkins, Patty, 193, 196, 305
Jesuits, 41, 217
Jesús, Teresa de, 60
Jesús María, José de
    De las excelencias de la virtud de la castidad, 113
Jews *see* Judaism
jive talk, 134-135
Joel, Billy, 295
John Tucker Must Die, 178, 187-188
journalism, 157
journey, 161, 166-167, 170
Judaism, 33-45, 143, 242
Judeo-Christian, 217
Judeo-Spanish, 39, 237-238, 242
judgment, 57-58, 101, 112, 164, 171-172, 183-185, 214
judicial system, 280
El juez de su causa 194, 205
juglar, 237, 242

justice
    appearance, 156; bring, 92, 116; call for, 146; deferral, 146; fighting for, 66; frontier, 218; poetic, 156, 183; resolution, 110, 156; sexual, 101; suppress, 155; twenty-first century, 156; vigilante, 54
    see also criminal justice system
Justice League, 11, 196-98
juxtaposition, 70-71, 76, 124, 211, 267

Keats, John, 21
Kerouac, Jack, 68-69, 79
kidnapping, 93, 110, 115, 124, 287
Kierkegaard, Søren, 73
killing, 51-53, 219
    see also murder
King of Naples, 150, 180
Kiss of the Spider Woman (film), 250
knights, 70-71, 73, 78-79, 161, 165, 172, 204, 210, 211, 213, 215, 219, 224, 292
knowledge
    basic, 258; disciplinary, 49, 156, 264; historical, 153; production, 294
Kurosawa, Akira, 222

L2 learners, 268
    see also second-language learners
laissez faire, 71, 77
language
    archaic, 169, 263; figurative, 235; code-switching, 37; L2, 268; learning, 249-262, 264; comput-

er-assisted learning, 260; markers,137; medical, 55; Judeo-Spanish, 237; non-rhotic, 137; nuance, 164; profane, 217; target, 178-179, 232, 251-252, 254; vulgar, 59

Larsson, Stieg, 53-54

las Casas, Bartolomé de, 213

Latin America, 206, 302

Latinos *also* Latinx, 290, 276, 290-291, 293-296, 298

law

anti-converso, 41-42; application, 112, 117; civil, 89, 114-115; court, 101; criminal and procedural, 115; enforcement, 54, 92; letter of the law, 113, 152; and order, 94; punitive, 96; religious, 117; Spanish, 112

Laws of Toro, 115

Lazarillo de Tormes, 48, 54-55, 59, 298, 309

leaders, 41, 126, 195, 197, 204, 299

learning *see* teaching approaches

Leave it to Beaver, 135

Legion (television), 261

Legitimacy, 142

Leone, Sergio, 214, 219-220, 222

lesson planning, 298

see also classroom discussion and teaching approaches

letrilla, 138, 308

LGBTQ *see also* queer theory, 152

liars *see* dishonesty

libro de caballerías, 211, 215, 224

Libro de los ejemplos del conde Lucanor y de Patronio, 49

life

American, 213; everyday, 138, 159, 180; experience, 298; horrors, 81; private, 82; public, 11; stage, 178

"Like a Prayer," 264, 268-270

limpieza de sangre, 40-42, 310, 143

see also blood purity and *pureza de sangre*

linguistics, 131-143

liras, 235

literacy

cultural, 35, 259; gap, 253; media, 26; reality, 48-49

literary criticism, 153, 250, 255

literature

American, 242; classic, 65; colonial, 252, 253; contemporary, 239, 293; Hispanic, 229, 264, 276; in translation, 296; and society, 27; Western, 176

see also Golden Age

The Lone Ranger (television), 211

The Lone Ranger (2013), 209

Lope *see* Vega, Lope de

love

and beauty, 93; blind, 100; courtly, 27, 165, 182, 210; Neoplatonic, 182; relationships, 201; perverse, 93; selfless, 154, 280; tragic, 278; of violence, 214

lovers

amistad torpe, 281-282; deceitful, 52, 181; female, 94; fickle, 182; former, 51, 189; would-be, 275

low culture, 27, 161, 257

lust, 108, 113-114, 123, 179, 182, 278

Luther, Martin, 274
lyric poetry, 131, 141-142, 230, 239, 241
lyricism, 68, 265
lyrics, 50, 72-75, 131, 201, 240, 266, 268-269

M. Butterfly, 257-258
Madonna, 263-271
magic *see* witchcraft
El mágico prodigioso, 275, 278
maidens, 114
mainstream, 69-70, 75, 79, 102, 176
male-to-female transformation, 255-256, 260
man
idea, 173; ideal, 56; leisure, 121
Man and Superman, 179, 184, 189
Man of La Mancha (theater production), 65-83
Man of La Mancha (film), 65-83, 168
The Man Who Killed Don Quixote, 79, 173
The Man Who Shot Liberty Valance, 213
Mancing, Howard, 159, 210, 216-217, 264, 266-267, 271
manliness, 195
Mann, Anthony, 222
Manuel, Don Juan, 49-50
La margarita del Tajo, 206
marginalization, 89, 94, 143, 167, 293
Maria Manuela of Portugal, 121
marriage

arranged, 90-91, 100-101, 181; between rapists and victims, 102, 110; customs, 91; death trap, 51; deceitful, 99; denunciation, 51, 202-204; false promises, 89-90,182-183; free will, 90; gender hierarchy, 49-50; happy, 98, 110; institution, 92, 101, 115; laws, 91, 107; as a prison-house, 52; sex, 114; unhappy, 121
Martínez Guijarro, Juan, 41
martyrs, 54
Marxism, 148
El más buscado (Chapo Guzmán), 241, 248
masculinity, 50-51, 124, 155
materialism, 79
McCarthyism, 66
McLuhan, Marshall, 162, 173
meaning
affect with, 196, 198, 264, 268; contradictory; discover, 50, 201, 206, 239, 250, 253, 256, 260, 292-293, 295; instability, 242; personal, 26, 160, 178, 299; symbolic, 124
see also Reception Theory
media
culture, 160; literacy, 26; mass, 22, 160, 177, 211, 250; misinformation, 173
see also social media
medialogy, 48
El médico de su honra, 51, 62
medieval

hero, 229, 242; late; literature, 49, 229, 252; period, 231; poetry, 239, 242; Spain, 42, 213, 242; texts, 230, 232, 292

Los melindres de Belisa, 277

memes, 293

memoirs, 70-71, 224, 295

men
Black, 135; cruelty, 52, 112; Indian, 167; powerful, 116-117, 125-126; simple, 222; white, 136, 215, 286, 294, 299; women, 87, 91-92, 97, 179

mental illness, 67, 163, 256

mesa de trucos, 48

mesmerism, 59

mester de clerecía, 242,

mester de juglaría, 242

mestizaje, 294

Metamorphoses, 119-120, 123

metaphors, 24, 45, 83, 160, 224, 265, 267-268

methodology, 131, 264

#MeToo movement, 48, 61-62, 87-88, 96, 101-102, 106-108, 109, 111, 116-117, 126, 146, 156

Mexico, 209, 213-215, 230, 239-241, 280

Mi marido tiene familia, 293

Middle Ages, 39, 89, 231

middle class, 94, 133, 135

"Mientras por competir con tu cabello," 61, 295

Miguel, Luis, 50

milieu, 22, 143, 146, 183, 294

militarism, 71

Millennials, 159

Millennium series, 53

Miller, Arthur, 65-66, 74, 80

Miller-Wasserman debate, 66

mimicry, 132, 134, 138

Minkus, Ludwig, 71

minorities, 36, 39, 116, 143, 291

minstrelsy, 134, 138, 141-142

mirroring, 67, 164-165, 168, 172, 213, 296

misappropriation, 133, 215

miscegenation, 36

misdeeds, 279

mise-en-scène, 74, 83

misogyny
authors, 54, 93; denunciation, 60; institutions, 54; men, 57; pleasure, 117, 146; practices, 61; systemic, 96

missing link, 254

model
behavioral, 50, 222; Calderonian, 51; conventional, 160, 179, 261; exemplary, 212; femininity, 135, 154; practice, 141, 162, 212; ready-made, 62; violent masculinity, 50
see also role models and practices: modeling

Modern Family, 167

modernity, 87, 89

molestation, 101

Molina, Tirso de, 88, 101-102, 176, 179-184, 194, 198, 250, 281, 298
see also Antona García and *El burlador de Sevilla*

moments

"Aha!", 255, 297; cultural, 147, 258-259; current political, 66, 155, 291; historical, 62, 83, 150, 153,196; teachable, 148, 156, 157

monarchy, 39, 117, 121, 155, 180

money, 56, 79, 81, 95-97, 102, 212

Moors, 39, 214, 234-239, 245-246, 279

Morales, Alonso de, 249, 252, 254-259, 262

Morales, Pedro de, 255-259, 262

moralists, 54-55, 90, 108, 113, 122

morals
alternative, 240; ambiguous, 62; code, 219, 222-223; corrupt, 239; crimes, 89; health, 60; reservations, 240; superior, 55; victorious, 236, 238

moriscos, 39, 214

moro see Moors

Moro alcalde, moro alcalde, /el de la veyuda barba, 237, 246-247

motherhood, 89, 92

mothers, 43, 70, 98, 100, 163, 196

motivation, 210, 270-271, 295

movements
Black Lives Matter, 57, 269; Chicano, 241-242, 248; feminist, 152-153; #MeToo, 48, 62, 87, 95-96, 101-102, 106-109, 111, 116-117, 126, 156; social, 108; #TimesUp, 61, 146, 150; "turn on, tune in, drop out," 69; youth, 69

movies
action, 169; animated, 161-162; contemporary, 230; gangster, 51; road, 48, 161, 171; superhero, 193; Western, 209, 212, 216
see also film

Moulton, Charles, 193, 198

mujer esquiva, 195, 202-203, 205

mujer varonil, 193-206, 305

Las mujeres sin hombres, 196

multiple literacies approach, 251

multiple personality disorder, 58

murder, 34, 52, 58-59, 67, 91, 94, 97-99, 102, 107, 183, 206, 220, 223, 285
see also killing

music
contemporary music as a teaching tool, 132, 229-243, 263-270, 298, 238, 271; court, 235, 237; examples, 296-297; pop, 74, 131-132, 136, 263, 265-267, 270, 293; sampling, 231, 238; videos, 241, 268-269.

musicals, 67-83

My Cid see Cantar de mio Cid

My Darling Clementine, 214

mysticism, 23, 27, 263-270

mystification, 48

myths, 125, 177, 190, 202, 239

mythology, 117, 120, 123, 199, 204

the n-word, 36, 138

Nabokov, Nicolas, 71

narcissism, 189

narcocorridos, 229-48, 298, 308-309

narrative

broad-brush, 152-153; canonical, 157; first-person, 55; frame, 53-54, 57, 93, 204; epic, 240; frameworks, 88-89, 94; Golden Age, 147; historical, 147, 153; inverted picaresque, 94; master, 42; road, 161; space, 57, 96; structures, 94, 151; take control, 57; terrifying, 81; verse, 240; visual, 240, 269

narratology, 260-261

narrator, 52-56, 97, 100, 218, 234, 279, 284

nationalism, 232

Native Americans, 37, 214-215, 219

nature
chivalric, 170; complex, 101; formulaic, 210; gender, 49-50, 82; individualist, 215; monstrous, 52; mystic experiences, 263; reality, 163, 172; vs. nurture, 195; structural, 102

Nazis, 37-40, 45

neo-liberalism, 78

neo-Transcendentalism, 69

Netflix, 57, 94, 147, 293

New Compilation of the Laws of the Kingdoms, 116

New Left, 71, 77

The Newsroom, 82

nihilism, 68

Nobel Prize, 21-22, 166, 239

noble, 45, 51, 73, 214

nobility, 90-91, 100, 102, 109, 116, 123, 176-177, 179-181, 187, 202
see also aristocracy

"Noche oscura," 264, 266-267, 269-271

norms
cultural, 112, 116-117, 125, 241; feminine, 195; gender, 194, 204-205; patriarchal, 49; social, 180-182, 194, 232, 256; subvert, 181; traditional, 180; transgress, 117; violence, 106

North America, 165, 168, 229, 252, 257, 261

nostalgia, 21, 36

novels
chivalric, 162, 165, 168-169, 172; early modern, 164; exemplary, 51, 100, 254; original, 60, 67, 82

novela, 87, 98, 100

nudity, 117, 119-120, 122-123, 217

El Nuevo Mundo descubierto por Cristóbal Colón, 48

Núñez de Coria, Francisco, 114

O Homem de la Mancha, 82
see also Don Quixote

Obama, Barack, 283

Obedience, 49-50, 97, 100, 267, 279

objects
of desire, 261; of exchange, 126; of hate, 93; passive, 118; of reflection, 103, 135
see also women: objectification

obligation, 50, 68

obsession, 38, 41-42, 96, 100, 169, 180, 182, 184, 261

occult, 275, 277

OITNB see Orange is the New Black

Los olvidados, 298

ontology, 150, 271

opera, 212-213, 253, 257

oppression, 52-53, 67, 107, 151, 193, 213

orality, 238, 266

oral transmission, 237

Orange is the New Black, 88, 94-97, 101-103

order

law, 94; natural, 53, 156; patriarchal, 52-54; social, 91, 156, 180-181, 190; symbolic, 88

Orlando furioso, 169, 256

Ortega y Gasset, José, 184

orthodoxy, 267

otherness, 23, 36-37, 140, 167, 294

outcasts, 167

The Outlaw, 218

The Outlaw Josey Wales, 222

outlaws, 214, 216, 220, 223

Ovid, 119-120, 123-124

painting, 117-124, 240-241

Palmerín, 210

Panopticon, 42

paradigms, 148-149, 163, 166

paradigmatic elements, 160

paradoxes, 50, 117, 124, 269, 286

parallels, 24, 38, 51, 87, 94, 155, 188, 190, 194, 206, 210, 213, 261, 265, 269, 296

pariah, 34

parodies, 67, 134, 138, 160, 170, 218

passing, 42

passion

carnal, 99, 182, 187, 265; crime, 98; justice, 81; perverse, 124

passivity, 112, 118, 125, 150, 154, 161, 202

Paterfamilias, 115

paternity, 189

patriarchy,

dominance, 89, 97, 152; ideology, 153; institutions, 89-90; norms, 49, 94, 157, 181, 280; order, 52-54, 147, 154-156; society, 49, 280; structures, 147, 155-156

pay gap, 276

Peckinpah, Sam, 217, 221

peasants, 90, 102, 168, 181

pedagogy, 21-28, 33, 48, 73, 90, 99, 140, 156-157, 160, 230, 250, 252, 260, 264-268, 271, 291-294, 298 *see also* classroom discussion and teaching approaches

pedophilia, 91, 101, 176

penance, 60

Penny, Michael, 80

perceptions, 40, 77, 82, 108, 143, 147, 156, 166, 250, 262, 266

perfectionism, 203

performativity, 50, 138, 165, 172, 259

Peribañez y el comendador de Ocaña, 51

perpetrators, 51, 53-54, 106, 110-111, 113-115, 118, 125-126, 155, 269, 275, 285

persecution, 40, 43, 214, 270

personification, 74, 176, 180

perspectives

critical, 22; disciplinary, 156; diverse, 261; feminist, 152-153; historical, 231; modern, 90; multiplicity, 242; pedagogical, 90, 140

perversion, 54, 91-94, 113, 118, 123

Petipa, Marius, 71

phantasy *see* fantasy

pharmakon, 55-56

Philip II, 41, 108, 116, 117, 119-121, 123, 125

Philip III, 214

Philip IV, 123

Photoshop *see* airbrushing

La pícara Justina, 55-62

pícara, 56

picaresque, 54, 56, 59, 94

Picatrix, 276

pitfalls, 147-148, 261

plays, 48, 50-51, 80, 102, 201, 203-205, 249, 255, 277, 295

pleasure, 106-108, 111, 117, 119-120, 125, 269, 296

pliegos sueltos, 235

plot, 51, 89, 92-94, 97, 99-100, 111, 125, 218, 222, 235, 237, 255-256, 259-260

Pocahontas, 48

Poe, Edgar Allan, 53

Poema de Mio Cid see *Cantar de mio Cid*

Poesie, 117, 120-121, 123-124

poetic license, 237

poetry
American, 76; as a weapon, 61; court; early modern, 239; epic, 27, 230, 235, 240-241; Golden Age, 131-132, 235; lyric, 230; mystic, 27, 263-271; Spanish, 139, 142; teaching, 178; writing, 60

point of departure, 39, 45, 151, 180, 185

polarization, 147, 150, 157

police, 96, 111, 285

political messages, 79-80

politically correct, 164

politics, 53, 65-83, 87, 97, 119, 126, 132, 141-142, 146-157, 294

pop culture
allusions, 271; analysis, 23, 48, 107, 178, 257; in the classroom, 24, 26, 107, 210, 225, 229-232, 242, 249-251, 253-254, 257, 259, 264-265, 271, 283, 286-288, 291-294, 295-298; elitism, 74, 258; critical and connective value, 26, 57, 132, 250, 269, 275, 293-294, 296, 299; engaging, 135, 230, 257, 261, 178, 185, 257, 259, 302-312; entertainment, 134; vs. folk culture, 241; imaginative applications, 256; media, 28, 125, 132; modern, 106, 125, 231-232, 261, 270, 299; non-U.S. based, 298; production, 147-150, 154, 159, 235; references, 82, 135, 169, 199, 229-31, 250, 265, 271, 293, 299; relationship, 152, 154, 163, 265; savvy, 24, 271; shelf life, 253; U.S., 133-34, 141, 258

pop music, 23, 74, 131-132, 136, 263-271

Pope Paul IV, 41

pornography, 176, 188

Porres Velázquez, Martín de, 269

portrayals

problematic, 108, 117-118, 132, 134, 137, 140-141, 167, 214, 195; realistic, 118, 221; revisionist, 66, 120, 123, 223; romanticized, 179, 232; sympathetic, 110, 112, 179; violence, 107, 111, 117-119, 123

possession, 58, 120-121, 279-280

postcolonial theory, 36, 310

postmodernism, 160-162, 270

poverty, 57, 59, 115-116

power

allegory, 119; apparatus, 96; differentials, 50, 280; dynamic, 287; female, 57, 87, 89, 118; industrial, 213; natural, 275; magic, 34-37, 162, 274-281, 283, 286-288; male, 87, 117, 125; occult, 277; political, 119; relations, 23, 87-88, 92; religious, 119; seizure; sexist, 88; surrender, 151

powers that be, 277

practicality, 50, 160, 242

practices

cultural, 74, 138, 173; juridical, 87, 90, 92, 102; discursive, 35, 146, 153, 156; institutional, 88, 102, 150; intellectual, 60, 71, 294; Jewish, 42; legal, 89, 96, 102, 107; misogynist, 61, 146; modeling, 88, 141, 162, 211; political, 294

praxis, 152

preconceived notions, 265

pregnancy, 110

prejudices, 57, 164, 271

present

conceptions, 184, 224; contradictions, 66-67, 78, 150-152, 240; historical moment, 83; and past, 178, 256; struggles, 157

presidency, 117, 146, 151

pretext, 67, 154

pride, 76, 89, 151, 171, 181

priests, 167-169, 211, 216-217, 219, 267

primogeniture, 97, 100-102

print, 45, 80, 101, 121, 173, 211

prison, 38-39, 52, 69, 77, 80-83, 93-96, 116, 155, 202, 269, 280

privacy, 51, 82, 114, 117, 121, 123, 125-126

The Private Life of Don Juan, 190

problems

confront, 157, 267; current, 77, 88, 157, 178, 190; solving, 140, 157, 259

progress, 106, 113, 146-147, 151, 157

promiscuity, 110

promises of marriage, 89-90, 98, 118, 181-182

prompts, 143, 154-155, 157, 186, 258

propaganda, 71-72

prose, 99, 232, 267

prosecution, 88-92, 96, 99, 101

prostitution, 59, 120, 285, 287

protagonists, 42, 54, 57, 136, 155, 163, 165, 168, 172, 176, 179, 183, 185-190, 193, 204, 221, 229, 233, 236, 256-257, 260-261, 269

protection, 42, 50-51, 53-54, 57, 60, 106, 109-110, 126, 151-152, 155, 181, 183, 213, 219-220

Protestantism, 270

prudence, 155, 199, 212, 278

psychoanalysis, 256, 259

psychology, 112, 155, 166, 263

psychotic behavior, 54, 257-258

public
awareness, 158; demonstrations, 126; exposure, 88, 95, 106, 113; institutions, 149, 299; life, 82, 111; money, 96; opinion, 222, 232; profile, 95; scorn, 116; shame, 88, 102, 110, 116, 118; speaking, 204-205; sphere, 114, 291; treatment of women, 121; changing tastes, 237

Puig, Manuel, 250

punishment, 51-52, 88-94, 96, 101-103, 112, 115-116, 123, 156, 179, 183, 195, 279

pureza de sangre statutes, 33, 35, 39, 45
see also limpieza de sangre

queer theory, 253, 259

quests, 44, 79

questioning, 57, 62, 67, 87-90, 102, 133, 136, 164, 172, 185, 237-242

Quevedo, Francisco de
feud with Luis de Góngora, 27, 143; quevedesque, 144

Quiroga, Gaspar de, 42

Quixote/Quijote *see* Don Quixote

Quixote (film), 72

Quixote (magazine), 71

quixotesque, 160-163, 169, 172-173

quixotism, 65, 68, 71, 73, 78, 83

race
ethnicity, 35-37, 39, 94; performance, 44, 134-143; representation, 35-37, 132, 167

racism, 36, 70, 137-138, 142, 195, 213, 269,

radio, 74, 79, 136-137, 297

Ramírez, Ana, 107-109, 112, 126

rap music *see* hip-hop

rape
accusation, 114, 116; "act of love," 124; aesthetically pleasing, 107, 111, 117-118, 124; condemnation, 107, 112-114, 126; crime, 52, 88-92, 97, 102-103, 110, 112, 115-116, 155; culture, 155, 275, 287; depictions, 117, 121, 123; discrepancy between reports and quantity, 109, 111; "heroic rape tradition," 117; laws regarding, 88, 107, 112-116, 126; legalized, 91; motif, 117, 119, 125; private issue, 126; private pleasure, 117; proving, 114-115, 126; public complaint, 113; rapists, 92, 101-102, 110, 113, 116, 118-119, 126, 156; reluctance to identify, 109, 111, 277; repercussions, 125-126; representations, 90, 92, 107-108, 117-119, 275; scenes, 123; serial, 91; survivors, 101, 103, 107, 111, 117; use of force, 114; victims, 101, 110-111, 114-116, 155

The Rape of Europa (1562), *117-119, 122-123*

reading

between the lines, 251, 260; chi-valric novels, 165-169, 172; close, 131, 156, 211; comic books, 165; comprehension, 26; contextualize, 62, 132, 134, 140, 230, 151; context-limited, 266-267; countercultural, 78; course, 254, 258; critical, 243; double, 264; Freudian, 91; guides, 252, 276, 280; literal, 164; place of familiarity, 264; poetry, 131-132, 178, 235, 241-242, 263, 265-266, 270-271; postmodern, 161; reality, 48-49, 161, 164

Reaganomics, 79

reality literacy, 48-49

reality vs. fiction/fantasy, 67, 73, 161-173

Reception Theory, 148-149, 237

recognition, 143, 160,

re-contextualization, 71, 79, 304

redemption, 99-100, 220

references

cultural, 82, 135, 169, 199, 229-31, 250, 265, 271, 293, 299; mixing, 169; phallic, 259; recognizing, 185, 194, 229, 250, 254, 271

reflection

critical, 103, 154; inviting, 120, 155, 157; self, 50, 152, 162

rejection

advances, 89, 166, 181, 205; body, 165-166; *laissez faire* capitalism, 177; literary, 70, 281; mainstream U.S. values, 69; social conventions, 68, 179, 214

relatability, 172, 177, 268, 293

relations

kinship, 49; homosocial, 167, 259; power, 23, 87-88, 92; sexual, 97; social, 96

relationships

art and artist, 102; Christians and Jews, 39; between male power, feminine victimization and sexual violence, 88, 92, 117, 126, 277; God, 115, 182, 263, 265, 267, 268-270; interpersonal, 189, 222; issues, 196, 198, 201-202, 205; with literary canon, 27, 75, 141, 249, 260-261; past and present, 178, 185; physical, 188, 269; politics and art; pop culture, 152, 154, 163, 265; Quixote and Sancho, 160, 163-168, 170, 216, 219-220

relativism, 239

relevance

personal, 194, 242, 294, 296, 299; political, 146; present, 69, 81, 132, 159, 173, 177-178, 185, 190, 229-231; of texts, 101, 131, 199, 231, 239, 287, 297

religion

Catholicism, 39, 41-42, 189, 204, 217-218, 270; Judaism, 33-45, 143, 242; male-dominated, 270; obedience, 50, 267; orthodoxy, 267; sex, 263-271

Remington, Frederic, 215

Renaissance, 119, 131, 164, 173, 180

representations

aesthetic, 27-28, 107; audiovisual, 256; conventional, 61, 75, 179; homosexuality, 167, 257; inaccurate,

231; law enforcement, 54, 92; male sexual aggression, 101, 157; masculinity, 50-51, 124; race and ethnicity, 35-37, 132, 167; rape, 90, 92, 107-108, 117-119, 275; women, 57, 92, 94-95, 101-102, 108, 118, 126, 154-155, 181, 195, 255, 279

repression, 59, 72, 78, 87-88

reputation, 109, 112, 155, 183-184

resentment, 40, 93

resolution, 110, 156, 258

responsibility, 87, 88-89, 94, 113, 154

Respuesta a Sor Filotea, 60, 305

retention of materials, 25, 196, 291

revolution, 69, 173, 266

El rey moro que reta a Valencia, 245

rhetorical devices, 91, 97, 100, 251, 278

rights, 81, 152, 154, 198

"Rinconete y Cortadillo," 298, 309

rituals, 51, 94, 99, 111, 280

Rizi, Francisco, 107

road narrative, 161

Rojas, Agustín de
    Viaje entretenido, 255, 258

Rojas, Fernando de
    La Celestina, 275-280, 298 275-278, 298, 307, 309

Roland, 212

roles
    active, 24; art, 79; assigned, 71, 93, 121; audience, 27; authoritative, 57, 116; borders, 240; culture, 78, 232, 241; exhibitionist, 125; gender, 48-49, 54, 61-62, 178, 181, 195, 197, 204, 259; hero, 82, 230, 239; language, 132, 134; perform, 43, 71, 135, 255, 262; self-assigned, 55, 161; scapegoat, 88, 92; student, 154, 157, 303; women, 82, 97, 99, 154, 168, 195, 197, 255, 262; writer, 66, 71, 75, 80

role models, 28, 89, 206, 239, 306

role play, 50

romance
    chivalric, 67, 76, 211, 311; popular culture, 165, 187, 230

romancero tradition, 235, 241

romances, 230, 235, 237-238, 240-241, 245

romantic
    approach, 162; Don Quixote, 67, 71, 162, 219; content, 50; idealization, 76, 82; literature, 153; pair, 167; poetry, 266; portrayals, 179, 185, 187-188, 214-215, 219, 232; relationships, 188, 201; success, 213

Roosevelt, Theodore, 215

Rowling, J.K., 33-45

Rubens, Peter Paul, 118, 121-122

Rueda, Lope de, 255

Ruiz de Pereda, Gaspar, 283

Russia, 71, 95, 304
    see also Soviet Union

sadomasochism, 194

saints
    Augustine, 93-94; Martín de Porres Velázquez, 269; John of the Cross, 271; patron, 213; Sebastian, 204

Salazar, António de Oliveira, 40-41

Salt, Waldo, 70, 72

salvation, 102, 269, 292

sampling in music, 231, 238

San Juan de la Cruz, 263-271, 308
   see also St. John of the Cross

Sandinistas, 79

sanity, 163-164

sarcasm, 162, 164, 171

Satan *see* devil

satire, 67, 69, 76, 78, 81,

The Savage Guns, 221

Saving Private Ryan, 35

scaffolding, 224, 249, 253, 311

scandals, 59, 61, 123, 217

scapegoats, 87-88, 92, 99

Schindler's List, 35

science fiction, 161, 165-166, 261

Second War of Castilian Succession, 197

second-born son, 100

second-language learning, 249-254, 256, 259-261
   see also L2 learners

seduction, 89-90, 99, 108, 110, 176-177, 181, 184, 187, 199, 236, 238-239, 296

Seinfeld, 160, 163, 310

self-determination, 97, 287

self-expression, 270

self-reflection, 50, 152, 162

selfie generation, 154

sensationalize, 101, 283, 287

sense of
   danger, 284; inevitability, 94; movement, 119; urgency, 252

sensuality/sanctity paradox, 269

Sentencia-Estatuto of Toledo, 41

Sephardic diaspora, 39, 242

sequencing of course materials, 255

La serrana de la Vera, 198, 200, 204

sex
   abuse, 102, 112-113, 146; assault, 101, 111, 114, 116, 125, 151, 195, 274, 276-277, 283; consummation, 269; crimes, 52, 88-92, 97, 102-103, 110-116; desire, 100, 119-120, 123, 125, 156, 277, 179; discrimination, 152, 277; economy, 95, 99; encounters, 182, 277; exploitation, 275, 277; fantasy, 125, 193, 275; imbalance, 125; injustice, 87, 92, 101, 150, 154, 156; lack of interest, 165; object, 118-119, 121, 125, 261, 280; pleasure, 108, 111, 117, 119-120, 269, 296; politics, 193, 275; predator, 102, 111, 182, 284; relations, 97; religion, 263-271; undertones, 95; unwanted, 277-278; virtue, 50, 183

sexism, 88, 95-96, 152, 277

sexual violence
   aestheticization, 87-89, 97, 103, 107, 111, 117-118, 124; campus, 277, 287; condemnation, 87, 107, 112-114, 126; cycle, 125-126; cultural acceptance, 103, 107-108, 112, 126, 150; destigmatizing, 116; exposure, 51, 54, 59, 87-88, 109; *see* #MeToo; prevalence, 109, 111, 116; sanitization, 118; systemic, 89, 91, 96; *see* #TimesUp; trivialization, 107; *see* victims
   see also rape

sexuality, 94, 111, 119, 167, 257, 264

Shakespeare, William, 49, 164, 188, 292

shame, 58-59, 68, 110-111, 116, 118, 278-279

shamelessness, 59

Shaw, George Bernard, 179, 184, 189

Shrek 1 & 2, 162, 296

Shteyngart, Gary, 21-22

Sidi *see* Cid

Siete Partidas, 114-115, 126

Siglo de Oro
  see Golden Age

signifier and signified, 256

silencing, 101, 103, 106, 108, 155

Silence Breakers, 106-108, 116, 126

The Simpsons, 292-293

sin, 60, 102

singers, 21, 200, 235, 237-239, 255, 265, 268

skepticism, 280, 286

skills
  acquisition, 242, 252; analytical, 185, 293, 303-304; developing, 23, 260, 298; linguistic, 259; public speaking, 205

slang, 137

slavery, 205, 214-216, 276-277

Sleeping with the Enemy, 48

slut-shaming, 99

social media, 90, 101, 133, 148-150, 152, 156, 173

social class, 94, 110, 115-116, 176, 178, 181-182

social status, 53, 110-111, 116, 133,

societies
  aristocratic, 52-53, 87, 89, 97, 100, 102, 115; collective, 154; contemporary, 75, 77, 80, 87, 108, 157, 229; contradictions, 66-67, 78, 94; controversies, 77-78, 193-194, 222, 239, 268, 270; corrupt, 54-55, 67, 74, 81, 96, 153, 180; debased, 73, 76, 79; heterogeneous, 50, 241; late modern, 101; male-dominated, 82, 270; open, 66; patriarchal, 49, 53, 89-90, 94, 97, 147, 153-156, 181, 280; pluralistic, 37; Spanish, 54, 101, 109, 154, 180, 182, 286; spectacle, 76-77, 111; stratified, 36, 240; truths, 55, 73, 164-165; U.S., 135, 213, 77

sociolect, 133

solemnity, 164, 268

solidarity, 280, 287, 291

solitude, 268

Sonata de invierno, 176, 190

songs, 21-22, 24, 72, 74, 136, 168, 199-201, 231, 235, 239-240, 242, 250, 255, 264-270, 284, 287, 295-298

sonnets, 60-61, 235, 295-296

Sor Juana Inés de la Cruz, 60-62, 140, 254, 305-306

sorcery, 279-280

soul, 44-45, 54, 58, 93, 98-99, 154, 219, 263, 265, 278

sources
  critical, 210; humor, 164-167, 173; inspiration, 257; primary, 254, 292-293, 296; secondary, 136, 254

South America, 284

Soviet Union, 66, 71
  see also Russia
spaces
  of agreement, 78; enclosed, 170,
  205; extradiegetic, 96; male, 198,
  121; metaphysical, 44-45, 265;
  open, 123; private, 121, 125; social,
  97, 157; uncontroversial, 78; virtual, 157
Spaghetti Western *see* Western
Spain
art, 27, 108; artists, 99, 107, 123-124;
  colonial, 153; Counter-Reformation, 88, 94, 97, 101, 108, 116-117,
  121, 180, 184, 267; cultural production, 27-28, 286; early modern, 22-23, 28, 35, 90, 106-110, 113,
  116-117, 142-143, 156-157, 184, 193-
  194, 211, 253, 275-276, 308-312;
  imperial, 153, 180, 212-213, 253,
  286; inquisitorial, 55, 286; literature, 229, 264, 276; medieval, 42;
  theater, 255
Spanish Inquisition *see* Inquisition
Spanish Golden Age
  see Golden Age
spectacle, 50, 75-77, 80, 111, 216, 268
spectators, 59, 66, 72-74, 77, 160,
  161, 172, 185, 205
speech
  Black, 131-143; direct, 261; freedom, 55, 71; hate, 36
spiritual
  activities, 264; catharsis; conception, 73, 156, 265; guidance, 269
St. Augustine, 93-94, 317
St. John of the Cross, 271

St. Martín de Porres, 269
Stagecoach, 209, 214
staging, 67, 79, 141, 251, 255, 262
standards, 89, 181, 188, 206, 291
Standard English, 135, 138
Standard Spanish, 140
Star Trek, 162, 164-167, 169-172
Star Wars, 149, 163
status quo, 22, 103, 309
stereotypes, 37, 135, 141, 160, 167-
  168, 172, 188, 195
Stewart, Rod, 295-296, 309
stigma, 37-38, 44, 56, 59, 111, 116, 293
stigmata, 269
story
  frame, 53; interpellated, 157; love,
  278; origin, 206, 239
storyboarding, 260-261
storytelling, 261
strangeness, 231
The Stranger, 213, 219-220
strategies
  aesthetic, 91; alternative, 154;
  communication, 179; defensive,
  112; moral; pedagogical, 156, 210-
  211, 264, 267, 271
strength, 124, 198, 201
structural
  feedback loops, 53; impunity, 117,
  151; injustices, 92; nature of gender inequality, 102; reading, 94;
  similarities, 90
structures
  grammatical, 231, 251; institutional, 88, 103; legal, 88; linguistic,

138, 240; narrative, 55, 94, 255; patriarchal, 147, 156, 305; power, 95, 305; racist, 134, 141; sexist, 95; social, 308

students
agency, 295-97; anxiety, 264, 266; confidence, 230, 264, 295-296; centering, 230; of color, 299; connecting with the text, 230, 266; cultural circumstances, 156; empowering, 24, 154, 298-299; encouraging, 48-49, 147, 233, 266, 268, 291; experience, 24, 140, 142, 147, 155, 240, 251, 253-254, 293-298, 309; faculty racial disparity, 299; identities, 276; low income and first generation, 276; meeting them where they are, 22, 230, 271; modern, 235; motivation, 270-271, 295; output, 253; preparation, 292; reflection, 120, 155, 157; relationship with pop culture, 152; relatable material, 172, 268; touchstone, 211

studies
contemporary, 250; cultural, 102, 148-149, 250, 259, 303; drama, 251; early modern, 250; literary, 295, 303, 309; Siglo, 290

Sturm und Drang, 41

subjectivity, 256, 259

subjugation, 275, 281, 307

submersion, 94, 120,

submission, 49, 275, 283-287

suffering, 68, 107-108, 118, 188, 280

suicide, 70, 93, 99, 258

superheroes, 194, 197-205, 229

see also comic books; heroes

superiority, 55, 76, 93, 166

Superman, 180, 189, 197, 199, 204, 229

symbolism, 50-51, 70, 88, 119, 124, 141, 146, 176, 193, 213, 271, 285, 308

synthesizing, 27, 147,

systemic racism, 269

systems
aristocratic, 52, 91; belief, 180; broken; caste; Counter Reformation, 101; devaluing women's work, 277; education, 276-277, 299; Hollywood studio, 218; honor, 52; judicial, 280; justice, 88, 94-95, 150, 155, 101-103; legal, 54, 110, 115-116, 285; oppression, 89, 91, 96-97, 116, 132, 213; organized, 79; political, 146; prison, 81, 96; rating, 217; signs, 160; unjust, 57, 96, 132, 280

taboo, 165, 257

Taming of the Shrew, 49, 188

"Tan largo que me lo fiáis," 146-157, 180

target language (TL), 178-179, 232, 251-252, 254

taste, 97, 121, 235, 237, 257, 297

teaching approaches, 22-28, 77, 87-88, 131-132, 142, 153-154, 157, 160-162, 178, 182, 210, 229-230, 251, 259, 261, 264, 269-271, 276, 295, 297-298

see also pedagogy

technology, 149, 152, 159, 170, 173, 189, 275, 294

television

adaptations of classic literature, 65-68; *Alias Grace*, 57-59; *Atlanta*, 136-138; audiences, 201; *The Big Bang Theory*, 159-173; crime shows, 74, 92, 51; critics, 65; history, 65; networks, 149; *Orange is the New Black*, 88, 94-97, 101-103; programs, 51, 135-137, 160-162, 193, 198-199, 211-212, 221, 292-293; homosexuality, 167; sitcoms, 162, 167; viewers, 68, 96, 148, 162, 164, 170, 172

tendencies

Baroque, 181-182; discursive, 35; dogmatic, 184; heteronormative, 256; idealist, 180

tensions, 67, 72, 144, 181, 222, 267

terminology

critical, 148; legal, 114; up-to-date, 152; vulgar, 59

terror, 52-54, 89

testimony, 66, 75, 109-112, 115-116, 285

texts

analysis, 53, 27, 101, 229, 233, 296, 302-304; antisocial, 55; artifact, 87, 97, 157, 249-261, 278; canonical, 51, 118, 147, 157, 230, 249-254; challenging, 229, 233, 251, 263-264; decipher, 235, 295-296; early modern, 143, 230, 249-250, 252, 278; elite, 250-251, 253, 260-261; foundational, 88, 178, 180; medieval, 49, 229-232, 239, 242, 252,

292; iconic, 218; primary, 254, 292-293, 296; secondary, 136, 254; seminal, 72, 74, 125; Siglo de Oro, 291, 297-299, *see also* Golden Age works; unorthodox 261

text to text/text to self/self to world, 264

theater, 23, 51, 65-83, 166, 182, 249, 253, 255, 262

Thelma and Louise, 48

themes

abandonment, 93; American literature, 242; central, 182, 237; Cervantes, 169, 173, 210; chivalric, 210; Don Juan, 180, 184, 188; hero, 230; honor, 182, 184, 188; law; love, 182, 184; music, 196, 198-201, 206; philosophical, 81; rape, 118, 121; reframing, 82; relevant, 178, 205, 231, 239, 242, 269-270; religious, 121, 182, 183, 269; of self-expression; struggle, 203; traditional, 178

theology, 73, 90, 94, 97, 100, 113, 156, 217, 270, 274, 280,

theory

Cold War, 77; feminist, 151; legal, 107; and practice, 24, 27-28; postcolonial, 36, 310; queer, 253, 259; reception, 148-149, 237

Thomas, Angie, 57

#TimesUp, 146-147, 150, 155
see also #MeToo

Tirant lo Blanc, 209

Titian, 107, 117-126

Title IX, 151

Tolentino, Jia, 101, 117

tone, 51, 72, 117, 236, 269-270

Toole, John Kennedy, 70

torture, 52-53, 217

toxic masculinity, 155

Toy Story I & II, 161-162

traditionalism, 74-76

traditions

ballad, 201, 230, 232, 235, 238; changing, 102, 230, 235; *corrido*, 241; cultural, 43, 102, 241; established, 101, 125, 163, 242; anti-Semitic, 35, 37-38, 41; gender, 194, 204; Greco-Roman, 231-232; "heroic" rape, 117, 121; lyrical, 131; musical, 21, 133, 233; mystic, 268; poetic, 76, 230, 233, 239; religious, 180, 183; *romancero*, 235, 241; Spanish, 35, 42, 141, 238, 242, 266; Western, 141-142, 161, 165, 210, 218

tragedy, 256-257

transformations

character, 95, 255, 260, 261; journey, 161, 166-167, 170; personal, 140, 170, 230; reality, 173

transgression, 112, 117, 181-182, 269, 308

translations

English, 196, 210, 252-253, 257, 296-297; literal, 53; literature, 295

transvestism, 194, 257

trauma, 44-45, 79, 125

Treatise on the Use of Women, 114

trials, 38, 43, 77, 118, 126, 241

trickery, 155, 179, 187, 239, 279

Tridentine doctrine, 91

trigger warning *see* disclaimer

tropes

aesthetic, 89; Baroque, 60; of "blood purity", 35; Iberian, 40; linguistic, 137; literary, 55, 77; poetic, 235; pop culture, 250

True Grit (1969), 214, 223

Trump, Donald, 48, 61, 117, 126, 146, 151

truths, 43, 45, 55, 58, 61, 67, 73-76, 82, 98, 164-165, 170, 202, 270, 297, 311

Tudor, Mary, 121

Turner, Frederick Jackson, 215

TV *see* television

Twitter, 146, 149, 152

Ubeda, Francisco López de, 54-55
see La pícara Justina

Uncle Sam, 79, 81

unconscious, 44, 71-72, 76, 82, 277, 279-280

under-represented groups, 39, 276, 291, 294

underdog, 219

understanding

character, 100; common, 157; nuanced, 152; progressive, 78; reality, 49; student, 132, 147, 190, 196, 253, 270, 303

undertones

homosocial, 167; sexual, 95

unfamiliar material, 22-23, 132, 230-231

upper class, 115

U.S.

contemporary, 27, 82, 132, 229, 302; cultural history, 133-135, 150, 215, 221-222; culture, 131-134, 141, 143, 211-212, 312, 241; foreign policy, 79, 81, 209; imperialism, 70, 214; political history, 150; political system, 146, 117; positive image, 71; racism, 70, 134, 138, 142, 214, 286; society, 135, 213, 77; universities, 28, 276, 290; values, 69-70, 215
see also America

Valle-Inclán, Ramón del, 176
valor, 198, 234, 237
Valor, agravio y mujer, 194, 205
values
aristocratic, 115; challenge existing, 71; gendered, 50, 98, 157, 203; pedagogical, 73; semantic, 40
vaquero see cowboys
Vatican, 218
vaudeville, 160, 215
Vega, Lope de, 50, 107, 111, 194, 196, 209, 249, 254, 277, 305, *Arte nuevo*, 194; *La Arcadia*; feud with Cervantes, 27, 66, 220, 222, 224; *Fuenteovejuna*, 89, 197, 309; *Las mujeres sin hombres*; *El Nuevo Mundo descubierto por Cristóbal Colón*, 48
Velázquez, Diego, 121
Vélez de Guevara, Luis, 196
La serrana de la Vera, 199
vengeance, 183, 197
Venus and Adonis, 119-121, 123
El verdugo de su esposa, 51

Viaje entretenido, 255, 258
victims, 92, 96, 100, 110, 112-113, 115-116, 118, 124, 155, 200, 206
victory, 146, 219, 234-236, 238
La vida es sueño, 194, 205
video, 199, 211, 231, 233, 240-241, 261, 268-270, 283-287
video games, 161, 171
viewers, 66, 68, 96, 119-125, 135, 148, 162, 164, 170, 172, 188, 220, 223, 310
villains, 43, 202, 218, 220, 223, 235, 285
violence
aestheticization, 87-89, 97, 103, 107, 111, 117-118, 124; catalyst, 100; decry, 107; domestic, 48-49, 52, 54, 89, 107, 110; enforcing gender roles, 49, 54; gender, 126, 206, 271; glorification, 51, 118; hidden, 88-89, 103, 112; husbands, 49, 52, 280; legitimized; masculine, 51-52, 115; sexual, 87-90, 103, 107-108, 110-113, 116, 118, 125-126; structural, 89
see also victims
violence against women, 53, 94, 106-108, 111, 118, 125
virginity, 89, 110-111, 114-115, 278, 296
visions
chivalric, 67; of decay, 53; of society, 70, 182, 190; of the West, 214-215, 221-222
visual arts, 123

voice, 54-62, 91, 106, 108, 111, 137, 150, 156, 164, 169, 219, 241, 280, 288, 292

voluntad, 109, 114, 278-279, 281, 284 *see also* free will

war, 39, 196-197, 206
warrior, 120, 195, 197, 199
warnings, 51-52, 56, 59, 100, 182, 258, 279, 306
Wasserman, Dale, 65-83, 311-312

Wayne, John "The Duke", 213, 221-224
    feud with Clint Eastwood, 212, 222-224
weakness, 101, 109, 180-181, 187, 201, 213
wealth, 49, 97, 101
web culture, 173
wedding, 49, 200, 219-220
Weinstein, Harvey, 88, 90, 101-102, 108, 116, 125-126, 147, 156
Welles, Orson, 72
Welsh, Irvine, 21
West Coast Beats, 69
West World (HBO series), 209
Western (genre)
    American, 216, 221, 223, 311; European, 209, 212; historical figures, 216; history, 210; Italian, 209, 211; revisionist, 223; silent, 212; Spaghetti, 209, 221-222; stars
white
    America, 135, 215; artists, 132, 134, 136-139, 142; cowboys, 214; culture, 138; men, 136, 151, 215, 276, 286, 294; people, 141, 299; privilege, 36, 133, 138, 141, 294, 299; superiority, 308; supremacist groups, 36, 140; women, 94, 135, 137, 140, 299
whitewashing, 91
whiteness, 36
widows, 115, 188, 189
Wister, Owen, 215
wives, 49-52, 92-94, 97-98, 121, 199, 222
will *see* free will
Will and Grace, 167
windmills, 71, 77, 79, 81
witchcraft, 34-45, 275-278, 280-281
witnesses, 110, 269
wizards, 34-45
Wolf Pack case, 112-114
women
    aberrant, 114; abuse, 53-54, 58, 61, 77, 87, 102, 111-113, 116-117, 126, 146, 150-152, 155, 157, 180, 283, 306; actors, 256; advances, 118, 166, 202, 205; airbrushed images, 60-62; aristocratic, 87, 97, 115; authors, 48, 51-57, 59-62, 87-88, 90, 95-103, 111-112, 140, 194, 196, 205, 254, 274, 276, 279, 282-284, 286, 298, 304-307, 309; bodies, 53, 61, 93, 112, 120-121 124-126, 194, 204, 218, 261, 277, 279; brave, 111-112, 116, 126, 198-199; characters, 92, 94, 101, 154, 181, 195, 255, 279, 305; Chicana, 276; criminal acts, 92-93; desire, 92, 100, 119-120, 125, 168, 181, 203,

261, 275, 277-280; discomfort, 119; disfigured, 93; errant, 89; exclusion, 153; flesh, 52, 61, 120, 125; free, 55-56, 287; galvanization, 62; hatred, 53, 57, 93-94; inappropriate, 60, 123; innocent, 51-52, 238, 280; imprisoned, 52, 93, 95-96, 155; kidnapped, 93, 110, 115, 124; liberation movement, 199; marginalized, 89, 94; married, 98-101, 115, 256, 307; and men, 87-92, 97; #MeToo, 48, 61-62, 87-88, 96, 101-102, 106-108, 109, 111, 116-117, 126, 146, 156; *mujer varonil*, 193-206, 305; "natural state," 108; objectification, 118-119, 121, 125, 261, 280; opportunity, 59; passive, 112, 118, 125, 154; peasant, 90, 102, 168; perception, 108, 147, 262; pride, 89, 181; political activists, 62; presidency, 61, 117, 146, 151, 305; *see* rape; and rapists, 92, 101-102, 110, 113, 116, 118-119, 126, 156; religious, 115; representations, 108, 118, 126; reputations, 112, 155, 183-184; responsibility, 88-89, 94, 113, 154; rights, 135, 151-152, 196, 199, 306; right to vote, 152, 154; seducers, 108, 238-239; shame, 59, 110-111, 116, 118, 278-279; solidarity, 280, 287; status, 53-55, 94, 110-111, 116, 153; stories, 94, 201 280, 287; strong, 118, 195, 197; subjects, 107, 118, 153, 157; suffering, 107-108, 118, 280; survival, 54, 112; temptation, 108, 114; treatment, 23, 61, 88, 93, 102, 121, 153-154; unconscious, 93, 277, 279-278, 284; unequal, 53-54, 61, 88, 102, 147, 152, 198, 202, 277; unreliability, 108; violence against, 53, 94, 106-108, 111, 125; virgin, 89, 110-111, 114-115, 278, 296; voice, 54-59, 62, 106, 108, 111, 156, 280; volition, 280; warriors, 195, 197; white, 94, 135, 140; womanhood, 135; work, 277; young, 53, 59-61, 109, 112, 160, 187

Women's March, 151

Wonder Woman, 193-206

Wonder Woman (2017), 193, 198

Wonder Woman (1975-1979), 193

works

canon, 51, 118, 147, 157, 230, 249-254, 302, 309; drama, 50, 180, 182, 194, 235, 242, 249, 251, 253-254, 258-259, 261; Golden Age, 22, 48-49, 51, 101, 131-132, 138-139, 142, 147, 153, 157, 197, 210, 215, 235, 297; mythical, 117; non-canonical, 230, 249-262, 309; theological, 73, 90, 156; traditional, 131, 230, 241

world

as it is, 67; of comics, 168, 171; corrupt, 81, 153, 180; domestic, 52, 110, 124, 203; Hispanic, 23, 27; of knight errantry, 210; male-dominated, 53, 82; modern secular, 73; ordered by sexual imbalance, 125; outside, 23-25, 80-81, 87, 168, 242; patriarchal, 97; perception, 166; real, 36, 81, 293; realistic, 251; of reality and fiction, 168; science, 169; Spanish-speaking, 27, 111, 232, 297; tired and cynical, 65,

68; view, 23, 56, 166, 171; visual,
173; war-torn, 196

World War I, 196

World War II, 38-39, 196, 209, 218

writers *see also* author
female, 48, 51-57, 59-62, 87-88,
90, 95-103, 111-112, 140, 194, 196,
205, 254, 274, 276, 279, 282-284,
286, 298, 304-307, 309; intentions, 81, 94; roles, 55, 75, 80;
serious, 66

writing
avant-garde, 71; component,
258; colonial, 37, 252-253; critical,
73; masculine realm, 60; proto-
feminist, 152; Spanish, 275, 283; as
a weapon, 57

Yankee imperialism, 79

Yojimbo, 222

yolo (you only live once), 155

youth, 24, 60-61, 68-69, 133, 169,
178, 190, 264, 291

YouTube, 70, 72, 199, 211, 275, 283-
284, 293

Zayas, María de, 48, 51-54, 62, 87-
88, 90, 95-103, 111-112, 194, 196,
205, 274, 276, 279, 282-284, 286,
298, 304-307
see also Desengaños amorosos

zeitgeist, 25

Zen, 69

Zorilla, José, 153-154
see also Don Juan Tenorio